SCIENCE AND THE PERCEPTION OF NATURE

SCIENCE AND THE PERCEPTION OF NATURE

BRITISH LANDSCAPE ART
IN THE LATE EIGHTEENTH AND EARLY NINETEENTH CENTURIES

CHARLOTTE KLONK

Published for
THE PAUL MELLON CENTRE
FOR STUDIES IN BRITISH ART
by
YALE UNIVERSITY PRESS
NEW HAVEN & LONDON

Designed by Gillian Malpass
Printed in Hong Kong

Library of Congress Catalog Card No.: 96-60715
ISBN: 0-300-06950-2

A catalogue record for this book is available from
The British Library

Frontispiece: John C. Nattes, *Fingal's Cave*, 1802.
Detail of plate 49.

CONTENTS

ACKNOWLEDGEMENTS   vii

INTRODUCTION.   I

I   AESTHETICS, PHILOSOPHY AND PHYSIOLOGY:
    THE ROAD TO PHENOMENALISM   9
     London: The Body and Society   12
     Scotland: The Culture of Sensibility   18
     The Development of a Critique of
       Efficient Causality   20
     The Rise of Phenomenalism   22
     The Picturesque Controversy   26

II   THE TEMPLE OF FLORA   37
     Robert John Thornton   38
     Thornton and Erasmus Darwin   39
     'All the Most Eminent English Artists'   41
     The Plants and their Backgrounds   49
     Ordered Continuity: The Arrangement
       of the Pictures   60
     The Failure of A New Illustration   64

III   FROM PICTURESQUE TRAVEL TO SCIENTIFIC
     OBSERVATION   67
     The Wonders of Nature   68

The Picturesque Tour in Scotland   70
Naturalist Travellers in Scotland and the
   Geological Controversy   74
The Western Isles   80
The East Coast: Tantallon Castle and the
   Bass Rock   95
Artists and Geologists   99

IV   SKETCHING FROM NATURE:
    JOHN AND CORNELIUS VARLEY AND
    THEIR CIRCLE.   101
     The New Role of Sketching   105
     Cornelius Varley   113
     The Scientific Outlook   126
     The Proto-Photographic Gaze   130
     Phenomenalism and the Retreat from
       Social Conflict   135
     The End of Phenomenalism   145

CONCLUSION.   149

NOTES.   154

BIBLIOGRAPHY.   182

INDEX.   193

Der Bann, den das Subjekt um Natur legt, befängt auch es:
Freiheit regt sich im Bewußtsein seiner Naturähnlichkeit.

The spell which the subject casts around nature captures the subject itself:
freedom arises in the awareness of its own naturalness.

Theodor Adorno, *Ästhetische Theorie*

ACKNOWLEDGEMENTS

During the work, first on my thesis, and then this book, I have accumulated an enormous number of debts, both to individuals and to institutions. My research for the thesis was made possible by the Studienstiftung des Deutschen Volkes, the Deutscher Akademischer Austauschdienst and the British Academy. During the year I spent after the completion of the thesis at the Museum van Hedendaagse Kunst in Ghent, Jan Hoet and the staff at the Museum productively questioned many of my assumptions about art and thus helped to inject new fuel into my work. I am grateful to Christ Church, Oxford, which, by electing me to a Junior Research Fellowship, gave me the opportunity to carry out the work required in order to publish the thesis as a book. The College, together with the Paul Mellon Centre for Studies in British Art, also contributed considerably to my photographic expenses and I would like to express my thanks to both institutions for this essential support.

The quantity of treasures available in British libraries was a source of continual delight to me, and I am grateful to the staff of the Cambridge University Library, the British Library and the Bodleian Library for their help. I owe thanks also to the librarians and archivists at the Royal Institution of Great Britain, the Royal Society of Great Britain, the Geological Society of London, and to those who work in the Prints and Drawings Rooms of the British Museum, the Victoria and Albert Museum, the Ashmolean Museum, and, in particular, to Jane Munro at the Fitzwilliam Museum. The Colnaghi Gallery was particularly helpful for the research on Cornelius Varley. Michael Spender, the former director of the Bankside Gallery, kindly let me see an important manuscript in the possession of the Royal Water-colour Society, and his successor, Judy Dixey, gave me permission to quote from it. I spent many happy hours with Mrs Joan Linnell Burton, Mr and Mrs Walker, Mrs Fleetwood Walker and others who wish to remain anonymous, while working on material in their collections. Those hours are certainly among the highlights of my research and I am grateful to Mr and Mrs Walker, Mrs Fleetwood Walker and to the Trustees of the Linnell Trust for their kind permission to quote from the material in their collections.

The following either read parts of the material and made valuable comments or helped me with their special knowledge: John Brewer, Janet Brown, Marianne Heinz, Nick Jardine, Paul Langford, Lucy Malein, John Pickstone, Michael Pidgley, Richard Sharpe, Heinz Otto Sibum and Monika Wagner. To Andrew Hemingway, Harry Mount, Christiana Payne, Michael Rosenthal, Simon Schaffer and Jim Secord I am particularly grateful for their careful reading of my work at different stages; their often brilliant suggestions made me re-think several topics and their perceptive criticism spared me embarrassing mistakes. I am grateful, too, to an anonymous reader on behalf of Yale University Press, whose constructive suggestions, I have tried my best to take to heart. The shortcomings of the book are mine alone and often stubbornly remain despite the efforts of these individuals. Very many thanks must also go to Gillian Malpass at Yale University Press who has made this book possible. Her professionalism, kindness and personal engagement have made the publication aspect of the work a very enjoyable experience. Ruth Thackeray's careful copy-editing has contributed substantially to the final form of the book.

But most of all I owe very sincere thanks to three persons. First, my former supervisor, John Gage, whose encyclopaedic knowledge set the research on its course. His unique combination of penetrating criticism and solid support saw me through the years of research. My father taught me how to see! Without him the book would have been far poorer in its visual perceptions. It is moving for me to recognise that he was able to comment so effectively on a text written in a language which is foreign to him. Finally I must mention Michael Rosen. It is he who helped me turn my Germanic writing into a readable English text. He challenged me when statements came too easily, he argued with me until thoughts took on shape, and he consoled me when they failed. Where would the book be without his sharp intellect and verbal skills?

This book is written in memory of my mother, who died at the outset of the work, but whose enthusiasm for its subject-matter I remembered in difficult times.

INTRODUCTION

Two landscapes. One (plate 1) directs the gaze through a screen of trees into a brightly sunlit golden cornfield. The village and the white church in the background are thrown into even sharper relief by the horizontal line of a dark green wood. The sky is blue, although distinct rain clouds emerge from the right-hand corner of the background. Only as it returns towards the foreground does the eye notice some tiny figures, coming to rest on a small man in a reddish jacket on the edge of the wooded path at the left-hand corner. Embraced by his surrounding environment and blended into it through the use of colour and brushstroke, this wanderer contemplates the landscape before him, implicating our own gaze in his. It is an environment in which nothing is startlingly individual: the trees, ground and vegetation melt into each other. They are just sufficiently marked to be ideal examples of their kind, but they are not specific representatives of their genera. From here the viewer, like the wanderer, can calmly contemplate the changing light and weather in the middle ground; the foreground is, in fact, strangely exempt from it – a different illumination reigns here, one in which light and shadow are not the effects of a real light source but part of an overall chiaroscuro which balances the structure of the composition. Yet this foreground frames and makes possible the view of a fresh summer day; in this way, the latter's changing reality is depicted as an integral part of a higher, stable order, one which is to be found in but yet can be seen as pointing beyond the given scene. The painting is Thomas Gainsborough's *Wooded Landscape with a Seated Figure*, in the Tate Gallery, London. It was painted around 1747, when Gainsborough (1727–1788) was still living in his home county, Suffolk.

While Gainsborough depicts a generalised landscape, the second painting is identifiable as a specific view of Suffolk (plate 2). Now light and colour do not highlight a single focus of attention, nor does the arrangement of objects direct the progress of the viewer's gaze, notwithstanding the path which leads into the background towards the mill houses and the canal running parallel to it. A range of subjects are emphasised equally across all the planes of the picture space: there is the little boy on a horse in the left foreground, apparently waiting for the barges on the canal behind him. The efforts of the bargeman attract the gaze as much as the red houses of the mill, thrown into sharp relief by the varied green tones of their surroundings. The figure with a dog halfway down the path which runs towards the lock by the mill houses provides another focus of attention, as do the weathered tall tree, grouped with a bare, forked tree-trunk, in the middle ground, and the slightly rotten timber of the shallow bridge over the stream at the right-hand foreground. The bright yellow-greenish hayfield with the sun shining on it and a mower at work on the right of the middle ground draws our attention, as do the work scene in the foreground and the houses in the background. The imaginary diagonal of the horse and the barge and the mooring-post of the left-hand foreground is echoed and balanced by the carefully delineated timberwork of the shallow bridge and vegetation next to the little stream in the right-hand corner. Reflecting on this summer day, our gaze wanders from one piece of artistic narration to another, from one prominent feature to the next; and yet the quality of light is present only for an instant, and the shadows and spots of sun will change with the moving clouds. Very soon, perhaps, the bright green field may fall into shadow, and then our gaze will seek out different points of attraction altogether.

The painting is John Constable's famous *Flatford Mill*, which he exhibited at the Royal Academy in 1817, now

1   Thomas Gainsborough, *Wooded Landscape with a Seated Figure*, c.1747, oil on canvas, 625 × 781, Tate Gallery, London.

also in the Tate Gallery in London. In contrast to Gainsborough's landscape, Constable (1776–1837), who made a close study of Gainsborough's works, places an almost pedantic emphasis on specifics that undermines the hierarchical order of the pictorial space. Its decentralisation leaves the gaze to find its own order of visual attention. Instead of Gainsborough's uniform tonality of greens, yellows and browns, Constable's colours and forms appear to be conditioned throughout the picture by the peculiar quality of light on this particular summer day. Though the painting is certainly a studio work, a combination of several outdoor sketches, it is repre-

sented as portraying a particular moment and the atmosphere of an actual location as it appeared to the observing artist. While Gainsborough's summer field was depicted as part of a pre-established order, Constable's scene gains its unity only by being rendered as the perception of one individual, the artist.

This book develops its narrative in the space between these two modes of depicting landscape and the radical change of perception which divides them: from the belief that the representation of nature must be framed within some objective ordering principle, to an acceptance of the receptivity of the individual subject as the

2   John Constable, *Flatford Mill*, 1817, oil on canvas, 1017 × 1270, Tate Gallery, London.

sole point of unity for artistic activity. *Science and the Perception of Nature* is guided by the belief that these striking changes were not the outcome of a logic internal to art alone. They are interwoven with changes in the understanding of nature which took place more broadly at this time, in particular, in contemporary natural philosophy and science.[1] The argument here is that the traditional modes of landscape art were sustained by an epistemology which in one way or another saw reality as mediated by a single, underlying common principle. As we will see, however, the credibility of such world-views came to be called into question, for a

variety of reasons, and a more subject-centred approach, such as is found in Constable's *Flatford Mill*, provided a short period of unstable synthesis at the beginning of the nineteenth century between the scientific observation of nature and the personal response of the perceiver. At a certain point after the turn of the nineteenth century, I hope to show, a moment in history obtained at which subjectivity-claims and objectivity-claims achieved a precarious balance.

★   ★   ★

In the past, art historians treated the development of British landscape art less as a matter of the changing social character of perception than as a product of artists' increasing technical mastery in the imitation of nature. This line of argument was put forward in 1949 by Sir Kenneth Clark in his pioneering *Landscape into Art*.[2] In Clark's view, Constable's work was the first truly successful manifestation of 'naturalism' in the history of landscape art. Constable's 'genius', according to Clark, 'first discovered and still justifies the art of unquestioning naturalism'.[3] Clark locates Constable's greatness in the way in which fidelity to nature ('the impressions received from actual objects are the essential point of departure') is transformed by the emotional force of moral vision.[4] It is this moral vision which is the focus of Clark's attention and he leaves the problems involved in his simple (some would say, naive) realist idea of mimesis undiscussed.

Eleven years later, in *Art and Illusion*, Sir Ernst Gombrich responded with a much more sophisticated account of naturalism.[5] For Gombrich, what constitutes landscape art is 'not the nature of the physical world but the nature of our reactions to it'.[6] The latter, in his view, are informed by the peculiar demands of the artists' tools and the means of representation, such as colour and perspective, available to them as well as being mediated by other visual representations. Thus Gombrich judges that 'Constable saw the English landscape in terms of Gainsborough's paintings'.[7] Gombrich replaces Clark's static ideal of the reflection of external reality with a conception of artistic mimesis as a dynamic progress towards reality which is never completed. For Gombrich, too, Constable represents progress from Gainsborough, not because he achieved an ultimately objective representation of nature, but because he was aware in a way that Gainsborough was not that 'only experimentation can show the artist a way out of the prison of style toward a greater truth'.[8] Experimentation of this kind challenges received conventions and inherited preconceptions, but it does not thereby clear the way for a simple mirroring of nature 'as it really is in itself'.[9]

Notwithstanding its subtlety, Gombrich's theory of landscape art still remains, in the end, an account of mimesis which assumes the existence of a reality in itself as the *terminus ad quem* of the experimental quest. For both Clark and Gombrich a binary structure divides the world into an objective and a subjective domain. So it comes as no surprise that both identify two divergent artistic traditions emerging at the beginning of the nineteenth century, initiated by the creative genius of J.M.W. Turner (1775–1851) and John Constable respectively. Both agree that the tradition following Turner led to an increasingly subjective kind of representation, while Constable's followers concentrated on the effort to represent the world before them.

The presumed essentialism behind these two interpretations has been sharply criticised in recent times.[10] This has been for two reasons. Firstly, it has been objected that history and society play a role in theories such as Clark's or Gombrich's only as a changing backdrop whose alterations do not affect the underlying and immutable substratum of reality. The pioneer of this critique in England was John Berger.[11] Secondly, it has been objected that, in so far as Clark and Gombrich rely on a dualistic epistemology, this has the effect of defining 'the world as anterior and masterful, and the painter's function before it as the secondary instrument'.[12] Influenced by such post-structuralist writers as Jean-François Lyotard and Jean Baudrillard, the latter type of critique holds that, because our operative concepts and categories depend upon certain linguistic and culture-specific norms, all truth-claims must be understood and analysed as merely the construct of this or that collective mind-set.[13]

To the extent that this criticism argues that the Gombrichian account of the artist's quest for truth naturalises or objectifies culturally relative constructions I agree with it. However, while I concede that knowledge about reality is always subject to the constraints of the prevailing social discourse and that it may for this reason be extremely hard to come by, this is not, I think, a sufficient reason to deny the existence of any reality outside the collective mind-set whatsoever. Indeed, such theories as Gombrich's, which interpret experience as governed by the quest for objectivity, are merely inverted into subjectivist scepticism in theories like Lyotard's, Baudrillard's, Norman Bryson's or W.J.T. Mitchell's, which leave no room for any fundamentally different realm outside and in relation to the subject. My own sympathies lie with the writers of the Frankfurt School and, in particular, with Theodor W. Adorno and Walter Benjamin, whose writings contain, in my view, an important alternative to the homocentricity of both the naive realist and radical anti-realist view of the subject and its experience.[14] In his *Ästhetische Theorie* Adorno prohibits any discourse about nature in positive terms. But this restriction is not because he doubts the existence of a subject-independent reality; quite the contrary. Adorno's prohibition is a product of his criticism of an understanding of the self as an agent which takes control of what is other than itself in order to come to terms with itself. Benjamin's conception of a 'mimetic capacity' offers an alternative to this Enlightenment view of the self, inasmuch as it identifies a mode of experience which seeks a relationship with what lies outside the subject without thereby subordinating it. I will come back to this theme at the end of the book, because one of its major objectives is to argue that the radical division between subjective and objective realms implicit in the naive realist and radical anti-realist accounts is not the only possible epistemology. Indeed, the binary structure which dominates our discourse regarding the relationship between mind and world today is itself a historical phenomenon, one which came into being in the early nineteenth century. What I wish to do in this book is to reanimate the period of transition which preceded this binary epistemology.

I shall use the term *phenomenalism* to denote the complex of attitudes concerning the relationship between mind and nature that grew in force at that time. According to phenomenalism, artists or scientists must confine themselves strictly to what is given to the perceiving subject, without making any prior suppositions concerning the underlying mechanisms by which what is observed is connected. For phenomenalism, generalisation is permissible only on the basis of the painstaking accumulation of particular instances. I choose the term phenomenalism rather than *empiricism* or *naturalism*, which are more frequently associated with this period, since the latter carry the (in my view misleading) suggestion that the mind responds passively to reflect unproblematically a mind-independent, objective realm. It is, however, important to emphasise that phenomenalism is not a form of *subjectivism*. It is true that, in placing the emphasis so heavily on the observer, phenomenalism can lead to subjectivism – the idea that reality is always refracted through the perceptions and emotions of the individual – but, in its (arguably unstable) original form, the role of the observer is consciously confined to being a screen for the way that reality is given. In other words, phenomenalism attempts to capture reality faithfully, not as it is in itself or in its underlying essence (if it has one) but *as it appears*.

Implicitly, my approach assumes that there is common ground behind what is alleged to be the radical division in artistic practice between the 'poetic' imagination of Turner's and Constable's 'objective' quest. For both Turner and Constable (in contrast to Gainsborough, for example) the artist's chosen subject-matter is always anchored within the realm of observable natural phenomena. Moreover, the implicit position of the perceiving subject is clearly marked in the practices of both artists. While Gombrich's conception of naturalism interprets the development of art in terms of an interplay between the techniques of representation and forms of perception available within the art world alone, phenomenalism denotes a complex of attitudes whose effects can clearly be seen in other areas of the culture, most notably (though not solely) in the natural sciences. This allows us to bring change in artistic practice into connection with other cultural practices, and *Science and the Perception of Nature* aims to do this by exploring the links between British landscape art of the late eighteenth and early nineteenth centuries with contemporary science.

★ ★ ★

Work on art and science is currently mushrooming. It is an enterprise that is more complex than sometimes acknowledged, however. To ask how a culture represents what it knows, and how what it knows affects what it sees, is to open a Pandora's box of methodological questions. Does science's more powerful quest for truth affect art unilaterally? Does art's visualisation of the world in any way shape or inform scientific understanding? Are they both to be conceptualised in relation to economic structures and political forces? Or are art and science simply two parallel strands in the fabric of the broader culture, each revealing something about its underlying beliefs and governing discourse?

Since the late 1960s, when art historians started to call the separation of science and art into question, investigations of the relationship between art and science have often focused on a structural comparison of their respective processes of creation and discovery.[15] Broadly based studies, such as Timothy F. Mitchell's recent *Art and Science in German Landscape Painting 1770–1840*, often appear to operate on the assumption that the two are held together by the unifying power of a vaguely conceived *Zeitgeist*.[16] But by far the most frequent assumption has been the existence of a privileged grip of science on art. Studies which have undertaken a historical analysis of the relationship between science and art have ended up by exploring unilaterally the impact of scientific or technological developments on art.[17] A pioneering work of this sort is Barbara Maria Stafford's *Voyage into Substance*.[18] Although our accounts share some material, Stafford's overall interpretation is quite different from my own. She traces a direct line of progress from the empiricist programme, first advanced by Bacon, through eighteenth-century natural histories and travel accounts, to nineteenth-century aesthetics.[19] One consequence of this schema is that a high proportion of the artistic productions of the late eighteenth century are characterised by Stafford only negatively, principally by their failure to match the empiricism of the naturalists to which she implicitly attributes intellectual (and perhaps also causal) priority.[20]

While some arguments appear to identify science as the underlying cause of artistic developments, another strand of contemporary art-historical research locates that cause in socio-economic structures. In this case, the process of agrarian enclosure and the emergence of bourgeois interests are given causal priority in the explanation of the changes taking place in landscape painting in the late eighteenth and early nineteenth centuries.[21] In exploring the connection between science and art, it would be reductive, I believe, to attribute a unique causal priority to one or the other: art is more than a reflection of social or scientific developments. Equally, I believe that the discursive structures by which art and science are linked turn out to be more subtle and unpredictable than the idea that they are both products of a homogeneous, underlying *Zeitgeist* or expressions of socio-economic forces.

In the face of such difficulties, one might think that Michel Foucault's approach represents an alternative to reductionism or oversimplification. Foucault approached the history of culture in terms of an analysis of the different regions of knowledge as they depend on and participate in certain general discursive formations which, in his view, structure social life without identifying causal connections or assigning explanatory primacy to one or the other. Of particular importance for the relationship between science and art is *Les mots*

et les choses, published in 1966.[22] Foucault has become a major figure who is invoked repeatedly (and often uncritically) in cultural studies, so that it seems to me important to discuss his position, and, indeed, my reservations about it, at some length – not least because Foucault was also the single most influential author for me when I started research on this book in the late 1980s.

In *Les mots et les choses* Foucault describes the study of language, of wealth and of nature in the eighteenth and early nineteenth centuries, not in order to determine which of these discourses influenced the other, but to articulate what he sees as the common ordering structure underlying life, language and labour – what he calls the *episteme*. This common ordering structure is, however, much more complex and specific than the vaguer notions of *Zeitgeist* which Foucault's critics often attribute to him. Foucault argues that in the eighteenth century these three domains of general grammar, natural history and the analysis of wealth were all structured by a common fundamental understanding of what he terms the 'indispensable link between representation and things'.[23] The mediation between things, representation and knowledge is, for Foucault, the homogeneous structure of all the discourses in the eighteenth century, which he calls the 'Classical *episteme*'.

In his exposition of the Classical *episteme* Foucault concentrates on the search for a common structure governing the relationship between knowledge and representations. He does not discuss the character of the relationship between representations and objects themselves (which, for a modern post-structuralist like Foucault, must, of course, be deeply problematic). Nevertheless, there is no doubt that the way in which the relationship between the human realm and non-human entities was conceived did play a fundamental role in the discursive economy of the eighteenth century. Here too the search was for a common underlying principle to connect apparently heterogeneous domains: a mediation between object, representation and knowledge. In some of the cases which I shall discuss – for example, in eighteenth-century treatises on the nervous system – this principle takes the form of belief in the existence of a single, mediating substance, in others it is understood as a single form of being which divides up into a hierarchy of different genera and species under the assumption of the continuity of nature. In natural history the existence of such a continuity allows the scientist to infer from visible structures to a taxonomical order. In landscape art it leads the artist to select and define nature in categories such as the sublime, the picturesque and the beautiful.

Foucault diagnoses the dissolution of the Classical *episteme* as taking place at the turn of the nineteenth century. The various theoretical shifts in discourses occurring at that time serve as an index (though not as a cause) of 'this profound breach'.[24] The Classical *episteme*, based on a system of representations, comes to be replaced by a conception of objects as structures: knowledge of objects is a knowledge of their causality, their history and their origin. To define objects of knowledge causally and historically leads, according to Foucault, to a separation of knowledge into different domains of inquiry, which become independent entities. At the turn of the nineteenth century natural history and philosophy separated into the different branches of the natural sciences and social sciences, which became autonomous. At that point, according to Foucault, knowledge could no longer be taken to be co-extensive with representation. This rift in turn leads to the reflection and projection of man himself as the cognitive subject and thus marks the advent of the subject in the order of discourses[25] – 'an invention of recent date'.[26] From now on, it is the investigation of empirically acquired content which forms the object of the positive sciences, while the social sciences reflect on the link between empirical content and the transcendental question of the conditions of knowledge.

My own analysis, like Foucault's, depicts a transformation, one which ultimately leads to a tension between the generalising observation of scientists and the more individualistic responses of artists. However, my understanding is that this opposition did not emerge immediately with the break-up of the eighteenth-century epistemology, as Foucault suggests. On the contrary, the early nineteenth century saw the spread of phenomenalism which brought these two aspirations – towards 'subjectivity' and 'objectivity' – together, albeit only temporarily. Phenomenalism retained the aspiration towards scientific generality, but on the basis of the individual and particular observations made by the subject; there was no assumption that a single principle would eliminate the diversity of reality. This attitude, I will argue, did not appear at all locations at the same time. In Chapter I, for example, its emergence is traced in the sphere of philosophy and aesthetics at the end of

the eighteenth century. In the third chapter, however, it only becomes apparent in landscape depictions of geological features towards the end of the second decade of the nineteenth century, at a time when this approach had already by and large been abandoned by the artists' circle in London which is the subject of my last chapter.

In *Les mots et les choses* Foucault adopts a method of analysis, which he calls 'archaeology', and which is assumed to be neutral and disinterested because observation is carried out from a standpoint of temporal and structural distance.[27] Consequently, specific changes are not accounted for and remain unmotivated. My own approach abandons such an abstract external viewpoint in favour of the reconstruction of particular cases. The price for such an involvement is perhaps the loss of those clear patterns in which changes appear, in Foucault's phrase, as 'profound breaches in the expanse of continuities'.[28] But what is gained is the possibility of grasping motivations and of developing causal explanations – causal explanations which, however, do not aim to account for all the changes in the discursive network.

For this reason, the book is divided into four somewhat self-contained case studies, each of which will seek to demonstrate a change in the perception of nature within differing discursive frameworks. The first chapter focuses on an analysis of theoretical texts. It links eighteenth-century aesthetic theories to contemporary physiological and philosophical investigations. I will argue that an understanding of the physiological account of the nervous system, the belief that there must be a direct connection between the mind and objects in the outside world, is crucial for our understanding of eighteenth-century aesthetics. But different presuppositions regarding the causal connection between mind and world also had differing social implications, as is apparent, for example, in Joseph Priestley's materialist opposition to Thomas Reid's metaphysical philosophy. Similarly, the aesthetic dispute between the politically much closer Uvedale Price and Richard Payne Knight shows that the adoption of varying physiological assumptions reflects a difference in their attitude towards the social problems of the 1790s. Around the turn of the century, however, the status of the mind-independent realm became problematic in all three fields – aesthetics, physiology and philosophy. A new understanding of the relationship between the mind and the world, associated with a new conception of causality, replaced the eighteenth-century belief in a unifying common medium which all previous accounts, despite their differences, had shared. This chapter introduces some of the central social concerns and debates of the period and in this way provides a framework for the following, much more narrowly conceived, case studies.

The second chapter is devoted to a detailed analysis of the genesis and meaning of one particular project in which art and science were consciously brought together under the auspices of a unitary metaphysics. Dr Robert John Thornton's famous botanical treatise, *The Temple of Flora*, whose publication was conceived in an initial *Advertisement* (1797) and culminated as Part 3 of *A New Illustration of the Sexual System of Linnaeus* (1807), locates the flowers it depicts in a landscape setting. Thornton commissioned the artists who executed the illustrations to depict the plants against landscape backgrounds which were, as we shall see, not those of their original environment. The taxonomical structure of these backgrounds becomes intelligible when interpreted in terms of established eighteenth-century aesthetic formulae. Thornton's publication shows the way in which taxonomy in the eighteenth century could be more than just an exercise in classifying the natural world. The taxonomist's hierarchies of genera and species formed systems that underpinned the unity of nature and guaranteed the place of the subject within it.

Chapter III develops further the argument, outlined in Chapter I, that enterprises such as Thornton's were coming to seem increasingly fanciful after the turn of the nineteenth century. In order to establish the nature of the change in the visualisation of landscape, contemporary geological treatises and their illustrations are compared and counterposed with landscape art. By examining the depictions of one area, Scotland, we will see that, on the one hand, in terms of the conventions of depiction that they adopted, geological illustrations lagged behind the texts which they accompanied. On the other hand, the emergence of a phenomenalist approach in geology seems to have stimulated landscape artists (notably William Daniell, J.M.W. Turner and Alexander Nasmyth) to perceive landscape in ways that went beyond received aesthetic formulae.

While Chapter III offers a diachronic perspective on the epistemological shift, tracing through changes in the pictorial representations of a single area over time, the last chapter again presents a less linear and more synoptic picture. It concentrates on the well-known circle of artists around John and Cornelius Varley in London. Cornelius Varley was an artist with original scientific interests, particularly in the field of optics, who had a noticeable influence on the landscape depictions produced by the circle. His novel approach to landscape depiction was not adopted as a consequence of scientific or technical developments, however; on the contrary, it is my contention that the 'photographic' mode of depiction practised by Cornelius Varley was a major factor behind his development of an optical device, the Graphic Telescope, which in turn formed a step towards the development of the photographic camera.

Chapter IV brings together and reinforces, I hope, two results from the previous chapters. First, it illustrates the way in which painters of this period came increasingly to concentrate on a specific local area and the representation of its changing appearance under different conditions (rather than seeing in the elements of a landscape an illustration of general pictorial principles). Second, it argues that the abandonment of belief in a common principle mediating the outside world with subjective reality leads to two modes of response to the experience of nature: an increasingly individualistic mode of perception, on the one hand, and a generalising attitude towards observation on the other.[29]

I

AESTHETICS, PHILOSOPHY AND PHYSIOLOGY: THE ROAD TO PHENOMENALISM

Aesthetics is for art what ornithology is for the birds.
— Barnett Newman

During the eighteenth century there was a remarkable expansion in the production and appreciation of landscape art in Britain. A central part of the explanation for this is social and economic: the rise of an increasingly prosperous and self-confident landed gentry. It was the gentry who sustained the demand for depictions of the English countryside (much of which they owned) and it was their self-understanding as part of a European cultural élite, nourished on the Grand Tour, that led to the steady import into Britain of landscape works by admired Continental masters. At the same time, drawing and sketching out of doors, as a genteel diversion or as a record of travel, were increasingly seen as desirable accomplishments for refined gentlemen – and gentle-women – and so professional artists found employment as drawing-masters.

British artists responded to the demand for landscape art in several ways. The existing tradition of topographical depiction was continued and expanded. Paul Sandby (1731–1809), for instance, experimented with different ways of incorporating the conventions of Continental landscape depiction into the indigenous topographical tradition. Other artists started to produce idealised treatments of the British landscape designed to hang alongside the paintings by Claude and Poussin that their richer patrons owned, or to act as a more afford-able substitute for those with lesser means.

The artists' search for appropriate conventions within which to depict the British landscape took place along-side an aesthetic debate regarding the nature and status of landscape art. The issues at stake here included the relative value of landscape painting in relation to other forms of art; the separation of different forms of land-scape art; the specification of the characteristic objects which form the subject-matter for each genre of land-scape art and the appropriate techniques for its compo-sition and depiction. Finally – and this is the particular focus of this chapter – there is the attempt to identify the nature of the connection that links aesthetic objects to the perceiving subject.

Initially, the debate regarding the forms of landscape art centred on two categories, each of which was iden-tified with the work of a seventeenth-century artist who worked in the area around Rome. Depictions of wil-derness by Salvator Rosa (1615–1673) came to be taken as paradigmatic examples of the *sublime*, while the works of Claude (Claude Gellée, called Le Lorrain, 1600–1682) were held to epitomise the ideal of land-scape *beauty*. It was these artists who provided the yard-stick for eighteenth-century academic landscape painting, as well as the reference points for aesthetic judgements of actual landscape. In a letter written in 1753, Mrs Elizabeth Montagu, the distinguished 'blue-stocking', describes the following scene:

Mr. Pitt [. . .] ordered a tent to be pitched, tea to be prepared, and his French horn to breath Music like the unseen Genius of the woods [. . .]. After tea we rambled about for an hour, seeing several views, some wild as Salvator Rosa, others placid, and with the setting sun, worthy of Claude Lorrain.[1]

This glamorous outing took place not on the Roman Campagna but near Tunbridge Wells.[2]

Richard Wilson (1714–1782) was the first eighteenth-century painter to follow up this new view of the British countryside by transposing Continental models onto native scenery. In *View near Wynnstay* (Llangollen) of 1770–1 (plate 3) Wilson depicts the Welsh landscape as smoothly undulating classical scenery and bathes the whole scene in a soft supernatural light that recalls Claude's highly generalised and stylised evocations of beautiful arcadia. Wilson's idealised British landscapes did not immediately convince his fellow-artists. According to Joshua Reynolds (1723–1792), the first President of the Royal Academy of Arts and the most influential spokesman for British artists, Wilson's British landscapes were 'too near common nature' to be successfully treated in the grand style of his Roman predecessors.[3] Nevertheless, although his impact on his contemporaries was limited, Wilson was to be one of the major influences on the next generation of artists, such as Turner and Constable.

The Swiss artist Philippe Jacques de Loutherbourg (1740–1812), who moved to London in 1771, was more successful. In such paintings as *An Avalanche in the Alps* of 1803 (plate 4) Loutherbourg takes up the threatening and life-destroying elements of Rosa's sublime *terribilità*. The spectators are effectively cut off from the action

3   Richard Wilson, *View near Wynnstay, the Seat of Sir Watkin Williams-Wynn, Bt.,* 1770–1, oil on canvas, 1804 × 2447, Yale Center for British Art, Paul Mellon Collection, New Haven.

4   Philip James de Loutherbourg, *An Avalanche in the Alps,* 1803, oil on canvas, 1099 × 1600, Tate Gallery, London.

by the gap between the pictorial foreground and the picture frame. Thus they can safely contemplate the dramatic scene unfolding before them from a vantage-point of apparent safety. The figures depicted on the left-hand side of the foreground, however, are desperate to escape this natural catastrophe which is overwhelming in relation to them. One, who was on the bridge when it collapsed under the impact of the avalanche, has lost the struggle already, and only a disappearing arm is visible. Through the stark contrasts between the dark left-hand side of the picture and the bluish-white of the breaking avalanche on the right, the force of this natural event is played off.

Although the sublime and the beautiful were the central categories for the appreciation of landscape in the early and middle part of the century, later another category, the *picturesque*, was added. The term 'picturesque' itself is an anglicisation of the French *pittoresque* or the Italian *pittoresco* and came into vogue in the early eighteenth century. Initially, it meant just whatever was suitable for painting, with no particular reference to landscape, and even the Reverend William Gilpin (1724–1804), whose published journals of his tours around Britain in the late eighteenth century established the craze for picturesque tourism, did not restrict the term exclusively to landscape aesthetics.[4] Gilpin made his first tour along the River Wye in 1770, although his description of it was not published until 1782. After several more such journeys, including one to the Lakes in 1772 and a tour into the Scottish Highlands in 1776, he set out to give his notion of the picturesque a more extended theoretical discussion in *Three Essays*, published in 1792.[5] By the time that the *Essays* appeared in print Gilpin had created a fashion for which the public had developed an insatiable hunger: the search for the picturesque. At the same time, the term was applied retrospectively to re-evaluate paintings such as Gainsborough's *Wooded Landscape with a Seated Figure* (plate 1), done in the 1740s, which did indeed depict what Reynolds described as 'common nature'.

In this chapter we will concentrate on the aesthetic theories that accompanied these developments. The eighteenth century was the heyday of grand theories, both in the natural sciences and in the sciences of man. Both spheres were dominated by the endeavour to establish a single underlying relationship between all the constituent parts of nature, whether between mind and body or between living beings and their environment. For those who started from a sensualist epistemology of a Lockean sort, the connection between human beings and their surroundings became crucial. From the physiological point of view, the consequence of this epistemology was an increased interest in neurology and the nervous system – the link and point of transition between human beings and the world in which they lived. As the century progressed, aesthetics came increasingly to occupy a central place in discussions concerning the relationship of human beings with their surroundings, since it was in this discipline that the character of the subjective reaction to objective stimuli was placed under the most intense investigation (indeed, aesthetics itself, as a term signifying investigation into the experience of art and beauty, is a product of the eighteenth century).

By the end of the century, however, the understanding of the interaction between man and nature was to change significantly. Instead of looking for a single underlying medium or principle of connection between the objective and the subjective realm, an increasing number of authors, first in Scotland and later in England, came to accept the idea that it was possible to look at subjective phenomena merely descriptively. We shall see that the changes associated with this shift took place across a range of discourses. Nor were its consequences immediately apparent to those who were responsible for the change. Some of the authors who depart most radically from the ruling eighteenth-century assumptions, like Dugald Stewart and Archibald Alison, presented their enterprise as merely continuing the work of

earlier writers, while others, who claimed to establish radically new approaches (Thomas Reid, for example) still remained within the established epistemological framework in fundamental respects.[6]

There is nothing new in identifying a major change at the turn of the nineteenth century; the majority of studies of the period emphasise the radicalism of the break – indeed, it has been called the 'Copernican Revolution in aesthetics'[7] – but the focus here is different. Much of the work on eighteenth-century aesthetics written by historians of ideas follows a teleological schema, whose central motif is the emergence and increasing dominance of 'subjectivity'.[8] This chapter will approach the period from a different point of view. It will ask what happened concurrently to the understanding of the non-human realm. In so doing it will emerge that not only is it the concept of 'subjectivity' which changes, but that the status of the object side becomes problematic around the turn of the century. I shall look particularly at the physiological explanations regarding the connection between mind and world that lay behind the aesthetic theories of the middle to late eighteenth century. I will first discuss the theories of three authors who were prominent in London in the second half of the eighteenth century: David Hartley, Edmund Burke and Joseph Priestley, and then move on to a discussion of similar theories in Scotland.

Although, of course, the wider goals and implications of their theories differed substantially, it is important at the outset to draw attention to certain features that these authors had in common. First, they all assumed in one way or another the contiguity of cause and effect; that is, an understanding of causal processes whereby cause and effect are required to touch each other in space and time. Where cause and effect were apparently separate, it was assumed that some as yet undiscovered chains of connecting causes must bind the two together. Above all, they assumed some intermediary which possessed the capacity to relate subjective perception with the objective realm. What was at issue between them was the nature of this medium. It was not just the physical character of such a medium which was called into question – whether it was a fluid, aether, or an elastic cord; quite often, as will become apparent in the discussion of the Scottish physiologists, its purely mechanical status was modified by the postulation of the existence of some 'sentient principle' in some way capable of the attributes of mind and matter.[9]

Yet we will see that this assumption came to be challenged, first in Scotland, implicitly by Thomas Reid and explicitly by his successors, Archibald Alison and Dugald Stewart. Finally, we shall return to England and the debate regarding the nature of the picturesque that took place in the 1790s between Uvedale Price and Richard Payne Knight. Some commentators, both contemporary and recent, have regarded the argument as a matter of hair-splitting between rival connoisseurs.[10] But the issues at stake are deeper and more revealing. The argument between Price and Knight illustrates the extent to which eighteenth-century aesthetics depended on specific physiological assumptions to account for the relationship between the perceiving subject and nature. It also shows how different presuppositions regarding the causal connection between mind and world corresponded to different social attitudes during the politically tense period of the 1790s. Price, I shall show, interpreted the picturesque in terms of an adaptation and continuation of Burke's physiological approach to aesthetics, while Knight's approach called into question the legitimacy of any attempt to provide an account of subjective phenomena in physical or physiological terms. To this extent, he was a pioneer or precursor in England of the phenomenalist stance.

London: The Body and Society

During the seventeenth century the Aristotelian theory of matter and motion in terms of substances thought to be capable of acting at a distance was displaced by corpuscularian and mechanist theories, according to which causation operates continuously and contiguously throughout the physical realm. Thus the fact that Isaac Newton (1642–1727), whose work by common consent represented the culmination of the scientific revolution, should have allowed for dynamic forces acting at a distance (in *Principia*, 1687) could not fail to prove controversial. Indeed, Newton himself found his position unsatisfactory. In the *Queries* appended to his *Opticks* (3/1717/18) he postulated the existence of a system of efficient causes operating through the medium of the *aether*. The aether, by virtue of its extreme subtlety and elasticity, was held to account for the transmission of motion without the loss of energy, and could thus be used to explain a variety of phenomena, such as refraction and reflection in optics,

electricity and magnetism.[11] It was also extremely influential on contemporary physiology where it was used to give an explanation of processes in the human body and of perception in particular. While Cartesian mechanists had explained the nervous system in hydrodynamic terms, assuming that perception involved a direct physical impact on the sense organs, which in turn set in motion a fluid in hollow nerves, the aether theory explained perceptions as the result of indirect impacts of external objects via their emission of aether.

David Hartley (1705–1757) adopted the Newtonian conception of the aether as part of a comprehensive theory of the human mind. He took Newton's hints in the *Queries* further than any of his contemporaries and applied them to the idea of 'association' propounded by Locke and Gay, thereby greatly expanding its scope. While Locke saw contiguity as a principle of association which only accounted for irrational processes of the mind, Hartley, in his *Observations on Man* (1749), uses it to explain all of the habits and customs of human beings, as well as the rational operations of the mind.[12] Ten years earlier, David Hume (1711–1776), in the *Treatise of Human Nature* (1739–40), had also identified association as the ordering principle of mental life, but, while Hume had based his account of mental processes and contents on the hydrodynamic model of Descartes (1596–1650) and Malebranche (1638–1715),[13] Hartley believes that associations are the effect of vibrations in a Newtonian aether which is suffused through the nervous system in virtue of its great elasticity and subtlety. For Hartley, the whole process of perception is achieved through the interconnection of vibrations:

> First then, We are to conceive, that when external Objects are impressed on the sensory Nerves, they excite Vibrations in the Aether residing in the Pores of these Nerves, by means of the mutual Actions interceding between the Objects, Nerves, and Aether.[14]

Hartley assumes that the nerves are solid and refers to the medullary substance of the brain, spinal cord and nerves as a single extended system which mediates sensation, motion and mental activities. Through attraction and repulsion, a sensation is propagated by the aether to the medullary substance, without causing any gross vibration in the nerves. With repetition, these vibrations in the brain contribute to the development of miniature vibrations, which are 'Vestiges, Types, or

Images of themselves, which may be called simple Ideas of Sensation'.[15] Complex ideas are the result of simple miniature vibrations which have run into complex vibrations and cause corresponding ideas.[16] They are not supposed to be merely a diminished version of those motions caused by external stimuli, but to be equally vivid.[17]

It is important to note that for Hartley, as for most of his contemporaries, the impact of external objects, either directly or through their emission of aether, causes vibrations, which *are* the sensations. Ultimately, therefore, all objects affect each of the senses in the same way by being uniformly 'decoded' as vibrations, and Hartley subsequently describes each sense in turn. Visual perception is achieved, he claims, through 'the variations of light and shade'.[18] According to Hartley, light, being transmitted through attraction and repulsion in particles of the aether, causes vibration in the aether of the optic nerve. This account has implications for the perception of painting. Because real objects establish 'vibratiuncles' (a complex set of vibrations),[19] caused by the rays of light, in the medullary substance, painting can affect us through the shaping of figures in light and shade by the rays which proceed from the plane surface. Since these rays are the result of the imitation of nature they fit the already established traces produced by equivalent light situations in nature and so affect man in the same way.[20]

Hartley's association theory is very frequently seen as a precursor of the Benthamite theory of progress.[21] His work does include statements like the following, in which he depicts human beings as developing through a learning process: 'Thus Association would convert a State, in which Pleasure and Pain were perceived by Turns, into one in which pure Pleasure alone would be perceived'.[22] It is probably due to Joseph Priestley's later edition of Hartley's theory that this and similar statements have been misinterpreted.[23] Priestley omitted the more speculative parts of Hartley's physiology and the theological elements which appeared particularly in the second volume of the original publication. It is there that Hartley qualifies his more apparently politically progressive statements. For example, he states that 'the bulk of mankind are not qualified for unmixed happiness'.[24] For Hartley, the significance of the gradual accumulation of knowledge through association is not that it will lead to social progress, but as a sign of Divine Providence. Given the gradual, trial-and-error character of the process of association, Hartley infers the operation of Divine Providence: the first man would have died before he had time to learn how to keep himself alive, had God not intervened miraculously.[25] The process of association simply describes the divinely established means by which each individual in turn ought to work towards spiritual perfection (a perfection which, if achieved, would re-establish the lost paradisiacal state). But, given that such perfection is unachievable by human beings without the intervention of divine grace, corruption and inequality are a permanent human condition, at least until the Last Judgement.[26]

A more secular endorsement of the *status quo* appeared eight years after Hartley's theory. Edmund Burke (1729–1797) published the first edition of his exceptionally influential *Philosophical Enquiry into the Origin of our Ideas of the Sublime and Beautiful* in 1757. Burke, like Hartley, attempted to give his theory a physiological grounding, but he seems not to have taken notice of Hartley's treatise.[27] The idea of a common unifying principle to unite the subject and the outside world was equally important to Burke, but, for a politician and future Whig parliamentarian, it held different implications.

Burke is concerned in the *Enquiry* with the sublime and the beautiful as forms of aesthetic response. They are identified as products of a taxonomy of human experience, which he classifies according to the forms of pain and pleasure. These categories, in turn, are based on two even more general principles, 'self-preservation' and 'society'.[28] Thus Burke constructs a general taxonomy of human emotions in analogy with the hierarchical classificatory tree of botany, with the sublime at the top: 'the sublime [. . .] is productive of the strongest emotion which the mind is capable of feeling'.[29] He specifies the ingredients which make up the sublime:

> Whatever is fitted in any sort to excite the ideas of pain, and danger, that is to say, whatever is in any sort terrible, or is conversant about terrible objects, or operates in a manner analogous to terror, is a source of the *sublime*.[30]

What is sublime causes the idea of pain, while beauty is what effects pleasure: 'By beauty I mean, that quality, or those qualities in bodies by which they cause love, or some passion similar to it'.[31]

Burke saw in the sublime an emotion which was

entirely the effect of an outside cause.[32] His object is to establish a theory which will identify the primary causes of the aesthetic emotions as well as dealing with their wider effects. It is in Part IV of the *Enquiry* that Burke deals with such primary causes. Here he articulates the physiological conception which is fundamental to his argument. His aim is to explain the efficient causes of pleasure and pain. Burke's system is a particular form of the vibration model which explains the nervous system by reference to gross movements along the nerve fibres. This model had largely been abandoned by physiologists by the time that Burke published his treatise because of the lack of evidence for such movements.[33] Burke does not appear to have based his version of this theory on one particular physiological source. His model is notably simple and might well have been something that he picked up casually. It is also intuitively quite comprehensible (in comparison, for example, with Hartley's version of the Newtonian aether). Burke takes up what had become a standard criticism of Newton's theory of the aether when he writes that the latter was just a hypothesis about ultimate causes which goes beyond 'the immediately sensible qualities of things'.[34] He seems not to have noticed that his own physiological model of the tone of the nerves is not confined to a purely descriptive account of observed phenomena either, but itself assumes just such ultimate, efficient causes.

Burke generally refers either to the different 'tones' of the nervous fibres or to variations in their vibrations. He states that 'pain and fear consist in an unnatural tension of the nerves',[35] while 'the genuine constituents of beauty, have each of them separately taken a natural tendency to relax the fibres'.[36] The feeling of terror, the main ingredient of the sublime, is understood to be the effect of the operation of the mind suggesting the idea of danger and thus producing an unnatural tension in the bodily organs.[37] This, however, would account only for the ideas associated with the sublime and thus not be a sufficient explanation according to the standards of Burke's theory, which aims to identify a chain of causes and effects between object and perceiver. Shortly afterwards, Burke identifies just such a direct connection as being characteristic of the sublime: 'a source of the sublime [. . .] relate[s] to such things, as are fitted by nature to produce this sort of tension, either by the primary operation of the mind or the body'.[38] But a necessary condition for the feeling of the sublime is that the idea of terror should come without immediate danger; thus horror can be followed by delight in order to produce 'one of the strongest of all the passions',[39] the sublime. This too is explained physiologically by Burke: when the source of pain and terror produces the tension, and then proves not to be physically destructive, the strain disappears and this produces release, which is delight, but not pleasure, pleasure being qualitatively different in that it actively produces a relaxation rather than a release.[40]

Burke then goes on to argue, like Hartley, that those natural properties that are productive of the sublime and the beautiful affect all the different senses in the same way, namely, by a physical impulse which is translated into a specific tone of the nervous fibre. Vision, however, poses a particular problem for models based on the existence of actual physical impulses. In rejecting the aether theory, Burke must face the problems which it was meant to circumvent: the mediation of the space between objects when that is not occupied by gross bodies capable of acting upon each other. Consequently, Burke talks of vision as being caused by the 'stroke' of light.[41] An effect of sublimity is, for instance, said to be produced by a vast object, each point of which emits a ray of light. However, because of the excessive number of strokes on the retina, tension is increased to the point at which it becomes painful.[42] Beauty, for Burke, is caused by smoothness and gradual variation in objects. In the case of vision, this means that the rays of light reflected from a softly varying surface continually excite the sense organ in different degrees and thus tend to produce an effect of relaxation through a 'gentle oscillatory motion, a rising and falling in the nerve'.[43] Because Burke is arguing on the basis of a gross body theory, his explanations of optical perception sometimes read as if he assumes that not only light rays but the objects themselves strike the retina:

> Another principal property of beautiful objects is, that the line of their parts is continually varying its direction; but it varies it by a very insensible deviation; it never varies it so quickly as to surprise, or by sharpness of its angle to cause any twitching or convulsion of the optic nerve.[44]

Although lacking the sophistication of Hartley's theory, Burke's physiology forms the heart of his aesthetics. His theory shares with contemporary works on physiology the idea of a common unifying principle –

in this case the elasticity of the nervous fibres – which is capable of mediating the outside world with the human mind by partaking of and transmitting the former's properties. Burke's attempt to produce a classification of human emotions is built on the same premises: to find, first, the most basic common emotions from which all other human reactions and sentiments are derived; their efficient causes, which are to be found in what is common between the human body and the outside world, can then be established.

After the *Enquiry*, Burke directed his energies wholeheartedly into politics. In fact, his aesthetic is not disconnected from his growing political concerns. In the *Essay on Taste*, which Burke prefixed to the second edition of the *Enquiry*, he held that the basic capacity for taste 'is the same in all, high and low, learned and unlearned',[45] a point on which he was in agreement with most of his contemporaries.[46] Taste, according to Burke, has two components: judgement and sensibility. The nervous system – the link between the human mind and the natural world – was the common factor that guaranteed the transmission to the perceiving subject of a stable, divine order. For taste to be good, however, both 'rectitude of judgment' and an appropriate sensibility are required.[47] He denies rectitude of judgement to those who are 'heated in the chace of honours and distinction', the climbers in society.[48] Burke's second condition for good taste is a proper sensibility: 'though a degree of sensibility is requisite to form a good judgment, yet a good judgment does not necessarily arise from a quick sensibility of pleasure'.[49] In contrast to correct judgement, sensibility is something which even education and good fortune cannot produce or amend: 'There are some men formed with feelings [. . .] so blunt, with tempers so cold and phlegmatic, that they can hardly be said to awake during the whole course of their lives'.[50] According to Burke, those occupied 'in the low drudgery of avarice' will always be found to be incapable of aesthetic feelings,[51] but so will some of those who have the means to refinement and the acquisition of good judgement but have a too 'quick sensibility of pleasure' or who lack it altogether.

From his first publications, the *Vindication* and the *Enquiry* in the 1750s, through to his sympathy for the American colonies and his involvement in the investigation of the East India Company in the 1780s, Burke's political energies were directed towards the faults and irresponsibilities which followed from the artificial 'refinement' of the establishment.[52] In *A Vindication of Natural Society*, Burke's concern, as Peter Melvin points out, had not been:

> [to justify] a primitive 'state of nature' as man's proper abode, which the misleading title implied, but his scorn for the excesses of artificial society. There is a full-blown attack on unduly complicated judicial procedures [. . .] along with a bitter review of the cost to mankind of all unmeaning forms and ceremonies.[53]

Here are the origins of a position that Burke later made explicit. For Burke, the natural ruling class consisted of the hereditary landed aristocracy and other men of independent means, because good education and leisure were the necessary conditions for good government (for example, breadth of vision and the capacity to command); but they were not a guarantee of it, because, as he had argued in the *Enquiry*, sensibility was also a necessary condition for good judgement, something one could not acquire. Thus men without property but of exceptional virtue, wisdom and sensibility – as Burke presumably saw himself – are required to act as a potential corrective as well as to guarantee advances in science and increases in wealth.[54] Like good taste, the good society has two essential parts – one inherited, the other acquired – but each needs the other for balance, in order not to deviate and become what Burke calls 'artificial'.

Later, however, Burke's argument shifted. The accusation of artificiality subsequently came to focus on those opposing the establishment: the radical dissenters and philosophical materialists, all those who supported the 'world of illusion and crude spectacle' of the Jacobin theatre.[55] Many of the latter, like Tom Paine (1737–1809), had been Burke's close friends before 1789. Yet Burke's *Reflections on the Revolution in France* do not represent a complete U-turn; rather, one side of his contradictory intellectual personality was brought to the fore by the crisis of the French Revolution.[56] The activities of the Bowood circle, under the patronage of William Petty, Marquis of Lansdowne (better known as Lord Shelburne),[57] with its mixture of natural philosophy and aspirations towards political reform, appears to have been a major cause of the redirection of Burke's rhetoric.[58] Joseph Priestley's work and writings were central to the Bowood circle from the time he became Shelburne's librarian in 1772. It was in that year that Burke and Priestley clashed politically for the first time. Priestley (1733–1804) was prominent among the group of radical dissenters who drafted the so-called Feathers Tavern Petition in an attempt to relieve themselves from the disabilities consequent upon failing to subscribe to the 'Thirty-Nine Articles'. In his speech to Parliament on 6 February 1772 Burke denounced any deliberately introduced changes in the fundamental institutions of society whatsoever:

> I would have a system of religious laws, that would remain fixed and permanent, like our civil constitution, and that would preserve the body ecclesiastical from tyranny and despotism, as much at least as our code of common and statute law does the people in general; for I am convinced that the liberty of conscience contended for by the petitioners would be the fore runner of religious slavery.[59]

Cunningly, Burke's rhetoric depicted the radical dissenters' demand for liberty as a step towards tyranny. He invokes the claims of tradition in the way which he would later develop so extensively in the *Reflections*: reason is to be rejected if it advances its claims at the expense of tradition. This, however, was an argument which, despite all the shifts of balance in his political thinking, was already present in the *Enquiry*: God's wisdom and Providence had made the world; therefore there was no reason to distrust the feelings and unreflective attitudes of human beings.[60] It was the central role of the nervous system in the *Enquiry* which guaranteed the knowability of that divine order.

Priestley's work challenged just that. After the failure of the Feathers Tavern Petition, Priestley's scientific work took on political radicalism through his commitment to philosophical materialism. Two of Priestley's publications from this period are relevant here: his *An Examination of Dr. Reid's Inquiry into the Human Mind on the Principles of Common Sense* (1774) and his edition of *Hartley's Theory of the Human Mind* (1775).[61] Priestley saw political implications in Reid's doctrines. For Priestley, appeals to 'common sense' could be used to legitimise politicians' repressive actions by making them immune to criticism:

> But if this talk should not be undertaken by some person, I am afraid we shall find these new principles extending their authority farther than the precincts

of metaphysics, morals, religion, christianity, and protestantism, to which they have been hitherto confined [. . .]. [P]oliticians [. . .] possessing themselves of this advantage, may venture once more to thunder out upon us their exploded doctrines of passive obedience and non-resistance. For having now nothing to fear from the powers of *reason*, and being encouraged by the examples of grave divines and metaphysicians, they may venture to assert their favourite maxims with the greatest confidence; appealing at once to this ultimate tribunal of common sense, and giving out their own mandates as the decisions of this new tribunal.[62]

Arguments of this kind had had practical consequences for Priestley, for they led to the rejection of the Feathers Tavern Petition.[63] Burke had responded to the demand for free thought raised by Priestley and other Dissenters with a plea for the intrinsic legitimacy of the *status quo*. As Fruchtman puts it, for Priestley, 'it all fitted neatly together: common sense provided a retrogressive epistemology which inexorably led to the acceptance of the *status quo*, no matter how immoral or ungodly that *status quo* might be'.[64]

By the time that Burke wrote the *Reflections* the French Revolution was well under way and he had singled out Priestley as 'the leader of a plot to subvert the English social order as the French had subverted theirs'.[65] Yet, at the outbreak of the Revolution, Burke wrote to Fox that Priestley had contacted him to ask if he (Fox) would be prepared to approach the Prince of Wales to ask for permission for Priestley to dedicate his *Experiments and Observations on Different Kinds of Airs* to the Prince. Burke took the view that science could do no harm and advised Fox:

> to gain entirely some of these dissenters, who are already, I fancy, inclined to come over to you. This Offer to dedicate to the Prince is a strong overt act of that disposition. Even if they cannot be wholly reclaimed, it would be something to neutralize the acid of that sharp and eager description of men.[66]

Burke made no connection at that point between Priestley's scientific work (which he had admired from the 1770s)[67] and his political position, although Burke had come to associate Priestley's politics with the fall of the Rockingham Administration in 1782 and the ruin of his own political career. Two years later, however, this combination of natural philosophy and politics received some of Burke's most sarcastic attacks.[68] From now on, whatever looked like a system of ideas appeared dangerous to Burke, even if, like Price's *Essay on the Picturesque*, it was written entirely from within his own conceptual framework.[69]

Priestley's interest in natural philosophy came increasingly to be intertwined with his political radicalism. He appears to have responded favourably to the implications of Hartley's theory for the endeavour to reform mind and society. He also endorsed Hartley's attempt to show that all the diverse phenomena of the human mind were only different modes of association and that these, in turn, were the effects of the nervous system. Yet there were major differences between Hartley and Priestley. As explained earlier, the religious considerations in the *Observations on Man* were a decisive element in Hartley's theory. In Priestley's view, however, these aspects of Hartley's thought only obscured the work's true significance.[70]

For Hartley, the process of association made possible the individual redemption from the fallen state of 'those who have eaten of the Tree of the Knowledge of Good and Evil, back again to a paradisiacal one'.[71] But, for Priestley, its true significance was to show the necessity of political change as the human mind progressed. Both writers argue that moral judgements are acquired by associating pleasurable sensations with some objects and painful ones with others and, for both, it is God's wisdom and providence which secures the right causes for the right associations. Priestley writes:

> Who can help admiring the admirable simplicity of nature, and the wisdom of the great author of it, in this provision for the *growth of all our passions*, and propensities, just as they are wanted, and in the degree in which they are wanted through life? All is performed by the general disposition of the mind to conform to its circumstances, and to be modified by them, without that seemingly operose and inelegant contrivance, of different original, independent instincts, adapted to a thousand different occasions, and either implanted in us at different times, or contrived to lie dormant till they are wanted.[72]

While, for Hartley, this determinism was necessary to open the possibility of redemption, Priestley's theology, though millennialist, is directed towards this world. Not only does the association theory account for the

achievement of common virtue, it also naturalises existing differences in opinion, since the latter depend on the different circumstances encountered by human beings:

> This opinion of the gradual formation of the ideas of moral right and wrong, from a great variety of elements, easily accounts for that prodigious diversity in the sentiments of mankind respecting the objects of moral obligation; and I do not see that any other hypothesis can account for the facts. If the idea of *moral obligation* was a *simple idea*, arising from the view of certain actions, or sentiments, I do not see why it should not be as *invariable* as the perception of colours or sounds. [. . .] Now a thing that varies with education and instruction as moral sentiments are known to do, certainly has the appearance of being generated by a series of different impressions, in some such manner as I have endeavoured to describe.[73]

Thus Priestley turned Hartley's system into a legitimation for political toleration and endowed it with a secular dynamism it had not previously had. Since a diversity of opinions is generated by impressions formed in different circumstances, and these in turn influence and create further changes, any belief in a static human order, be that belief socially or biologically based, is untenable. Only thanks to God's providence does this dynamism evolve coherently rather than leading to chaos. This difference of emphasis led Priestley to omit parts of Hartley's treatise. Hartley, for instance, had maintained a strict division between body and mind:

> The first is subjected to our Senses and Inquiries, in the same manner as the other Parts of the External material World. The last is that Substance, Agent, Principle, &c. to which we refer the sensations, Ideas, Pleasures, Pains and voluntary Motion.[74]

In consequence, progress, for Hartley, can take place only in the spiritual realm. Priestley, however, argues that 'man does not consist of two principles, so essentially different from one another as matter and spirit'.[75] He maintains that, since the brain and the nerves are of the same substance: 'the affection of a nerve during the transmission of a sensation and the affection of the brain during the perceived presence of it, are probably the same', and he reasons that 'ideas themselves, as they exist in the mind, may be as different from what they are in the brain, as that peculiar difference of texture

[. . .] which occasions difference of colour, is from the colours themselves, as we conceive of them'.[76] Thus the change from one state to another is not a qualitative one for Priestley, but structural. Priestley replaced materialistic models of explanation with a dynamic mechanism which, as Schofield puts it, assumed matter to be 'nothing but the geometry of space and the interaction of forces'.[77] Thus there is no room in Priestley's system for an agent, like the Newtonian aether employed by Hartley to mediate between mind and matter, for mind is not to be thought of as a qualitatively different substance but is assumed to be merely a structural 'result (whether necessary or not) of such an organical structure as that of the brain'.[78]

Isaac Kramnick has argued that a close parallel exists between Priestley's scientific world-view and his theory of the liberal state.[79] In contrast to Burke's understanding of the state as an organism which constitutes the final purpose of communal existence, the sole function of Priestley's liberal state lay in the protection of individuals and their rights. Like his account of the interaction of substances, the state for Priestley, as Kramnick puts it, 'consists of nothing but material matter that attracts and repels according to the gravitational laws of interest'.[80]

Priestley's advocacy of social reform went hand in hand with his criticism of the received model of physiological explanation: theories that assume efficient causes in the form of substances (such as aether or fluid) are branded as mere speculation.[81] But he does not reject the possibility of causal explanation altogether.[82] As in his understanding of the diversity of opinions in society acting together and affecting each other, Priestley perceives the distinction between matter and mind as a structural difference between interacting forces, not a qualitative difference, fixed for ever.

Although Priestley makes the relationship between human beings and their environment a dynamic one, it was in fact the Scottish School of Common Sense, so fiercely attacked by him, which cut the physiological link between mind and body altogether.

Scotland: The Culture of Sensibility

The intellectual milieu in Scotland in the eighteenth century was not polarised between progressivism and traditionalism in the same way as it was in England. The intellectual élite which had emerged by the mid-eighteenth century, centring around the three university towns of Edinburgh, Glasgow and Aberdeen, was almost exclusively Whiggish in tendency and in various ways committed to the improvement of the backward Scottish community.[83] Almost without exception, the members of the élite were no revolutionaries, and, particularly during the 1790s, when, in the wake of the French Revolution, a Tory government had come to power and repression of reformist thinking set in, they were at pains to affirm their loyalty to the British constitution and to distance their desire for reform from calls to revolution.[84] Fundamental to the Scottish Whigs' creed was an understanding of the capacity of human beings to respond emotionally and sensually to their environment. David Hume and Adam Smith (1723–1790) both placed the passions at the centre of their progressive understanding of society. The development of sympathy is the necessary means by which humanity moves from a coercive to a cooperative political order. Sensual responsiveness, in the form of the body's nervous system, became the key object of investigation for Scottish physiology.[85]

It was Robert Whytt (1714–1766) who, when appointed Professor of Medicine in Edinburgh in 1749, first introduced research on the nervous system into Scottish academic life.[86] In 1751 Whytt published his *Essay on the Vital and other Involuntary Motions of Animals*, in which he states that:

> the human body ought not to be regarded (as it has too long been by many Physiologists) as a mechanical machine, so exquisitely formed, as, by the mere force of its construction, to be able to perform, and continue, the several vital functions; things far above the powers of mechanism! But as a system, framed indeed with the greatest art and contrivance; a system! [sic] in which the peculiar structure of each part is not more to be admired than the wise and beautiful arrangement of the whole; nevertheless, as a system whose motions are all owing to the active power, and energy, of an immaterial sentient principle, to which it is united, and by which every fibre of it is enlivened and actuated.[87]

Thus it has been claimed that, in contrast to the English and Continental physiological theories mentioned so far, Whytt 'reintroduced the soul into the body'.[88] He postulates the existence of a 'sentient principle', which he also ('in compliance with custom') called 'animal or vital spirits', though this should not, he says, be taken to imply any 'particular nature or manner of acting; it being sufficient [. . .] that the existence of such a power is granted in general'.[89] This principle has the power to operate mechanically, while at the same time being a non-mechanical, vital force, able to mediate soul and body. It is assumed to be endowed with the power to feel and to act as a gentle, steady force with a mild, tonic effect on muscles. The energy of the mind is supposed to make an immediate impact on the sentient principle.[90] Thus Whytt assumes the soul to be co-extensive with the body.[91]

Having represented the sentient principle as the controlling power necessary to integrate the bodily functions, Whytt then went on to publish a second treatise in which he attempted to construct a *nosology* – a classification of nervous disorders – claiming that 'in almost every disease, the nerves suffer more or less, and there are very few disorders which may not, in a large sense, be called nervous'.[92] Characteristically, Whytt argued that, since the sentient principle was reactive in response to outer stimuli, such nervous diseases could usefully be treated by external action on the body.[93]

In many ways, Whytt laid the foundations for all his successors at Edinburgh, although none of them shared his own radical scepticism regarding the natural philosopher's ability to explain the nature of nervous power. In the endeavour to establish physiology as a strong and autonomous science, however, most of Whytt's medical followers in Edinburgh were not prepared to follow him in the assumption that there existed an immaterial sentient principle which did not follow natural laws.[94] Nevertheless, as we shall see, his scepticism was a major influence upon Reid's philosophical critique of efficient causality.

Whytt's successor in Edinburgh, William Cullen (1710–1790), was probably the most influential eighteenth-century British writer on physiology. His theory shows the variety of models of explanation which were current by the middle of the century and the way in which different models were often not treated as mutually exclusive. Cullen's theory of the nervous system moves between the idea of a 'nervous power' in the sense organs (said to be the result of the action of external bodies, 'propagated from the place of impulse along the course of the nerves')[95] and the idea of a nervous fluid, which was assumed to be a modification of Newton's universal aether.[96] Yet Cullen also characterises the latter in more Whyttian terms as what 'may be otherwise properly enough termed the vital principle' on which the immaterial soul can act.[97] As Lawrence explains, Cullen 'retained all the characteristics of Whytt's sentient principle – purposeful action, coordinating ability, and, most importantly, unconscious feeling – without introducing second substances into physiology'.[98] In consequence, Cullen's nosology embodied a far more mechanical view of the nervous system than Whytt's; the nervous system contains nothing that is not subject to physical laws. Thus the nervous system not only became accessible to research, but was also supposed to be controllable to the extent that physical events can be influenced. Cullen saw the origins of diseases in processes of excitement and collapse – states of increased and decreased mobility of the nervous power or fluid in the brain – which in turn affected the body's sensitivity.

For both Whytt and Cullen the understanding of the body's reactive capacity and the sensitivity of the nervous system to internal and external stimuli became the key to their medical systems. As for the professors of medicine, so too for Scottish writers on society and authors of aesthetic treatises: sensibility was fundamental. According to Henry Home, Lord Kames (1696–1782), investigation 'into the nature of man as a sensitive being'[99] was to discover the 'principles, common to all men'.[100] However, like Burke, Home argued that although sensibility was a universal property of human beings, this was not sufficient for the development of taste.[101] Alexander Gerard (1728–1795) takes the same position in his *Essay on Taste* (1759).[102] What is also needed, according to Gerard, is 'a vigorous abstracting faculty, the greatest force of reason, [. . .] a deep knowledge of the principle of human nature' and 'it is only in the few, who improve the rudiments of taste which *nature* has implanted, by *culture* well chosen, and judiciously applied, that taste at length appears in elegant form and just proportion'.[103] Home specifies that this is 'chiefly [. . .] the duty of the opulent, who have leisure to improve their minds and their feelings'.[104] Those who have 'education' and 'reflection',[105] the gentry and the learned, are also those entitled to form the ruling élite, because taste and a moral sense are 'allied'.[106] Home thus, in effect, endorsed the political supremacy of the social élite which had come to dominate the Scottish culture, composed of the landowning gentry and the members of the traditional learned professions, such as lawyers, doctors, the clergy and university professors.

Scottish thinkers from Hume to Stewart, although they differed in many respects, were agreed on one point: the need for innovation and change in society, although without thereby challenging the established hierarchical order.[107] In the years of anti-French-Revolution propaganda, when the Whiggish intellectual élite was set in opposition to the Tory domination, this commitment did not cease. During these years, as Chitnis puts it:

> the party politicisation became so much more marked [. . .] when the law sported a clutch of reactionary judges hell-bent on suppressing Jacobins, when the ruling Moderates in the Kirk adhered to their old war-cry of order but for political not ecclesiastical reasons, and when university professors had to watch what they said in lectures for fear of being branded as revolutionaries and perverters of the youth.[108]

Among those professors who came under suspicion of subversion was the Common Sense philosopher Thomas Reid (1710–1796), whose doctrine had been so severely attacked by Priestley for its reactionary implications. In 1794 Reid had to distance himself publicly from the egalitarian utopianism that had been attributed to him.[109] His student, Dugald Stewart, was accused of being in sympathy with the spirit of the French Revolution and the content of his lectures was placed under strict supervision. Nevertheless, both men continued to hold significant positions in the Scottish intellectual milieu. The idea of progress and the gradual diffusion of political liberty to all levels of society remained under discussion in Scotland in a way which had become unthinkable in England at the time.

The Development of a Critique of Efficient Causality

The fundamental similarity between the Scottish and English physiological theories discussed so far is their basic presupposition of the transfer of feeling by way of some mediating agency from 'impression' to 'idea'. It was within one of the Scottish élite's social circles, however, that a fundamental critique of the nature of causality was first developed. The Scottish Common Sense School grew out of the discussions of the Philosophical Society of Aberdeen, which met twice a month between 1758 and 1773.[110] When its founder, Thomas Reid,[111] published his *Inquiry into the Human Mind* (1764), he was not in the first place attempting to refute models of explanation of natural events which drew on efficient causes but to oppose the kind of philosophical scepticism which had been advanced in Scotland by Hume and in Ireland by Berkeley (1685–1753). Like his associates, Reid took a progressive view of society. But in contrast, for example, to Hume or Adam Smith (although Smith's position is more ambivalent than sometimes assumed) Reid was unhappy with commercial society and looked forward, as Davie puts it, 'to a Third Age of Humanity achieved by a communal effort of will, which would reinstate some of the lost virtues of the primitive'.[112] This utopianism was interpreted in egalitarian terms by Reid's contemporaries, but, as regards contemporary society, it was not. Although Reid rejected the assumption of a common unifying principle which mediated the reactive response of human beings to their environment, he arrived at the same hierarchical conclusions as his contemporaries via a different route. For Reid, for reasons that will be explained below, the sense of sight was esteemed highest in the process of perception. From this, as Davie puts it, Reid went on to extend to natural philosophy:

> Hume's principle that the key to the problem of ethical standards in a commercial age is to recognise the complementariness of the respective standpoints of the vulgar and the learned. The way to harmonise the respective roles of sight, and of touch in the mastery of nature was to note that [. . .] the specialists engaged in manufacture or experiment had an incomparably deeper knowledge of the detail of the bodies involved than the spectators could have.[113]

Those, on the other hand, not engaged in specialist manual tasks, but who were in a position to survey the whole process of manufacturing in society, were able 'to correct the experts' blind spots, and even suggest to them fruitful hypotheses'.[114] Thus Reid's argument, although based on the difference between the sense organs of sight and touch, rather than on sensibility as a common principle, also gives privilege to those who are not engaged in manual (and thus narrowing) work, by virtue of their literal 'far-sightedness'. But he does so via a different kind of theory, one which eventually would open the way to new developments.

For Reid, Hume's and Berkeley's scepticism was the necessary correlate of unacknowledged assumptions made by them about the nature of causation. Although Hume and Berkeley denied the certainty of our knowledge of external objects, they nevertheless maintained that sensations and feelings had to have external causes. Reid's strategy for meeting their criticisms lay in abandoning certain assumptions which Hume and Berkeley shared with their contemporaries: in particular, he rejected the assumption that an effect in the human mind or body has to have a cause which touches the body or mind directly in space and time – that is, the notion of the contiguity of cause and effect. Instead, Reid posits the existence of an innate disposition in human nature, 'common sense',[115] which contains pre-established knowledge of the world, to the extent that the outside world can make an impact upon us without the intervention of any mediating substance. Thus Reid simply removes what had been the foundation of the theories of his contemporaries – the claim that things could affect the mind and be represented there only by means of the senses. Reid states:

> For effects and causes, in the operations of nature, mean nothing but signs, and the things signified by them. We perceive no proper causality or efficiency in any natural cause, but only a connection established by the course of nature between it and what is called its effect.[116]

Like many writers before him, Reid claims Newton's authority for his ideas, but, while those physiologists who had based their theories on the idea of an efficient cause had drawn on Newton's *Queries*, Reid asserts that he alone takes up the real Newton of the *Principia*, in which Newton repeatedly states that, for him, to talk of forces was to speak only of mathematical physical laws, not causes.[117] Reid's ambition was to find just those laws for the mind that Newton had found for physics:

> Are there any principles with regard to the mind, settled with that perspicuity and evidence, which attends the principles of mechanics, astronomy and optics? These are really sciences, built upon laws of nature which universally obtain. What is discovered in them is no longer matter of dispute: future ages may add to it, but till the course of nature be changed, what is already established can never be overturned. But when we turn our attention inward, and consider the phaenomena of human thoughts, opinions and perceptions, and endeavour to trace them to the general laws and the first principle of our constitution, we are immediately involved in darkness and perplexity.[118]

Reid's critique of the inconclusiveness of physiological models of perception is very likely to have been formed when he studied under Robert Whytt, whose idea of a sentient principle, as we have seen, functions merely as a receptacle for the unknown. But Reid goes further: he attempts to show that to identify a mediating principle which transmits ideas as the last step in a chain of contiguous physiological impressions does not solve the problem but postpones it. There will always be an ultimate gap between the idea as a physiological entity and the processes of the mind. For Reid, the sensory fact is without any reference to the object and the mental fact is itself as original as the sensory fact:

> However these things may be, if Nature had given us nothing more than impressions made upon the body, and sensations in our minds corresponding to them, we should in that case have been merely sentient, but not percipient beings. We should never have been able to form a conception of any external object, far less a belief of its existence. Our sensations have no resemblance to external objects, nor can we discover, by our reason, any necessary connections between the existence of the former, and that of the latter.[119]

Such an understanding ultimately leads to dualism, which most of the other eighteenth-century theories, whether philosophical or physiological, avoided. Reid breaks down the process of perception into three independent constituents: the object world, which can be explained by recourse to physical laws; the sense organs, which can be explained according to physiological laws (not, it is important to note, efficient causes); and independent mental facts.

Yet, despite these major innovations, Reid remains anchored within the discursive structures of his time: his questions are fundamentally the same as those of his predecessors; it is his answers that differ. For Reid, reflections on the certainty of knowledge and the connection between object world and human realm are the proper topics of inquiry. Reid replaces speculations about mechanical causes with metaphysical or theological ones, for he goes on to identify 'God as being the efficient cause, either directly or indirectly, of all changes in the physical world'.[120] It is characteristic of this conventional aspect of Reid's work that the *Inquiry* should offer an analysis of the five senses whose structure corresponds to the writings of his contemporaries. Nevertheless, in contrast to those writers who explained the processes of perception by reference to a single unifying principle, Reid argues that each of the sense organs functions according to different laws; they embody different kinds of sensation which cannot be unified on the physiological level. Reid is adamant in his insistence that the senses of taste, smell and hearing do not transmit knowledge of the object but merely register some quality caused in an unknown way in the outside world. The sense of touch, on the other hand, *does* give knowledge of primary qualities (hardness, and so on) as well as secondary ones (heat and cold). As mentioned earlier, the sense of vision has a special position in Reid's system, as it does in his understanding of society. The optical organ had, of course, always played a prominent role in treatises dealing with perception, as being the chief means for the transmission of ideas. For Reid, however, vision is the only sense whose impressions transmit essential knowledge about the object.[121] Michel Malherbe explains the special role of the sense of vision in Reid's treatise as follows:

But, whereas, like other senses, touch requires the distinction between sensation (a subjective reality) and the secondary or primary quality which, determined or not, is taken as being real, because it is felt, sight introduces a second structure of designation or signification, which is superimposed on the first, without being confused with it. Undoubtedly, sensation is the subjective sign of the quality of the thing; but this objective quality, such as it is offered, (for instance, the side of a cube which I look at) is itself the sign of the appearing thing (the cube with its six sides). The objective determination itself here includes the representation of the thing by its visible quality.[122]

Thus the sense of vision involves more than simple sensation. It is the only sense which is already knowledge, since the image presented is already a full representation of the thing's visual structures: 'it is the real

and external object to the eye'.[123] Though colour is clearly a secondary quality, being the sign of an unknown quality in the object,[124] it also indicates the position of the cause to the eye, which produces no sensation like the general figure:

Thus we proceed in orderly fashion from simple to complex, from sensation to knowledge, from a subjective content of sensation indicating some unknown quality of the thing to a sensation losing its subjective presence, but gaining in objective character, in the case of touch and, *a fortiori*, in the case of seeing, where the sensation itself is not reachable but by complete concentration, for the benefit of a presence of the thing henceforth complex and informed enough to enclose the relationship between appearing and being.[125]

In his later publication, the *Essays on the Intellectual Powers of Man* (1785), Reid concentrates on the operations of the mind rather than on the organs of sense.[126] He distinguishes between sense organ and sensation, and considers mental facts to be distinct from them both. Malherbe has pointed out that, by giving the sensation a purely subjective function which feeds on but is not itself a conception in the mind, 'Reid carries on his endeavour to make every kind of representation disappear from the mind, as if what has already been fought on the side of sensorial impression, must be again hunted down in the sentient subject itself'.[127]

Thus Reid's philosophy abandons the search for the physiological link between mind and body and outside world: the gap between them cannot be closed by reasoning. Yet his final aim is to argue, in eighteenth-century fashion, that something must be capable of bridging the gap simply because it is in fact bridged, and that this must be due to a metaphysical cause: God.

The Rise of Phenomenalism

At the turn of the nineteenth century two treatises on perception entered the discussion in Scotland which, on a superficial level, may seem simply to extend the type of thinking that had been going on for nearly a hundred years. Archibald Alison's *Essays on the Nature and Principles of Taste* (1790) and Dugald Stewart's *Elements of the Philosophy of the Human Mind* (1792–1827) were both written within the formal constraints of the established mode of investigation.[128] Nevertheless, they redirected the nature of the questions posed to such an extent that they in effect undermined the whole genus.

Both writers acknowledged the influence of Reid, whose lectures they had attended while students in Glasgow; all three became friends.[129] Like Reid, Alison (1757–1839) and Stewart (1753–1828) both criticise assumptions which postulate the existence of a hidden connection between disparate elements in the subjective and objective realms. But what separates them from Reid's metaphysics and gives their work an entirely new direction is their rejection of his traditional approach to questions of epistemology. Reid, writing against scepticism, was motivated philosophically by the desire to find a solution to questions concerning the certainty of human knowledge. Alison and Stewart, however, seek to bypass such problems. According to Hipple, the abandonment of physiological and normative preoccupations means that these texts achieve a 'logical coherence unmatched in British aesthetics'.[130] Because they rejected what they saw as the speculative inclinations of their predecessors, Hipple describes them as using an inductive method and (in the case of Alison) anticipating John Stewart Mill's 'Joint Method of Agreement and Difference'.[131] In my view, however, to the extent that these texts do indeed embody a positivistic conception of scientific method, this is not because they represent the conclusion to a continuous argument so much as because they result from a shift in the understanding of the subject-object relationship. This change marks a break with tradition, rather than a conclusion to it.

Archibald Alison, having been a vicar in England, returned to Edinburgh in 1800 as minister of the episcopal chapel of Cowgate. His *Essays* were originally published in 1790, but their reception by the public was very slow and the work did not achieve recognition until 1811 with the appearance of the second edition.[132] In contrast to all previous British aesthetic theorists, Alison no longer argues that objects outside the subject are the efficient causes of sublime, beautiful (or picturesque) emotions. He states that the 'Qualities of Matter are not to be considered as sublime or beautiful in themselves, but as either sublime or beautiful from being the signs or Expressions of qualities capable of producing Emotion'.[133] Thus the role of nature or other objects (such as paintings) is reduced to that of a mere occasional cause in the process of aesthetic appreciation.

A stimulus is necessary to set a train of association in motion, but it is the latter which produces the aesthetic emotions: 'That unless this exercise of imagination is excited, the emotions of beauty or sublimity are unfelt'.[134] Although otherwise very different, Alison's relocation of aesthetic experience in the free play of mind, instead of in a correspondence between the qualities of mind and matter, does indeed display some similarities with his German contemporary, Immanuel Kant.

Alison's association theory has frequently been linked to Hartley,[135] but, apart from the fact that both use the principle of association to explain mental processes, very little else unites their reasoning. Alison's theory is not concerned with explaining how trains of associations are started or formed and so does not appeal either to Hartleian or Humean principles. The limit of Alison's ambition is to give examples of what actually happens: 'Trains of pleasing or of solemn thought arise spontaneously within our minds, our hearts swell with emotions, of which the objects before us seem to afford no adequate cause'.[136]

The fact that he does not raise the question of how knowledge of the expressions of matter comes about is Alison's major step away from the eighteenth-century tradition and takes him beyond even Reid. Alison's self-restriction to the enumeration of various instances in which sublime, beautiful or picturesque associations are set in motion amounts to a phenomenological stance and this has led critics to see him as a romantic subjectivist.[137] His theory emphasises the uniqueness of individual experience and the particularity of the determinants of the trains of association. But he also follows Adam Smith's account of the division of labour in emphasising the influence of occupational experience on the character which associations have: 'there are probably few men, who have not had occasion to remark how much the diversity of tastes corresponds to the diversity of occupations'.[138] This argument potentially represents a major problem for the appreciation of landscape art; if Alison had followed his line of argument through, it might well have led to the rejection of the public role of art, for he argues that the painter's experience in front of the object is unique to him, perhaps sharable by colleagues, but not communicable to non-artists:

The pleasure, for instance, which the generality of

mankind receive from any celebrated painting, is trifling when compared to that which a painter feels, if he is a man of any common degree of candour. What is, to them, only an accurate representation of nature, is, to him, a beautiful exertion of genius, and a perfect display of art.[139]

But Alison does not entirely go down this road. In perceiving sublime and beautiful events, he says, the painter's capacity for aesthetic appreciation is the same as everybody else's and thus such scenes are, he argues, universally appreciated in the same manner. Alison, like his predecessors, believed in the universality of certain standards of taste, but his system has more room for individual variations. The chain of association differs in different individuals, while its quality remains the same – except, of course, he hastens to add, conventionally enough, in those 'who, by their original constitution' are unable to exercise 'enlarged and extensive thought' altogether, and whose efforts of imagination are either feeble or slow.[140]

Using the same well-worn argument, Alison explains why it is that only those in 'higher stations' can develop taste:

It is only in the higher stations [. . .] or in the liberal professions of life, that we expect to find men either of delicate or comprehensive taste. The inferior situations of life, by contracting the knowledge of men within very narrow limits, produce insensibly a similar contraction in their notions of the beautiful and sublime.[141]

And he continues to stress particularly the disabling influence on taste of life in the modern commercial cities, thus excluding all those involved in commerce from what Barrell has called 'the republic of taste'.[142] As conventional as this argument is, it was sharply at odds with social reality by the time Alison wrote. During the second half of the eighteenth century, middle-class men and women, not only of the 'liberal professions of life' but also from the supposedly 'contracting' sphere of trade and manufacture, were steadily assuming important political influence – particularly (but not just) in the cities – and the gentry and Parliament were increasingly accommodating the demands of those they thought they were patronising.[143] Alison, however, still writes that 'they who have been doomed, by their professions, to pass their earlier years in populous and commercial cities, and in the narrow and selfish pursuits which prevail there, soon lose that sensibility'.[144]

Dugald Stewart's theory contains no such justification of social hierarchies based on the uniform capacity for taste and of its refinement under privileged conditions. Instead, he emphasises the possibility of developing the individual's endowments through education. Stewart, Reid's most influential disciple, became Professor of Moral Philosophy in Edinburgh in 1785. He argued for a phenomenalist position in response to received theories of mind and perception. In the first volume of his *Elements of the Philosophy of the Human Mind* Stewart reiterates Reid's critique of efficient causes in theories of perception:[145]

they all evidently proceed on a supposition, suggested by the phenomena of physics, that there must of necessity exist some medium of communication between the objects of perception and the percipient mind; and they all indicate a secret conviction in their authors, of the essential distinction between mind and matter.[146]

For Stewart, as for Alison, it is enough that the registration of the phenomena tells us of the existence of some connection, although we cannot account for its character:

It seems now to be pretty generally agreed among philosophers, that there is no instance, in which we are able to perceive a necessary connexion between two successive events; or to comprehend in what manner the one proceeds from the other, as its cause. From experience, indeed, we learn, that there are many events, which are constantly conjoined, so that the one invariably follows the other: but it is possible for any thing we know to the contrary, that this connexion, though a constant one, as far as our observation has reached, may not be a necessary connexion; nay, it is possible that there may be no necessary connexion among any of the phenomena we see: and if there are any such connexions existing, we may rest assured that we shall never be able to discover them.[147]

Thus Stewart, too, goes beyond Reid's criticism of efficient causes. In contrast to Reid, however, Stewart claims to sidestep questions regarding the certainty of human knowledge; he sets out to discuss the laws of the operations of the mind, deduced from observation, without raising questions of causation. The success of this method in the physical sciences, he claims, makes it the paradigm for every other science, including the philosophy of mind:

> In the investigation of physical laws, it is well known that our inquiries must always terminate in some general fact, of which no account can be given, but that such is the constitution of our nature [. . .]. The case is exactly the same in the philosophy of mind. When we have once ascertained a general fact; such as, the various laws which regulate the association of ideas, of the dependence of memory on that effort of the mind which we call Attention; it is all that we ought to aim at, in this branch of science.[148]

Reid was concerned with the problems raised by the metaphysical connection between mind and matter and so it was unnecessary for him to explain the operations of the mind in the production of empirical knowledge; he appealed to association only to explain such secondary phenomena as variations in habit. Stewart, however, saw his enterprise as the positive counterpart to Reid's critique: to give a scientific account of the laws governing the operation of the mind itself, and a version of association theory came to play an important role in this. Stewart's description of the sense of vision differs from Reid's in this respect. While Reid emphasises the limited nature of the information transmitted by the senses, Stewart concentrates on the process by which an image in the mind is generated. Obviously informed by William Cheselden's account of a boy born blind, published in the *Philosophical Transactions* of 1728,[149] Stewart states that 'this sense, prior to experience, conveys to us the notion of extension in two dimensions only'.[150] It is not only in the perception of distance that an anticipatory judgement, acquired through association, is required. In the perception of an extended figure, too, Stewart infers the prior operation of the mind. According to him, the mind cannot conceive a complete figure at once, but conceives every point of the outline on the retina after each other: 'Every point, by itself, constitutes just as distinct an object of attention to the mind, as if it were separated by an interval of empty space from the rest'.[151] Thus he concludes that not only a faculty of attention but also a faculty of memory must be assumed to be at work in the mind which 'stores' the different acts of attention and without which we could have 'no perception of visible figure'.[152] For Stewart, there is no

essential character in the objects of the senses which produces their image in the mind. The image, as he argues in the first two volumes of the *Elements*, is in fact the product of different acts of the mind working together, as the faculties of attention and memory combine in the case of vision.

It is not only in the philosophy of mind that Stewart continues the tradition on the one hand while abandoning its basis on the other. This applies equally to his publication of two essays on the sublime and the beautiful.[153] Stewart had argued vehemently in the first volume of the *Elements* against the traditional view of a correspondence between particular material characteristics and associated subjective emotions; thus he had to reject the existence of such essential connections between the objects of aesthetics and the aesthetic emotions. Stewart's aesthetic essays can be considered to be a rejection of the epistemology with which emotion-based theories had been supported. In a passage which has become famous he expounds an understanding of the sublime and picturesque as based on a linguistic relationship rather than an essential one:

> I shall begin with the supposition that the letters A, B, C, D, E, denote a series of objects; that A possesses some one quality in common with B; B a quality in common with C [. . .; and so on]; – while, at the same time, no quality can be found which belongs in common to any *three* objects in the series. Is it not conceivable, that the affinity between A and B may produce a transference of the name of the first to the second; and that, in consequence of the other affinities which connect the remaining objects together, the same name may pass in succession from B to C; from C to D; and from D to E? In this manner, a common appelation will arise between A and E, although the two objects may, in their nature and properties, be so widely distant from each other, that no stretch of imagination can conceive how the thoughts were led from the former to the latter.[154]

Here Stewart makes it clear that 'sublime' and 'beautiful' are words which have acquired their meaning by being applied to a variety of objects which otherwise share no single feature. Thus for both Alison and Stewart it is no longer something innate in the object which initiates aesthetic emotions. But while for Alison these emotions are a feature of the mind, and beauty is found in objects which fit this human significance, for

Stewart, beauty is not even an 'objective correlative' of the human world any more, because beautiful objects do not resemble one another; in fact, they may have no characteristics in common at all but receive their significance only through what he called 'transitive meaning'.[155] His essay employs a bold strategy for dispensing with most of the problems which adhere to the by now familiar distinction between the sublime qualities of an object and the sublime experience. Stewart is interested instead in the rules of association which constitutes the process whereby language yields new or expanded meanings of the sublime and beautiful through use. However, Stewart refrains from giving any account of sublimity and beauty whose claims go beyond the investigation of the 'associations, in consequence of which the common name of Sublimity has been applied to all of them; and to illustrate the influence of this common name in reacting on the Imagination and the Taste'.[156]

Such phenomenalism, which aims to abstain from speculative theorising and withdraws into the realm of mere observation, aspires towards the status of science. For Stewart, this shift of ambition allows the philosophy of mind to leave the confines of pure reason and become applicable to society. He states repeatedly throughout the *Elements* that knowledge of the mind's laws can influence education by illuminating the possibilities for the training of the mind. In the wake of the rise of a significant middle class, such a commitment to general education represented a clear step away from the previous generation's conviction of the exclusive merits of the propertied élite. Stewart's system of mental science, although committed to reform, stays well clear of any hint of controversial or heterodox views on human nature. At a time when philosophical systems had become closely associated with the materialism and radical politics of people such as Priestley and the French *philosophes*, theoretical speculations were very often used by the Tory Town Councils in Scotland to refuse university appointments to their political opponents.[157] Despite his commitment to intellectual liberalism, this did not affect Dugald Stewart. During the period in which he published the *Elements* – between 1792 and 1827 – the intellectual atmosphere in Edinburgh, and particularly the medical profession, was dominated by his form of Scottish Common Sense philosophy, propagated to a wider audience by his Whig disciples in the *Edinburgh Review*.[158] Stewart rep-

resents our first encounter with an important feature of phenomenalism: his was a successful strategy of withdrawal from a debate which had increasingly acquired politically dangerous connotations.[159]

For Stewart, the external object, previously firmly established as the *cause* of perception, has become ambiguous. When he analyses the operation of the mind, the object to which he is referring is left entirely unclear. Is it the object of perception – for example the image on the retina – from which the faculties of attention and memory take their conceptions? Or is it the object as identified by physical scientists (whose knowledge Stewart takes to be paradigmatic)? In both cases the question of what secondary qualities (such as colours) are remains unclear. Are they the result of the interference of light waves,[160] as they were for the scientists, or are they the colours as perceived by the eye? In the latter case, the scientific object, postulated as the scientific cause of perception, becomes a kind of *Ding an sich* in the Kantian sense, something whose true nature is withdrawn for ever beyond human experience. Thus Stewart's theory exposes a tension in the relationship between the human realm and non-human entities which was foreign to eighteenth-century discourse. Such a tension has, of course, severe implications for art. Because wavelengths were not suitable subjects for painting at the time, art was drawn to confine itself to the realm of experience.

Richard Olson has argued that, from the beginning of the nineteenth century, the Common Sense School of philosophy came to determine the methodological and epistemological attitudes of the 'exact sciences' not just in Scotland but subsequently throughout Britain.[161] The debate between Uvedale Price and Richard Payne Knight regarding the nature of picturesque beauty illustrates how it came to make an impact on aesthetic debates south of the border.

The Picturesque Controversy

As we have seen, the aesthetic of the picturesque came into vogue in the 1780s. Initially, the term was used to describe landscape regarded as a series of views whose most important characteristic was the variety they offered to the brushstroke. Gilpin had identified roughness and irregularity as the chief ingredients of the picturesque. Gilpin himself, however, remains indecisive regarding the precise meaning of the term. On the one hand, he identifies as 'picturesque' whatever is suitable for pictorial representation, on the other he tentatively attempts to identify an essential difference between the beautiful and the picturesque in natural objects:

> As this difference therefore between the *beautiful*, and the *picturesque* appears really to exist, and must depend on some peculiar construction of the object; it may be worth while to examine, what that peculiar construction is.[162]

But Gilpin does not offer a full-scale theory to support his aesthetic distinction. In particular, he does not try to identify the efficient causes of the picturesque, in the way that Edmund Burke had done for the sublime and the beautiful.

It is just this task that Uvedale Price, a Hereford squire, undertook when he published his *Essay on the Picturesque* in 1794.[163] The *Essay* was intended to complement Burke by distinguishing the new category of the picturesque from the sublime and the beautiful and to complete Gilpin's work by establishing, as Gilpin himself had not, its efficient causes. 'I hope to shew, in the course of this work', Price writes, 'that the picturesque has a character not less separate and distinct than either the sublime or the beautiful, nor less independent of the art of painting'.[164]

While Burke had characterised the beautiful by smoothness and gradual variation, picturesque objects, for Price, as for Gilpin, display variety and intricacy. Roughness, sudden variation and irregularity are the characteristic causes for the picturesque, and Price goes on to enumerate the objects which display them: old cottages, gnarled trees, 'beggars, gypsies, and all such rough tattered figures [. . .] and other objects of the same kind'.[165] Such objects were in fact depicted – although Price never makes this point directly in the *Essay* – by the painter Thomas Gainsborough. In his youth, Price had accompanied Gainsborough on sketching expeditions into the country around Bath. Gainsborough's watercolour *Wooded Landscape with Gypsy Encampment* (plate 5), done in the early 1760s, shows the kind of figures Price identified as prime examples of the picturesque. By the time Price wrote his treatise such figures had indeed become the staple of picturesque staffage. For example, in *Interior of Ruins, Buildwas Abbey, Shropshire* of c.1785 (plate 6) by Michael

5   Thomas Gainsborough, *Wooded Landscape with Gypsy Encampment (Country Lane with Gypsies Resting)*, early 1760s, graphite, watercolour and bodycolour on pale brown prepared paper, 287 × 235, Yale Center for British Art, Paul Mellon Collection, New Haven.

Angelo Rooker (1746–1801), it is the gypsies who give colour and life to the otherwise overpowering and solemn ruin.

Following Burke, Price claims that the connection between the subject and the outside world is extremely simple: it lies in the ability of the nerves to transmit gross physical impacts. He repeats Burke's explanation that it is 'overstretched' nerves which cause ideas of pain and terror, the ingredients of the sublime, and that beauty is the effect of the relaxation of the normal nerve tone. Since he had earlier defined the picturesque as holding 'a station between beauty and sublimity',[166] it does not come as a surprise that Price sees the picturesque as being caused by what

> neither relaxes, nor violently stretches the fibres, but by its active agency keeps them to their full tone; and

6   Michael Angelo Rooker, *Interior of Ruins, Buildwas Abbey, Shropshire,* c.1785, graphite and watercolour, 251 × 295, Ashmolean Museum, Oxford.

thus, when mixed with either of the other characters corrects the languor of beauty, or the horror of sublimity.[167]

Walter Hipple has pointed out that this notion poses a difficult question: 'How does the stimulus of the picturesque, which keeps the fibres to their natural tone, midway betwixt languor and tension – how does this differ from no stimulus at all?'.[168] One could add: how does the picturesque impression differ from everyday perception? But, these epistemological questions aside, it is noticeable that in Price's physiological account, as well as in his aesthetic explanations, the picturesque emerges as that category which is capable of representing everyday matters, that is, social reality when seen from an idealised vantage-point, rather than taking exceptional events as its subject-matter, as in the sublime and beautiful.

Since Price's physiology rests on the assumption that the impulses that act on the fibres do so in the same way throughout the body, he does not make a clear distinction between the perceptions of the different organs. Through association they inform and melt into each other:

> The sense of seeing (as I before observed) is so much indebted to that of feeling for a number of its perceptions, that there is no considering the one, abstractedly from the other: he therefore would reason very ill on the effects of vision, who should leave out our ideas of rough and smooth, of hard and soft, of thickness, distance, &c., because they were originally acquired by the touch.[169]

Price's claim that the senses operated uniformly throughout the body formed the most obvious point of contention between himself and Richard Payne Knight. In 1794, the same year as Price's book appeared, Knight published a poem, *The Landscape*, which seemed to be in perfect harmony with Price's treatise. It too endorsed an aesthetic experience which is predicated on variety and intricacy. Both works argued for a reform in landscape gardening according to picturesque principles and strongly condemned the mechanical improvements of Lancelot ('Capability') Brown and Humphry Repton.[170] But a year later, in the second edition, Knight began his polemics against Price in a footnote.[171] Price responded with *A Dialogue on the Distinct Characters of the Picturesque: In Answer to the Objections of Mr. Knight* in 1801.[172] Although they were later to be reconciled, the two friends fell out over the issue. Price felt that Knight was being patronising by presuming to point out to him his own superior 'metaphysical skills'.[173]

Some recent commentators appear to agree that it was only Knight's greater philosophical sophistication which lay behind the quarrel.[174] But more is at stake. There are substantial differences between the protagonists' viewpoints. This difference, however, is not one between an old-fashioned conservative, who sentimentally 'harkened back to a golden age',[175] as some commentators have made Price out to be, and a revolutionary primitivist, who called for 'the liberation of repressed nature', as others have described Knight.[176] As we will see, the differences between Price and Knight are more complex and are the result of a confluence of political, physiological and metaphysical assumptions.[177]

Before discussing the two authors' differences, it is worth pointing out a similarity, however, because it is illuminating for the way in which picturesque depictions were, at the time, understood to please. Perhaps rather surprisingly for us today, typical picturesque depictions of the late eighteenth century were held to be pleasing in virtue of the direct physical pleasure that they were supposed to produce on the retina. Knight, like Burke and Price, maintained that light produced an 'irritation' of the retina and that this could produce instantaneous pleasure or pain:

> That the irritation, produced in the membranes of the eye by vision, is proportioned to the quantity of light poured into it, we may perceive by the dilation and contraction of that membrane called the iris.[178]

It is for this reason, Knight argues, that painting can delight, being capable of causing the same pleasurable irritation on the retina as the outside world. Although Price's and Knight's conceptions of perception are in other respects quite different, they share the same physiological justification for the intricate play of chiaroscuro – the contrast of light areas with dark ones – which dominated picturesque depictions of the time. A striking example of the late eighteenth-century taste for a virtuoso chiaroscuro is John Robert Cozens' *Cetara, on the Gulf of Salerno* of 1790 (plate 7). In 1776 Cozens (1752–1797) had travelled through Switzerland to Italy as the artistic companion to Richard Payne Knight on his Grand Tour (something Cozens was to do again with William Beckford in 1782). Cozens later worked up many of the sketches he made on these tours and *Cetara, on the Gulf of Salerno* is one of them. If this picture were to be bathed in a more uniform light – highlighting perhaps the crown of the mountains but throwing the village into full shadow – it would be a totally dull scene. What makes the drawing interesting is the stark contrast of light and shadow on the mountains and the intricate variation of dark and light areas in the village at the foot of the mountains by the sea.

This dramatic interplay of chiaroscuro was thought to give physical pleasure in virtue of its irritation of the retina in a well-managed and subtly gradated manner. Colour, Knight believed, could be understood in a similar way: it was, he maintained, 'only collections of rays variously modified, separated, and combined, according to the different textures of the surface of the bodies from which they are reflected'.[179] Thus for colours to be pleasing they had to present the viewer's visual apparatus with moderate and subtle variations within the range from dark to light.[180]

While they shared this physical understanding of the pleasures of picturesque depictions, Price and Knight disagreed fundamentally, however, regarding the way in which perceptions in general and, more particularly, tastes are formed. In contrast to Price's theory, which identified irritation and vibration as the agencies connecting the outside world, via the sense organs, with ideas in the mind, Knight rejected the existence of any physical connection, or indeed resemblance, between the objects themselves on the one hand, and sensations and ideas on the other. In 1805 Knight published his *Analytical Inquiry into the Principles of Taste* in order to present his own understanding of perception more systematically. Here he rejected the implicit essentialism of Price's position, with its assumption that certain qualities inherent in objects produce a direct physiological effect and that it is this that constitutes the aesthetic experience. According to Knight, aesthetic experience is a perception in which the mind plays an active, judging role, fed by, but independent from, the sense data. Moreover, he argued, Price did not make a sufficiently clear distinction between the sensations of the different sense organs:

> These [the senses] painting also separates; and, in its imitations of objects, which are pleasing to the eye but otherwise offensive, exhibits the pleasing qualities only; so that we are delighted with the copy, when we should, perhaps, turn away with disgust and abhorrence from the original.[181]

He pointed out that, in failing to separate the sense organs, Price's position would be led *ad absurdum* when dealing with picturesque objects which were obnoxious to the sense of smell. If all senses were equally relevant to the aesthetic experience, then how could it be that 'the rotting shed, or fungous tree, Or tatter'd rags of age and misery', strongly repulsive in smell, were nevertheless aesthetically pleasing?[182] Knight himself restricts the picturesque to 'that kind of beauty which belongs exclusively to the sense of vision; or to the imagination guided by that sense'.[183]

Knight's dualism owes a great deal to the Scottish Common Sense School, in particular to Reid. Knight's book seems to have been the first English aesthetic treatise to take up their criticism of efficient causes. Nevertheless, Knight did not entirely follow the restric-

tions of this school, and in so doing he exposed himself to the ridicule of other writers influenced by it.[184] A sharp distinction between mind and body was congenial to Knight's extreme social élitism. The activity of painting itself was downgraded in value – its proper task was no more than the accurate delineation of an image on the retina[185] – while judgement upon the work of art was left to those who had developed the faculty of taste, the artists' patrons – an argument which sustained Knight's prejudice against the aspirations of artists in the Royal Academy.[186]

Like the Scottish writers, Knight places the passions at the centre of both his aesthetic theory and his understanding of society.[187] From Adam Smith and his Scottish contemporaries Knight takes over the view that human beings move from one stage of social development to another by virtue of their desires and not their reasoning, and that, in the process, the disruptive and primitive passions will come to be replaced by the more stable, orderly and predictable interests that are the characteristic motivating forces behind civilised human beings.[188] At this point, however, when 'instinct to intellect is slowly brought, And vague perception methodized to thought',[189] Knight invokes Hume's theory of association. By this process custom and habit shape our taste. As Knight points out:

> there is scarcely any subject, upon which men differ more than concerning the objects of their pleasures and amusements; and this difference subsists, not only among individuals, but among ages and nations; almost every generation accusing that which immediately preceded it, of bad taste.[190]

Knight criticises Hume for his assertion in *Of the Standard of Taste* that there is no universal standard for beauty (this, incidentally, appears to be a clear misreading of Hume). Nevertheless, while for Hume the general rules of beauty are best acquired by the steady accumulation (and organisation) of particular experience, Knight believes that such rules are no more than coagulated habits and customs. Indeed, Knight believes, the habits and customs which evolve in a society are nothing more than artificially stagnated forms of social refinement, overlaying the natural passions of human beings. In this way, not just taste but societies in general become, in Knight's view, rigid and incapable of further development, leaving them prone to despotic rule,

7　John Robert Cozens, *Cetara, on the Gulf of Salerno*, 1790, graphite and watercolour, 366 × 527, Gift in honor of Paul Mellon by the Patrons' Permanent Fund with additional support from Dick and Ritchie Scaife, Catherine Mellon Conover, Rachel Mellon Walton, Mr. and Mrs. James M. Walton and an anonymous donor, ©1994 Board of Trustees, National Gallery of Art, Washington, D.C.

either by a single tyrant or by the people acting as a mob.[191] The natural thus becomes the artificial and the artificial the selfish. Addressing himself to contemporary British society, Knight states:

> For, come it will – the inevitable day,
> When Britain must corruption's forfeit pay,
> Beneath a despot's, or a rabble's sway.[192]

The 'rabble's sway' was, of course, Knight's reference to what was happening in France. At such a point in the history of society what was needed, he claimed, was an aristocracy in the true sense, capable of rising above the fixed habits and rigid prejudices of the common people:

> [. . .] created being's boasted pride,
> The polish'd nation's intellectual guide,
> Who, mild and steady, active and sedate,
> With power infelt directs some happy state.[193]

In fact, Knight ventures, if France had had such men as Washington, Franklin and Adams, it might now – he is writing in 1796 – be as happy and free as America.[194] An important qualification for Knight's 'special men' is their ability to cut through what is artificial. Thus Knight does believe in a universal good: the natural passions and affections of the human mind as guided by the senses, which for most people are buried beneath the layers of social refinement.[195]

This conviction has consequences for art, and somewhat modifies my initial account of Knight's views. Good paintings are not confined to the simple physical pleasure experienced by the sense of vision:

> for, not only the passions and affections of the human mind, but the natural modes of expressing them, are the same in all ages, and all countries; and the less their natural modes are connected with those local and temporary habits, the more strong and general will be the sympathies excited by them.[196]

There is progress in the arts, as there is in society.[197] The great breakthrough in art came quite suddenly, according to Knight, when the Venetian and Lombard School, followed by the Dutch and Flemish, became aware of the distinction between what the mind knew and what the eye saw.[198] Their massing of light and shade expressed knowledge of the objects as they appear to the eye only. So far, painting is still understood as an 'artificial retina'. But there is a second stage of excellence, which distinguishes the genius from the mere mechanic, and this corresponds to 'the natural mode of expressing' the human passions of the mind. So, if art is not to degenerate into unnatural imitation and artificiality, it must first check its representations against nature as it appears on the retina. At the second stage, however, it must be true to the passions which set the laws of motion of mental life.[199] The data that are subject to these laws are given by the senses. They can change from individual to individual, from generation to generation, and from nation to nation, but the laws of motion themselves remain the same. In fact, the more content that is left to the imagination, the freer the man of broad experience is to bring that experience to bear on the depiction, and the more pleasure he will receive from it.[200]

Knight was consciously opposed to the first President of the Royal Academy, Reynolds, and his general ideal of form, but in other ways he comes much closer to Reynolds than he thinks, not just in his opposition to contemporary historical painting, but also in the priority he assigns to the expression of feeling and sentiment – the quality which, according to Knight, distinguishes the liberal from the mechanical arts. But Knight is adamant that, while art and good taste can bring moral improvement, on their own they are not enough to reverse the direction of social development:

> The only moral good, that appears to result from either poetry, music, painting, or sculpture, arises from their influence in civilizing and softening mankind, by substituting intellectual, to sensual pleasures; and turning the mind from violent and sanguinary, to mild and peaceful pursuits.[201]

This is because taste has, according to Knight, nothing to do with reason: 'taste depends upon feeling and sentiment, and not upon demonstration and argument'.[202] Yet it is reason, not in the narrow mathematical sense, but in a broader, Humean sense, as reasoning on the basis of habitual association, that the greatest statesmen must possess. Knight celebrates this quality in his *A Monody on the Death of the Rt. Hon. Charles James Fox*.[203] We are back to Knight's élitist dualism: the greatest artists, like Rembrandt, have the ability to depict not only what the eye truly sees, but also the fundamental human passions, stimulated by these sense data. It is, however, left to the exceptional connoisseur (like Knight himself) not just to take pleasure in the range of associations which come with such paintings, but also to judge them correctly, and so to detect the universality in such depictions. This is precisely the capacity which, in Knight's view, distinguishes the greatest statesmen and justifies their authority over others.

Knight himself had aspirations as a statesman. In his political career, as a Member of Parliament for Leominster, and, from 1784, for Ludlow, Knight was closely allied with Fox and so was often in opposition, for example over the war with America. In *The Landscape* he presents the ordered landscapes of Capability Brown as analogous to political despotism, which inhibits man's spontaneous growth and freedom, and passages like the following have been read (by Horace Walpole, for example) as supporting the French Revolution:[204]

> So when rebellion breaks the despot's chain,
> First wasteful ruin marks the rabble's reign;
> Till tired their fury, and their vengeance spent,
> One common interest bids their hearts relent;
> Then temperate order from confusion springs,
> And, fann'd by freedom, genius spreads its wings.[205]

Knight, however, made it clear that he had no sympathy with the 'armed rabble, which now govern and lay waste France', seeing them as a danger to 'civilized society'.[206] In the second edition of the poem he felt

forced to distance himself explicitly from the 'endeavour to find analogies between picturesque compositions and political confusion'.[207] While Knight admits that, theoretically, the rabble might be the means by which tyranny is overthrown, its very existence is itself a sign of the degeneration of society, to be met by a firm assertion of power on the part of the élite. In his Sicilian diary of 1777 Knight had written that he was inclined to think 'that nothing less than another general Revolution in Europe' could effect a return to the purity of the ancients, although 'that does not seem likely to happen'.[208] But this statement was not as radical as it now sounds. Even within the Anglican Church, the view that, although government was of divine ordinance and normally required political obedience, rebellion was permissible in certain circumstances was widely accepted.[209] After all, the Glorious Revolution had to be justified. But that revolution was bloodless and no threat to property. Neither was true of the French Revolution. When the latter took place, twelve years after Knight's diary entry, he, like most of his English contemporaries, had only contempt for it.

Nor was Knight's opposition to revolutionary politics merely theoretical. He led a successful military operation against a collier uprising in his home county, and, at the age of seventy, long after having retired from Parliament, still wrote that the lower classes and 'redundant population of the manufacturing Districts' are 'as Ingredients of the Mob [. . .] utterly contemptible'.[210] He writes in *The Progress of Civil Society* about the danger of the rising manufacturing mobs, against which 'barracks are now erecting near to every great town':

> This is an easy and obvious expedient, not unlike that of the sailor, who finding his horse liable to stumble, tied a stone to his tail. – [. . .] I cannot but think, that by arming and embodying the principal householders, and thus making a militia of property in the great towns, a more safe, constitutional, and effectual guard for the public peace might be obtained.[211]

For Knight the self-interest of the propertied classes would be a more reliable peace-keeper than a professional army, which he describes as

> [. . .] a rabble, faithful to their pay,
> Prepared alike to serve, or to betray.[212]

The 1790s were tense times in England. There had been threats of invasion from France, English sailors had mutinied at Spithead, and revolutionary clubs had sprung into existence all over the country. Prices for corn rose to an unprecedented height and agriculture proved more lucrative than ever for the landed gentry. Yet rural poverty was rising. The recurrent food shortages of the second half of the eighteenth century culminated in the disastrous year of 1795, the year Price and Knight began their argument. For many contemporary observers, the enclosure of open fields and commons and so-called 'improved' agriculture were seen to be responsible.[213] For Knight the solution to unrest lies in the intervention of an exceptional élite with the capacity to disconnect itself from the misled mass of human beings. For Price, also an ally of Fox, on the other hand, the political solution lies in a rural paternalism which actively embraces the poor and emphasises care and management, rather than militant repression.

Price was himself a committed agricultural improver, continuing the rationalising and modernising his father had begun at Foxley.[214] His strategy, however, was to promote duty and responsibility on the part of those who owned the land. He recalls 'a beloved uncle', whose 'benevolence towards all the inhabitants around him' proved a better strategy against the spread of democratic rebelliousness than the assertion of superior force:

> Such attentive kindnesses are amply repaid by affectionate regard and reverence; and were they general throughout the kingdom, they would do much more towards guarding us against democratical opinions, 'Than twenty thousand soldiers arm'd in proof'.[215]

In 1797 Price published a pamphlet, addressed to men of property in his county, Herefordshire, in which he advocated a voluntary county militia which would, he argued, forestall the internal rebellion a French invasion might precipitate more effectively than a professional army with no attachment to the county.[216] As we have seen, Knight too thought that armed men of property would be a better means of keeping down a rebellious mob than a professional army, but Knight was more concerned with the unrest of the industrial labourers than the agricultural poor. This was pertinent to his own estate, whose wealth stemmed not just from agriculture, like Price's, but also from a considerable mining industry. In contrast to Knight's detached view of the self-interest of property, Price emphasised the wider sense of connection such a militia, whose members would range from the small farmer to the squire, would bring about: 'Whatever promotes that union and intercourse [between men of the greatest and of the smallest property], promotes the essential happiness and security of individuals, and of the state at large.'[217] Indeed, such a union would also benefit the labouring people of the county, 'whose welfare is intimately connected with our own',[218] because it would 'watch over them',[219] not by force but with concern and benevolence, and thus block the inroads of revolution at the root. It was also part of Price's strategy as an agricultural improver to preserve the number of small farmers and cottagers on his estate who had local knowledge and an attachment to the land, rather than adopting the large-scale strategies of other landlords, who dispossessed smallholders, absented themselves and thereby empowered irresponsible wealthy tenant farmers who relied increasingly on seasonal labour.[220] As Price puts it: 'Vast possessions may give ambitious views, and ambition destroys local attachments'.[221]

Price was far from alone in his fear that large sections of the gentry were opting out of their responsibilities at the very time when commercial farming and the social changes it produced most demanded attendance to duty. By mid-century, control of the counties had virtually passed into the hands of a narrow group of comparatively lowly, middle-class men.[222] However, by the time Price was writing, this change was seen as the source of rural unrest and much effort, both on the part of the government and of the gentry themselves, went into re-establishing the links between the gentry and their counties.[223] Price's and Knight's aesthetic systems match their respective political concerns. In Knight's picturesque theory, raw nature is celebrated. But this is a matter solely of the sense of vision and its associated emotions; Knight denies any efficient connection between the object of sensation, sensation itself and ideas. Thus abstracted, the celebration of unrestrained nature takes place in the mind alone, and good taste, like good political action, lies in the intellectual capacity to disconnect oneself from the concrete impact of life. Price, on the other hand, envisages society as being brought into harmony by the caring management of the landed gentry, just as in his picturesque theory those

objects which bear the marks of decay and disruption are integrated through the unifying effects of light and shade. Fundamental to both spheres was the assumption of a common ordering principle which had the capacity to bridge and bind disparate elements.

Price's assumption of a common unifying principle is characteristic of eighteenth-century theories. Knight's dualism, on the other hand, foreshadows the emergence of a phenomenalist approach which attempts to restrict itself to the merely observable. This more theoretically (although not socially) radical stance is not yet fully articulated by Knight, who still upholds a form of universalism in his assumption that there are stable natural passions to which exceptionally gifted men have access. Such assumptions were relegated to the realm of mere speculations by such writers as Dugald Stewart in the early nineteenth century, who restricted themselves to the laws governing the operation of the mind itself, selfconsciously avoiding questions regarding the connection between mind and matter. But when Knight complains, for example, about the 'practice of our students in landscape-painting' who 'in making only slight sketches from nature, and finishing them at home, must effectually prevent their excelling in that art',[224] he is endorsing a phenomenalist artistic strategy which would come to fruition both in the circle around the brothers John and Cornelius Varley and, independently, in the paintings of John Constable.

In this chapter we have seen how far eighteenth-century writers on aesthetics felt the need to identify an intermediary to underpin the subjective response to the objective realm. By the end of the century this assumption came to be questioned in the phenomenalism of Alison, Stewart and Knight. We will see in the following chapters that such a phenomenalist position emerged contemporaneously in landscape art and science. But, as Stewart's treatise already makes apparent, such a position brings inherent tensions to the surface. It was to lead to tensions between two realms: the realm of the generalising observation of the scientists and the more individualistic responses of the artists. Phenomenalism represents a transitional position at a time of social and political change in English and Scottish culture.

8 Philip Reinagle, *Cupid Inspiring the Plants with Love*, 1805, stipple engraving (T. Burke) printed in colour, hand-finished, plate size 514 × 422, from R.J. Thornton *The Temple of Flora*, by permission of the Syndics of Cambridge University Library.

II

THE TEMPLE OF FLORA

Dr Robert John Thornton's *A New Illustration of the Sexual System of Carolus von Linnaeus* was produced between the years 1797 and 1807. It consisted of three parts, the first two being Thornton's account of Linnaeus' system. The third part, with the title *The Temple of Flora: Or, Garden of Nature*, contained hand-coloured prints of plants, executed in a variety of media ranging from stipple and line engraving to mezzotint and aquatint.[1] These engravings are accompanied by botanical and mythological explanations along with appropriate poetry.

The proliferation of new species, brought back to Europe from foreign travel and from colonial expansion in the seventeenth and eighteenth centuries, stimulated an upsurge in interest both in horticulture and in attempts to order and classify plants. This reached a highpoint in 1735 when Carolus Linnaeus (1707–1778) published his *Systema Naturae* which introduced a new classification of plants which instantly caught the imagination of the European public (the book had sixteen editions during his own lifetime). In the wake of this, publication of botanical treatises with illustrations soared, particularly on the Continent. Georg Dionysius Ehret's *Trew's Plantae Selectae* (1750–73) was the most celebrated and ambitious.[2] In England, however, it was a more modest publication which first achieved major success, William Curtis' *Botanical Magazine*, issued in periodical parts in 1787. All of these publications depicted ideal specimens outside their specific environment. It was not until the nineteenth century that plants were shown in their original scenery, although depicting plants after real models became popular somewhat earlier.[3] Thornton's grandiose conception was an attempt, it seems, to produce as ambitious and sumptuous a work of botanical illustration as those appearing elsewhere in Europe, and perhaps even to supersede

them in virtue of its unique feature: the introduction of landscape settings for the plants.

The artists Thornton employed (with the exception of Sydenham Teak Edwards, who executed only a single print) were not professional botanical draughtsmen but known chiefly for the production of landscapes and portraits. Thornton's *Advertisement to the New Illustration*, issued in 1797, placed great emphasis on the landscape settings. The images, he wrote, 'will not only express the different gradations of the flowers, but will generally have, what has not been before attempted, Back-Grounds expressive of the situation to which each naturally belongs'.[4] But the relationship between the plants and their settings is by no means as straightforward as this might lead one to assume. While Thornton abandons the tradition of showing specimens in isolation of any context, his introduction of the landscape backgrounds is not yet a straightforward depiction of the plants' actual environment. There is frequently a discrepancy between the contexts in which the plants would actually be found growing and those in which they are represented, and this is, indeed, no accident. Together with the pictorial conventions within which they are depicted, these discrepancies reveal a characteristically eighteenth-century conception of nature, in whose terms they are comprehensible.[5] Thornton's prints relate his botanical specimens to the three dominant pictorial formulae of the second half of the eighteenth century: the sublime, the beautiful and the picturesque.

Thornton's work shows that these categories are much more than a pictorial classification of the natural world. As we will see, they are sustained by a metaphysics which identifies a common unifying principle acting throughout nature; a sublime landscape, for example, can naturally produce a sublime plant and – just as naturally – sublime emotions in the spectator. *The Temple of Flora* reveals the common ground on which both botanical taxonomy and landscape art were operating, before a phenomenalist attitude challenged the unitary metaphysics which governed such understanding.[6] The taxonomist's hierarchies of genera and species were an attempt to unveil the system which underpinned the unity of nature, a system in which each subject had a definitive, yet interconnected place.

Robert John Thornton

Thornton's family background and early career were somewhat eccentric. His father, Bonnell Thornton, was one of the most famous and influential journalists of the 1750s and 1760s. As a major shareholder of the twice-weekly *St. James Chronicle* and chief adviser to Henry Sampson Woodfall's *Public Advertiser*, Bonnell Thornton enjoyed enormous access to and influence over the press. He belonged to the Nonsense Club, which cultivated a rebellious and irreverent attitude towards the establishment for which the newspapers under the club's members' influence formed an outlet. The group allied itself with Wilkes' libertine cause in the 1760s, and their control over parts of the press was of central importance to the popularity of Wilkes' campaign.[7] Bonnell Thornton was also a close friend of Hogarth, and together the two men staged an anti-exhibition in 1762 which could have stood comparison with any twentieth-century dadaist happening.[8] Two items in the exhibition, for example, were placed behind blue curtains which the public was requested not to open. If they did, however, they found two boards, on one of which was written 'Ha! ha! ha!' and on the other 'He! he! he!'. The display mocked the traditional way in which erotic art was displayed in private collections, but it also clearly poked fun at the voyeurism of exhibition visitors themselves.[9] Bonnell Thornton possessed independent money. After the death of his mother and older brother, Robert John Thornton became his father's sole beneficiary; the inheritance of the family fortune allowed him to embark on his major publication, *A New Illustration*.

Conventionally enough as a younger son, Robert Thornton (1768?–1837) was first intended for the Church and for this purpose was sent to Trinity College, Cambridge. However, once there, he apparently gave more attention to Thomas Martyn's lectures on botany than to the study of divinity and he seems to have altered his objective to a career in medicine. He received the degree of MB in 1793, having written a thesis in which (he later claimed) he showed that oxygen was vital for human life, being the source of what he called 'animal heat'. The ideas in his thesis made Thornton an easy convert to Dr Thomas Beddoes' therapeutic method of administering 'factitious airs' to patients, a practice by which he would make the sufferers inhale various intoxicating gases. In fact, as Beddoes (1760–1808) and James Watt (1736–1819) (who designed a breathing apparatus for Beddoes' experiments) believed, Thornton intended to set himself up as the leading exponent of Beddoes' pneumatic medicine in London.[10] Beddoes was regarded with suspicion by the medical establishment because of his Brunonian[11] methods and he was ridiculed in the Tory press because of his radical politics.[12] It is not clear if Thornton was fully aware of Beddoes' politics – he would have had no sympathy with them – but he distanced himself explicitly from the Brunonian aspects of Beddoes' therapy.[13] None of Thornton's writings shows any of the anti-establishment rhetoric that his father had made his hallmark. On the contrary, Thornton seems to have been at pains throughout his career to show himself true and loyal to King and Country.

From Cambridge, Thornton went on to Guy's Hospital to complete his studies. But afterwards, having come into his inheritance, he seems to have contemplated a political career and published his first book, the thoroughly Whiggish *The Politician's Creed, Being the Great Outline of Political Science: From the Writings of Montesquieu, Hume, Gibbon, Paley, Townsend, &c.&c. by an Independent* (1795).[14] He soon abandoned these ambitions, however, and set up in medical practice in London in 1797, the year in which he started to commission for *A New Illustration*.

In *The Politician's Creed*, Thornton sets out to discuss 'the Advantages and Disadvantages of the different Forms of Government' which, over the course of history, have been created by man who 'by nature is truly a social animal'. He concludes:

> It may therefore be pronounced as an universal axiom in politics, that an Hereditary Prince, a Nobility without vassals, and a people voting by their

representatives, form the best monarchy, aristocracy and Democracy.[15]

Like Burke, Thornton venerates the British Constitution as a bulwark against the pressures of particular interests. Only an equal balance between the monarch, the aristocracy and the people prevents, he writes, the undermining of 'the best constitution in the world, and disordering that wise system of Laws, institutions, and customs' which has developed over 'so many centuries'.[16]

During 1795, the year in which *The Politician's Creed* was published, there was strong protest against the repressive legislation enacted in response to the French Revolution; English radicals, like Priestley, had been demanding changes in the Constitution for some time. Thornton's defence of the British Constitution appears to be aimed against such demands and he warns explicitly against 'levelling ideas'.[17] Thornton's view of society is traditional: hierarchical but equitable, productive but pleasurable, manifesting variety within an overall order. Above all, such a society is 'natural'.

Thornton and Erasmus Darwin

At the heart of Thornton's conception of nature is the ontological continuum between human beings and their environment. In another publication, *The Philosophy of Medicine*, he writes:

> Everything in this world is systematical; all is combination, relation, affinity, connection. There is nothing but what is the immediate effect of something preceding it, and determines the existence of something that shall follow it.[18]

Thornton shares with other characteristically eighteenth-century theorists the assumption of the contiguity of cause and effect in nature. This is most explicitly articulated in *The Philosophy of Medicine*. According to Thornton (and in contrast to the theories discussed in the previous chapter) the mediating substance between the external world and the human body is 'electric fluid'.[19] On this point he disagrees with the author who was the major influence behind *The Temple of Flora*, Erasmus Darwin (1731–1802).

Darwin first gained fame as a doctor practising in Derbyshire. He was one of the founders of the Lunar Society, a famous group established during the 1770s in the Midlands which brought together natural philosophers, like Priestley, industrialists, like Josiah Wedgwood, and inventors like Matthew Boulton and James Watt, with the aim of fostering the progress of society through scientific knowledge, particularly in areas relevant to industry.[20] Although Darwin had already been made a Fellow of the Royal Society in 1761, he became a public celebrity with the publication of *The Botanic Garden* in 1789 and 1791, a long poem of speculation on natural philosophical matters in heroic couplets.[21]

The Botanic Garden gave Thornton the idea for *The Temple of Flora* and it is quoted extensively in *A New Illustration*.[22] Darwin's underlying theme is the shared properties of plants and humans. In his view, plants, like animals, possess sensation, movement and a certain degree of mental activity:

> Have vegetable buds irritability? have they sensation? have they volition? have they associations of motion? I am persuaded they possess them all, though in a much inferior degree.[23]

And further:

> To these must be added the indubitable evidence of their passion of love, and of their necessity to sleep; and I think we may truly conclude that they are furnished with a brain or common sensorium belonging to each bud.[24]

Linnaeus had shown that plants were sexual creatures, just like human beings. That plants possessed sexuality was most important to Darwin, for whom 'sexual reproduction is the chef d'oeuvre, the masterpiece of nature'.[25] It is through the principle of sexual production that 'new varieties, or improvements, are frequently obtained'.[26]

The Botanic Garden appeared in two parts. 'The Loves of the Plants' of 1789 gives a highly anthropomorphic account of the sexuality of plants, in the context of which scientific discoveries are presented. 'The Economy of Vegetation' of 1791 uses a 'Goddess of Botany' to address the Nymphs, Gnomes and Sylphs of the four elements, and this again becomes the occasion for extensive accounts of contemporary science, given in the footnotes ('The Economy of Vegetation' formed the first part of the completed work). In 'The Loves of the Plants' Darwin explains the contraction of leaves as parallel to the capacity of animals to fall asleep, describing this as the abolition of voluntary powers. The mimosa, or 'sensitive plant', which retreats from touch and closes its leaves at night, stands as an example for the possession of such voluntary powers and indicates the existence of a common sensorium in plants.[27] Climbing plants show that even the ability for 'spontaneous movement', the 'voluntary power of motion', is present in the vegetable kingdom.[28]

In the two volumes of his most famous work, *Zoonomia*, published in 1794 and 1796, Darwin classifies bodily actions into four classes: irritation, sensation, volition and association. In his view, these motions are the necessary conditions of all life. His explanation of how these processes are stimulated by an outside object and then transmitted within the nervous system, however, is like Cullen's: he takes physical and chemical processes to be responsible for inducing the initial reaction, but then assumes that the mediating substance at work within the nervous system is something entirely peculiar to living organisms. For this reason Darwin rejected Galvani's recent theory of the electrical properties of the nervous system. Thornton, however, was totally convinced by it.[29] But although they disagreed on the precise nature of the mediating principle, both of them assumed the existence of a common denominator which possesses the capacity to mediate between organisms and the outside world. In Darwin's case some elements are understood as being specific to living organisms, while some are shared between them and other parts of the material world, such as chemical and physical processes.[30] Thornton, on the other hand, believes that electric fluid acts through the whole of the natural world.[31]

Darwin's writing contains a dynamic element which is absent from Thornton's. Already in 'The Economy of Vegetation', but most explicitly in the *Zoonomia*, Darwin connects the increasing variety of species with evolutionary development and progress in scientific knowledge.[32] Influenced by James Hutton's *Theory of the Earth*, he reflects on the similarities between species, despite the great morphological changes they have undergone.[33] From this he concludes that 'the earth began to exist, millions of ages before the commencement of the history of mankind' and that 'all warm-blooded animals have arisen from one living filament'.[34] With the aid of the four fundamental modes of response to the outside world that he posits – irritation, sensation, volition and association – Darwin develops an understanding of causal interactions as being permanently in progress towards perfect adaptation. The living filament is, says Darwin:

> The Great First Cause endued with animality, with the power of acquiring new parts, attended with new propensities, directed by irritations, sensations, volitions, and associations; and thus possessing the faculty of continuing to improve by its own inherent activity, and of delivering down those improvements by generation to its posterity world without end.[35]

Yet this is by no means a conception of evolution in the manner of Erasmus' grandson Charles (1809–1882), in which development is in the end produced by accidental mutations. Erasmus Darwin's thought presupposes a natural world whose 'propensities' have been designed by the 'Great First Cause' to offer a range of available possibilities to be exploited for progress and improvement. Darwin's notion of improvement was influenced by the mercantile management of natural resources advocated by his industrialist friends in the Lunar Society.[36] Thornton's traditional Whig view of improvement, on the other hand, draws on a vision of an ideal *status quo*, presented as under threat from individual aspirations. In *The Politician's Creed* his main concern had been to warn against those 'who kindle up the passions of their partisans, and under pretence of public good, pursue the interest and ends of their particular faction'.[37] While Darwin sympathised with the French Revolution, at least at the outset, Thornton took care in his writings to assert his patriotism.

In the course of the 1790s, as anxiety about the spread of revolutionary ideas increased in Britain, Darwin's work became subject to severe criticism, particularly for its rejection of the Mosaic account of natural order.[38] Although he had a strongly deistic appreciation of God, Darwin's dynamic biological system appeared to undermine notions of stability and order. Given how eager Thornton was in general to distance himself from radical politics,[39] it is somewhat surprising that he appears to have been oblivious to the presence of these implications of Darwin's work and that he was apparently not deterred by Darwins having fallen from political favour by the time of *A New Illustration*.[40] One might perhaps have supposed that Thornton's attempt to vindicate the traditional Mosaic standpoint and his demonstrative patriotism would have helped to produce a more positive appreciation of his own enterprise. However, as we will see, it too turned out to be a failure.

'All the Most Eminent English Artists'

Thornton advertised the publication of *A New Illustration* for the first time in 1797 in order to gain subscribers. He continued to commission artists and issue prints until 1804, after which only one further artist joined the project. In that year Thornton mounted a private exhibition which opened on 14 May 1804 at 49 New Bond Street and was accompanied by a catalogue.[41] The show included all the paintings executed for Thornton which were eventually published as engravings in the final edition of *A New Illustration* in 1807. Eight years later, the paintings were shown once again to the public, apparently for the last time.[42] On this occasion they formed the first prize in a lottery, drawn on 6 May 1813 by the State Lottery at Cooper's Hall, Basing Street.[43]

One can be sure that Thornton, in recruiting his artists, presented his project to them in terms of the same high aspirations as he was later to express in the catalogue when he exhibited the commissioned paintings: 'This Work is designed to be a National Work, all the most eminent English Artists have been engaged'.

Only one artist is mentioned specifically in the *Advertisement* for the flower pictures of *A New Illustration*, Philip Reinagle (1749–1833), who was not particularly eminent, while John Russell (1745–1806), who was engaged to work on allegorical depictions at the opening of *The Temple of Flora*, did enjoy some fame.[44] In the end, none of the prints executed by Russell alone were included, although Thornton did manage to engage two genuinely 'eminent' artists, John Opie (1761–1807) and Maria Cosway (1759–1838), to work on the two allegorical illustrations that did appear. Opie and Cosway, both prominent Royal Academicians, had succeeded in establishing themselves in the most highly regarded contemporary artistic category, history painting. Opie collaborated with Russell on the picture *Aesculapius, Flora, Ceres and Cupid Honouring the Bust of Linnaeus*, and, in 1807, Maria Cosway's *Flora Dispensing her Favours on the Earth* (plate 9) was printed. The engraving is signed simply 'Cosway', and Ronald King states that it was done after a painting by Richard Cosway, Maria's husband.[45] This is very unlikely, since Richard was a portrait painter; Maria, however, was a

9   Maria Cosway, *Flora Dispensing her Favours on the Earth*, aquatint and stipple engraving (T. Woolnoth) printed in colour, hand-finished, plate size 483 × 382, from R.J. Thornton *The Temple of Flora*, by permission of the Syndics of Cambridge University Library.

painter of allegorical subjects. The third allegorical painting, *Cupid Inspiring the Plants with Love* (plate 8), was by Reinagle, who, together with Peter Henderson (active 1799–1829), painted most of the plants for Thornton. However, he, Henderson and the two other artists employed around the turn of the century for the plant depictions in *The Temple of Flora*, Sydenham Teak Edwards (1769?–1819) and Abraham Pether (1756–1812), can hardly be called the 'most eminent English Artists'.

Of all of these artists, Reinagle seems to have been the most suitable choice. He had become an Associate of the Royal Academy in 1787 and he had shown his skill in life drawing, both in his portraits and, more particularly, in his animal and sporting pictures. He was also trying to establish a name as a landscape artist. Those of his paintings that are known today show that Reinagle's work falls entirely within the eighteenth-century taste for landscape backgrounds in muted colours with feathery trees and generalising rather than particular features, the latter being reserved for a central scene in the fore- or middle ground.[46] Evidently Thornton was looking for an artist who did not specialise exclusively in landscapes or flower pieces.[47]

Reinagle's versatility stands in marked contrast to two far more specialised artists employed by Thornton: Sydenham Teak Edwards and Abraham Pether. Edwards was one of the most famous botanical draughtsmen of the time.[48] However, at the Royal Academy he mainly exhibited sporting pieces of horses and dogs.[49] There is only one reference to a flower painting by him in a Royal Academy exhibition catalogue (in 1799, with the title *A Group of Hyacinths*). Although Edwards was trained exclusively as a botanical draughtsman, he seems to have been capable of depicting landscapes. These, like Reinagle's, tended to be rather sombre in colour, generalising in outline and evocative of a sublime or picturesque atmosphere.[50] Edwards' fame as the first botanical draughtsman who was 'constantly resorting to nature' might have suggested his employment to Thornton.[51] But, in fact, Edwards executed only one print for Thornton, the *Hyacinths* (plate 10), which I take to be also the 1799 exhibit in the Royal Academy mentioned above. It places the plants in front of a rather crude and unelaborated landscape with three levels: a dark brownish-green foreground with undifferentiated growth, a river in the middle ground, and a background with very much the same covering as the foreground, just slightly lighter in colouring. At the edge of the river, on the left, picturesque details appear, although the small houses are barely visible next to the masts of sailing boats. The whole picture which is rather flat (including the sky) does not come near the interesting effects that Reinagle's best designs produced.

Thornton apparently had more elaborate landscape settings in mind for three other plants. In 1800 Reinagle showed *The Night-Blowing Cereus* at the Royal Academy. Shortly afterwards, Thornton commissioned a second version for which Abraham Pether was employed to execute the background. Pether subsequently painted two other plants as well, *The Snowdrops* and *The Persian Cyclamen*. However, he never exhibited any of Thornton's commissions at the Royal Academy or elsewhere.[52] Nowadays, there are hardly any paintings by Pether in public galleries and only a few have appeared on the art market. Those that are known show that Pether produced quite ambitious landscapes conforming closely to the current genre conventions, particularly the sublime.[53] That he was widely known at the time, however, is clear from the fact that Edward Dayes (1763–1804), a watercolour painter, included him in his biographical notes on contemporary artists. Dayes states that 'no man, since the days of Claude, could paint a distance with so much sweetness as this artist [. . .] and as he seldom resorts to Nature for his materials, his forms are often repeated'.[54]

Pether's capacity for dramatic effects in his paintings and in particular his penchant for moonlight scenes gained him the sobriquet 'Moonlight Pether'.[55] This must have induced Thornton to ask for Pether's participation when he planned to add a background scene to the second version of the cereus, a plant whose flower opens at night. This painting provides an example of how the original natural setting of the plants was often ignored in *A New Illustration*. The Moon Cactus, or 'Night-Blowing Cereus' as Thornton calls it, is a native of Jamaica and Cuba and only grows in greenhouses in Great Britain.[56] Yet Thornton shows it in the open with a church tower that indicates an English setting (plate 11). Reinagle painted this golden flower very dramatically, in strong contrast to Pether's gloomy background (which is, in fact, more a *backdrop*, since it lacks any depth). The ramshackle church, adorned with an owl on the top left-hand side and a tree on the right, through whose branches the silvery moon can be glimpsed, are more like characterising attributes than parts of a real landscape. The moonlight on the river below the flower is only a pale reflection, and is contrasted with the golden presence of the cereus. As in Loutherbourg's painting *An Avalanche in the Alps* (plate 4), the sublimity of the scene lies in the stark contrasts employed to give dramatic effects. Highly generalised trees surround the church, leaving only the upper half of the tower with the clock visible. This is shown as standing at five minutes past twelve, indicating that the flower has opened at night-time. The collaboration of the two painters was evidently extremely successful, as this print became the best remembered of the whole cycle.[57]

Probably because Pether was also known for his snow scenes, Thornton asked him to paint those plants which appear at the beginning of the year, breaking 'the way

10   Sydenham Teak Edwards, *Hyacinths*, 1801, aquatint, stipple and line engraving (T. Warner) printed in colour, hand-finished, plate size 548 × 453, from R.J. Thornton *The Temple of Flora*, by permission of the Syndics of Cambridge University Library.

11 Philip Reinagle and Abraham Pether, *The Night-Blowing Cereus*, 1800, mezzotint (R. Dunkarton) printed in colour, hand-finished, plate size 486 × 366, from R.J. Thornton *The Temple of Flora*, by permission of the Syndics of Cambridge University Library.

12   Abraham Pether, *The Snowdrop*, 1804, mezzotint (W. Ward), hand-finished, plate size 485 × 347, from R.J. Thornton *The Temple of Flora*, by permission of the Syndics of Cambridge University Library.

through the frozen soil' as Thornton later described them,[58] *The Snowdrop* (plate 12) and *The Persian Cyclamen* (plate 13). These are two of the five prints which actually show the plants growing in a landscape. In all other cases the stems are cut off by the bottom of the picture plane. Compared with the others, the plants here occupy very little picture space. Pether places the snowdrops together with colourful crocuses in a hilly landscape which is still covered with snow, stretching to the horizon. On the right in the middle ground appears a small and simple cottage in front of a bare tree. Further behind, a settlement, including a church, can just be perceived. The sky shows a sun that is either rising or setting, tinting the horizon orange. Although there is still a tiny stretch of blue sky, heavy clouds massively crowd in, signifying that more snow is on the way (a

13   Abraham Pether, *The Persian Cyclamen*, 1804, aquatint, stipple and line engraving (W. Elmes) printed in colour, hand-finished, plate size 497 × 406, from R.J. Thornton *The Temple of Flora*, by permission of the Syndics of Cambridge University Library.

14   Peter Henderson, *Indian Reed*, 1804, aquatint, line engraving (J. Caldwall) printed in colour, hand-finished, plate size 535 × 405, from R.J. Thornton *The Temple of Flora*, by permission of the Syndics of Cambridge University Library.

point Thornton makes with regard to the clouds in *The Superb Lily*).[59] The cyclamen is shown in a mountainous landscape, next to a tree (which ranges into the picture space from the right). In this case Thornton obviously advised Pether to embellish the landscape with palms and a pagoda to indicate its origin. Since a similar building appears in the depiction of the *Indian Reed* (plate 14), Thornton, like Curtis, who published a picture of this plant in the *Botanical Magazine* in 1788, obviously believed that the plant is a native of the East Indies, although the depicted plant is more likely a wild form from the Near East.[60]

By 1800, Thornton's main artist, Reinagle, had ceased to exhibit paintings from *The Temple of Flora*, and Thornton's intensive employment of him seems to have slowed down drastically. But at this point a replacement entered the project. It is probably one of the first indi-

15   Peter Henderson, *The White Lily*, 1800, aquatint (J.C. Stadler) printed in colour, hand-finished, plate size 533 × 400, from R.J. Thornton *The Temple of Flora*, by permission of the Syndics of Cambridge University Library.

16   Philip Reinagle, *The Superb Lily*, 1799, mezzotint (W. Ward) printed in colour, hand-finished, plate size 475 × 352, from R.J. Thornton *The Temple of Flora*, by permission of the Syndics of Cambridge University Library.

cations that Thornton's publication lacked the sub-scription for which he was hoping that he should have employed an entirely undistinguished artist, Peter Henderson, for the major part of the remaining work. From 1801 until 1803 Henderson showed only paint-ings done for Thornton at the Royal Academy.[61] Before that, he had exhibited only once, a *Portrait of a Gentleman* in 1799.[62] Henderson was obviously trained for the project by Thornton himself, and developed his technique by copying Reinagle's work.

The first painting he appears to have executed is *The White Lily* (plate 15), which was engraved in 1800. Here the composition of the background is closely oriented towards Reinagle's *The Superb Lily* (plate 16) of 1799. In both prints the background is chiefly formed by the dark foothill, leaving only the top right-hand corner

open, filled by Henderson with a feathery tree and a round temple surrounded by water, and by Reinagle with sky, showing a trace of blue among darker clouds and other hills. Henderson also continued the series of passion flowers which started with Reinagle's *The Blue Passion Flower* (plate 17), shown ranged around the bottom of a huge fluted column. Henderson, in his *The Winged Passion-Flower* (plate 18) shows, by pictorial analogy, the middle part of this same column. His section of the column, like Reinagle's, is flanked on both sides by a landscape, although in Henderson's illustration parts of the temple painted for *The White Lily* are once again displayed. Henderson also executed a third painting in this series, *The Quadrangular Passion-Flower* (plate 19), which is shown wrapped around the top of the column, with only a glimpse on the right of

17   Philip Reinagle, *The Blue Passion Flower*, 1800, aquatint, stipple and line engraving (J. Caldwall), printed in colour, hand-finished, plate size 515 × 382, from R.J. Thornton *The Temple of Flora*, by permission of the Syndics of Cambridge University Library.

18   Peter Henderson, *The Winged Passion-Flower*, 1802, aquatint, stipple and line engraving (T. Warner) printed in colour, hand-finished, paper size 562 × 428, from R.J. Thornton *The Temple of Flora*, by permission of the Syndics of Cambridge University Library.

another building. Contemporaries would have recognised the architectural tokens of sacred classical buildings as elements belonging to the pictorial stock of the beautiful as it was developed by the Roman landscape painters of the seventeenth century. Both Henderson's paintings were exhibited and published in 1802. However, by 1804 all the artists seem to have more or less stopped working for Thornton (except for Maria Cosway whose *Flora Dispensing her Favours on Earth* (plate 9) was engraved in 1807).[63]

There is, however, one further artist who appears in connection with a painting for *The Temple of Flora*. This artist is the watercolourist Edward Dayes, who enjoyed some fame for his topographical drawings in the picturesque fashion. Dayes' name does not appear on any print in *A New Illustration*, but the last painting in the

exhibition, *Roses* (plate 23), depicted by Thornton himself, was described as follows: 'time is at the break of morning, when Phaeton (the sun) is but just risen, (from Dayes) and Zephyr is crowning Spring with roses (from an Old Master)'. Thornton clearly copied the various elements of the painting from different sources, among them an allegorically described depiction of the sun by Dayes.[64] Thornton obviously admired Dayes' work. He enthusiastically subscribed to 25 copies of *The Works of the Late Edward Dayes* (1805) according to a list attached by Dayes' widow to the compilation. Dayes' writings include a treatise describing his method of making tinted drawings in muted colours, a style characteristic of the second half of the eighteenth century, but which had largely been abandoned by the beginning of the nineteenth century in favour of brighter

19 Peter Henderson, *The Quadrangular Passion-Flower*, 1802, aquatint, stipple engraving (J.S. Hopwood) printed in colour, hand-finished, plate size 538 × 412, from R.J. Thornton *The Temple of Flora*, by permission of the Syndics of Cambridge University Library.

colours applied directly onto paper without an underdrawing. Thornton's enthusiastic subscription to Dayes' book, as well as the choice of the artists he employed for his project, show that Thornton's taste for landscapes was of the eighteenth century rather than the nineteenth, favouring muted colours and generalising approaches.

The Plants and their Backgrounds

The most notable characteristic of the illustrations in *The Temple of Flora* is the clear-cut, precise and colourful delineation of each plant illustrated. Their flowering parts are shown so close up that their roots in the surrounding landscape are in most cases obscured,

allowing no pictorial space between observer and plant. Thus the plants take up the whole foreground, so that, when set against a muted coloured background, they assume an almost heroic appearance. Yet, at the same time, the landscape setting never really develops into three dimensions. Rather, one perceives two different levels of expression.[65] On the level of the plant, the delineation of the flowers is both precise and idealised. Thornton makes sure that all the parts of the fructification are clearly visible. As is to be expected in a botanical drawing which should permit the classification of the plant, Thornton tries to show the buds, flowers and, where applicable, fruits (as in the case of the passion flowers, plates 17–19). Quite often we even find that a leaf has been depicted turned upside down (plate 13), obviously in order to allow more precise identification of the plant. The plants are thus shown as perfect specimens, a point that Thornton explicitly emphasises in his footnote describing *A Group of Auriculas*. In instances which are supposed to depict varieties developed through cultivation, he even shows different species next to each other which would never grow together naturally (this is so in the case of the prints of the tulips, plate 20, roses, plate 23, hyacinths, plate 10, auriculas, plate 21, and carnations, plate 22). Although all the plants are shown in their ideal state, most of them seem to have been taken from specific forms in nature or represent compilations made from studies of observed plants. With perhaps one exception, I could not identify models for the depictions in other botanical treatises preceding *A New Illustration*.[66] All the plants shown had been introduced into England by the end of the eighteenth century (the first seven prints show highly cultivated European forms but none of the rest is of European origin) and thus it is perfectly possible that Thornton had his pictures designed without recourse to other botanical publications. Three times Thornton himself recounts in the text where he has seen the plants. The carnations are said to be copies 'of the exact size of Nature, from out of the choice collection of Mr. Davey, of the King's Road, Chelsea, as were the Tulips from that of Mr. Mason, certainly the first florist in the world'. *The Aloe* (plate 24) (which is in fact an agave) was, he says, taken from a plant which was reputed to be seventy years old and apparently flowered in September 1790 'at Smith's nursery, at Dalston, near Hackney'.[67]

In a letter sent to the *Philosophical Magazine*,

20 (above left) Philip Reinagle, *Tulips*, 1798, mezzotint (R. Earlom) printed in colour, hand-finished, plate size 476 × 353, from R.J. Thornton *The Temple of Flora*, by permission of the Syndics of Cambridge University Library.

21 (above right) Peter Henderson, *A Group of Auriculas*, 1803, aquatint, stipple and line engraving (F.C. Lewis and J.S. Hopwood) printed in colour, hand-finished, plate size 551 × 411, from R.J. Thornton *The Temple of Flora*, by permission of the Syndics of Cambridge University Library.

22 (right) Peter Henderson, *A Group of Carnations*, 1803, aquatint, stipple and line engraving (J. Caldwall) printed in colour, hand-finished, plate size 525 × 404, from R.J. Thornton *The Temple of Flora*, by permission of the Syndics of Cambridge University Library.

23 (facing page) Robert John Thornton, *Roses*, 1805, mezzotint, line engraving (R. Earlom) printed in colour, hand-finished, plate size 483 × 372, from R.J. Thornton *The Temple of Flora*, by permission of the Syndics of Cambridge University Library.

24 Philip Reinagle, *The Aloe*, 1798, aquatint, line engraving
(T. Medland) printed in colour, hand-finished, paper size 597
× 454, from R.J. Thornton *The Temple of Flora*, by permission of the Syndics of Cambridge University Library.

Thornton gives further details as to how the depictions
of the plants were obtained:

> First, take, for example, the oblique-leaved Begonia.
> A plant was obtained from the Physic Gardens at
> Chelsea. It had only *female* flowers. This was sketched
> in, and Mr. Reinagle went with me in a chaise ten
> miles off to obtain a branch with *male* flowers, in
> order to complete the picture. The blue Passion-
> flower contains *eleven stages* of that flower, from its
> first appearance in the bud to the perfect fruit. No
> one branch showed these gradations. The flowers
> were obtained at Barr's nursery, at Dalston, and the
> perfect fruit from North's nursery, near the Asylum.
> The superb Lily, &c. required the same
> observances.[68]

However, the main concern of the depictions does

not seem to be to show the plants as they would
spontaneously grow in a specific natural setting. Even in
the case of the snowdrops (plate 12), one of the very few
depictions showing plants rooted in the landscape, their
isolated and unprotected position on a slope would not
have been likely to produce the highly cultivated
arrangement here displayed alongside a group of crocuses. In fact, it seems clear that when Thornton talks of
the 'situation to which each [plant] naturally belongs',[69]
he does not mean a botanically true landscape, that is, a
landscape suitable for the plants' flourishing. Rather, in
a broader sense, the backgrounds express the perceived
situation of the plant, and we can explore these situations through the landscape.

Five of the flowers, which are native to the much
warmer climes of India, Africa and Asia (*The Queen*,
plate 25, *The Nodding Renealmia*, plate 26, *The China
Limodron*, plate 27, *The Sacred Egyptian Bean*, plate 28,
The Blue Egyptian Water-Lily, plate 29), have a gentle
mountain background, bare of any particularities,
sometimes with calm water in view. Only palms and
occasionally religious buildings, like temples, pagodas,
pyramids or mosques, indicate their foreign origin. The
sky often shows a golden tint near the horizon. It seems
as if those features which in the eighteenth century
were taken to be characteristic of landscape within the
aesthetic category of the beautiful – smoothness, gentle-
ness, a golden sky and the presence of sacred buildings
– have here ossified into mere formulae or conventional
tokens used in order to ascribe meaning to the plants.
Not only do these attributes allude to the plants'
extraordinary beauty, they are also meant to express the
ancient status of the flowers, just as Claude Lorrain's
paintings denote an eternal harmony in the Italian landscapes he depicts. In the case of the *Indian Reed*, *The
Sacred Egyptian Bean* and *The Blue Egyptian Water-Lily*,
this is made explicit in the accompanying texts, in
which their ancient status and the celebration of them
in pagan religions are mentioned, as is the beauty of the
subjects depicted. In other examples the beauty is
expressed solely through the images (plates 17–19): the
column stands metonymically for an ancient temple,
and symbolises eternal support for the flower; in the
text, the flower itself is explicitly linked to what was
perceived to be the most beautiful and eternal kind of
reality – Christ's martyrdom. *The White Lily* (plate 15),
on the other hand, is shown in front of a dark mountain, a design which was made necessary, as Thornton

25 Peter Henderson, *The Queen*, 1804, stipple and line engraving (R. Cooper) printed in colour, hand-finished, paper size 556 × 435, from R.J. Thornton *The Temple of Flora*, by permission of the Syndics of Cambridge University Library.

26 Peter Henderson, *The Nodding Renealmia*, 1801, aquatint, stipple and line engraving (J. Caldwall) printed in colour, hand-finished, plate size 521 × 396, from R.J. Thornton *The Temple of Flora*, by permission of the Syndics of Cambridge University Library.

says, to enhance the effect of the white flowers. Yet there is a glimpse of a temple in the background, again signifying the religious associations of the plant: 'our blessed Saviour [. . .] alludes to it [the flower], when addressing his faint-hearted disciples'. In the text for the roses (plate 23), Thornton refers to their association with eternity through long quotations of myths, stories and poems which celebrate them.[70] Again, no landscape background is shown in this print except a temple on a hill and the rising sun at the left-hand side of the depiction.

Not only have some of the landscapes in *The Temple of Flora* plainly been created according to the canons of the eighteenth-century category of the beautiful, but the two complementary categories of the sublime and the picturesque are also represented. These conventions

lead to a characterisation of the plants in terms that are not derived from orthodox Linnaean botany. A sublime background is given to the engravings *The Superb Lily*, *The Dragon Arum* and *The Night-Blowing Cereus*. In *The Superb Lily* (plate 16) the flower is shown in a threatening environment. Dark mountains rear up behind it and the stormy sky, pierced only briefly by blue, is full of clouds bearing snow (as Thornton describes them in the introductory 'Explanation of the Picturesque Plates'). The accompanying poem describes the plant as complaining of its shady surroundings; it is then exposed by God to the sun, which leads to its death. In *The Dragon Arum* (plate 30) the plant itself is the focus of attention, while the landscape is kept very simple, consisting of mere hints of mountains which gradually fade into the dark and nebulous sky. The yellow tint in the

27 (above left)   Peter Henderson, *The China Limodoron*, 1802, aquatint, stipple and line engraving (J. Landseer) printed in colour, hand-finished, plate size 529 × 396, from R.J. Thornton *The Temple of Flora*, by permission of the Syndics of Cambridge University Library.

28 (above right)   Peter Henderson, *The Sacred Egyptian Bean*, 1804, aquatint, stipple engraving (T. Burke and F.C. Lewis) printed in colour, hand-finished, paper size 570 × 470, from R.J. Thornton *The Temple of Flora*, by permission of the Syndics of Cambridge University Library.

29 (right)   Peter Henderson, *The Blue Egyptian Water-Lily*, 1804, aquatint (J.C. Stadler) printed in colour, hand-finished, plate size 520 × 398, from R.J. Thornton *The Temple of Flora*, by permission of the Syndics of Cambridge University Library.

30 (facing page)   Peter Henderson, *The Dragon Arum*, 1801, mezzotint (W. Ward) printed in colour, hand-finished, plate size 476 × 352, from R.J. Thornton *The Temple of Flora*, by permission of the Syndics of Cambridge University Library.

background throws the purple of the plant into stark relief. In the text Thornton gives full play to the horrific properties traditionally attributed to it. (In reality the dragon arum prefers a sunny location and is a perfectly harmless plant; only its berries – not shown in the picture – are poisonous). Clive Bush in his interpretation of the picture has stressed the darkly erotic, hermaphroditic connotations of this plant:

> The purple hood, with its crenelated outline, achieved characteristically with the opposition of light and dark color, envelops along its whole length which dominates the page, in labia-like folds, the black phallus of the core.[71]

The dark and threatening background gives

this sexualised depiction its malign and repellent associations.

As with the category of the beautiful, the sublime landscapes do not serve a botanical purpose but interpret the plants' perceived character. The landscape settings never impinge upon the pictorial authority of the flower itself and it is precisely because the backgrounds play a subsidiary role that we can find such clear tokens of the beautiful and the sublime in them. Indeed, in the case of *The Night-Blowing Cereus* (plate 11), the background is simply a collection of motifs from the repertoire of the sublime (a church tower with a clock standing at midnight, a moonlit wood) which do not even form a coherent spatial whole.

The backgrounds to the snowdrops, hyacinths and tulips, on the other hand, show features of the pictur-

31 Peter Henderson, *The Maggot-bearing Stapelia*, 1801, aquatint, stipple and line engraving (J.C. Stadler) printed in colour, hand-finished, plate size 523 × 402, from R.J. Thornton *The Temple of Flora*, by permission of the Syndics of Cambridge University Library.

32 Philip Reinagle, *Pitcher Plant*, 1803, aquatint, stipple and line engraving (R. Cooper) printed in colour, hand-finished, paper size 557 × 438, from R.J. Thornton *The Temple of Flora*, by permission of the Syndics of Cambridge University Library.

ebrated in treatises of the picturesque such as those of Price and Knight. Since the importance of variety had been consistently stressed in theorising about the picturesque, it is not surprising to find that this category is employed in just those prints that emphasise the innate variety of the species depicted.

The beautiful, the sublime and the picturesque were often not as distinct as I have presented them as being. While eighteenth-century aesthetic theory might seek to separate them, practice would often elide them, and this is also the case in *The Temple of Flora*. While some images clearly evoke the beautiful, the sublime and the picturesque alone, others, like *The Persian Cyclamen* (plate 13), combine the categories. *The Maggot-bearing Stapelia* (plate 31) is set in a picturesque Alpine setting, while the plant itself is shown as having a sublime character. Thornton states that it is a plant of poisonous,

33 Philip Reinagle, *The Narrow-leaved Kalmia*, 1804, aquatint, stipple engraving (J. Caldwall) printed in colour, hand-finished, plate size 538 × 410, from R.J. Thornton *The Temple of Flora*, by permission of the Syndics of Cambridge University Library.

34 Peter Henderson, *The American Cowslip*, 1801, aquatint, stipple and line engraving (T. Warner) printed in colour, hand-finished, paper size 565 × 427, from R.J. Thornton *The Temple of Flora*, by permission of the Syndics of Cambridge University Library.

esque. In contrast to the beautiful, these picturesque landscapes display more textured surfaces and show features of secular human life, such as the cottage in the winter setting of *The Snowdrop* (plate 12), the village to the right in the print of the *Tulips* (plate 20) and boats in the case of the *Hyacinths* (plate 10). Thornton states in the introductory text that the hyacinths and tulips 'are placed in Holland, where these flowers are particularly cultivated, embellishing a level country'. According to Gilpin, the arch-advocate of the picturesque, flatness itself was not picturesque. But Dutch seventeenth-century paintings had come to be considered as the quintessentially picturesque counterparts to the Roman classical landscapes. They displayed the textured surfaces, light distribution and secular subject-matter cel-

deceptive animal appearance, which grows 'over the arid wilds of Africa' (the Alpine background is all the more surprising, then). In other cases, as we will see later, this contrast of categories seems to have been introduced by Thornton to make a deliberate point.

In other prints, however, which show species from America, the landscape backgrounds are reduced to unspecific ranges of mountains, as in the illustration of the *Pitcher Plant* (plate 32), or *The Narrow-leaved Kalmia* (plate 33). *The Aloe* (plate 24), although it is a native of tropical America, is placed in front of a bare rock in a green hilly landscape with a river in the far background. A mountainous landscape was thought suitable to

36   David Allan, *Thomas Graham, Baron Lynedoch*, c.1769, oil on canvas, 1384 × 984, Yale Center for British Art, Paul Mellon Collection, New Haven.

35   Joshua Reynolds, *Commodore Keppel*, c.1753–4, oil on canvas, 2390 × 1475, National Maritime Museum, London.

express 'its stately form'. In *The American Cowslip* (plate 34) the coastal setting serves to allow the depiction of ships, which Thornton intends to denote its American origin, though, in fact, this plant grows in woods and on prairies.[72] What these examples have in common with the other landscapes is that they operate in a connotative way, rather than displaying a homogeneous setting for the plants. To this extent the backgrounds not only embody a condensed meaning distilled from the different forms of landscape painting, but also function like backgrounds in eighteenth-century portrait paintings.[73]

Portraiture was the most financially rewarding genre from the 1780s onwards,[74] and both the leading figures in the development of British portrait painting,

37   Jacques-Antoine Vallin, *Dr Forlenze*, 1807, oil on canvas, 2096 × 1283, reproduced by courtesy of the Trustees, The National Gallery, London.

Gainsborough and Reynolds, frequently placed their figures in a natural setting. However, as in Thornton's plant depiction, the sitters, firmly delineated as they are, remain separated from their surroundings.[75] The background serves to elicit a meaning which then alludes to the sitter, thus characterising him or her by connotation. A case in point is Reynolds' portrait of *Commodore Keppel* (plate 35) of c.1753–4. The Commodore, who had recently escaped shipwreck,[76] is shown in front of a stormy sky and rugged seashore. In the background broken timbers are tossed in the waves. Here, as in Thornton's *The Superb Lily* (plate 16), the sublimity of the landscape evokes the heroism of the sitter. Another source of vocabulary for the interpretation of such idealised landscape settings is the seventeenth-century tradition of royal portraiture. For example, when Anthony Van Dyck depicted Charles I riding through an idealised English oak forest, he at once suggested the king's close relationship with the territory he governs and his connection with an acardian past which 'places him within a moral orbit beyond that of mere affairs of state'.[77] In eighteenth-century portraits this association of nobility with an arcadian past is sometimes hinted at by introducing an ancient temple into an otherwise unelaborated background, as David Allan (1744–1796) did in his portrait of *Thomas Graham, Baron Lynedoch* (plate 36) of c.1769. Thornton adopted these conventional strategies in his flower depictions when he attempted to attribute timeless meaning to some of his flowers (plate 15). In portraiture we can also find the key to another feature of some prints: those in which Thornton alludes to the place of origin of the plants via token references rather than homogeneous landscape settings. When, in 1807, Jacques-Antoine Vallin (active 1791–1831) painted a portrait of *Dr Forlenze* (plate 37), famous in Paris for his occult performances, he placed him in front of the Molo in Naples, signified by one of the lighthouses, and filled the background with a depiction of Vesuvius, thus referring to Forlenze's home town. Vallin was here using well-recognised tokens to evoke a specific connotation. In just the same way, ships flying the American flag are introduced in *The American Cowslip* (plate 34). Thornton's strategy in *The Temple of Flora* is clearly anthropomorphic: the pictures are portraits whose subjects are plants because for him there is an ontological continuum between plants and human beings.

Therefore it is not surprising that some of Thornton's characterisations of plants can carry significant political implications:

> Some Flowers rear their heads with a majestic mien; and overlook, like sovereigns or nobles, the whole parterre. Others seem more moderate in their aims, and advance only to the middle stations; a genius turned for heraldry, might term them, the gentry of the border. While others, free from all aspiring views, creep unambitiously on the ground, and look like the commonalty of the kind. – Some are intersected with elegant stripes, or studded with radiant spots. Some affect to be genteelly powdered, or neatly fringed, while others are plain in their aspect, unaffected in their dress, and content to please with a naked simplicity. Some assume the monarch's purple, some look most becoming in the virgin's white; but black, doleful black, has no admittance in the wardrobe of Nature. The weeds of mourning would be a manifest indecorum, when Summer holds an universal festival.[78]

Thus the snowdrops, which are shown much smaller in Thornton's print than any of the other plants, are taken to display the modesty properly associated with the position of the lower classes. Their humble status is seen to reflect the natural necessity of variety of status within an overall order. The complaints of the Superb Lily in the poem, her desire to be let out of her shadowy surroundings and her consequent death, become a warning against revolt which would upset the existing order, an order considered by Thornton to be a 'universal truth'.[79] Each subject must bow to this truth for the sake of the general happiness.[80] Thornton's work sets out to show a divinely established natural order which structures the vegetable kingdom in the same way as it does the human kingdom.

Ordered Continuity: The Arrangement of the Pictures

The extent to which his understanding of the continuity between man and nature was influential for Thornton can also be seen from the order of those exhibits shown at the Royal Academy done for *The Temple of Flora*. The Royal Academy exhibition catalogue reveals that the *Large Flowering Sensitive Plant* (plate 38), the mimosa, was the first to be shown (1797)

38   Philip Reinagle, *Large Flowering Sensitive Plant*, 1799, aquatint, stipple and line engraving (J.C. Stadler) printed in colour, hand-finished, plate size 473 × 358, from R.J. Thornton *The Temple of Flora*, by permission of the Syndics of Cambridge University Library.

and thus was possibly the first to be commissioned. Presumably *The Aloe* (plate 24) and the *Tulips* (plate 20), which both bear 1798 as their date of engraving, came next. In the text of *A New Illustration*, accompanying *The Aloe*, Thornton expresses astonishment at the rapidity of its growth:

> It was supposed to be about 70 years old, at which time, it displayed its scape, or trunk, arising from the center of the leaves, increasing with astonishing rapidity, until it reached nearly the height of 30 feet, resembling the mast of a ship.

Just as the mimosa, in virtue of its sensitivity to touch, gives evidence in favour of Darwin's belief in the existence of a sensorium in plants, so the aloe provides Thornton's own illustration of their potentiality for

movement. The tulips, on the other hand, illustrate the importance of sexuality in plants, the central ordering principle of Linneaus' taxonomy. Because the tulips have two sexes (stamens and pistils) they can generate a variety in the offspring – something which both Darwin and Thornton celebrated.[81]

However, not only do plants display the same bodily functions as animals and human beings, they also interact with their surroundings in virtue of their stimulus-response system.[82] But in Thornton's *The Temple of Flora*, these stimuli are not of a purely botanical character. Recalling that, for Thornton, an 'electric fluid' was the common bond between all living beings and their environment, it is possible to read his combination of beautiful landscape settings with plants that he takes to be timeless and grand in a way that parallels Burke's account of the effect of beautiful objects on the mind. A balanced and gentle (that is, beautiful) landscape, in which no strong opposition prevails, affects the plant in a correspondingly even, unexcited way and hence sustains the eternal, stable existence of the species of plant depicted. In the case of other species, their more varied character reflects more varied impacts and so is matched by the richer textures of picturesque landscapes, while a foetid plant, *The Dragon Arum* (plate 30), is given a horrific setting. Here the sublimity of the setting expresses an affinity in the plant.

Sometimes a contrasting mode of depiction is used to produce a heightened effect of opposition between the plant and its setting. Thus the beauty of *The Superb Lily* (plate 16) is offset by its sublime background. Similarly, the darkness of the background in *The Night-Blowing Cereus* (plate 11) accentuates the effect of a glamorous shining flower. Reference to Darwin's ideas makes it clear that this is by no means an inconsistency on Thornton's part, however; the opposition between habitat and species is represented as being as productive as the opposition of the sexes is in interaction within species. It is in *The Philosophy of Medicine* that Thornton is most explicit about the correlation between the pictorial category of the sublime and what he sees as an important principle of life, the interaction of opposites. The example that he chooses is, not surprisingly, taken from one of his own former artists:

> This [the potentially productive effect of oppositions] is also very finely exhibited in some sublime paintings by Pether. He has represented an irruption of Mount

Vesuvius during a full moon, each mingling their different lights upon the heaven and on the waters. In another picture we have a village on fire with a moon-light scenery; and in a third, a moon-light with the warm emanation from a forge of a blacksmith's shop. That these paintings owe much of their effect from the principle we are endeavouring to prove by a variety of arguments, we think no one can deny, and the principle itself is generally known and allowed by painters themselves.[83]

In Thornton's view there is no threatening aspect to these subjects:

The Divine Mind, which at once comprehends all the relations of things, saw from the first the true good. Therefore there is not in the universe any such thing as absolute evil; because it contains nothing in itself but what is the cause of some good, which could not have existed, as things are, without the possiblity of evil.[84]

With a world-view which conceives of the world as a 'truly good' Divine creation, in which 'everything is systematical' and in 'combination, relation, affinity, connection', it is impossible for any display of it to be brought to systematic closure.[85]

For this reason, Thornton's arrangement of the pictures is an open-ended play. Neither the order in which Thornton commissioned the paintings, as shown from the order of their exhibition at the Royal Academy, nor the dates of engraving to be found on the prints, match their final placing in *A New Illustration*, and the catalogue to Thornton's 1804 exhibition follows a different sequence yet again, implying a changing argument on his part each time.[86] It is notable, however, that what might have seemed the most obvious order – Linnaeus' own – is not adopted by Thornton at any stage.

In the final arrangement of *A New Illustration* Thornton begins with a theme which had become well established by that time. The first section is an account of those plants which start to flower immediately after the end of winter. It is arranged in sequence by months and dates and is illustrated with snowdrops and crocuses, the cyclamen, hyacinths and, finally, roses. Such an order of presentation had become very popular in garden treatises since the appearance in 1732 of Robert Furber's *Twelve Months of Flowers*, a work which was intended to advise on planting throughout the year.[87]

Darwin himself finished 'The Economy of Vegetation' with a last canto which celebrated the regular appearance of plants after winter.[88] Thornton concludes this section by introducing some stanzas against the war, drawing a parallel between the war with France and winter. While winter is understood as a natural period of silence and the signs of spring are explicitly celebrated as manifestations of the providence of the Creator, who always assures the 'regular succession' of life, the war is seen as an artificial interruption by men and out of accord with nature.[89]

Yet at this time, when patriotism was at its highest and violation of it threatened to be treated as an act of treason,[90] Thornton seems to have felt obliged to add the following remark:

Yet I hope it will be understood, that neither the Poet Laureate, nor myself, wish to inculcate pusillanimity. 'Dulce et decorum est pro patria mori'. We deplore only that ambition and folly in rulers which create Wars, from jealousy of trade, or for territorial aggrandisement!

What Thornton condemns is thus not participation in the war as such, but the action of individuals (specifically Napoleon, as the poems make clear) in violating what he considers to be natural law. *The Sacred Egyptian Bean* at the end of *A New Illustration* gives him another occasion to show his patriotism with a reference to Nelson's victory at the Nile in 1798.

This lofty note is followed by a section which, as I see it, displays plants which best illustrate the variety of species and which Thornton was later to describe as follows: 'Each allows himself a little particularity in his dress, though all belong to the one family; so that they are various, and yet the same'.[91] This order is not stringent and exclusive, and illustrates only one dimension of a larger and more comprehensive order, as is shown by the overlapping of these sections. For example, plants like hyacinths, which appear in the seasonal section, could just as easily appear in the variety section, since they also display different forms under cultivation. The third sequence is even more difficult to interpret precisely. From *The Queen* onwards Thornton shows all those plants which bear remarkable analogies with animal organisms. *The Queen* (plate 25) is a plant whose flower can be seen as visually mimicking tropical birds, such as parrots. I take this section to end with the *American Bog-Plants* (plate 39), a type of predatory plant

39   Philip Reinagle, *American Bog-Plants*, 1806, aquatint (T. Sutherland) printed in colour, hand-finished, paper size 556 × 427, from R.J. Thornton *The Temple of Flora*, by permission of the Syndics of Cambridge University Library.

40   Peter Henderson, *The Pontic Rhododendron*, 1802, aquatint, stipple and line engraving (J. Caldwall) printed in colour, hand-finished, plate size 526 × 401, from R.J. Thornton *The Temple of Flora*, by permission of the Syndics of Cambridge University Library.

in that they eat animals, and the last section starts with *The Pontic Rhododendron* (plate 40). The text which accompanies the illustration of this shrub introduces it as a plant which grows during winter:

> In the dreary season of winter, nature has partially indulged the eye with ever-greens, the presage of the resurrection of animated beings, and of the returning zephyr: and none of this class claims our attention, for the beauty of its flowers, and wisdom of its contrivance, more than the Pontic Rhododendron, which was introduced into our gardens from the Levant in 1763.

With this plant and the next one, the American cowslip, Thornton emphasises what he calls the 'Providence' of the Creator, which makes its presence felt even during 'dreary seasons' or difficult circumstances. The

American cowslip is celebrated for just this quality, its 'principal design, being intended upon the continuance, and preservation, of the species'.

In the last three pictures Thornton illustrates plants which were known to have been admired by followers of ancient heathen religions and which could therefore stand for the unchangeable and eternal presence of Divine Revelation. Darwin had also employed a range of expressions from ancient religions and mythologies as a proof of the existence of eternal laws. Both he and Thornton believed that it was a sign of the advances made by modern natural philosophy that it should be possible to decipher ancient expressions into more comprehensible and complete notions.[92]

The fact that Thornton arranged the pictures according to different architectonic principles at different times shows that their order remained to some degree open. In *The Religious Use of Botany* of 1824, Thornton again explores different aspects of the botanical world. He introduces his subject-matter in a paratactic manner, moving from one topic to the next without apparent connection: 'There is another subject of the verdant kingdom',[93] he writes for example, or, again, 'Our next observation will be upon a general property'.[94] In fact, some plants, like the lily or the rose, are actually presented under different categories altogether. He writes:

Adore the supreme BENEFACTOR for the blessings HE showers down upon every order of beings; adore HIM for numberless mercies which are appropriated to thyself; but, above all, adore HIM for that noble gift of a rational and immortal soul; which constitutes us masters of the globe, and gives us the real enjoyment of its riches, which discovers ten thousand beauties which otherwise had been lost, and renders them both a source of delight and a nursery of devotion. By virtue of this exalted principle, we are qualified to admire our MAKER's works, and capable of bearing HIS illustrious image.[95]

Man, in Thornton's view, is able to perceive and understand the Creator's work, but does not play the primary role in determining the course that nature takes. Thus, although human beings 'are qualified to admire our MAKER's works', they themselves form part of that work and so can never rise to a vantage-point from which that order can be comprehended in its entirety. Any human appropriation of the divine order will be limited and incomplete.

The Failure of A New Illustration

A New Illustration was designed by Thornton to be a truly grand composition, 'a National Work', as he claimed in the exhibition catalogue in 1804. But the public received it differently. In May 1804 the following criticism appeared in the *Monthly Magazine*:

Dr. Thornton is proceeding in his great national work, as he pompously calls it, 'A new Illustration' of the Linnean [sic] system. Seventeen numbers are already before the public, whose expectations, it is believed, are egregiously disappointed. The work was evidently not intended for common readers: it is dressed out for the levee and the drawing-room of

princes and the nobility. The plates are finished with exquisite delicacy, and will immortalize the vanity and insufficiency of Dr. Thornton.[96]

The same issue contains a further criticism, which challenges the scientific value of the enterprise:

Expensive performances like this can recommend themselves only to persons, who, with a taste for the polite arts, possess also the means of indulging it; and to public libraries, the archives of what is curious in a country.[97]

In the end, *A New Illustration* was a failure.[98] Thornton evidently could not find enough subscribers to sustain the project, and, when the edition was finally completed in 1807, it contained only a third of the material apparently intended. By 1812 Thornton was forced to hold a lottery with the paintings from which the prints were taken as first prize in a final attempt to escape financial ruin.[99] Yet even this did not succeed. It is certain that not enough tickets were sold in the course of 1812,[100] since the final drawing was announced in the *London Gazette* for 16 March 1813.[101] Today the prints of *The Temple of Flora* are extremely popular and sell for astonishing prices. But at the time the project proved to be a disaster and ruined Thornton personally. His obituary in the *Annual Register*, twenty-five years later, states that: 'the results [of the lottery] were not sufficiently successful to restore his fortune, and he was ever after a beggared man'.[102]

Thornton himself blamed the war: 'The once moderately rich very justly now complain they are exhausted through taxes laid on them to pay armed men to diffuse rapine, fire, and murder, over civilized Europe' (*A New Illustration*). This was quite a common complaint at the time. The income tax which William Pitt the Younger had introduced to pay for the war affected people more than ever before. Most noticeable, however, were the effects of inflation. For the labouring classes, real wages declined during the war years and did not rise again until much later.[103] Inflation bore most heavily on the poorest classes and those of the middle class who were on fixed or relatively inflexible incomes.[104] Landowners, on the other hand, who were able to increase their rents and to profit from the substantial rise in corn prices, as well as those merchants and industrialists who profited from the needs of the war economy made significant gains during these years.

Thornton's publication, as the critic of the *Monthly Magazine* pointed out, was not for the common reader, but 'dressed out for the levee and the drawing-room of princes and the nobility',[105] and this market could still easily have absorbed an enterprise like Thornton's, had it corresponded to its taste. The reason for the lack of interest in Thornton's project cannot have been purely economic.

Nor was it the lack of a prestigious printer. Thornton took his project to one of the most famous printers in London, Thomas Bensley, who had his headquarters in Bolt Court, off Fleet Street, and was renowned for his production of the finest typographical work. Bensley printed the book on behalf of the author, who then undertook the distribution himself by subscription, a practice which was not at all unusual in the eighteenth century, particularly for ambitious natural history publications. Eliminating a middleman, the bookseller, had the advantage that financial gain could be maximised.[106]

Accusations of pretentiousness were not, of course, helpful to ambitious literary or artistic projects. As discussed in the previous chapter, in the 1790s grand speculative systems like Thornton's and Darwin's (with some justification in the latter case) had become associated with the natural philosophy and radical politics of people like Thomas Beddoes and Priestley and were thus treated with suspicion.[107]

Thornton's understanding of nature shared with Darwin and the political radicals a conception of the subject as something that is defined by a realm outside it; in both, we find the notion of the individual as a *tabula rasa*, to be written upon by whatever is outside it.[108] Such a position is not intrinsically radical; it was held by a wide range of eighteenth-century writers influenced by Locke. But combined with a dynamic understanding of nature it could be turned to radical ends. *A New Illustration* was animated by the endeavour to trace the contours of a single, self-differentiating principle, running through the human and the natural realm alike, celebrating the realisation of an ideal order, as intended by Divine Providence. The assumption of a single unifying principle is what motivates Thornton's use of the landscape categories, the sublime, the beautiful and the picturesque, as backgrounds to the plants depicted. *The Temple of Flora* shows particularly clearly that these eighteenth-century categories were much more than pictorial classifications, or expressions of human sentiments projected onto nature. As in Burke's discussion of the sublime and the beautiful or in Price's analysis of the picturesque, aesthetic qualities are perceived to be features innate in the outside realm, capable of effecting a similar response in living beings. But such investigations were losing credibility with the rise of a different kind of natural philosophy, one in which the 'ardent pursuit of analogies', as one critic of *A New Illustration* put it, was consciously abandoned.[109]

Staffa

III

FROM PICTURESQUE TRAVEL TO SCIENTIFIC OBSERVATION

By the time Thornton's *Temple of Flora* was completed in 1807, striking changes had begun to appear in the depiction of British landscape. Between 1790 and 1830 pictorial formulae like the sublime, the beautiful and the picturesque lost their privileged place in the perception of nature and were gradually displaced by a more phenomenalist mode of representation. In this chapter we shall examine ways in which this transformation corresponded to changes in the rhetoric and self-understanding of one particular science, geology.

Geology was one of the earliest areas of study in which eighteenth-century assumptions about common unifying principles acting uniformly throughout the realm of natural phenomena were called into question. A geological discourse arose at the beginning of the nineteenth century, which, as in the theories of perception of Archibald Alison and Dugald Stewart, attempted to restrict itself to mere observation, rejecting any prior suppositions concerning underlying mechanisms by which what is observed is connected. Since both geologists and landscape artists were concerned with the appearance of the natural world, it is not surprising that it is here that we should find some of the most direct connections between scientists and artists during this period.

A comparison between two images produced by William Daniell (1769–1837) epitomises the changes which will concern us in this chapter. Daniell had established his reputation with paintings and drawings of India, which he visited with his uncle Thomas Daniell (1749–1840) between 1784 and 1794. He subsequently became an Associate of the Royal Academy in 1807 and a full Academician in 1822, being elected in preference to Constable. Between 1807 and 1812 Daniell compiled a publication to which he gave the title *Interesting Selections from Animated Nature with Illus-*trative *Scenery*.[1] He included in it a print of *The Cave of Fingal* (1807) (plate 41) at Staffa.[2] It shows the entrance to the major cave on the Isle of Staffa as if one were looking into the nave of a huge cathedral, with a vault-like formation of earth resting on even, rectilinear columns. *The Cave of Fingal* is shown as a natural and divine wonder, analogous to but more perfect than the products of human activity.

Between 1814 and 1825 Daniell produced a further publication, *A Voyage round Great Britain*,[3] a project which, in contrast to the *Interesting Selections from Animated Nature*, brought him considerable fame. In its third volume (1818) Daniell again showed a series of illustrations, aquatints printed in colour, displaying different views of the Isle of Staffa, but these are entirely different from his previous representations.[4] In the second picture of this series, the *Entrance to Fingal's Cave* (plate 42), the columns have become reduced in size and the earth formation above them no longer alludes to a cathedral vault. It has now become simply a massive layer of strata lying above the columns. What is most conspicuous is the lack of any emphasis on those features that could have curiosity value. The sea, this time calm and settled, forms a layer parallel to the columns and the earth strata above. Nothing is particularly startling, everything represented in the picture is equally important to the overall impression. The latter is enhanced by the calm weather which facilitates a clear observation of the actual distribution of light and shade. The eighteenth-century fashion for tinting the drawing in a muted brownish or bluish colour to distribute an overall effect of chiaroscuro has been abandoned in favour of subtle local colours in blue, green, brown and yellow. In contrast to the earlier print, which emphasised architectural structures in order to evoke astonishment at nature's curiosities, this depiction conspicuously stays clear of such implications; it is plainly meant to appear as a neutral delineation of what has presented itself to the artist's eye. In the accompanying text Daniell makes the following statement, which can be read as an implicit criticism of his own former approach:

> This celebrated spot seemed the more worthy of attention, because those graphic delineations of it which have obtained most circulation are now found to be inadequate to the subject, and in many respects utterly erroneous. This remark will be understood to apply to the engravings in Mr. Pennant's tour, from drawings by his servant, Moses Griffiths, which have been so carelessly copied in several publications on the continent, that the various objects have been reversed in their position, and their relative proportions still more incorrectly given than in the originals.[5]

As we shall see, Daniell copied his own earlier depiction of Fingal's cave from one of the illustrations in Pennant's publication. This shows a view of the cave looking into its mouth which places the island on the viewer's right, while, in fact, as Daniell's second print rightly depicts it, the island lies to the left. Daniell is mistaken in his assumption that Griffiths designed the engravings in Pennant's section on Staffa. This section was taken from an account by Joseph Banks and the depictions were executed by Banks' own draughtsman. Daniell goes on to say that:

41 William Daniell, *The Cave of Fingal*, 1807, engraving (W. Daniell) from W. Daniell *Interesting Selections from Animated Nature*, vol. 1 [1812?], Radcl.19981 c.33/1, Bodleian Library, Oxford.

To those who have perused the enthusiastic descriptions of Staffa which have been given by various tourists, it may be a source of some disappointment to find that the reality by no means justifies the notions they had been led to form, and that the optics of a poet's fancy must be requisite to convert the scene before them into the end of an immense cathedral, whose massy roof is supported by stupendous pillars formed with all the regularity of art.[6]

He then introduces a description of Staffa by the geologist John MacCulloch (1773–1835). MacCulloch was an early member of the Geological Society of London, set up in 1807 to promote a fieldwork approach to geology against what its founders saw as the purely speculative theories concerning the earth current at the end of the eighteenth century.[7] MacCulloch's research on Staffa took place between 1811 and 1813 while he was employed by the Board of Ordnance.[8] He subsequently published his account in the *Transactions of the Geological Society of London*,[9] and Daniell seems to have read this paper while preparing for his own voyage there. Daniell states:

> It is for this reason [Daniell's distrust of the exaggeration of former accounts] among others that the preference is due to his [MacCulloch's] paper on Staffa over those which have so long challenged the wonder of the public; he has forborne to stimulate curiosity by hyberbolical comparisons, and delivering his statements in plain and direct language, has reduced the prevalent opinions on the subject to a more just and reasonable standard.[10]

Daniell's abandonment of pictorial conventions in the delineation of his engravings in *A Voyage round Great Britain* is here clearly linked to the new fieldwork approach in geology which dismissed theoretical explanations that invoked causes and connections beyond the realm of the visible.

The Wonders of Nature

In contrast to *A Voyage round Great Britain*, Daniell's earlier work was predicated on the same kind of analogical thinking as had structured Thornton's enterprise. Most of the pictures in the *Interesting Selections* show animals in a landscape setting and the accompanying

42   William Daniell, *Entrance to Fingal's Cave, Staffa*, 1817, aquatint (W. Daniell) printed in colour, hand-finished, from W. Daniell *A Voyage round Great Britain*, vol.3 (1818), G.A.Gen.Top.b.33 (opp. p. 34), Bodleian Library, Oxford.

texts to the engravings are short taxonomical accounts referring rather generally to the animals' habitat. In the introductory comments Daniell describes his selection as having been guided by the desire to depict nature in its variety and beauty, insofar as this was 'thought capable of a picturesque illustration'. Although he acknowledges that such depictions are not new, he claims that the placing of the subjects in their habitat is:

> for by placing the different subjects apparently in situations and under circumstances where they are usually seen in nature, a new interest is communicated even to familiar objects, and an air of truth given to all, much more impressive than without such local acompaniments.[11]

Daniell does not mention Thornton, but it is almost certain that he knew of his enterprise, since most of Thornton's artists had exhibited paintings executed for engravings in *A New Illustration* at the Royal Academy or the British Institution.[12] Not only is the conception behind Daniell's publication reminiscent of *A New Illustration*, the pictures, too, are similar. Daniell's landscapes are less of a backdrop than Thornton's. They provide a coherent spatial setting for the animals and his depictions of exotic scenery are more convincing (not surprisingly, since he had travelled to India). Nevertheless, the landscape settings still function in an attributive way, to characterise the essential features of the animals. So, for example, Daniell shows *The Storks* in front of pyramids, although he states that storks are also common in Europe, and he refers in his accompanying text to the fact that the Muhammadans hold the stork:

'in great veneration; it is almost as sacred among them, as the ibis was formerly with the Egyptians'.[13] Reference to ancient religion had led Thornton to place his representation of water-lilies in front of pyramids. By similar reasoning, we find *The Goose* (like the snowdrops in *The Temple of Flora*) in a picturesque setting, since it is a 'well known inhabitant of almost every village green'.[14] The accompanying texts to the engravings give a short taxonomical account of the animals and refer to their natural environment only in passing, again without specific details of their habitat.[15]

The *Cave of Fingal* is one of five prints in this publication that show bizarre earth formations. The others are *Basaltic Columns, Interior of a Salt Mine and Giant's Causeway* (all vol. 1) and *Grotto of Antiparos* (vol. 2).[16] Although three of the five are linked to specific locations – the Cave of Fingal at Staffa; the Giant's Causeway, County Antrim, Northern Ireland; and the Grotto of Antiparos – these places are shown only generically, just as the animals depicted by Daniell are shown as particular species which stand for their respective genera. The reason for their inclusion is stated clearly in the text accompanying *Basaltic Columns*:

He who travels to discover the wonders of nature, and unravel her mysteries, will not readily find any thing more likely to arrest his attention, or better calculated to give scope to conjecture, than the gigantic columns of basaltes.[17]

However, eleven years later, Daniell, influenced by the new fieldwork approach in geology, was to dismiss his own previous thought as 'hyperbolical comparisons' stretching impermissibly beyond the realm of what is observable.

In what follows I shall concentrate on Scotland in exploring the intersection of artists' depictions and geological discourse. This is not an arbitrary choice. The most wide-ranging geological controversy of the time took place in relation to Scotland. This was partly due to the simple fact that James Hutton (1726–1797) and Robert Jameson (1774–1854), the two main theoretical protagonists, were active in Edinburgh. But Scotland also displayed a far greater range of geological phenomena than any other part of Great Britain, from sedimentary formations of different ages in the Lowlands to stratified and unstratified formations and volcanic rock in the Highlands and Western Isles region.[18] In no other region can one find so many illustrations of the same locations by different naturalist travellers as in Scotland – most other parts of Great Britain were not illustrated in any detail by more than one geologist. It is thus no coincidence that Martin Rudwick, in his pioneering article 'The Emergence of a Visual Language for Geological Science 1760–1840', illustrates his brief discussion of documentary landscape drawings with delineations of many of the locations that I too am going to discuss.[19] Rudwick argues that, by the beginning of the nineteenth century, geologists more and more illustrated their accounts with 'realistic' landscape drawings rather than schematised sketches 'in order to counter the premature construction of theoretical "systems" by those who had never seen the relevant evidence'.[20] But, as will become clear, these 'scientific' landscape drawings, particularly when set against contemporary artistic productions, often prove to be strikingly at variance with the expressed intentions behind them, and revert to the pictorial formulae of an earlier period. Immediate connections can be established between geological accounts and artists' practices only in a few cases. But even if direct interaction between artists and geologists was rare, we will see that both groups possessed at least a superficial knowledge of each other's activities.

The Picturesque Tour in Scotland

Scottish artists in the second half of the eighteenth century mainly depicted their own country according to the established classical formulae of Claude Lorrain or Salvator Rosa.[21] Three of the most prolific Scottish artists, Alexander Runciman (1736–1785), Jacob More (1740?–1793) and Alexander Nasmyth (1758–1840), had all spent some time in Rome. Thus the more abundant fertility of the Lowlands was a more suitable subject for their art, and locations like Loch Lomond and the waterfalls of the River Clyde (especially the three most impressive: Bonnington Linn, Cora Linn and Stonebyres Linn) appeared repeatedly in their paintings. Often the scale of the scenery was drastically enlarged to increase the feeling of grandeur. Foreground figures in classical garb were added and the place and time evoked were remote and indefinite, just as in a Claudian arcadia. Alternatively, particularly when the waterfalls of the River Clyde were being illustrated, the depiction could turn into a Salvator Rosa-like savage wilderness, with its broken tree staffage and low viewpoint.

Scottish scenery first became known to the English public, however, through Paul Sandby. The naturalist traveller Thomas Pennant (1726–1798), to whom Daniell refers in his criticism of previous depictions of Staffa, published several of Sandby's pictures in his *Tour in Scotland* in 1771.[22] In 1778 Sandby issued his own magnificently engraved *Virtuosi's Museum* which contained a number of images showing locations in Scotland.[23] Sandby became familiar with Scotland right at the beginning of his career when he was employed as chief draughtsman of the Scottish Ordnance Survey, established in September 1747. Working under Colonel David Watson, Sandby's task was to provide the army with reliable information of Scottish topography.[24] In the summers he travelled with the survey teams, seeing more of the Scottish countryside than any English or even Scottish artist before him. The winters he spent in Edinburgh, preparing finished copies of maps and topographic views.[25] Despite his heavy employment by the Ordnance Survey, Sandby found time to sketch extensively, depicting both the countryside he was travelling through and its inhabitants.

Paul Sandby represents a tradition of British landscape art mentioned only in passing so far, one which preceded the mid-eighteenth-century fashion for depicting the native landscape according to the classical formulae of the sublime and the beautiful. Although Sandby also experimented with such Italianate landscapes (in oil, as well as bodycolour and watercolour) he worked chiefly in a tradition of topographical depiction which was Northern in origin. Several Dutch and Flemish artists came to England in the seventeenth century, to paint the country houses of their English patrons. The object of these works was to show accurately the details of the estates, displaying proudly the extent of the property. The tradition of topography was given new impetus in the 1740s when Canaletto (1697–1768) arrived in England. As Claude Lorrain's conventions were adapted to the English countryside, so Canaletto's served as a model for clear, sharp, well-drawn and brightly coloured views of the urban scenery. Paul's brother and teacher, the artist Thomas Sandby (1721–1798), produced such urban views of London (often in collaboration with his younger brother). The delineation or description of a particular locality is the characteristic of topography, but the breadth of the description varied. It could encompass a complex terrain, with buildings, hills and water as well as human activity, all skillfully arranged according to the demands of composition. Or, it might concentrate on a single recognisable feature which then forms the focal point for a generalised composition. Most of the illustrations Pennant published in his *Tour of Scotland* in 1771 after drawings by Sandby fall into one of these two patterns.

One of the drawings that Sandby produced in Scotland while off-duty is the watercolour *South Prospect of Leith* of 1747 (plate 43).[26] The town, which lies just north of Edinburgh, is shown in the middle distance. To the right some isolated buildings, among them a smoking kiln and a windmill, border on the sea in the background. A road with several figures and a coach leads diagonally from the left foreground to the right middleground. The right foreground is taken up by darkly drawn bushes and vegetation behind which a cornfield with harvesters appears. This drawing (which was obviously intended to be engraved) shows how indebted Sandby was at this stage in his career to the Northern tradition of landscape depiction. Like Dutch seventeenth-century landscapes, its composition presents a recognisable view, structured diagonally and not at right angles to the picture plane. Whatever style Sandby was later to adopt, his work always displays a strong sense of compositional patterns and a predeliction for pellucid light in the sky. Just as the sublime and the beautiful evoke eternal conditions, so topography stabilises the depicted scene, either by restricting itself to a limited range of harmonising colours independent of any characteristics that might stem from specific weather or time effects, or by strong compositional structures, which visually assert stability in the face of changing atmospheric conditions. Even in his most informal and atmospheric watercolours, Sandby never abandoned these stabilising pictorial strategies. One of the earliest such studies is another view of Leith (plate 44), drawn in 1747. Again the town is set in the middle distance behind brightly lit fields. The sea and hills appear on the horizon, above which rises a brilliantly coloured sky whose colours range from dark blue to red and yellow where the sun is setting. The sweeping parallels that run through this composition are initiated by the line of buildings which appears in the foreground, punctured horizontally only by some trees. Among them figures are faintly indicated. In stark

S outh Prospect of Leith

43　Paul Sandby, *South Prospect of Leith*, 1747, graphite, black ink and watercolour, 219 × 391, Ashmolean Museum, Oxford.

contrast to the background, this area lies in deep shadow, from which only the strong red in the roofs of the houses stands out. As we will see in the next chapter, the capturing of atmospheric effects was to become of great importance to landscape artists after the turn of the century and, to some extent, Sandby anticipated this development. But with Sandby one never has the sense that a fragment of nature's appearance is being captured, as is often the case in studies by artists after the turn of the century. Even in such apparently spontaneous sketches as this one, the depiction is constructed according to pictorial conventions of arranging and mediating the fore-, middle- and background. Sandby's watercolours always adhere to the demands of scenic representation. Although such studies have clearly been observed from nature, they were most certainly not coloured on the spot, as would become customary among later artists. In this sketch of Leith the dramatic colour effects of the sky are superimposed in chalk on

the watercolour washes, which indicates that Sandby reworked the drawing at home after it had dried.

By the time that the twenty-seven prints of Scottish subjects in the *Virtuosi's Museum* appeared in 1778, the topographical tradition, in which exactitude of delineation was paramount, was merging with the demands of the picturesque for roughness and variety. The popularity of Sandby's engravings did much to spread the taste for the picturesque. Sandby's depictions in this publication excel in the artful overall distribution of alternating areas of light and shade which Price's picturesque theory was to promote as the unifying strategy for pictorial compositions. The prints exhibit recognisable views, mostly of castles, ranging from Stirling Castle to Dunstaffnage Castle at Loch Etive, then moving north-west and northwards into Banffshire. They also include views of the main waterfalls on the River Clyde, which Sandby had sketched in the late 1740s and which were to become firmly established as picturesque subjects on

44   Paul Sandby, *Leith*, 1747, graphite, chalk and watercolour, 162 × 453, Ashmolean Museum, Oxford.

the Scottish tourist circuit. Although Sandby published engravings which showed subjects from nearly all over Scotland, later picturesque travellers from England seem hardly to have got beyond Blair Atholl and Loch Lomond.

Joseph Farington (1747–1821), the great socialite of the Royal Academy, visited Scotland in 1788 and 1790. In 1788 he accompanied John Knox, a Scottish-born bookseller living in London, who intended to publish Farington's drawings. However, Knox died in 1790 and the project was never carried out. Farington nevertheless seems to have hoped for another opportunity and continued to compile sketchbooks of Scottish subjects with detailed antiquarian and topographical notes. Judging by the contents of his *Sketchbooks*, on these first journeys he seems not to have travelled further north than St Andrews on the east coast and Loch Katrine to the west.[27] He depicted extensively the more varied countryside and richer vegetation around Lanark, Glasgow, Loch Lomond and Kilmarnock and wrote in his journal: 'I recollect in no part of the world such a length of country witht [sic] objects to engage notice [. . .] a continuation of barrenness and drearyness'.[28] To Farington, whose own style was topography turned picturesque, large parts of Scotland appeared devoid of any visual interest.

William Gilpin, too, undertook one of his tours in search of the picturesque in Scotland in 1776.[29] He seems to have travelled slightly further into the Highlands than Farington dared. From Edinburgh Gilpin went to Stirling, Kinross, Perth and from there to the Highlands, going as far as Blair Atholl and returning via Inverary, Loch Lomond and Glasgow. Gilpin, however, quite in contrast to Farington, found the mountains of the Highlands suitable ingredients for picturesque compositions:

> Their broken lines and surfaces mix variety enough with their simplicity to make them often noble subjects in painting; tho as we have observed, they less accommodated to drawing. Indeed these wild scenes of sublimity, unadorned even by a single tree, form in themselves a very *grand species of landscape*.[30]

The aquatints in this publication, which were prepared by Samuel Alken after Gilpin's drawings, show mountains, most often flanking a lake, but sometimes a castle or ruin. These scenes would not have been identifiable as specific locations had they not been reproduced facing the text. Gilpin's sole interest lay in the artful distribution of chiaroscuro over the pictures, which emphasised their rugged features (plate 45). It is likely that it was Gilpin's freer use of tone and his abandonment of topographical delineation that made him more prepared to appreciate the Highlands than Farington, who, like the earlier watercolourists, relied on a more linear treatment more suited to areas of richer vegetation and texture.

What the itinerary and depictions of Sandby, Farington and Gilpin show is that the mainland of Scotland was firmly established from the 1780s onwards

45   William Gilpin, *Dumbarton*, 1789, aquatint (S. Alken), from W. Gilpin *Observations*, vol. 2 (1789), by permission of the Syndics of Cambridge University Library.

as an artistic subject for picturesque travel. Even Farington came to appreciate the Highlands as picturesque in 1801, when he undertook his third journey, now emphasising tone, like Gilpin, rather than topographical delineation: 'my attention was engaged in watching the effects of light & shade on the Mountains', he now stated.[31] In Farington's opinion, the proper itinerary for a picturesque traveller to the Highlands should start in Edinburgh or Glasgow and should cross the Forth to Kinross, Perth, Dunkeld, Blair Atholl, Kenmore, Killin, Tyndrum, Dalmally, Inverary and finally Dumbarton.[32] Scottish scenery had come to be regarded as the equal of Wales and the Lake District as a subject for picturesque views, eventually even outstripping them in popularity by the 1850s.[33]

From 1785 onwards Scottish scenes were on show nearly every year at the Royal Academy exhibitions in London. Initially the preferred subjects were the mainland castles, but from 1809 Loch Lomond and Loch Katrine became very common.[34] But the coast and islands, where the earth crust is laid bare and so the features of Scotland's distinctive geological formations are most palpably visible, did not attract the attention of artists in the eighteenth century. William Daniell was the first artist to exhibit drawings of the west coast and its islands, which he did intermittently from 1816 until 1825. The same lack of interest in the Scottish coast and islands prevailed in Scotland itself. Artists' exhibitions were institutionalised in Edinburgh in 1808, but it was

not until the 1820s that scenes of specific coasts or islands make an appearance in the catalogues.[35] Even Turner stayed on the mainland during his first visits to Scotland, not reaching the Western Isles until 1831. His first tour consisted of a brief excursion over the border in 1797. Turner consulted Farington before leaving for his second tour in 1801 and, following Farington's advice, started from Glasgow and went only slightly further north than Blair Atholl.[36] It was the naturalist travellers, particularly those with strong geological interests, who reached the Scottish coast and Western Isles at a time before artists discovered them as rewarding subject-matter.[37]

Naturalist Travellers in Scotland and the Geological Controversy

The first location on the west coast of Scotland to attract the attention of a naturalist traveller was the Isle of Staffa.[38] In the text to his earlier depiction of Fingal's Cave, Daniell includes a description of the island by the future President of the Royal Society of London, Sir Joseph Banks (1743–1820), the first visitor to publish an account of this remarkable island (1772),[39] which was followed by his more detailed report in Thomas Pennant's *A Tour in Scotland, and Voyage to the Hebrides* (vol. 2, 1776).[40] The very few earlier travellers to the Western Isles, such as Martin Martin,[41] were interested in the islands' nature in relation to their peoples and for this reason uninhabited islands like Staffa were neglected. Writing at the beginning of the age of the naturalist traveller, Banks concludes his account of Fingal's Cave with the following paean to nature:

> each hill, which hung over the columns below, forming an ample pediment; [. . .] almost into the shape of those used in architecture [. . .]. Compared to this what are the cathedrals or the palaces built by men! Mere models or playthings, imitations as diminutive as his works will always be when compared to those of nature. Where is now the boast of the architect! regularity the only part in which he fancied himself to exceed his mistress, Nature, is here found in her possession, and here it has been for ages undescribed.[42]

Pennant accompanied Banks' account with five engravings of the island. One, a panorama of Staffa and its surroundings, was probably prepared by his own draughtsman, Griffiths.[43] The four other prints were executed by John F. Miller, James Miller and John Cleveley, the professional draughtsmen who accompanied Banks in 1772.[44] One of these, *Fingal's Cave in Staffa* (plate 46), is obviously the model for Daniell's earlier depiction. Not only does it exhibit the same cathedral-like structures as Daniell's *The Cave of Fingal* (plate 41) but it is also taken from the same angle.[45] Banks' verbal description and pictorial delineation of Staffa in fact proved to be so powerful that all subsequent travellers known to me refer to them. The French naturalist Barthélemi Faujas de Saint-Fond (1741–1819) visited Staffa in 1784[46] and published three engravings of the island in his publication on Great Britain thirteen years later.[47] In preparation for his voyage he contacted Banks and asked him for a copy of his illustrated account of Staffa in Pennant's tour.[48] The effects of this are apparent, since Faujas de Saint-Fond's *Vue de la Grotte de Fingal* (plate 47), prepared by the artist Durand, seems to be a copy of Banks', even more exaggerated in its architectural features, the nave having become slightly more elongated; in fact, he even criticises Banks' otherwise esteemed draughtsman for having depicted it too 'irregulièrement'. He continues: 'mais il n'y a absolument que des colonnes'.[49] Faujas de Saint-Fond', like Daniell, also copied the reversed position of the cave from Banks' model, where it is wrongly suggested that the island is lying to the right. Indeed, it transpires from Banks' correspondence that Faujas might not even have seen Staffa himself. On 21 October 1784 James Dryander wrote to Banks: 'Faujas has not been to Staffa; when he came to the place of crossing to Mull he considered it dangerous and stayed on the mainland'.[50] Five days later, Sir Charles Blagden tells Banks that 'the conduct of Faujas de St. Fond on his Scottish tour will not easily be forgotten and he can never show his face again'.[51] Later, Richard Kirwan writes to Banks that he treats Faujas 'with contempt for his unfaithfulness'.[52]

The emphasis on the regularity, overwhelming size and artful construction of this natural phenomenon is also the dominant characteristic of the engravings in Thomas Garnett's *Observations on a Tour through the Highlands and Part of the Western Isles of Scotland*, which first appeared in 1800 with vignettes drawn by the artist who accompanied him, called Watts.[53] The same is true for Louis A. Necker de Saussure's depiction (plate 48),

46 John Cleveley or James Miller or John F. Miller, *Fingal's Cave in Staffa*, engraving (Major) from T. Pennant *A Tour in Scotland, and Voyage to the Hebrides*, vol. 2 (1776), Gough Scotl.277 (plate XXVII), Bodleian Library, Oxford.

47 Durand, *Vue de la Grotte de Fingal*, engraving (Boutrois) from B. Faujas de Saint-Fond *Voyage en Angleterre*, vol. 2 (1797), CC.21.Art.Seld. (plate III), Bodleian Library, Oxford.

which formed the frontispiece of his *A Voyage to the Hebrides*.[54] Necker de Saussure (1786–1861) travelled to the Western Isles in 1806, 1807 and 1808 and subsequently presented the first geological map of Scotland to the Geological Society of London. His book was not published until 1821, by which time he was professor at Geneva and only occasionally returned' to Scotland for further research.

48   (Louis A. Necker de Saussure), *Fingal's Cave*, engraving
(W. Read) from L.A. Necker de Saussure *A Voyage to the
Hebrides* (1822), by permission of the Syndics of Cambridge
University Library.

All these geologists echoed Banks in their sense of
wonder at the creations of nature. But it was Faujas de
Saint-Fond who first offered a causal explanation for
the geological phenomena on the island of Staffa, thus
going beyond the descriptive account of a naturalist
traveller like Banks. Banks had been drawn to the island
by a local report that pillars occurred there similar to
those of the Giant's Causeway in Ireland. Such basaltic
pillars had become the subject of a dispute in the mid-

eighteenth century. The French naturalist Jean Etienne
Guettard (1715–1786) had claimed, after demonstrating
the existence of extinct volcanoes in the Auvergne in
1751, that they were volcanic in origin, while Richard
Pococke (1704–1765) explained their formation as the
result of repeated precipitations from water or mud,
thus giving them an aqueous origin.[55] The volcanic
view was supported by Nicolas Desmarest (1725–1815)
and it was communicated to the Royal Society in 1770
when R.E. Raspe (1737–1794) gave his account of the
volcanic origin of basalt columns near Kassel.[56] This
interest in the phenomena of basalt seems to have determined Banks to visit the island; he arrived there on 12
August 1772. Although he was certainly aware of the
claims of volcanic origin for basaltic columns, Banks
did not commit himself fully to this view when he
described Staffa. He referred only cautiously to 'lava-
like material' and the 'appearance of a lava' in the strata
below the columns on the west side of the island, but
did not attempt to identify secondary causes for it.[57]
Faujas de Saint-Fond, like his countrymen Guettard and
Desmarest, had studied lava formations on the Continent and inferred from these observations that a similar
volcanic process must have produced the basaltic structures on Staffa. The study of volcanoes and their effects
had received new impetus after William Hamilton
(1730–1803) published his brillantly illustrated account
of an eruption of Mount Vesuvius in the *Philosophical
Transactions of the Royal Society of London* in 1775.[58]
Hence volcanic activity was easily accepted by later
geologists as the cause of the basaltic columns on Staffa.
The aqueous explanation, however, was reasserted in
1800 when Robert Jameson published his *Mineralogy of
the Scottish Isles*,[59] offering an explanation that belongs to
a theory known as *neptunism*. Neptunism was developed
by Abraham Werner (1750–1817) at the end of the
eighteenth century at the Bergakademie in Freiberg. It
explained the origin of rocks by arguing that a distinctive series of compositions and densities had precipitated
in temporal sequence from a universal ocean. Jameson
had been a partisan of the neptunist theories of Werner
since his time as a student in Edinburgh. He did not,
however, visit Staffa himself during his journey and
relied solely on Banks' account.

In the text accompanying his *Basaltic Columns* of 1807
William Daniell did, in fact, refer to the conflict
between 'vulcanist' and 'neptunist' theories which are,
as he put it, 'calculated to give scope to conjecture':

The theory of the primitive formation of these singular bodies is involved in much obscurity. Naturalists are divided in their opinions, and each party has an equal claim to superiority; where certainty is not to be obtained, every one feels himself justified to support his conjecture, and hitherto every attempt to fathom the causes which in some period of this globe's existence have contributed to produce such wonderful effects, has failed.[60]

However, none of the explanations current at that time seriously called into question Daniell's reverential attitude towards a creation full of mysteries and curiosities, which 'keep alive sentiments of admiration and reverence for the works of the Deity'.[61] Neither vulcanism nor neptunism presented an account of nature which was inconsistent with Christian natural theology. Volcanic phenomena, such as the earthquake in London of 1750 and the devastating earthquake in Lisbon of 1755, as well as the series of eruptions of Vesuvius in the later eighteenth century, had been treated as miraculous catastrophes outside the ordinary course of nature and were taken as a sign of God's presence.[62] In maintaining that the mineral formations with which the globe is covered were precipitated from a primeval ocean, the Wernerian system could also easily be linked to the Mosaic account of the Deluge.[63] Moreover, it was valued for its power and precision, and for its supposed ready applicability to every country. Indeed, even after the turn of the century, when geologists had come to question such comprehensive, mono-causal explanations of the earth, their investigations were conducted in much the same terms as Werner's.[64]

It was not until John Playfair's publication of the Huttonian theory of the earth in 1802 that the theological controversy which that theory had aroused reached a wider public.[65] Hutton presented his theory of the earth before the Royal Society of Edinburgh on 7 March and 4 April 1785, and published an abstract, describing the theory essentially in its final form, later that year. The first full version appeared in 1788 in the *Transactions of the Royal Society of Edinburgh*,[66] but it was not until 1795 that his *Theory of the Earth with Proofs and Illustrations*[67] appeared. As Stephen J. Gould states, the latter 'might have occupied but a footnote to history if his unreadable treatise had not been epitomized by his friend, and brilliant prose stylist, John Playfair'.[68]

Hutton argued that the facts of the history of the earth were to be found in natural history, not in human records, and he ignored the biblical account of creation as a source of scientific information. According to Hutton, the earth's formation of horizontal layers overlying vertical ones records two great cycles of sedimentation with two episodes of uplift caused by subterranean heat. The lines of disjunctions between two successive formations, a phenomenon which was later to be called 'unconformity',[69] were the direct evidence for Hutton's belief that the history of our earth included several cycles and that it was in a permanent state of degeneration and regeneration. New continents were forever being naturally created out of the debris of former ones, he thought, and the earth might wheel on indefinitely with 'no vestige of a beginning, – no prospect of an end'.[70]

It was not Hutton's postulation of the igneous origin of rocks like granite which brought vehement accusations of impiety on him (this, after all, had been argued before) but his presumption of an indefinite time-scale for the earth's origins, unbounded by any specific act of creation. Whereas the biblical account had made the history of the earth the outcome of one or more acts of divine intervention (for example, the Deluge) Hutton, a Deist, relegated divine action to the sphere of primary causes, beyond the scope of scientific investigation. In this way he prepared the path for the fieldwork geologists after the turn of the century, who, as we shall see, rejected theories of the genesis of the earth which assumed causes going beyond direct evidence. For Hutton, the evidence of God's perfection was that he had designed a world that could maintain itself indefinitely. He writes that it is in vain 'to look for any thing higher in the origin of the earth' than natural causes.[71] Hutton's denial of the role of divine causation in the history of the earth outraged writers like Richard Kirwan (1733–1812) and Jean André de Luc (1727–1817). They set themselves against the idea of an earth in permanent revolution and defended the traditional view, advancing what Roy Porter has called 'directionalist, catastrophist, Biblical theories of the Earth'.[72]

Hutton presents the earth's history as a natural economy of degeneration and regeneration in endless cycles which he interpreted as confirming the overall stability of the natural order. Hutton offers his theory as having been derived by reason from certain key premises and he treats his observations only as confirmation of these claims. His treatment of granite makes this clear. He writes:

> I just saw it, and no more, at Petershead and Aberdeen, but that was all the granite I had ever seen when I wrote my Theory of the Earth. I have, since that time, seen it in different places; because I went on purpose to examine it.[73]

Hutton did, however, travel widely to find the required data for the confirmation of his hypotheses.[74] He made his most important field journeys between 1785 and 1788, finding much of his evidence on the coast from Siccar Point in the east to the Isle of Arran in the west, as well as in the north at Portsoy, the most important exception being Glen Tilt in the Highlands. Hutton's observations were initially recorded in detailed sketches by John Clerk of Eldin (1728–1812); in 1787, on his trip to the Isle of Arran, Hutton was instead accompanied by Clerk's son John, and on the visit to Siccar Point in 1788, by John Playfair (1748–1819) and Sir James Hall (1761–1832), who made two pen drawings of the geological structures.[75] Only a few of the drawings which resulted from these journeys were finally engraved and published in the *Theory of the Earth*. Their relatively recent rediscovery, however, shows them to have been done in a manner highly congenial to Hutton's enterprise.[76] Clerk was a student of Sandby's in Edinburgh in the late 1740s and owned a collection of his teacher's drawings. The depictions he prepared in connection with Hutton's theory concentrate on sections of the relevant strata. They are drawn with a detail and precision similar to that which would have been shown by a topographical draughtsman. In this case, however, the feature on which the artist concentrates is the junctions of the earth's formation. Clerk also adopted Sandby's innovations in map making, indicating dramatic differences in the heights of mountains by adding gradually fading darker dabs of colour to the lighter background.[77] There are also a few panoramas among the drawings. Here, a much more artistic approach prevails, influenced by the taste for the sublime and the picturesque. Washes of muted colour create a generalised surrounding, which frames a central scene. The dramatic contrast of light areas against dark ones produces an interesting composition, whose lighting, however, could not correspond to the observed scene. Just as Hutton's theory provided the framework for the accommodation of particular evidence, so the generalised landscape in these drawings frames and establishes a context for its central subject-matter.

Although it was Hutton who first shook the understanding of earth's history as the result of divine causation, I want to argue that it was not Hutton but the fieldwork approach to geology after the turn of the century which most fundamentally affected the representation (and, ultimately, the perception) of nature. Hutton's method of using fieldwork evidence simply as confirmation for his hypotheses rather than as the means for their generation was much disparaged in the early nineteenth century by the phenomenalist geologists who founded the Geological Society of London in 1807. Kirwan had already accused Hutton's theory of reaching 'a priori conclusions unsupported by facts', but he himself argued for a divine cosmogony no less remote from observation.[78] The members of the Geological Society of London, on the other hand, responded to the struggle between vulcanists, neptunists and theologians by a withdrawal from wider theorising in favour of the accumulation of data, concentrating particularly on the stratigraphic appearance of whatever location was under examination. For them, the idea that natural processes – that is, secondary causes alone – could account for the origin and genesis of a particular locale was no longer a matter of dispute. But they went further: even if the evidence led to causal hypotheses, these must be restricted to the particular location under investigation, without leading to further generalisations. Their attitude has clear parallels to the restriction on the part of contemporary philosophers and aestheticians like Stewart and Alison with regard to the laws of the operations of the mind. At a time when Hutton's theory was being linked to the French Revolution as a threat to the existing social order, the restriction to the relations between natural formations in locally, temporally and causally confined areas represented a step away from religious and political 'counter-revolutionary turmoil'.[79]

The fieldwork geologists' position was clearly expressed in the introduction to the first volume of the Geological Society's *Transactions*: 'In the present imperfect state of this science, it cannot be supposed that the Society should attempt to decide upon the merits of the different theories of the earth that have been proposed'.[80] Instead, the *Transactions* were established to draw up and distribute:

a series of inquiries, calculated in their opinion to excite a greater degree of attention to this important study, than it had yet received in this country; and to serve as a guide to the geological traveller, by pointing out some of the various objects, which it is his province to examine.[81]

The Geological Society grew out of an earlier scheme for a national school of mines.[82] This initiative was typical of the late eighteenth century in bringing together individuals from a variety of backgrounds: wealthy landowners with mining interests, practical surveyors, and professional men whose occupations involved them in the analysis of minerals, like apothecaries, chemists and pharmaceutical manufacturers. As Paul Weindling has argued, there was no unified political agenda behind the project apart from its commitment to economic utility. The participants' political outlooks ranged from the conservative to the radical.[83] Collaboration was particularly important in geology, which required people with quite different skills for the collection and analysis of its data. The first public statement made on behalf of the Geological Society in the *Transactions* of 1811 recognises this and speaks self-confidently of bringing together the scattered efforts of all those engaged in the study of the earth: the miner, the quarrier, the surveyor and the traveller. The adoption of a phenomenalist rhetoric was well suited to this. Phenomenalism privileges observation, independent of theoretical and specialist knowledge, and so makes geology accessible to people from different backgrounds.[84]

Later, however, the same rhetoric was used to exclude those who tried to steer geology towards utilitarian applications. This was largely due to the Geological Society's first president, George Bellas Greenough. He and his followers were concerned to establish geology as an independent science with its own distinct method, descriptive stratigraphy, based on field observation alone. Although the *Annual Report* of 1815 still describes the role of the Geological Society as supervising the efforts of artists, natural historians and chemists, either for the sake of improvements in industry or as a branch of scientific research,[85] those pursuing geology without concern for economic utility increasingly came to dominate. In this case, the phenomenalist rhetoric served the establishment of a hierarchy, privileging those gentleman geologists who had the means and leisure to go on lengthy field-trips. Presenting geology in these terms was also useful in gaining public acceptance for it as an independent science, drawing on the old image of the leisured gentleman whose wealth allowed him to rise above factional interests. A fierce debate still continued within the Society, but, as James A. Secord has pointed out:

> The relatively homogenous social background of those at the center of British geology ensured a very broad consensus on religious and political issues. One scarcely expected to find freethinking secularists and Scriptural literalists frequenting the rooms of a scientific society in Somerset House.[86]

The phenomenalism of the Geological Society was, however, inherently fragile, as we shall see.

It was not only with respect to the perception of nature that geologists were influential for artists. They pioneered a new interest in the coast and islands long before artists discovered them as a subject. This was particularly the case in Scotland. As we have seen, Hutton had travelled from coast to coast. Robert Jameson spent the summer of 1798 exploring the Hebrides and the Western Isles and in 1799 he investigated the Orkneys and Arran. As a result of these journeys, he issued his *Mineralogy of the Scottish Isles* in 1800. Between 8 June and 25 October 1805, George Bellas Greenough (1778–1855), one of the founders of the Geological Society and its first president, set out on a tour through Scotland to examine critically the data on which the Hutton–Werner controversy was based.[87] The itinerary of the tour shows clearly that the major geological discussion focused on the coasts of Scotland. Greenough started off along the east coast and stopped at Dunbar to examine Siccar Point, where Hutton had found evidence for his theory of unconformity. He proceeded to Edinburgh and, after a prolonged stay, made his way to the west coast and islands to visit the locations which were at the centre of the debate between vulcanists and neptunists. At Staffa he made a careful study of the prismatic jointing in the basalt without committing himself to any theory concerning their origin. He confirms the volcanic character only of the lava stone which covers parts of the columns. After going up to the Isle of Skye and down to the southern part of the west coast again Greenough continued his travel northwards into the Highlands, crossing the country via Glenroy and Inverness to Aberdeen. He eventually went down along the east coast and returned to Edinburgh by way of Perth on 9 October. From here he made a last excursion to the Isle of Arran, where both Hutton and Jameson had found evidence for their theories. Later, another member of the Geological Society, John MacCulloch (who had been very influential for William Daniell) focused on the western coast and islands in his attempt to give a more complete and detailed account of their geological formations than had hitherto been undertaken.[88]

Given the extensive interest in the Scottish coast and Western Isles shown by naturalist travellers and geologists in the second half of the eighteenth century, it is somewhat surprising to discover that before the 1820s William Daniell was alone in providing illustrations of one of the islands or of the western coast. Indeed, Daniell made the point himself when he wrote in *A Voyage round Great Britain* that:

> The country on which we are about to enter is one of the most picturesque in the whole circuit of the island. It has been repeatedly explored and described; but the curiosity of the public respecting it is still unsatisfied, especially in whatever regards the illustration derived from the pencil. None of the tours on the west of Scotland now extant contain engravings at all worthy of their respective subjects; and it is a matter somewhat surprising, that a tract so inviting to the painter should not have called forth a single series of views.[89]

The only contemporary views of the Western Isles to be found are in geological publications, and it is very likely that Daniell's criticism is directed at them. By the 1820s, however, the coast and island had become an important destination for artists on their tour in Scotland. The reasons for this broadening of subject-matter are complex and best discussed in relation to specific examples.

The Western Isles

The single exception to the restriction of artists' subjects to the mainland before 1820 is the Isle of Staffa.[90] After Pennant's publication of Banks' account, Staffa became well known and was the only location in the Western Isles to be included in picturesque travel literature. A typical example of a picturesque appreciation of Staffa is the depiction of *Fingal's Cave* (plate 49) by John Claude Nattes (1765?–1822), published in James Fittler's *Scotia Depicta* in 1804, after the oil painting of 1802 had been shown at the Royal Academy.[91] Again, as in Banks' depiction, the entrance to the cave is shown with little figures and a boat appears in the foreground to establish the awesome size of the location. But, in contrast to the earlier prints, which emphasised regularity in order to display by analogy the purposeful character of nature's creations, this illustration attempts to capture an air of irregularity and grandeur more in tune with the increasing popularity of the sublime and the picturesque. The feeling of sublimity is evoked by a close-up view of the entrance, which opens like a black hole. A dramatic chiaroscuro is distributed over the depiction, which does not come from a real light source but appears as a mystical illumination. The picture bears witness to the shift towards an appreciation of architecture in its ruined state, emphasising the broken outlines in order to achieve a more textured appearance. However, this does not challenge the interpretation of Staffa as a mysterious wonder; rather it heightens it.[92] Nor, indeed, did the development of a causal explanation for Staffa's distinctive geological features call into question this kind of appreciation; such action could still be regarded as a miracle of nature.

When Robert Jameson undertook his journey to the Western Isles in 1800, he published two illustrations of the Isle of Eigg and the Isle of Skye. The depictions, executed by Jameson's friend Charles Bell, are interesting for they show clearly that his neptunist way of thinking did not lead him to challenge traditional perception. The engraving *View from Beinn, Na, Caillich in Skye* (plate 50) repeats picturesque conventions: a darker foreground is covered with rugged stones on which two groups of people rest and contemplate the view – a central ridge of mountains, with dramatic and abrupt features, flanked by the sea. The exaggerated depiction of the mountains shows them as sublime objects, an effect reinforced by the emergence of heavy clouds behind. Indeed, Jameson's verbal account explicitly adopts eighteenth-century conventions for describing a sublime experience, ultimately linking it to the incomprehensibility of divine power:

> Here, our most sanguine expectations were more than realised, every faculty for a while seemed arrested, until we could burst into an exclamation on

49   John C. Nattes, *Fingal's Cave*, 1802, engraving (J. Fittler) from J. Fittler *Scotia Depicta* (1804), Gough Maps 171 (plate 26), Bodleian Library, Oxford.

the vastness of the scene, and on the mighty and eternal power of him who framed so great a work.[93]

The second illustration is similar in conception, although here Jameson's geological interests are move apparent. The *Columnar Promontory of the Scure-Eigg* (plate 51) is composed of several layers of basaltic columns and, since Jameson supported the Wernerian theory attributing an aqueous origin to them, their depiction appears to emphasise the successive horizontal layers. As in picturesque depictions, the central object forms the main focus, yet according to Jameson's own description of the site, it is of sublime appearance.[94] The view of it is from below so that the Scuir of Eigg covers

nearly the whole page. On its top are placed three figures, so tiny that they are nearly invisible. They not only establish, according to convention, the scale of the formation, but also clearly enhance the imposing character of this natural phenomenon. The neptunists were mainly concerned with the precise taxonomical distinction and designation of rocks, less so with the explanation of their origin. Such an approach was therefore consistent with the eighteenth-century conception of general natural history of naturalist travellers like Pennant. Jameson, too, made his main aim the accurate identification of the rocks of the Western Isles and he does not seem to have had any difficulty in depicting his observations within the traditional pictorial formulae.

50 Charles Bell, *View from Beinn,Na,Caillich in Skye*, engraving (R. Scott) from R. Jameson *A Mineralogy of the Scottish Isles*, vol. 2 (1800), Vet.A5.d.223 (opp. p. 94), Bodleian Library, Oxford.

It is far more surprising to find that the pictures in John MacCulloch's publication on the Western Isles of 1819 are similar in character.[95] MacCulloch, as we have seen, criticised previous descriptions of the Western Isles as unsatisfactory. Belonging to the new generation of fieldwork geologists, he did not focus his research merely on the classification of objects, but on the variety of phenomena and their observed relations. MacCulloch's bias towards the identification of different minerals, rather than on the stratigraphy of the sites under study, was a bias he shared with eighteenth-

51 Charles Bell, *Columnar Promontory of the Scure-Eigg*, engraving (R. Scott) from R. Jameson *A Mineralogy of the Scottish Isles*, vol. 2 (1800), Vet.A5.d.223 (opp. p. 46), Bodleian Library, Oxford.

century mineralogists, who owed much to Werner's taxonomy. But, under the influence of the Geological Society's phenomenalist rhetoric, MacCulloch is keen to distinguish himself from the mineralogists' utilitarian attitude:

> It is moreover impossible, in the present state of the science, to foresee the utility of minute research, or the serious deficiencies which may hereafter be found to arise from the neglect of circumstances apparently trifling.[96]

Among the illustrations which MacCulloch prepared for the publication was another view of the Scuir of Eigg (plate 52). The mountain is here perceived from a different angle from that in Jameson's picture, although it is no less imposing. A traditional dark foreground forms the plateau from which the mountain and its summit of columns is viewed. Halfway up the mountain are two tiny figures and a further single figure is visible towards the foreground on the right-hand side. The depiction of the stones does not permit the viewer to draw any conclusions with regard to their varying geological character. It is the rugged character of the rocks, in contrast to the finer appearance of the vegetation, which gives the print its texture and hence the picturesque character of the whole. The stormy dark clouds behind the mountain induce a sublime impression. The focus of light on the middle ground reinforces the concentration on the main subject, the Scuir, plainly contradicting MacCulloch's expressed intention not to neglect any 'trifling circumstance' in his examination. In fact, MacCulloch's verbal account of the Isle of Eigg also falls short of this aim. Before a short description of its different mineral components, which does not add to Jameson's publication, he gives an introduction which asserts the sublime character of the Scuir, repeating the conventional eighteenth-century terminology derived from Burke's *Enquiry*:

> That resemblance to architecture is much increased by the columnar structure, which is sufficiently distinguishable even from a distance, and produces a strong effect of artificial regularity when seen near at hand. To this vague association in the mind of the efforts of art with the magnitude of nature, is owing much of that sublimity of character which the Scuir presents, even when divested of the accessary [sic] circumstances produced by the accidents of light and

52 John MacCulloch, *View of the Scuir of Egg*, 1819, engraving (H.F. Rose) from J. MacCulloch *A Description of the Western Isles*, vol. 3 (1819), G.A.Scotl.4.203, Bodleian Library, Oxford.

shade and by atmospheric effects. The sense of power is a fertile source of the sublime, and as the appearance of power exerted, no less than that of simplicity, is necessary to confer this character on architecture, so the mind, insensibly transferring the operations of nature to the efforts of art where they approximate in character, becomes impressed with a feeling rarely excited by her more ordinary forms, where these are even more stupendous.[97]

Only a single word in the text indicates that this evocation of the sublime is not an eighteenth-century one. When Banks had linked Staffa to architecture, this was not understood as simply the effect of an 'insensible' move of the mind, but the connection itself was presented as part of the objective realm, and thus gave objective grounds for the observer's admiration. MacCulloch's text, on the other hand, displays the influence of Alison's phenomenalist aesthetic, inasmuch as explanations of the sublime shift away from its source in nature towards the independent·operations of the mind itself. No longer restricted to recording given natural stimuli, MacCulloch allows his associations free play:

> Occasionally they [clouds] sweep along the base, leaving its huge and black mass involved in additional gloom and resembling the castle of some Arabian enchanter built on the clouds and suspended in the air.[98]

However, these associations cannot yet be felt in the engravings, whose character is still reminiscent of the late eighteenth-century formula of the sublime. While this early account reveals a tension between MacCulloch's professional aspirations towards phenomenalist descriptive stratigraphy and his narrative recourse to subjective associations, MacCulloch later published a second book on the Western Isles in which the latter, more subjective mode has taken over.[99] Here, his descriptions of the natural scenery no longer aim for geological accuracy, but are represented by introducing personal and literary associations, a procedure which is given theoretical legitimation through an explicit reference to Alison:

> I have compared the effects of natural scenery with those of purely moral impressions and feelings, on other occasions. How the former acts by means of the latter, has been well illustrated by many, but by none better than Alison.[100]

However, the discrepancies between geological purpose, pictorial representation and verbal account seem not to have been noticed by Necker de Saussure, whose *Voyage to the Hebrides* (1822) includes a view of *The Scuir of Egg from the East* (plate 53) which seems to be a straightforward copy of MacCulloch's (plate 52). Even the tiny figures from MacCulloch's print are included in this engraving; only the foreground rocks are bolder.

MacCulloch also included two depictions of Staffa in the third volume of his *A Description of the Western Isles* which did not appear in his previously published paper

53 (Louis A. Necker de Saussure), *The Scuir of Egg from the East*, engraving (W. Read) from L.A. Necker de Saussure *A Voyage to the Hebrides* (1822), 203.e.89 (2) (between pp. 50–1), Bodleian Library, Oxford.

54 John MacCulloch, *Entrance of Fingal's Cave, Staffa*, 1819, engraving (C. Heath) from J. MacCulloch *A Description of the Western Isles*, vol.3 (1819), G.A.Scotl.4.203, Bodleian Library, Oxford.

in the *Transactions of the Geological Society*. In these two pictures his delineation of the rock and strata is more careful than was characteristic of the tradition of Staffa depictions discussed so far. His *Entrance of Fingal's Cave, Staffa* (plate 54) shows the short basalt columns in the foreground leading up to the entrance not only as consisting of hexagonal stumps, but as having quite an irregular order and shape. The columns of the Isle itself also appear rather fragile, less solid, with breaks and irregularities. They support a massive stratum on top. The whole picture seems to be more like a drawing than an engraving, since stark contrasts are suppressed and light and shade are used only tentatively to produce the effect of volume. The junction between the huge top and the columns is indeed somewhat unresolved. MacCulloch himself states that he regrets not having illustrated the subject 'by engravings as finished and as numerous as it merits'.[101] Yet, compared with Daniell's depiction (plate 42), published a year earlier, this print still exhibits some picturesque exaggeration, for example, the darkening sky and the imposing mass of the uppermost bed. The Geological Society of London holds some of the original drawings MacCulloch prepared for his publications in the *Transactions*.[102] These too are characterised by a feature also present in his Staffa illustrations in *A Description of the Western Isles of Scotland*: it is the position of strata which interests him, not the materiality of the phenomena under observa-

tion. The strata are presented in clear strokes while the surrounding area is given picturesque interest through the varigated alternation of light and shade.

The text in *A Description of the Western Isles of Scotland* shows that MacCulloch was here attempting more consciously to give a new kind of depiction than he had done for the Isle of Eigg. He explicitly criticises 'that air of architectural regularity which [. . .] he has] censured in the published representations'.[103] In his paper in the *Transactions* he had already expressed his intention to enter

> minutely into the general description of the island, particularly since a second examination, besides confirming the remarkable fact I at first noticed, has enabled me to investigate its structure more completely. [. . .] A multiplicity of objects pressing at once for regard.[104]

MacCulloch does not just concentrate on the structure of the columns but also examines the strata on top, where he had found some alluvial fragments of older rocks. This perhaps explains the emphasis on this layer in the accompanying illustration in the book, which, however, does not show what he emphasises verbally:

> The last and uppermost bed consists [. . .] of a confused mass of small columns, much bent, often very obscure, and mixed with a large proportion of rock which can scarcely be said to have even a columnar tendency, but of which the exterior surface is broken into innumerable minute parts.[105]

55 John MacCulloch, *View of Staffa from the South West*, 1819, engraving (Byrne) from J. MacCulloch *A Description of the Western Isles*, vol.3 (1819), G.A.Scotl.4.203, Bodleian Library, Oxford.

56   William Daniell, *The Island of Staffa from the South West*, 1817, aquatint (W. Daniell) printed in colour, hand-finished, from W. Daniell *A Voyage round Great Britain*, vol.3 (1818), G.A.Gen.Top.b.33 (opp. p.47), Bodleian Library, Oxford.

Another view shows the island from the south-west (plate 55). Banks' account also contained two side views of Staffa, which, as with the engraving of Fingal's Cave, carry strong allusions to architecture, so that the strata over- and underlying the columns appear like floor and roof, with the caves as door-openings. MacCulloch's print in contrast exhibits more strongly than ever his interest in the relative position and formation of the different strata of Staffa. But, again, Daniell's aquatint from the same viewpoint (plate 56) seems more adequate, since MacCulloch's picture fails to convey a sense of the different textures. This is partly due to the fact that Daniell shows the scene in a realistic distribution of light and shadow, while MacCulloch presents it in a picturesque overall distribution of chiaroscuro.

Again, although less strongly so, MacCulloch's graphical design alludes to a tradition from which, at least verbally, he wants to distance himself. To depict an object within a framework of chiaroscuro, outside the real light situation, is to depict it as if in some pre-established order, be that order perceived as a divine one or as a Huttonian overall order of cyclic motions. But in the account in the *Transactions*, MacCulloch states that the appearances, which he had set out to grasp in their full complexity: 'are perhaps insufficient to enable us to decide between two difficulties of equal magnitude, nor is it here necessary to enter further on that question'.[106] He is here referring to the two current modes of explanation for Staffa, the igneous and aqueous theories, but refuses to decide between them, since

57　J.M.W. Turner, *Staffa, Fingal's Cave*, 1832, oil on canvas, 909 × 1214, Yale Center for British Art, Paul Mellon Collection, New Haven.

that would, he says, presuppose 'accumulating information on which a consolidated fabric may at some future time be erected'.[107]

Yet this attempt to unite the phenomenalist conception of the primacy of observation with the scientific ideal of objectivity is inherently unstable. A scientific approach which relies so heavily on observation by the individual who undertakes it opens the path to relativism. That its inner tensions could lead to a more subjectivist mode of perception is already evident from MacCulloch's own account. Having stated that previous descriptions of Staffa were misleading, he argues:

Let those who have a taste for the grand and the beautiful, and who, from the cause above mentioned, may have quitted Staffa with a sensation of disappointment, return to this cave again, and again view it, regardless of the descriptions of others and their own ill-founded anticipations. They will then become sensible of its beauties, and feel ready to describe it in terms which may excite equal disappointment in those who shall follow, and who may, like themselves, vainly expect that the feelings of one individual are the measure for those of another, or that any thing can exist which the imagination is not ready to exceed.[108]

MacCulloch's description falls into two parts, one in which he expresses the observations, and the other in which he allows himself to introduce subjective associations, as, for example, in his description of the Isle of Eigg.[109]

Even William Daniell's objective of simply noting what he perceived, without reference to pre-established patterns, presupposes the artist as a selfconscious subject, although the position of the perceiver is not, in this case, itself perceptible from the depictions. In 1831, when Turner went to Staffa, the implicit position of the perceiving subject had become a strong constituent of the depiction. A year after this visit he exhibited a painting at the Royal Academy with the title *Staffa, Fingal's Cave* (plate 57), in which the cave itself is hardly visible.[110] Some of the vertical structures of the island can be traced on the left-hand side of the picture, piercing through the mist and haze behind a turbulent sea. The steam of a dark steamboat on the middle ground towards the right mingles with the atmosphere. The moist impression is enhanced by the diffused light from the sun which is setting into the sea amidst clouds on the right-hand side. The colours of the columns – red, yellow, blue – are repeated in and thereby related to the halo around the sun.

This painting was sold in 1845 through C.R. Leslie to James Lenox of New York. After having received the picture, the new owner complained about its indistinctness and Leslie urged Turner to write to him about it. It is interesting to note that Turner replied with a description of his own experience on which the picture had been based. He stated that a strong sea was running and it was 'not very pleasant or safe to go into the cave when the wave rolls right in'. On the voyage back 'the sun getting towards the horizon burst through the rain-cloud, angry, and for wind'.[111]

However, a vignette executed in 1834 for Sir Walter Scott's poem *The Lord of the Isles* (plate 58) shows that Turner had an interest not only in the atmospheric effects which he encountered but also in the geological formations of the island.[112] The picture shows Fingal's Cave not from the usual standpoint (outside), but from inside looking outwards.[113] The columns are quite carefully depicted with breaks, or, in technical terminology, joints, in their structure. But here too the water and weather which enter the cave are strongly emphasised in their forceful movements. Thus Turner achieves a tension between the dynamism of the elements – the

58 J.M.W. Turner, *Fingal's Cave*, 1834, engraving (E. Goodall) from W. Scott *The Complete Poetical Works*, vol.10 (1834), by permission of the Syndics of Cambridge University Library.

water and the atmosphere – and the solidity of the stones.

The fact that, as John Gage has pointed out, the sun in the oil painting is haloed in a way which presages rain is significant.[114] This indicator of change, linked by colour to the columnar structure on the left-hand side of the painting, does not appear in the sketches which Turner made on the voyage.[115] Atmospheric changes of this kind, although not part of the perception of the moment, are nevertheless possible objects of experience. Their inclusion signifies a conception of nature as in a process of change, in which immediately given appearances point beyond themselves to the future – or, as in the case of the rocks, to the past. In Turner's painting, just as in the writings of MacCulloch, there is no viewpoint beyond the realm of the observable from which such changes could be understood. Turner's depiction of Staffa, however, unlike Daniell's, is strongly infused with his own attitude as an observing subject who perceives in the ongoing atmospheric spectacle the quintessence of a permanently forming and developing nature.[116] This dynamic understanding of nature makes the moment of encounter with the perceiver significant. It seems to have become established as the conventional mode of representing Staffa by the time that Anthony Vandyke Copley Fielding (1787–1855) prepared a series of drawings of it between 1845 and 1853.

There is a clear contrast between the strict phenomenalist position, with its prohibition on general theory and restriction to what is observed at a particular instant, and the conception of nature as dynamically evolving, implicit in Turner's depiction of Staffa. But that strict phenomenalist position is itself, it must be said, an abstraction or ideal type. As we have already seen with MacCulloch, phenomenalism is inherently unstable; without *some* kind of generalisation no science would be possible at all.

Even within the Geological Society of London, such a strict position was methodologically adhered to only in the first years of its foundation, most notably by George Greenough.[117] By the late 1810s and 1820s the Cuvierian approach to stratigraphy was being adopted by members of the Society. It was an attempt to go beyond the local descriptive stratigraphy which Greenough had been advocating, by correlating successions in different parts of the world, particularly by comparisons of fossil content. In this way palaeontological stratigraphy was committed to the establishment of a generalised geological schema of the earth which a strict phenomenalist position would not permit. However, it could still be presented as a strategy which is solely based on observation. Thomas Webster (1773–1844), Keeper of the Museum and later Secretary of the Geological Society of London, was the first to employ the method that Georges Cuvier (1769–1832) had used in his work on the Paris Basin, in order to determine the succession of the Isle of Wight. He immediately qualifies his conjectures by a warning straight from the phenomenalist rhetoric of the Geological Society. In the present state of the science of geology, he writes,

it is more important to examine the actual position of the several fragments of strata now forming the surface of the earth, and by connecting them together, to endeavour to ascertain the curved and broken forms into which they have been reduced by some unknown agent, than, finally, to dogmatize, in this scanty state of our knowledge, on the precise nature of this power, which can be rationally sought for only by a careful examination of the effects produced.[118]

By the 1820s, however, a number of geologists started, once again, to address questions of revolutions in the history of the earth. Most prominent among them were William Buckland (1784–1856) and W.D. Conybeare (1787–1857). Both advocated a diluvian theory of the earth's history, which assumed successive natural deluges, supposed to have caused the extinction of animal populations, and to have transported masses of debris across the earth's surface. Yet even this commitment to general theories was still couched in phenomenalist rhetoric. 'It is not the business of the present work to propose theories, but to record facts', writes Conybeare in his introduction to his and William Phillips' *Outlines of the Geology of England and Wales*, having presented a critical account of several such explanations.[119] It is clear that by that time phenomenalism amounted to very little more than paying lip-service to the principle that scientists should stick to the evidence before them – a methodological principle that hardly goes beyond the level of platitude.

When Turner reached the Isle of Staffa, Charles Lyell (1797–1875) was publishing his famous *Principles of Geology*.[120] Lyell's new theory of the earth did justice to its progressive character, while at the same time integrating Hutton's notion of an unchanging earth-history. In this way, Lyell's work was part of a larger move in the 1830s among scientists towards a renewed acceptance of conjectural and imaginative elements in scientific thinking.[121]

By this stage, MacCulloch too had abandoned his abstinence with regard to conjectures beyond the immediate data. But, instead of embracing one or other of the newly established secondary-cause models such as Lyell's or Cuvier's stratigraphic palaeontology, he harks back to former global cosmogonies, both those of divine final causation and the Huttonian model. In his last geological work, *A System of Geology, with a Theory of the Earth* (1831),[122] as well as in his *Proofs and Illustra-*

tions of the Attributes of God (1837) – like the *Bridgewater Treatises*, written as an attempt to infer God's handiwork from the perfection of geological appearances[123] – MacCulloch argues that, while neither a theory of the earth nor God's providence (which accounts for what even a theory of secondary causes cannot explain) can ultimately be proved, the attempt to develop such theoretical accounts is nevertheless worthwhile. Thus he now fully endorses what he had earlier rejected: speculations without immediate evidence.[124]

Although no depictions of Staffa between Daniell's publication of 1818 and Turner's paintings of 1832 seem to have survived, at least five artists exhibited this subject in the forty years after 1816 while there had been only one (Nattes' *Fingal's Cave*) in the first forty years following Banks' enthusiastic account.[125] Any attempt at explanation for this can only be tentative. One reason seems to be the emergence of an interest in the dynamic forces of nature, which Lyell's progressive account of earth-history emphasised. These exhibit themselves better in a place which is surrounded by the moving masses of the sea and which is constantly subject to changing atmospheric conditions than on the mainland. But this is certainly not a sufficient explanation, since Staffa was already on the itinerary of the naturalist traveller, as an example of an extraordinary feature of nature. Another more pragmatic explanation is the difficulty of reaching the island. From Banks' first account onwards, the dangers of landing on the island with a sailing boat were regularly described and Daniell too gives a dramatic account of his experience, which was not helped by the boatman available:

> In approaching this island for the purpose of exploring it, advantage must of course be taken of the state of the wind. If it be westerly, there must evidently be some inconvenience in navigating that part of the coast which is exposed to it, on account of the heavy swell, and the precipitous mass against which it beats: the same apprehension is to be entertained with regard to the east coast, if the wind blow from that quarter; in either case the aim must be to land on the leeward side of the isle. It is to be observed also, that the boats which usually offer themselves for this purpose are of a clumsy construction, and ill adapted to the navigation of these seas; the boatmen, also, are a slow-minded heedless race, by no means alert in the prevention of accidents, confident in their ability in

the last extreme of things to shift for themselves, and disposed to give a stranger the credit of being equally sea-worthy. Unmindful of the sudden gusts and squalls which occur in the most promising weather, they will belay their sheet whenever they can invent a pretext for doing so, unless prevented by a peremptory remonstrance on the part of their passenger. When such remonstrance is of no avail, it is incumbent on the latter to have his Knife ready for the purpose of cutting the rope instantly, in case of emergency.[126]

But such difficulties were removed with the introduction of steamboats in 1822,[127] which made the island accessible to a larger number of people. Turner was able to blend the steam of the boat with the mist of the atmosphere when he went, and, though he states that the entrance into the cave by foot was not safe, his journey was far more secure than it would ever have been before.

The introduction of a steamboat must also be a factor behind the appearance of depictions of the Isle of Skye from the late 1820s onwards, but the main cause certainly lies elsewhere. In 1814 Walter Scott (1771–1832) embarked on a journey along the west coast and islands and in January 1815 he published the poem *The Lord of the Isles* which contains a long description of the southern mountains of the Isle of Skye. He later wrote that 'the Poem cannot be said to have made a favourable impression on the public'.[128] But, by the end of the 1820s and the beginning of the 1830s, the impact of Scott's work had broadened to include the depiction of landscapes which had featured both in his poems and in the novels.[129]

Turner went to Staffa and the Isle of Skye in 1831 to prepare drawings for the illustrated edition of Scott's *Complete Poetical Works* which appeared in 1834; engravings of Turner's *Fingal's Cave* (plate 58) and *Loch Coruiskin* on Skye were published as the frontispieces to the tenth volume.[130] But the first depictions of scenes on the Isle of Skye are once again to be found in literature with a specifically geological interest. The earliest is again in Thomas Pennant's *Tour in Scotland, and Voyage to the Hebrides* and was drawn by Moses Griffiths. It shows a *View from Beinn, Na, Caillich in Skie* towards the south.[131] The panorama of the hills and Cuillin mountains in the background exhibit a strikingly serrated formation. It seems that this bizarre appearance attracted

Pennant as he was attracted to other 'natural curiosities'. The picturesque *View from Beinn,Na,Caillich* in Robert Jameson's *Mineralogy*, discussed earlier (plate 50), is in fact modelled on this print. Jameson did not reach the Cuillin hills themselves on the southern end of the island, and it was MacCulloch who first published a detailed description of them and the Lochs Coruisk and Scavaig in the *Transactions of the Geological Society* in 1816 and 1817.[132] This paper was read in January 1815 and MacCulloch states that it was based on observations made during five weeks spent on the island, which must therefore have been in 1814. In his 1819 publication MacCulloch claimed to have been the first non-native to have visited the area, which previously had 'never been seen by a stranger, and was indeed known to few even of the inhabitants of Sky [sic]'.[133]

But, although Scott had been a friend of MacCulloch since the 1790s, the two seem not to have met when Scott arrived on Skye on 23 August 1814. According to Scott's travel diary of 1814, it was the owner of Dunvegan Castle, the chieftain Maccleod, who told Scott and his friends about the 'fine romantic' Loch Coruisk.[134] Since MacCulloch became a friend of Maccleod while he was staying on the island, it is possible that Maccleod's suggestion was derived from MacCulloch. However, Loch Coruisk, which is difficult to reach from the land, only became really well known and popular after Scott's publication of *The Lord of the Isles*.

MacCulloch's description in the *Transactions* is concerned only with an accurate account, bare of 'premature' conclusions.[135] He attempts to give 'a general sketch of the several rocks which form the island, noting their geographical positions as accurately as circumstances permit; after which I shall attempt to trace their geological arrangement'.[136] His description of the range of the Cuillin hills refrains from dramatic associations, but he was much impressed by the 'spiry and rugged forms of its outline, which presents a series of naked rocks and towering cliffs destitute of vegetation, and rising dark through the mists which seem for ever to hang on its stormy summit'.[137]

Although MacCulloch published two pictures of the Isle of Skye in 1819 in the third volume of his *A Description of the Western Isles*, neither shows this area. Both are again highly picturesque, one a *View of the Storr in Sky* (plate 59), which shows this rock in exaggerated bizarre forms, the other of *Dunvegan Castle*. Once again,

59 John MacCulloch, *View at the Storr in Sky*, 1819, engraving (I. Stewart) from J. MacCulloch *A Description of the Western Isles*, vol.3 (1819), G.A.Scotl.4.203, Bodleian Library, Oxford.

it is Daniell's series of views of this spot, which he published in 1820, which best matches MacCulloch's geological description.[138] That Daniell knew MacCulloch's account of the Isle of Skye is made clear in the text:[139] his view of *The Coolin Taken from Loch Slapin* (plate 60) shows the dark and rugged mountain in the background, as described by MacCulloch. In the foreground the lake is surrounded by strata which are not bare like the mountains but tinted in light green and brown to indicate vegetation, and the yellowish tints of sunlight give the scene its calm and undramatic impression. This rather static impression is also predominant in *Loch Coruisg near Loch Scavig* (plate 61), although here the dark mountains reach straight down to the lake. Spots of sunlight illuminate parts of the foreground of the loch and parts of the mountains, thus emphasising their solid character. The mist which seems to hang permanently on the summits (according to MacCulloch) reaches from behind the mountains and is appropriately depicted in Daniell's picture.

It has been alleged that Daniell, in his aquatint *Loch Coruisg near Loch Scavig* of 1819, failed, 'despite the height, darkness, and sawtoothed edges of his hills, in conveying the effect of complete seclusion and self contained unity which visitors usually felt, or in expressing the curvilinear character of the mountain ridge'.[140] This judgement is interesting, because it reflects the endurance – even in the late twentieth century

60 William Daniell, *The Coolin Taken from Loch Slapin*, 1819, aquatint (W. Daniell) printed in colour, hand-finished, from W. Daniell *A Voyage round Great Britain*, vol. 4 (1820), G.A.Gen.Top.b.33 (opp. p. 37), Bodleian Library, Oxford.

61 William Daniell, *Loch Coruisg near Loch Scavig*, 1819, aquatint (W. Daniell) printed in colour, hand-finished, from W. Daniell *A Voyage round Great Britain*, vol. 4 (1820), G.A.Gen.Top.b.33 (opp. p. 40), Bodleian Library, Oxford.

– of a perception of the Cuillin hills which came to be established under the influence of Scott's *Lord of the Isles*. But with regard to Daniell, it is, of course, quite anachronistic. While it is true that Daniell quotes the poem, it did not yet influence his perception of the scene. In Scott's poem the area around Loch Coruisk is the place from where the rightful Lord of the Isles sets out to regain his former territory:

> No marvel thus the Monarch spake;
> For rarely human eye has known
> A scene so stern as that dread lake,
> With its dark ledge of barren stone.
> Seems that primeval earthquake's sway
> Hath rent a strange and shatter'd way
> Through the rude bosom of the hill,
> And that each naked precipice,
> Sable ravine, and dark abyss,
> Tells of the outrage still.[141]

Scott here acknowledges what by this time, as we have seen, had become a commonplace among geologists, that the earth's formation was due to violent processes of nature, the date being left undiscussed. Scott's heroes, the Bruce (the Lord) and Ronald (his ally) traverse this solemn area on their way to pursue their lonely and dangerous task and the landscape thus becomes the projecting screen for the protagonists' own fate:

> Answer'd the Bruce, 'And musing mind
> Might here a graver moral find.
> These mighty cliffs, that heave on high
> Their naked brows to middle sky,
> Indifferent to the sun or snow,
> Where nought can fade, and nought can blow,
> May they not mark a Monarch's fate.[142]

Scott uses landscape in the same way as he uses history: as a projected reality, abstracted from the given scene. What is important is not an accurate account of the landscape's geological features, but its suitability for the reflection of the situation and emotions of his subjects.

62   George Fennel Robson, *Loch Coruisk and the Cuchullin Mountains, Isle of Skye*, c.1828, watercolour and bodycolour, 642 × 1118, by courtesy of the Board of Trustees of the Victoria and Albert Museum, London.

George Fennel Robson (1788–1833), an English watercolourist who published *Scenery of the Grampian Mountains* in 1814, produced at least four watercolours of the Cuillin hills around 1828 (plate 62).[143] Three of them are very similar: the foreground is formed by a detailed depiction of massive stones which almost microscopically exhibit their breaks and texture. The dark, mirroring surface of the lake in the middle ground reflects the darkness of the huge mountains in the background. The impenetrable solidity and ruggedness of the mountains encloses the spot completely, and these are further emphasised by the appearance of a sunset sky just behind their summits. This small shaft of light is on the verge of being covered once more by the dark clouds which have piled up on top of the mountains. The difference between the pictures consists only in the arrangement of the stony foreground and the slight variations in characterisation of the mountains. Thus what appears to be a careful observation of the rock formations is actually a studio product, and intended merely for effect. In the drawing in the Victoria and Albert Museum, here illustrated, two men dressed in traditional Highland costumes are placed on the edge of one of the massive stones which surround the lake in the foreground (a further figure stands just below them). One of the men points to the mountains. A sickle moon at the top right hand of the drawing adds to the impression of a theatrical scene with the well-lit foreground as the stage and the rather flat contours of the background as its backdrop. In this way the Cuillin hills have become the setting for the dramas of individuals, whether Scott's protagonists themselves or visitors informed by the associations generated by his work.

A similar seclusion is the predominant feature in the oil painting *Loch Coruisk, Isle of Skye* (plate 63) by John Knox (1778–1845).[144] No figure appears in this painting, which again shows the foreground as a stony platform on which an observer might stand, the lake as a dark mirror surface, and the mountain as an enclosing and impenetrable background. What distinguishes this depiction, however, is the exactitude with which Knox renders the weather-beaten surface. At some points the sun highlights spots which exhibit sparkling cracks and downward pointing grooves, as if water running downwards had worked for centuries on the mountains. Here again one notices the endeavour to convey a geologically convincing appearance, but this is betrayed by the fact that the mountains appear uniformly sparkling and

63   John Knox, *Loch Coruisk, Isle of Skye*, oil on canvas, 505 × 710, photo Sotheby's.

textured and by the fact that the picture is tinted in an orange hue, which gives it a somewhat sensational and supernatural appearance. Daniell had not been interested in conveying the effect of texture and yet his *Loch Coruisg near Loch Scarig* (plate 61) showed the mountains in a variety of forms. Such differentiation is abandoned in Knox's painting in favour of the illusion of materiality. As in Scott's description, the place has become a desert region, in contrast to Daniell's image in which seagulls and a boat showed the lake to be visited and gave scale to the mountain. Thus emptied out, Knox's depiction, like Robson's, invites the projection of subjective associations onto the landscape. It seems that only when landscape features had become the projection screen for subjectivity, rather than being admired for their significance in revealing the processes of nature's creation, was it possible to dare to paint such emptiness.

None of these paintings has as its objective the accurate delineation of the geological formation of the Cuillin hills and Loch Coruisk; the specific characteristics of the location have merged into a backdrop for subjective sensations. However, Turner's watercolour *Loch Coruisk, Skye* (plate 64) was esteemed for its geological accuracy after John Ruskin (1819–1900) claimed that he would prefer it to a geological drawing as a means of explaining structure.[145] Though the title is *Loch Coruisk*, the main subject of the depiction is the extensive course of the ridge of the Cuillin hills. The artist has climbed to the top and shows their summits in

64   J.M.W. Turner, *Loch Coruisk, Skye*, watercolour, 89 × 143, National Gallery of Scotland, Edinburgh.

yellow-reddish hues reaching into the background. The lake, in a blue tint, lies deep down on the right-hand side of the picture. Although the dramatic build-up of the mountains is the main feature, it is not, as Ruskin calls it, a 'marking' of 'its strata stone by stone'.[146] Turner immerses the mountains in a curling mist which prolongs their toppling structure to the right and makes them seem to sweep over. The rosy light and the purple haze which dissolve the solidity of the mountains is in closer adherence to Scott's verses than to MacCulloch's description of the black, bare and solid appearance of what he had called the 'hypersthene rock'.[147]

Turner had probably known MacCulloch from 1814 onwards and he owned the first two volumes of the *Transactions of the Geological Society*.[148] These volumes included MacCulloch's account of Staffa but not his work on the Isle of Skye, which appeared in the third and fourth volumes. Turner is, however, very likely to have come into possession of MacCulloch's last book on the Western Isles, *The Highlands and Western Isles*,

conceived as a series of letters to Scott, through the poet himself. But by this time, as we have seen, MacCulloch's purely geological interests have given way to the second and rather unintegrated aspect of his writing: the description of the pleasures of the subjective associations to which the geological observations give rise. MacCulloch's account of the spot around Loch Coruisk reads as follows:

> So suddenly and unexpectedly does this strange scene break on the view, so unlike is it to the sea bay without, so dissimilar to all other scenery, and so little to be foreseen in a narrow insulated spot like Sky, that I felt as if transported by some magician into the enchanted wilds of an Arabian tale, carried to the habitation of the Genii among the mysterious recesses of Caucasus.[149]

MacCulloch's earlier geological descriptions, which emphasise the dark and solid character of the Cuillin hills, seem, however, not to have made an impact on

Turner's perception of them. MacCulloch had stressed the unstratified character which gives the mountains 'a permanence by which it appears to brave the external war of the elements which surround it'.[150] In Turner's watercolour the mountains are characterised by cumulating gradations. Atmospheric action, mentioned by MacCulloch only as the cause of the serrated outline of the hills, has assumed a power in Turner's depiction which shapes and forms and gives a dynamic to the whole ridge.[151] Here, as in the Staffa painting, Turner shows the atmosphere as indicative of nature in a constant process of change, but, in restricting himself to the observable, he proceeds in a manner which is in keeping with MacCulloch's earlier rejection of theoretical presuppositions.[152]

Ruskin praised the intricately seamed faces of rocks and hills in Turner's drawing as geologically accurate. In fact the seams are more apparent in John Knox's and George Fennel Robson's pictures, although their rocks and hills come across as artificially differentiated rather than meticulously observed geological formations. It is not the detailed delineation of rock structures which gives Turner's drawing its geological character but his interpretation of nature's appearance as in constant change through the action of the elements.

Turner's depiction is characterised by its emphasis on the personal experience of the observing subject – the point of view he chooses places the viewer in such a singular (and dangerous) position that his situation cannot be forgotten. In making the implicit position of the perceiving subject an essential element of the depiction, Turner holds a station between MacCulloch's earlier phenomenalism and his later subjectivism.

The East Coast: Tantallon Castle and the Bass Rock

As Farington's sketchbooks show, the east coast of Scotland in the former Berwickshire and Haddingtonshire was already on the route of the picturesque traveller. Gilpin, too, had recommended coastal scenes in his tour of Hampshire, Sussex and Kent in 1774 as being particularly picturesque, since the sea offered a variety of changing light and shade hues, especially when viewed during storms.[153] As for the coastal rock formations themselves, he states that 'at best, the sea-coast rock, is

inferior to the land rock from its want of accompaniments'.[154] For the same reasons it was not the east coast of Scotland itself which attracted the attention of the picturesque travellers, but the series of castles on its shore. An engraving of *Tantallon Castle with the Bass & the Isle of May* (plate 65) appeared in Francis Grose's *The Antiquities of Scotland*, one of the few illustrations in the publication to be based on a drawing made by the

65 Francis Grose, *Tantallon Castle with the Bass & the Isle of May*, 1789, engraving (Sparrow), from F. Grose *The Antiquities of Scotland*, vol.1 (1789), by permission of the Syndics of Cambridge University Library.

author himself. Here, the character of the rocky coast on which the castle is built is played down.[155] The ruined building is shown as if at the flat edge of a lake. The Bass Rock is visible on the right-hand side, lying in calm water. This rock was the only purely natural feature of the coast to receive attention during the late eighteenth century, since it ranked, like Staffa, among the curiosities of nature, as Pennant's account makes clear:

> A little further, about a mile from the shore, lies the Bass Island, or rather rock, of a most stupendous height; on the south side the top appears of a conic shape, but the other over-hangs the sea in a most tremendous manner. The castle, which was once the state prison of Scotland, is now neglected: it lies close to the edge of the precipice, facing the little village of Castleton; where I took boat, in order to visit this singular spot.[156]

66   Alexander Nasmyth, *Tantallon Castle*, 1816, oil on canvas, 950 × 1405, National Gallery of Scotland, Edinburgh.

Farington too singled the Bass Rock out as the subject of two of his sketches and the broken line of his pencil shows that he was attracted by the rugged outline of the stone.[157] That a shift of perception must have occurred around the beginning of the nineteenth century is shown, however, in the painting of *Tantallon Castle* by Alexander Nasmyth (1758–1840) of 1816 (plate 66), which includes the Bass Rock.[158] Here the castle is viewed from a lower point of the coast in the foreground, standing on a cliff which reaches from the left into the middle ground of the painting. A turbulent sea surrounds the Bass Rock on the right-hand side. The dramatic clouds in the sky and the wreck of a boat on the beach in the foreground indicate that a rough storm has just passed. Underneath the castle a sailboat is visible; it seems to be in difficulties and a small boat appears to have gone to its rescue while two small figures watch it from the shore.

It is not the depiction of a shipwreck on an inaccessible coast under a stormy sky which is novel in Nasmyth's painting. This theme derives from an eighteenth-century tradition initiated by the French sea and landscape painter Claude Joseph Vernet (1714–1789). Gainsborough's *Coast Scene: Selling Fish*[159] of 1781 and De Loutherbourg's *Shipwreck*[160] of 1793 both exemplify the tradition of showing an unspecified small stretch of coast with highly generalised and exaggeratedly rugged outlines. The main subject of these paintings is usually the dramatically moving sea on which a ship is in danger. Nasmyth's picture departs from this formula in two notable respects. First, Nasmyth places the scene at a specific location, unmistakably Tantallon Castle, facing the Bass Rock. More importantly, the coast is now no longer merely the resisting shore but has become part of the drama at sea. The cliffs show an intricate structure of contrasting lines while the Bass Rock is not singled out merely for its astonishing outlines but is an integrated constituent of the scene. It seems as if the massive wave which dashes onto the cliff in the foreground is being used to signify the range of natural forces which must have caused the appearance of such a coastal structure.

The history visible in the structure of the coast in Nasmyth's painting could well have been perceived in the context of contemporary geological discussion. In his *Autobiography*, James Nasmyth recalls his father's acquaintance with Hutton's theory of the origin of the earth:

> During his sojourn in Italy, in 1783, he had the good fortune to make the acquaintance of Sir James Hall of Dunglass, Haddingtonshire. The acquaintance afterwards ripened into a deeply-rooted friendship. During the winter season Sir James resided with his family in his town house in George Street. He was passionately attached to the pursuit of art and science. He practised the art of painting in my father's room, and was greatly helped by him in the requisite manipulative skill. Sir James was at that time engaged in writing his well-known essay 'On the Origin of Gothic Architecture', and in this my father was of important help to him. He executed the greater number of the illustrations to this beautiful work. [. . .] Besides his enthusiasm in art and architecture, Sir James devoted a great deal of time to the study of geology. [. . .] These were the days of the Wernerian and Huttonian controversy as to the origin of the changes on the surface of the earth. Sir James Hall was President of the Edinburgh Royal Society, and established the true volcanic nature of the composition and formation of the rocks and mountains which surround Edinburgh. I have been led to speak of this subject, because when a boy I was often present at the discussions of these great principles. My father, Sir James Hall, Professor Playfair and Leslie, took

their accustomed walks round Edinburgh, and I clung eagerly to their words.[161]

If James Nasmyth's memory is correct, these meetings must have taken place around 1798, when Hall was preparing his publication on Gothic architecture. At this time Nasmyth was still the major Scottish representative of classically ordered pictures in the tradition of Claude Lorrain. Since Hutton's theory retained the notion of an overall stability in nature, it would not seem to have represented any challenge to Nasmyth's own perception. But, by the beginning of the nineteenth century, Hutton's followers were being urged to support their theoretical claims by the accumulation and closer examination of empirical evidence. Playfair added a range of new observations to his edition of Hutton's *Theory*, and Hall, in addition to proving the igneous origin of rocks by experiment, supported his papers in the *Transactions of the Royal Society of Edinburgh* with evidence taken mainly from close examination of the east coast of southern Scotland. It was also around this time, according to Martin Kemp, that Nasmyth 'was beginning to abandon the enamelled finish and schematized foliage of his early landscapes', and to develop a drawing technique which showed more of an interest in recording actual structures and appearances.[162] It is possible that the geological interests of his friend Hall, who concentrated on the close examination of specific locations on the east coast, induced Nasmyth to view such a famous spot as Tantallon Castle with eyes informed by the knowledge of the forceful changes on the earth's surface which the movements of the water laid bare. In contrast to eighteenth-century coastal views, Nasmyth shows that the coast is not just there, but that it is part of the drama of the shaping and forming of natural elements. But Nasmyth did not depict what, of course, was most important for Hall, the subject of his schematised drawings in his articles in the *Transactions of the Royal Society of Edinburgh*, namely, the vertical positions and convolutions of strata.

Turner's watercolour of *The Bass Rock* (plate 67) also owes more to the general geological debate and its emphasis on the relations between all the participating natural elements at a specific location than to any particular empirical discovery. Turner prepared sketches of the rock in 1818 and 1822, when he visited Scotland again in order to produce drawings for Walter Scott's

67   J.M.W. Turner, *The Bass Rock*, watercolour, 167 × 231, The Board of Trustees of the National Museums and Galleries on Merseyside (Lady Lever Art Gallery, Port Sunlight).

The Provincial Antiquities and Picturesque Scenery of Scotland.[163] This watercolour appeared as an engraving in 1826. As in the case of Staffa and Skye, Turner's principal motivation was neither a concern for geologically accurate depiction nor an eighteenth-century curiosity at the extravagant appearances of nature. The Bass Rock is shown from the angle at which (as Pennant had already noticed) it appears much less dramatic. A stormy sky shows lightning which seems to go straight into the rock. In the foreground, in front of the highly agitated sea and the conical shape of the Bass Rock itself, figures and the remains of a ruined ship appear. The fact that the shipwreck is not depicted supports the impression that it is the natural forces which form the true subject of the picture, rather than the dramatic scene taking place within it. Though the

storm and the sea envelop the rock, which is being struck by lightning, it is in the contrast with the ship-wreck victims in the foreground that one gets the impression that this little island, standing firm like a boulder in the breakers, is nevertheless involved in the drama and that its appearance depends on all the other elements. As in his later pictures of the Western Isles, Turner concentrates on the depiction of atmospheric forces, which indicates a view of nature made up of constantly changing but interlinked appearances.

By the 1820s the castles on the coast of East Lothian were, like the Western Isles, falling under the spell of Walter Scott's poems. John Thomson (1778–1840), for example, who, with Turner, prepared the most substantial number of illustrations for Scott's *Provincial Antiquities and Picturesque Scenery of Scotland*, took as his

98

favourite subject Fast Castle,[164] the castle reputed to have been the model for 'Wolf's Crag Castle' in Scott's *The Bride of Lammermoor*. He also painted Tantallon Castle,[165] which Scott describes in *Marmion*. Thomson and other artists depicted these castles in the light of Scott's poetical imagination, conferring on them a neglected and solemn atmosphere that is not apparent in earlier paintings.

Artists and Geologists

What I have attempted to show is that the changes in the artistic depiction of the Scottish landscape in the period from around 1790 to 1830 are linked to a broader shift in the perception of nature as manifested by contemporary geologists in particular. Coastal scenes were rarely depicted in the late eighteenth century, and then only in so far as they contained natural curiosities or castles. But, by the 1820s, in Scotland as elsewhere, coastal scenes were a common subject, providing an ideal opportunity for artists to illustrate the play of conflicting forces in nature. Generally speaking, at the beginning of the period, the style of depiction shows a concentration on a single, central feature; the rocks are represented with an emphasis on their bizarre character, in abstraction from their natural context and situation. By the end of the period, the structure of the depictions has become decentralised and the rocks are shown as a part of an environment whose natural history results from their particular context.

Although, as we have seen, there was a certain amount of interaction between artists and geologists, it is clear that the influence of geological research on artistic practice was indirect and variable. Even in the case of an artist like William Daniell, where direct interaction can be established, it would be too much to assume that his abandonment of conventional modes of depiction was due directly to his awareness of the new geological approach. It seems that when he first took up the idea of the *Voyage round Great Britain* he had already formed the intention of depicting and noting what had hitherto been neglected. But his encounter with the new approach during his preparations appears to have helped him perceive locations like Staffa in a way which went beyond the established formulae.

Even if the details of contemporary geological debate influenced only a small number of artists, geology does seem to have been of interest to them at a more superficial level, as in the case of Alexander Nasmyth. Farington writes in 1813 that '[t]he changes which have taken place in the formation of the earth of this our Globe was a subject of conversation' among English artists.[166] The increasing interest shown by artists in coastal scenes came about at least in part because geological discussion had led to a more general change in the understanding of natural developments. Coasts were no longer perceived as locations where the sublime effects of storms affect and victimise human action, but as places where purely natural forces have left their most visible traces. Although, as we have seen, the geologists pioneered this interest in the coast and islands, the visual language of their representation did not match up to their verbal accounts. Their illustrations were limited by formulae which corresponded to an earlier conception of natural history and it was artists like Daniell who first developed new ways of depicting nature.

By the end of the 1820s, the particularist depiction of the connected appearances of individual locations gave place to a more subjectivist emphasis on the perceptions of the artist, and scientists now once again endorsed the necessity of hypotheses. The phenomenalist approach, which first dismissed speculative theories in order to concentrate on recording the relation of different appearances to each other, was, as we have seen, an ephemeral stance; it placed such weight on the individual observer that, freed from scientific restrictions, the subject could express his or her personal associations in relation to natural phenomena. At this point, non-scientific discourses, like Walter Scott's writing, could influence the way in which places were perceived.

In discussing geological research and artists' work, I have traced several lines which sometimes run parallel and sometimes intersect. The way that fieldwork geologists gave their attention to a variety of phenomena at a particular location, rather than concentrating on a single feature of it, corresponded to a change in outlook by landscape artists after the turn of the century. This shift of emphasis is, in fact, characteristic of a change that took place more broadly in British landscape art in the early nineteenth century. One circle of artists, the group that formed around John and Cornelius Varley in London at the beginning of the nineteenth century, was, it can be argued, at the forefront of this change. The emergence of a phenomenalist stance in their work will be the subject of the next chapter.

IV

SKETCHING FROM NATURE:
JOHN AND CORNELIUS VARLEY AND THEIR CIRCLE

As we have seen, artists' tours changed their character after the turn of the nineteenth century and the search for picturesque views was modified in important respects. William Daniell's *Voyage round Great Britain* continued to treat characteristic picturesque subjects but showed them realistically lit, rather than embedded in an overall chiaroscuro. Such modifications, one might think, would require sketching which amounted to more than capturing the scene in rough pencil outlines. Daniell produced hundreds of sketches on his journeys, some of which have survived in two sketchbooks in the British Museum. These are traditional slight pencil sketches, sometimes heightened with white chalk, with colour occasionally noted in writing. Given Daniell's emphasis on natural light and colour in his prints, this is surprising. Daniell obviously worked up his final aquatints with the help of a very good memory for the atmospheric appearance of the locations he visited.[1]

Although Daniell's working procedure does not depart from traditional sketching practice, the decentralisation of subject-matter and the interest in atmosphere which his finished pictures display are features of early nineteenth-century British watercolours that distinguish them from their eighteenth-century predecessors. These aesthetic changes are often attributed to an important technical innovation within the art of watercolours. By the early nineteenth century, watercolour painting replaced the practice of tinted drawings. While the latter consisted of thin washes of colour on top of a completed monochrome drawing, the former were produced by applying colour directly to the paper. This allowed landscape depictions with richer colours and greater fluidity, producing the expansive atmosphere for which the British watercolourists of the early nine-

teenth century have become famous. The technique of building up a watercolour drawing could amount to quite an elaborate process. In the case of Turner, for example, it might involve letting wet washes run into each other and then perhaps superimposing another layer when dry again, or sponging or scratching out parts of the wash already applied. Such techniques led to works which appear exceptionally fresh, apparently spontaneous and fluid renderings of a particular moment, although they are, in fact, quite elaborate studio works. But while these technical developments may have been appropriate to the new attitude to landscape, they did not cause it; indeed, their complexity is somewhat at odds with the impression of immediacy and spontaneity at which they aim. It was with the emergence in the first decade of the nineteenth century of a change in the practice of sketching outdoors that the phenomenalism which was so influential upon early nineteenth-century British watercolours was first and most fully articulated.[2]

The works produced in the milieu of John and Cornelius Varley after 1800 provide the earliest British (and, arguably, the earliest international) examples of developed open-air artistic practice (including oil sketches) to have noticeable effects on the finished work produced after it. The Varley circle[3] modified the practice of sketching in two important respects: first, they sketched extensively in colour on the spot rather than just preparing pencil outlines; and, second, they elevated the status of the sketch done outdoors to a work in its own right which was worthy of exhibition. In so doing they introduced a new evaluation of the diversity of natural phenomena and the ephemeral appearances of landscape which had a lasting effect on

British landscape. As we will see, the Varley circle was at the heart of the artists' community in London in the early nineteenth century, and participated in, if they did not initiate, most of the formal or informal artists' societies of the time, from 'Monro's academy' to the 'Sketching Society' and the Society of Painters in Water-Colours. Almost all the artists, such as Peter de Wint (1784–1849), David Cox (1783–1859) and George Robert Lewis (1782–1871), who later became famous for their fresh atmospheric landscape depictions, came under the influence of members of the Varley circle at one time or another. Although by the time that these artists produced their most celebrated works the strict phenomenalism which informed the Varleys' sketching practice had been abandoned, its effects were long-lasting.

Since 1892, when Alfred Story ascribed the motto 'Go to Nature for everything' to John Varley (1778–1842),[4] he has been taken to be the father of *plein-air* painting in Britain.[5] But, in fact, John Varley himself seems not to have taken part fully in the development he initiated; his own work generally exemplifies another type of depiction, relying on the kind of schematised ideal composition which was to become typical of the works shown at the Society of Painters in Water-Colours.[6] It was, in fact, John's brother Cornelius (1781–1873), whose sketches pioneered the attitude which became characteristic of the work of John's pupils in the first decade of the nineteenth century. Although Cornelius Varley went on a tour of north Wales, the most canonical of the eighteenth-century picturesque tours, at the very beginning of his career, his sketches even then display a new appreciation of the scenery. Instead of searching for the sublime in the rough mountainous landscape, he concentrates on capturing various interacting aspects of a view in their actual light situation. Cornelius Varley's interest in the changing appearances of a location was, as we will see, informed by his scientific background and this in turn motivated his later development both as a scientist and as an artist.

The circle in its early years consisted of John and Cornelius Varley, William Mulready (1786–1863) and John's students John Linnell (1792–1882), William Turner of Oxford (1789–1862) and William Henry Hunt (1790–1864). Linnell was apprenticed to John Varley in 1804–5 in order to learn the depiction of landscape, William Turner of Oxford followed in 1805

and William Henry Hunt in 1806. William Mulready, who was not formally a student of John Varley's, had married his sister Elizabeth in 1803 and lived with him until 1805.[7]

The transition from the search for singular objects to a more sustained study of objects in their location through outdoor sketches seems to have occurred in the Varley circle at the same time as the geologists of the Geological Society were making it their programme. The practice of repeatedly sketching in the area around Twickenham and Millbank on the banks of the Thames, is a striking feature of their earliest work. Written evidence for this comes from both Linnell and Hunt. In his autobiography (written in 1863) Linnell describes Varley's pupils' drawing studies at Millbank and on the Thames at Twickenham, where Varley had rented a summer house: 'Hunt and I were always out when weather permitted painting in oil on millboard from nature'.[8] Similarly, a manuscript compiled by J.J. Jenkins, the secretary of the Old Water-Colour Society between 1854 and 1864, quotes a conversation with Hunt, who relates that when he was a pupil of Varley's, he and his fellow-students would 'sit down before any common object – a Cottage, Garden Rails, a Mossy wall, or an old Port, and endeavour to imitate them minutely / a rareful mode of practice not then recognized as it has since become' and thus 'much scoffed at by the Artists of the time'.[9] Some of this work has survived, both in the form of oil sketches and drawings by Varley's pupils. For example, the oil sketch by John Linnell *Study of a Tree* (plate 68) is almost identical in its focus on the structure and texture of a tree-trunk with William Henry Hunt's oil sketch *Study from Nature at Twickenham* (plate 69), both made in the same summer of 1806. Similarly unassuming in subject-matter and composition are chalk sketches by William Turner of Oxford, for example his *Trees on a River Bank*, and John Varley's *River Bank: Willow Tree and Figures* (sheet in a sketchbook), both in the Victoria and Albert Museum. In 1803 Cornelius Varley had made a sky study whose reverse side also showed a similar watercolour study of the texture of a tree-trunk.[10] All of these sketches are close-up studies of trees or river-banks, like John Linnell's oil sketch *At Twickenham* (plate 70). Although the subject-matter still reflects the late eighteenth-century picturesque taste for the variegated play of textures in rural objects, the composition in *At Twickenham* is de-hierarchised, concentrating on some

68　John Linnell, *Study of a Tree*, 1806, oil on board, 324 × 168, Tate Gallery, London.

69　William Henry Hunt, *Study from Nature at Twickenham*, c.1806, oil on board, 330 × 168, Tate Gallery, London.

apparently insignificant segment of a wider scene rather than developing an integrated representation in a picturesque framework. What is emphasised is the moment of encounter between artist and subject-matter. Although the use of subdued tones apparently keeps these studies within the eighteenth-century tradition, these may well have been more the result of the dazzling effects of outdoor light, a problem which has often been noted for those working in oil in the open air, rather than adherence to convention.[11] The attempt to render the distribution of light and shade more realistically would later dramatically modify artists' colour

70   John Linnell, *At Twickenham*, 1806, oil on board, 165 × 254, Tate Gallery, London.

selection – in the course of the first half of the nineteenth century the colour scale became noticeably brighter.

We will see, however, that the development of this mode of depiction was not the result of a conscious attempt to break with traditional ways of perceiving and representing, but was the product of the confluence of more than one factor. There were notable changes in the training of the artists involved, something apparent in Thomas Monro's teaching practice and its influence on his student John Varley, as well as in Cornelius Varley's early career as an artist. As Linnell's autobiography makes clear, the artists apprenticed to John Varley had a quite untraditional education: 'copying drawings formed no part of the pupils' employment; they were constantly drawing from nature or trying to compose'.[12] It was in the context of this rather *laissez-faire* system of training by sketching in the open air that Cornelius

Varley exercised an important influence and led the Varley circle towards a more phenomenalist mode of landscape depiction.

When a further generation of artists was apprenticed to John Varley in the second decade of the nineteenth century, he seems to have abandoned his earlier teaching practice. Francis Oliver Finch (1802–1862) describes Varley's students as copying in the studio[13] and Varley's advice is reported to have changed to 'Nature wants cooking'.[14] While Cornelius Varley told Jenkins that his brother John 'gained credit' for his earlier students because 'they distinguished themselves without showing any likeness with their master',[15] his later students all take a formalised approach to landscape art very similar to their teacher's. And indeed, when John Varley published his drawing manual, *A Treatise on the Principles of Landscape Design*, in 1821, he stated in the advertisement/subtitle that:

this work originated from the Author's own practice and experience, [...] after several years repeated solicitation from his pupils (who, in the retirement of the country, have found the difficulty of proceeding without some fixed principles to work on; and industry, without them frequently unavailing).[16]

This, and the fact that none of the artists who had been part of the Varleys' circle in the first decade of the century continued to produce such outdoor sketches, suggests that their early approach to nature was only a transitional stage in their careers.[17] Here, also, phenomenalism proved to be an unstable position.

The members of the Varley circle were not the only British landscape artists to practise outdoor sketching in oil. John Constable took up outdoor sketching in oil in 1802, so far as we know quite independently. In this year he wrote in a much-quoted letter that there was 'nothing in the [Royal Academy] exhibition worth looking up to – there is room enough for a natural painture', and he determined to return in the summer from London to his birth place, East Bergholt, to 'make some laborious studies of nature [...] to get a pure and unaffected representation of the scenes'.[18] The studies which resulted from this show, however, that Constable, in contrast to Cornelius Varley, approached landscape at this time informed by conventional pictorial formulae, such as the picturesque.[19] It was only after 1811 that his practice departed conspicuously from received pictorial models and noticeably informed his finished work. Indeed, he is reported to have finished a whole oil painting, *Boat Building* (now in the Victoria and Albert Museum), on the spot in the open air in autumn 1814.

We saw at the beginning of this book, in Constable's *Flatford Mill* (plate 2), a painting whose emphasis on specific details throughout the picture and attention to a peculiar situation of light amounts to the radical abandonment of pictorial conventions in favour of observation. The significance given to each element is not derived from an intrinsic order within the subject-matter, but by its relation to something outside itself, the observing subject. This is also characteristic of the work produced in the Varley circle in the first decade. The difference, however, is that the order derived from the relation between observed scene and observer is optical in the Varley circle, while in Constable's work it stems from the significance his homeland and its activ-

ities had for him. Constable builds up a narration through the detailed scenes delineated, which results in what Michael Rosenthal has called a 'georgic narrative', and this is absent from the Varley circle's work.[20] Thus, in Constable's case, the subjectivism which lurks beneath the surface of phenomenalism is already quite close to breaking through and this was to become the main characteristic of Constable's work shortly afterwards. Indeed (and once again there is a similarity here to the method of work of some members of the Varley circle) by the 1820s, when Constable's work appears to be freshest and most dedicated to the rendering of a fleeting moment, he had in fact abandoned his strict adherence to the principle of the primacy of observation. Although Constable and other artists had relinquished the phenomenalist method by then, the legacy of phenomenalism is apparent in the metaphysical understanding of nature as evanescent and in a process of constant change. By the time that *plein-air* sketching was more widely and successfully translated into finished pictures, in the second decade of the nineteenth century, the artists involved, as we will see, had come to interpret their practice within a corresponding system of aesthetic meanings, one which constitutes a significant move beyond phenomenalism. When Ruskin argued for the centrality of sketching to artistic practice (in the five volumes of *Modern Painters*, published between 1843 and 1860) sketching was presented as having autonomous value – it would show a truer picture of the artist's genius, being closer to the artist's source in nature, or give privileged access to the artist's working procedure.

The New Role of Sketching

In the previous chapter I was concerned to follow the effects of a single cause in the development from one mode of perception and depiction to another. This chapter will offer a less linear and more synoptic picture. Epistemological shifts of the kind that this book is concerned with do not occur in a straight line, nor are they the intended effects of the conscious acts of those who bring them about. Changes appear first in many different places, not always connected to one another, and their initial consequences (as in the case of the contacts between art and geology) may be diverse and even contradictory. Only later do these developments solidify into an orthodoxy, usually when further factors have taken hold. The sketching practice which concentrated on the meticulous transcriptions of 'any common object' provides a good example of such a pattern.

At the beginning of the nineteenth century, outdoor sketching was a loosely structured practice, adopted for a variety of reasons, more or less explicit. In 1802 the watercolour artist Edward Dayes, who was important to Thornton (as discussed above), published the first of his series of essays 'On Painting', in the *Philosophical Magazine*.[21] Here he repeated a principle that had become dogma since Reynolds' *Discourses*: to acquire artistic skills the student had to copy Old Master pictures, first in parts and then as a whole. Only after having achieved a certain level of formal knowledge in this way was one to be set free to 'apply to nature' one's skills; nature could not be depicted without a pre-established framework of rules.[22] Dayes' use of the word 'sketch' thus refers only to the practice of copying from other masters,[23] in the manner defined by Reynolds. The purpose of a sketch in this sense is to convey an overall impression or close study of a particular part of it.[24]

It was Gilpin, as many scholars have noted, who first rejected this academic tradition of referring to nature in terms of an inherited stock of received formal ideals, presenting nature instead as the source of archetypes.[25] With Gilpin the sketch from nature takes on an authority unprecedented in English writing. Because he addressed himself in the first place to a wider public, not to professionals, Gilpin's new evaluation of the sketch on the spot was particularly influential in the creation of a public acknowledgement of its role. According to Gilpin, the artist's first sketch is: 'the standard, to which, in the absence of nature, he must at least recur for his *general ideas*'.[26] But Gilpin, too, like Reynolds and Dayes, distinguishes in his own way between the full and careful study of a particular object and a sketch, whose purpose is simply to represent an overall impression or a generalised view:

> From this correct knowledge of objects arises another amusement; that of representing, by a few strokes in a sketch, those ideas, which have made the most impression upon us.[27]

Moreover, these two immediate functions of sketching cannot be communicated to others, but serve only to '*assist our own memory*': 'when a sketch is intended *to convey in some degree, our ideas to others*, it is necessary,

that it should be somewhat more adorned'.[28] Such an 'adorned sketch' allowed the artist to improve his depiction of a scene, as required by an established compositional principle, such as the picturesque. Picturesque composition, according to Gilpin, 'consists in uniting in one whole a variety of parts' by means of the skilfully distributed interplay of light and shadow.[29] Only in this modified form could the two modes of sketching practice, the careful study of a particular object and the capturing of the overall impression, be integrated.

Gilpin's theoretical discussion thus represents public acknowledgement of the importance of sketches from nature. But it does not yet correspond to what would emerge as the practice of the circle around Varley. For someone in search of the picturesque, in which chiaroscuro rather than colour played the paramount role, sketches on the spot did not require more than pencil or chalk. Linnell's oil sketch *At Twickenham* (plate 70), on the other hand, does not just give detailed examination to a single object on the river-bank or present a rough overall impression of the distribution of light and shadow. He also depicts in colour the complex structural relations within an apparently insignificant small scene viewed close-up – something which stands in contrast to Gilpin's doctrine that the 'unpicturesque assemblage of objects' is unsuitable for any kind of depiction other than 'plans' (that is, for technical purposes, such as Ordnance Survey).

Internationally, *plein-air* sketching in oil, such as Varley's students practised, was not in itself new and can be traced back to the seventeenth century. Earlier practice, however, always preserved a strict line of division between sketch and finished work; Dayes' and Gilpin's attitude towards drawings does not depart from this. Conisbee gives a picture of the range of conceptions behind earlier outdoor activities:

> There is no easy evolution of attitudes to *plein-air* painting before the Romantic period, and artists proceeded to paint from nature for a variety of reasons, often private and unsung: some works may have been only in part painted directly from nature (Claude; Dughet?); some studies were made with a view to incorporation into studio works, to give a heightened sense of veracity (Sandrart; Claude?; Desportes certainly; Vernet?); some studies were made as independent works, (a) to train the artist in

accurately or more convincingly matching in paint the effects of nature, and/or (b) for the pure pleasure of imitating in paint (which is also a projection of the painter himself), without the constraints normal in commissioned work (Velasquez; Dughet; Rosa; Desportes; Vernet?; Valenciennes; Jones; Granet). It was the subsequent generations of painters, from Constable and Corot to Cézanne, who would take this tradition as a starting-point, and who would bring a fusion of the landscape 'sketch' and the 'finished' work, where, as far as possible and increasingly so, the pure sensation of the first response to nature could be carried over into a grander scale.[30]

For the gap between sketch on the spot and finished work to be closed, the characteristic qualities of the sketch itself had to be appreciated first in its own right.

In fact, a number of works with titles such as 'sketch from nature' or 'study from nature' appeared with increasing frequency in the exhibition catalogues of the Royal Academy from the 1790s onwards. They are, however, now difficult to identify. Joseph Farington, for example, exhibited a *Sketch from Nature* in 1790 and a *Study from Nature* in 1791.[31] Most of Farington's work was in the topographical tradition (for example, his tour in Scotland, discussed in Chapter III). For topographical watercolourists the distinction between finished work and sketch on the spot was always more fluid than it was for artists working in oil, since the overriding aim, after all, was to present an accurate image of the scene observed. From the seventeenth century onwards, the practice followed was to make two drawings of each subject, one on the spot in pencil and a finished watercolour worked up in colour afterwards in the studio. Gilpin had made clear that a sketch which was to be shown to others had to be 'adorned'; thus we may infer that it was a composed sketch which was shown at the Royal Academy as a 'sketch from nature' and that this was closely associated with the topographical view.[32] A 'sketch from nature' could represent any view in nature that fell within the domain of the picturesque. We have seen that Paul Sandby's watercolour sketch of Leith (plate 44), although certainly observed from nature, was clearly constructed according to pictorial requirements and definitely not coloured on the spot. The pictures shown at the Royal Academy from the 1790s onwards

as 'sketch from nature' or 'study from nature' are likely to have been similar.

How unusual it still was in the first decade of the nineteenth century to use colour while working in front of the subject emerges from a letter the watercolourist John Sell Cotman (1782–1842) wrote to his Norfolk patron, Dawson Turner, from Yorkshire in 1805. He writes that his 'chief study has been colouring from Nature', adding that many of his works were 'close copies of that ficle [sic] Dame'. This suggests that he was not used to the practice and encountered difficulties.[33] Thomas Girtin (1775–1802), who, with Turner, was influential in moving the technique of watercolouring away from the tinted drawing, became famous in the early nineteenth century for his atmospheric drawings built up by bold, decisive penwork, and short, broad, layered brushstrokes. Significantly, it was Cornelius Varley who reported that Girtin, when sketching from nature, would 'expose himself to all weathers, sitting out for hours in the rain to observe the effect of storms and clouds upon the atmosphere'.[34] It is not known, however, whether Girtin really did develop an extensive outdoor sketching practice or not. Although he was renowned for his atmospheric drawings, their sweeping simplicity and the grandeur of the landscape convey a homogeneous emotional tone which a drawing strictly attentive to the varied appearance of nature would not produce (see plate 85 below).

Cornelius Varley's account of Girtin certainly reveals the importance he himself had come to attach to outdoor sketching. To capture the changing atmospheric effects observed in nature colouring on the spot was essential, and it was in the Varley circle that sketching in colour was most systematically practised. Moreover, around 1805, Cornelius Varley exhibited studies in which the gap between finished work and sketch is diminished. In so doing, Varley elevated the qualities characteristic of sketches (for example, giving attention to ephemeral phenomena and equal priority to diverse elements) into subjects worthy of works of art and so prepared the way for those developments in landscape art which have made the British artists of the early nineteenth century famous. Two such works are among Cornelius Varley's earliest exhibits, shown in 1805 at the newly established Water-Colour Society, of which he and his brother were founding members. *Ross Market Place, Herefordshire* (plate 71) bears the subtitle *A Sketch*

71 Cornelius Varley, *Ross Market Place, Herefordshire*, 1803, graphite and watercolour, 295 × 457, by courtesy of the Board of Trustees of the Victoria and Albert Museum, London.

on the Spot.[35] The other work has the title *S.E. View of St Albans* and, although it seems to have been lost, its probable appearance can be established from a surviving sketch at the same location (plate 72) albeit from a different angle. *Ross Market Place* was made on Varley's second journey to Wales in 1803 and the second drawing, very likely, on a sketching trip to St Albans in 1804. Both watercolours confirm that the topographical view and the sketch have now become closely associated. But they also show an interest in the particular disposition of the sunlight which goes beyond the compositional use of light and shadow in topographical depictions to define parts of the represented architecture, an interest which required the application of colour on the spot. In *Ross Market Place* the areas of shadow are represented through a grey wash over a pencil drawing; the highlights, however, are left unfilled-in, as are those areas to which Varley applies unbroken local colour of red,

yellow and beige. This approach serves in the first place to capture a real light situation, but, in addition, confers a luminosity on the drawing which leads beyond the dead coloration of traditional tinted drawing.

Perhaps the most remarkable feature of these two drawings is the attention which Varley gives to nearly every little detail in their depiction. In the drawing of *Ross Market Place, Herefordshire* the irregular dirt road in the foreground centre and the uneven features of the construction of the house on the right of the foreground are shown with exceptional clarity. Even apparently useless features, like the hook which hangs from the beam carrying the signpost on the house, are noted. Only where the sunlight is too bright or the objects too far distant to be distinctly perceived do they retreat into their general outlines (as in the case of the right-hand corner of the market hall in the background of the drawing). The drawing has the character of a section from a wider view; it lacks a central object within its own picture space. The side alley to the left of the picture is delineated just as sharply as the market hall and the house next to it in the centre of the picture, so that no feature is sufficiently dominant to provide a compositional focus. Thus, in its meticulousness, Varley's sketch made on the spot goes beyond the tradition of 'adorned sketches'. The drawing is explicit precisely with respect to those parts which Gilpin wished to suppress in the sketches which were to be shown in public. While Gilpin states that 'General ideas only must be looked for; not the peculiarities of portrait',[36] it is just the latter which Varley's watercolour depicts.

This careful attention to detail is also characteristic of some of John Varley's finished topographical work in the years between 1800 and 1804.[37] *Looking up the High Street, Conway*[38] and *View of St Peter's Church, Chester,*[39] 1803, both have closely corresponding counterparts in graphite drawings by Cornelius Varley: *A Street in Conway Seen from the Watergate*[40] and *The Rows at Chester* (plate 73), drawn in 1802, when the two brothers were travelling together to north Wales. As Lyles has stated, these dates suggest that John Varley finished his own versions only after their return.[41] Thus they are studio works, but they still retain a clarity of lighting absent from his later work which is usually aimed at achieving a more general effect. Compared with Cornelius' drawings done on the spot, John's depictions have been adjusted to received artistic formulae in the picturesque

72   Cornelius Varley, *St Albans, Hertfordshire*, 1804?, graphite and watercolour, 240 × 349, sold Colnaghi's, London, 21 February–16 March 1973, photo Dr Michael Pidgley.

73   Cornelius Varley, *The Rows at Chester*, 1802, graphite and grey wash, 400 × 584, by courtesy of the Board of Trustees of the Victoria and Albert Museum, London.

tradition. This becomes apparent if we compare *Looking down the High Street, Conway* (plate 75; the companion piece to the above-mentioned) with one of Paul Sandby's street scenes of the late 1770s. *Village Street, Old Charlton, Kent* (plate 76) is also structured around a central receding street. Sandby also gives great attention to detail. His depiction is enveloped in the warm, clear light of the evening sun, which at once unites the picture's elements and produces its harmonious effect, suggesting a world at peace with itself. The figure drawings, as in John Varley's work, add little narrative scenes which are absent from Cornelius' depictions. Sandby's street scenes seem to suggest that they are permanent and beyond change, while Cornelius' do not point beyond the immediate moment.

Two main elements are new in Cornelius Varley's exhibited sketches: both the setting of their subjects in actual light situations rendered in colour on the spot, and the attention given to apparently insignificant details throughout the picture place them outside the terms of Gilpin's category of the 'adorned sketch' and traditional topography. The use of actual lighting, however, is first noticeable in a watercolour made by John Varley in 1800 in the company of Dr Thomas Monro (1759–1833) (plate 74). Though it still retains a stageset-like assemblage of trees in the foreground and a figure on a path leading into the middle ground, the panoramic vista exhibits an inconspicuous stretch of land in clear sunlight, represented in light greens, browns and russet.[42] That it was meant to be more than a personal *aide-mémoire* is indicated by the extensive inscription 'View from Polesden near Bookham in Surrey, made in Company with Dr. Monro by John Varley, October 1800, Study from nature'. Cornelius Varley's statement that in 1800 'Dr. Monro took him [John Varley] to his house at Fetcham in Surrey to make coloured sketches in the neighbourhood particularly about Boxhill' confirms that John Varley came under Monro's influence at the start of his career.[43] Cornelius considered these sketches to be John's best work; significantly, they seem to have come closest to Cornelius' own ambition of transcribing rather than composing landscape.

Around this time Cornelius and John frequently visited the doctor in his house in Adelphi Terrace, in the artists' quarter in the West End, and Monro apparently suggested to John that he should live nearby.[44] According to Cornelius, he and John lived together in Charles Street, Covent Garden. Cornelius also relates how Dr Monro 'would stand while my Brother was drawing and dictated the tints he should use'.[45] This makes it clear that, although John Varley had shown pictures at the Royal Academy from 1798 onwards, he and his brother were still considered to be students. All of which suggests that Dr Monro played an important part in encouraging the two Varley brothers to produce coloured sketches directly from nature.

Monro is mainly known today by what has come to be called the 'Monro Academy'.[46] He set up evening

74   John Varley, *View of Polesden, Surrey*, 1800, graphite and watercolour, 160 × 210, Laing Art Gallery, Newcastle upon Tyne (Tyne and Wear Museums).

drawing sessions at his house at Adelphi Terrace which initially enabled Girtin and Turner to copy drawings by John R. Cozens. Later, the young watercolourists Varley, Cotman, De Wint, Hunt and others were able to learn from their predecessors' work in Monro's possession. In this way Monro made possible for watercolour artists what had traditionally been regarded as the prime form of artistic education: copying the work of previous masters.[47]

More unusually, however, it was also Monro's practice to induce the artists who stayed with him to sketch the surrounding of his houses in the country.[48] Surviving drawings of this kind by Hunt show an interest similar to the Varleys' in apparently insignificant detail and realistic light and shadow.[49] The sales catalogue of works owned by Monro at his death also contains a significant number of drawings of the areas around Fetcham made by Girtin, Turner, Thomas Hearne (1744–1817), Henry Edridge (1769–1821) and Varley in the early years and, later, of the areas around Bushey by Hunt and De Wint.[50] That Monro valued the depiction of what Gilpin would have called the 'unpicturesque assemblage of objects' is made clear in a sarcastic letter by Samuel Palmer (1805–1881) to George Richmond in 1828:

> Mr. Sherman went recommended by Mr. Varley to Dr. Monro [. . .]. The doctor led the way to that selected scene which he intended to commend first of all to his visitor's attention [. . .]. At last the picturesque tourist arrived at the Arcadia of their destination: – and Behold! – It was a BRICKFIELD!!!!![51]

Dr Monro's own drawing style does not show any traces of this apparent interest, however. His subjects are usually rural scenes, done with a Gainsborough-like picturesqueness. Nor did he colour his own drawings in front of the object. Palmer describes an occasion on which Monro returned to his studio to carry out finishing work, leaving the artist who had accompanied him to complete his own colouring in the open air.[52] There is also no certain evidence that Dr Monro ever used watercolour,[53] despite the fact that he was a patron of those watercolour artists, J.R. Cozens, Girtin and Turner, who abandoned the tinted drawing in favour of working with colour directly (an innovation, of course, which helped watercolour artists to establish their own identity as painters, manifest in the foundation of the Water-Colour Society in 1805).[54]

Monro's apparently strange mixture of the traditional

75   John Varley, *Looking down the High Street, Conway*, c.1802–3, graphite and watercolour, 368 × 5220, by courtesy of the Board of Trustees of the Victoria and Albert Museum, London.

with the new and unconventional has always been something of an enigma. The fact that his own medical career shows similar ambiguities suggests a possible interpretation. Monro's training as a doctor took place at a time of transition. During the eighteenth century the medical profession had come to be composed of three kinds of doctor: physicians, surgeons and apothecaries. Monro belonged to the physicians, the oldest, most respected and privileged of the groups. Under the auspices of the Royal College of Physicians they were an élite of doctors caring for the gentry, whose first requirement was the provision of good medical advice rather than the carrying out of surgical operations.[55] The common opinion among medical historians is that medical education in England was particularly poor

during the eighteenth century, but that it would have been sufficient to provide a reasonable degree of care had the tripartite system proved stable.[56] But it did not. For manifold reasons, of which the increasing prosperity in Georgian society is perhaps the most obvious, medicine 'expanded as part of the general growth of the service sector in a thriving consumer economy'.[57] At the same time, philanthropic initiatives led to the foundation of many new hospitals from around 1750 onwards. Though the College of Physicians was socially conservative and tried to prevent reforms for as long as possible,[58] it was affected by the change, since every hospital had one or more appointments for physicians. Such physicians needed a wider range of practical skills and hospital expansion thus gave rise to a more practical

76 Paul Sandby, *Village Street, Old Charlton, Kent*, late 1770s, graphite, ink and watercolour on laid paper stuck on board, 307 × 515, by courtesy of the Board of Trustees of the Victoria and Albert Museum, London.

orientation in medical education. Initially, this change took place only in the hospitals. The essential part of the hospital learning experience lay in the students accompanying physicians during ward rounds and observing surgeons during operations. This was supplemented by lectures on subjects such as anatomy, surgery and practical physic.

Dr Monro, on the one hand, was very much part of the traditional system of education. Having graduated from Oxford in 1787, 'he became a candidate of the College of Physicians in 1790, and a fellow in 1791'.[59] He then went on to assist his father, whom he later succeeded, as physician to the lunatic asylum Bethlem, the oldest in the country. For Monro to acquire his practical knowledge in a hospital for the mentally ill rather than as a practitioner to the gentry must have forced him to try to bridge the huge gap between his theoretical, academic knowledge and the practical problems involved in caring for cases of severe mental disorder from all social strata.[60]

There is a parallel between Monro's own education and his unconventional training of the artists under his patronage. Just as his acquisition of medical skills was completed only by being confronted with the brute facts of disease which he encountered in the hospital, so, too, Monro would take his artists, after they had acquired formal knowledge by copying, out into the open and confront them with 'any common object'.[61] Without wishing to push the argument too far, it seems likely that Monro had his own mode of learning in mind when he formed his 'academy': the acquisition of practical skills by a form of personal instruction more loosely structured than a traditional apprenticeship.

Cornelius Varley

Sketching was given an independent value in Cornelius Varley's work more than in that of any other artist of the time. In the sale of his work remaining after his death (Christie's, 15 July 1875), 163 out of 230 works were catalogued as sketches, most produced in the years before 1810. It is not the number of sketches in itself which is remarkable, but the high number of sketches in proportion to finished works. Varley rarely seems to have worked his sketches up into finished versions. Altogether, he exhibited forty pictures in the first dec- ade of the century,[62] of which several were themselves sketches done on the spot, such as *Ross Market Place* (plate 71). From the fact that Varley produced four times as many sketches as exhibited works in these years, it is reasonable to infer that for him *plein-air* sketching was more than simply a means to an end and certainly more than an *aide-mémoire*. Cornelius' exhib- ited work in 1805 comes closer than any of his contem- poraries to the characteristic features of outdoor sketches. He therefore played a more important role in the development of open-air art practice than his brother – or, indeed, than any other artist of the time.

This role, however, seems to have escaped notice after his death.[63] In a review of the sale of Varley's work at Christie's, the *Telegraph* of 16 July 1875 stated:

> The interest in this sale of pictures and drawings by Cornelius Varley is not of the kind in which dealers can have any great share. We have got far beyond such work as his; and an 'investment' would be much more judiciously made in the watercolour paintings of living men than in crude performances like these. Most, if not all, the lots put up yesterday fell to bids which were so low as to suggest the no doubt actual fact of their having been bought by friends.

As a comparison of titles makes clear, a large amount of this work did indeed remain with the family and was not sold until 1973. In 1894 Alfred T. Story wrote:

> As an artist Cornelius Varley did not come near his more celebrated brother. His works were few, and for the most part of a semi-classical and somewhat conventional character, introducing architecture and groups of figures. They were composed with care and generally finished with much elaboration. There was a quality in his work, however, which always gained for him the respect of his brother-artists.[64]

Martin Hardie appears to have been the first modern art historian to re-evaluate Cornelius' work, which he judges to be 'peculiarly satisfying'.[65] Iolo A. Williams, who, like Hardie, was engaged in tracing the history of watercolours from the point of view of its emergence into what they considered to be autonomy – that is, the point at which the colour was applied in transparent washes without underlying drawing or bodycolour – appreciates Varley's drawing for the 'fresh and lucid qualities of its washes'.[66] But it is only recently, in the wake of the interest in 'naturalistic' landscape depiction, that Cornelius has again attracted attention.[67] If it had not been for Michael Pidgley's rediscovery of Cornelius Varley's drawings in the family's collection, however, and a subsequent article and catalogue by him, Cornelius might have remained a footnote in the history of his brother.[68]

Part of the reason for Cornelius' more radical depar- ture from the traditional form of artistic practice may lie in the fact that, unlike his brother, he was not trained as an artist. John was employed at the age of fifteen or sixteen by the topographical draughtsman Joseph Charles Barrow for jobs and errands and was allowed to draw and copy Old Master prints with Barrow's other pupils in return.[69] Cornelius, however, lived with his uncle Samuel Varley after the death of their father in 1791. Samuel Varley was a watch and instrument maker and Cornelius later wrote in his own autobiography that

> it was my good fortune to be with him during the chief of his Philosophical and chemical progress and having to help in every thing my hands were put to all Kinds of work [. . .] I was delighted with the chemical wonders that were then opening on the world and also learned that Knoledge [sic] is no burden but lightens all other burdens.[70]

Cornelius claims that by his fourteenth birthday he had made his own microscope, and he continued to work on the improvement of lens making. His uncle conducted a series of chemical experiments and founded the Chemical and Philosophical Society at Hatton House, one of the many predecessors of the Royal Institution. The Royal Institution, founded in 1800, still stood largely in the gentleman-amateur tradi- tion of the Royal Society. But, in contrast to the Royal Society, it combined its social role with an interest in scientific improvement and the industrial application of science. According to Cornelius Varley, in 1800 his uncle agreed to work for Charles, 3rd Earl Stanhope, one of the few 'improving' aristocrats in the country

77 Cornelius Varley, *Lord Rous's Park*, 1801, graphite and watercolour, 264 × 373, by courtesy of the Trustees of the British Museum, London.

and a patron of the Hatton House Lectures.[71] So Samuel Varley gave up his own business and the Hatton House Lectures and Cornelius determined to become an artist like his elder brother. It is interesting to note that he did not think it necessary to go through a traditional training and claimed that he 'taught' himself by 'sketching from nature' and 'was soon engaged to teach others'. Through his brother, he seems to have come into contact straight away with Thomas Monro and, through Monro, met the Earl of Essex who 'recommended me to my first pupils and told me what to charge'. Within a year of the start of his new career he was invited with his brother to Gillingham Hall, Norfolk, to teach Mrs Bacon Schutz and her daughters. One of the earliest known works by Cornelius Varley is

the *Lime Trees at Gillingham* (plate 78), dated 1801.[72] From Norfolk he went to Suffolk and seems to have stayed with the Rous family at Henham Hall. There he produced a number of drawings in graphite and one also tinted in a greenish blue (plate 77), inscribed 'Lord Rouses [sic] park' and dated 1801.[73] These drawings demonstrate that, although he would have had the opportunity to copy other watercolours through his contact with Dr Monro in the previous year, Cornelius Varley approached landscape at that time unequipped with formal rules. The weight of these drawings is concentrated on capturing the trees in the middle ground. Neither the foreground nor the sky is given much attention. Nor does it seem as if compositional considerations were of any concern to Cornelius. What

78   Cornelius Varley, *Lime Trees at Gillingham*, 1801, graphite and grey wash, 346 × 260, Ashmolean Museum, Oxford.

79 Cornelius Varley, *Part of Cader Idris and Tal-y-Llyn*, 1803, graphite and watercolour, 254 × 368, by courtesy of the Board of Trustees of the Victoria and Albert Museum, London.

interested him was merely the capturing of the variety of tree structures in the middle ground.

The opportunity to engage immediately with the appearances of natural phenomena, unencumbered by the expectations surrounding scientific experiments conducted in the setting of Hatton House, was later described by Varley as a great and unprecedented liberty after the subservient role in which he had worked in his uncle's laboratories:

> This happy change was like a glorious holiday. The pure air The sence of liberty to ramble anywhere & to have the boundless works of creation open before me [. . .] has left an impression that time does not efface but has contributed to make me hold on the course I believed to be right amid all the crooks of life & urgencies to deviate.[74]

This passage has an almost Rousseauesque feel. In Varley's case, however, this was not a fantasy of escape from society but the product of his life in 'the midst of the most cultivated amiable Kindness' of the gentry with whom he was staying. Yet he must also have felt the limitations involved in constructing pictures just by transcribing observations, since he relates that, after having spent the winter in Suffolk in order to be able to sketch in frost and snow, he returned to London to learn the correct rules of perspective.[75]

In June 1802 Varley travelled to north Wales with his brother and Thomas Webster, at this stage still a young architect who had recently been employed to design the Royal Institution's lecture hall and who later became a prominent member of the Geological Society of London. He returned to Wales in 1803 with the artists

80 Cornelius Varley, *Mountain Landscape, North Wales*, 1803, graphite and watercolour, 225 × 369, sold Colnaghi's, London, 21 February–16 March 1973, photo Dr Michael Pidgley.

81 Cornelius Varley, *Sketchbook: Lime Rocks Llangollen* (p.10), 1802, graphite, 163 × 367, by permission of the Syndics of the Fitzwilliam Museum, Cambridge.

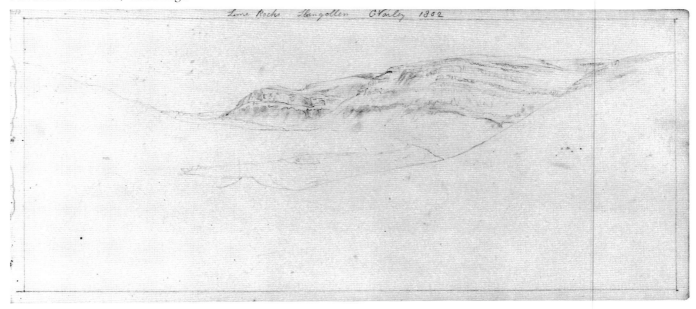

82   Cornelius Varley, *Evening at Llanberis*, 1805, watercolour, 200 × 238, Tate Gallery, London.

Joshua Cristall (1768–1847) and William Havell (1782–1857). Both artists are known to have had an early interest in open-air sketching, something which would have made them like-minded travel companions for Cornelius Varley. Indeed, a study by Cristall of the rocky features near Devil's Bridge in Wales is very similar in treatment to Cornelius Varley's sketch of the same subject in the British Museum (plate 89).[76] But these studies never informed Cristall's finished work, which is devoted to a revival of the classicist tradition. Havell's sketches, however, unlike Cornelius Varley's

or Linnell's, never departed from compositional formulae and are thus closer to John Varley.[77] Cornelius' watercolours now known to us from these years bear few traces of having been constructed according to the rules of linear perspective or compositional considerations. Most of his works from the trips to Wales, including a third one he did on his own in 1805, were left unfinished. He seems always to have concentrated on one aspect of the landscape as perceived, without attempting to integrate it into an overall composition. *Part of Cader Idris and Tal-y-Llyn* (plate 79) of 1803 is an

83 John Varley, *Mountain Landscape: View from Cader Idris*, c.1804, watercolour and bodycolour, 245 × 346, by courtesy of the Board of Trustees of the Victoria and Albert Museum, London.

example of this. Broad washes mark the mountainous landscape and the valley, of which only two areas are worked out in more detail. Similarly, in *Mountain Landscape, North Wales* (plate 80), also of 1803, a faint wash is laid over the scene and again only two areas, apparently chosen almost at random, are sufficiently finished for different species of trees and earth formations to be clearly discernible. A drawing in a sketchbook from 1802 with the title *Lime Rocks Llangollen* (plate 81) concentrates exclusively on capturing the rock formations. Another watercolour from his tour in 1805, *Evening at Llanberis* (plate 82), on the other hand, shows the different shades of the mountains as they appear in an evening sky. No detail of the landscape is noted. Since Varley does not build up his pictures according to any formal schema, it is possible for him to leave the

foreground as a mere coloured wash. None of these drawings develops a clearly defined pictorial space; they are fragments drawn here and there from the artist's surroundings.[78] In comparison with John Varley's *Mountain Landscape: View from Cader Idris* (plate 83), it is clear that Cornelius is trying to do no more than capture a phenomenon. Although a second version of the same scene by John Varley carries an inscription describing it as based on experience 'at Half Past 3 in the Morning',[79] his depiction is obviously composed according to the pictorial tradition of the sublime. The drawing is suffused with glowing light and a solemn figure in the foreground appears forlorn in the vast expanse of the mountain ranges, so that the picture conveys a uniform impression of awesomeness. Some drawings by Cornelius Varley could, at first sight, be

120

84   Cornelius Varley, *Barmouth Vale from Cader Idris*, 1803, graphite and watercolour, 298 × 462, sold Colnaghi's, London, 21 February–16 March 1973, photo Dr Michael Pidgley.

85   Thomas Girtin, *Kirkstall Abbey*, 1802, watercolour, 290 × 537, by courtesy of the Trustees of the British Museum, London.

86 Cornelius Varley, *Beddgelert Bridge*, 1802, graphite and watercolour, 298 × 454, by courtesy of the Board of Trustees of the Victoria and Albert Museum, London.

thought to be attempting the same effect.[80] They are different, however. They can never be reduced to a single mood, whether that of the sublime, or of a Claudian arcadia; they remain, rather, simply studies of an evening sky.

Even in those cases where Cornelius Varley shows a landscape as a whole, as in *Barmouth Vale from Cader Idris* (plate 84) of 1803, he proceeds similarly.[81] Here again, only on a wider scale, it is the intricate interaction between the different structures as observed in the landscape which takes his interest rather than the concern for one single impression or the construction of a successfully controlled pictorial space. Again, the picture space does not frame the view: it is entered in an immediate way. The curving rows of trees which lead the eye from the right foreground into the background enclose and define the spaces alongside them; the struc-

ture of the picture is derived from this interaction. Although this drawing possesses the decentralisation characteristic of a Girtinesque picture space, it is clear that there is a different guiding principle behind its construction. While Girtin's famous *Kirkstall Abbey* (plate 85), for example, is formed by broad sweeping areas, Cornelius Varley's depictions are far more detailed in the structures delineated. Even in those drawings which were brought to a nearly finished state (some of which were exhibited with the subtitle *A Sketch on the Spot*) it is impossible to identify a prevailing mood; they remain as descriptive in character as the rougher sketches. *Beddgelert Bridge* (plate 86) of 1802 is a good example, remarkable for the way in which Varley sets bright colours next to each other in an almost impressionist fashion, as in the pier of the bridge.

122

87   Cornelius Varley, *Sketchbook: Wrekin Shropshire* (p.4), 1802, graphite and watercolour, 163 × 367, by permission of the Syndics of the Fitzwilliam Museum, Cambridge.

88   Cornelius Varley, *The Traveller*, graphite and grey wash, 221 × 341, sold Colnaghi's, London, 21 February–16 March 1973, photo Dr Michael Pidgley.

It is clear that Varley was not simply ignorant of the picturesque formulae for landscape depiction, which he would have encountered in his patrons' collections and through his brother. Nor does the fact that he did not follow picturesque formulae in the main bulk of his sketches show that he rejected them in all cases. There are, indeed, some drawings by Varley which show that he tried his hand at traditional modes of landscape depiction. An example of an exercise in the more generalising, Girtinesque style of landscape, using rows of unspecifically depicted trees to indicate recession, can be found in a sketchbook of 1802, prepared during his first journey to Wales with his brother (plate 87). Another example is a graphite and grey wash drawing (plate 88), probably based, as was pointed out in Colnaghi's catalogue, on a drawing showing Wilton Castle, dated 1803.[82] But while Varley aimed in this latter sketch to catch the castle as it appeared in a clearly sunlit landscape, the watercolour based on it sets the ruin on a little hill in the middle of a highly generalised landscape setting. Dark clouds appear from behind the castle and a galloping rider in the foreground adds drama. In this way the picture contains the elements of a sublime formula picture and its imaginative character is highlighted by the inscription on the verso: 'The Traveller speeds his daring course along/ Eager to outride the fast O'er whelming storm'.[83] It is possible that this is the work exhibited by Varley at the Royal Academy in 1807, with the title *The Traveller*.[84]

To judge by the titles of his exhibited work, one may infer that Cornelius Varley had different aspirations as a professional artist to those shown in his early sketches. His first exhibits at the Royal Academy were two works, both with the title *Wood Scene: Composition*, which he showed in 1803 and 1804. Only in 1805 did he exhibit the watercolours of *Ross Market Place* and *St Albans*, mentioned earlier, which come closest to his sketching practice. It was not these more elaborate sketches, however, but his 'little studies in blacklead' (black lead, i.e. graphite, was, as we have seen, the traditional medium for sketching outdoors), which attracted the attention of the critic of the *Morning Post*, who wrote:

We are much gratified by a number of elaborate little studies in blacklead by C. Varley; this primary attention to correctness of detail is certainly the only way to become a great painter. 109, 'A Cottage,' and 119,

'Wimbledon', show the advantage that this young artist has already derived from pursuing this method of improvement.[85]

Perhaps partly because Cornelius did not sell as well as others during the first exhibitions of the Water-Colour Society,[86] his titles change increasingly from the names of particular places to poetic ones: for example, *Solitude* (1806) or *Evening*, to which Varley adds a line of poetry or the subtitle *Effect from Nature* (not, as in 1805, *Study from Nature*), thus indicating that they are compositions rather than transcriptions.[87] Part of the programme of the early Water-Colour Society was to put watercolour artists on an equal footing with their counterparts in the Royal Academy who worked in oil. One way to achieve this was by taking up what was then ranked highest in the hierarchy of genres, the historical or poetical depiction. It is clear that Cornelius Varley shared this aspiration, which manifested itself most plainly in the Sketching Society to which he belonged from 1808.[88] Moreover Basil S. Long has discovered a poem by Cornelius Varley among papers relating to the Water-Colour Society which seems to satirise the very thing that he himself pursued at that time. The poem is called *Song to the Generous in Art* and is based on *The Marseillaise*. The last verse ends as follows:

The Copyists like a looking glass
Reflect all Common things with pain
We wondering at them grieve alas!
To see such labours piled in vain
For painting still is Nature's language
If sent directly to our hearts
(Not tiring eyes with little parts)
Exalts the soul and quels the Savage
   Raise up Raise up your Minds
   Spread wide your eyes around
   Take in take in Poetic Stores
   For Nature does abound.[89]

Although these lines seems to incorporate a Reynoldsian understanding of landscape art as capturing the 'essence' of reality beyond its ever-varying appearances, most of the earlier drawings by Varley which he took beyond sketches show exactly the opposite. The sketch of *Devil's Bridge* (plate 89), dated 1803, concentrates on the dramatic interplay of dynamic structures in its centre. The attention is focused on the water falling over huge blocks of rock, overhung with tree branches.

89 Cornelius Varley, *Devil's Bridge*, 1803, graphite and grey wash, 409 × 309, by courtesy of the Trustees of the British Museum, London.

90 Cornelius Varley, *Devil's Bridge*, graphite and water-colour, 459 × 299, sold Colnaghi's, London, 21 February–16 March 1973, photo Dr Michael Pidgley.

To indicate the spots which should display highlights in a finished version, Varley has inserted in handwriting the words 'white spots'. The bridge itself, which would have occupied the centre in a picturesque depiction, is here only hinted at, being relegated to the top left corner.

This drawing is a rare example of a sketch by Varley which was developed into a finished watercolour. The final version (plate 90)[90] retains the dramatic interplay of lines and natural structures in the centre. Although Varley has now added a foreground, this is not a con-ventional stageset-like frame, serving to locate the observer and to focus on one central object; the branches of the overhanging trees merely project into the depiction, without framing the view. The structural interest in the picture focuses on the interplay of rocks, waterfall and tree branches, but this is not a picturesque

staging; the surrounding features are no mere frame-work. They are depicted in their own right as they appeared (note the bridge at the top left corner).

What might now be read as a purely formal exercise in the arrangement of counter-balanced structures is, in fact, an attempt to represent structures immediately perceptible in the given, natural scene. Cornelius Varley departs from the attitude which would see 'the world as a series of painterly motifs'[91] in order to capture the given moment as he observed it; however, his attempts to depict what is out there are only rarely successfully translated back into a pictorial space. There is, too, an inherent difficulty in reading such works; trying to capture specific moments as they present themselves to the perceiving artist, the pictures leave behind the inherited vocabulary of pictorial relationships in favour of a spontaneity which potentially escapes description altogether.

The main bulk of Varley's output shows an artist whose scrutinising gaze attempts to register closely whatever he encounters.[92] But because he is not following any particular aesthetic he seems to have had difficulty in combining the different moments of his detailed observations into one picture. Absorbed in the perception of one fragmentary aspect of the scene in front of him, he appears to be unable to give equal attention to the surrounding appearances. Only occasionally, as in the picture of *Devil's Bridge* and such street scenes as *Ross Market Place*, is Varley more successful. Particularly in subject-matter like the latter, his study of perspective was easier to apply, and, since topographical exactitude was the sole aim, he seems not to have been forced to decide between atmospheric or structural, focused or panoramic depiction.

The Scientific Outlook

Cornelius Varley's clear interest in the precise registration of natural phenomena, despite the contrary tendencies of his professional artistic environment, is related to his scientific interests. His scientific career continued after he had left his uncle's house and formed his main occupation from 1814 onwards, with art relegated to a part-time pursuit. In 1819 he had evidently not yet decided definitely which career would have priority, for he was given one of the first three prizes that the Old Water-Colour Society awarded to its members in order to encourage the production of 'important work'.[93] It is very likely that Varley's contacts with the scientific world were already established through his work with his uncle, but he explicitly mentions, both in his autobiography and in the account of his career given to Jenkins, that he, his brother and Thomas Webster met a group of London scientists on a geological tour while they stayed in north Wales in 1802.[94] Among this group were Mr and Mrs Lowry, listed later among the subscribers to Varley's publication *Shipping, Barges, Fishing Boats, and other Vessels* (1809),[95] and Arthur Aikin, the future secretary of the Society of Arts.[96] Both the engraver Wilson Lowry (1762–1824)

and Arthur Aikin (1773–1854) were members of the British Mineralogical Society, the forerunner of the Geological Society. Both were lapsed radicals, and both had a strong interest in the utilitarian application of scientific investigations and inventions, an interest which was also the prime concern of the Society of Arts with which both came to be associated. The Society was established in 1754 specifically to encourage the industrial application of scientific knowledge by awarding prizes.

Varley also became involved with the Society of Arts (his name appears on many of the engraved illustrations in its *Transactions* between 1804 and 1844) and the City Philosophical Society, where he would have met, among others, the famous chemist and physicist Michael Faraday (1791–1867). At the end of the second decade the members of the City Philosophical Society largely migrated to the Society of Arts.[97] Varley had already become a full member of the Society of Arts earlier, in 1814, after which he spent his time developing microscope technology and improving lenses, although he also worked on methods of preserving oil paintings and watercolours.[98]

His activity as a draughtsman for the Society of Arts kept him in touch with new inventions; his earliest scientific publications, however, were concerned with reporting and analysing observed phenomena. In 1807 and 1809 Varley published two articles in the *Philosophical Magazine* concerned with atmospheric phenomena, which connect closely with his artistic activity in the first decade of the century.[99] From the beginning of the nineteenth century meteorology had received 'increased attention', as Luke Howard (1772–1864) put it in his seminal article 'On the Modification of Clouds' in 1803.[100] In 1801–3 John Dalton (1766–1844) had described the laws of vapour pressure and showed that clouds are formed by the expansion and cooling of ascending damp air, while in 1802 Howard published an attack on Hutton's 'Theory of Rain', in which Hutton had attempted to explain the formation of clouds by subterranean heat (the principle which governed his entire *Theory of the Earth*). Howard, like the fieldwork geologists, criticised Hutton for over-ambition, claiming that it was far too early to formulate a unified theory for such an apparently complex phenomenon.[101] Howard concludes the first part of his second article with an appeal for more thorough collection of empirical data:

The relations of rain, and of periodical showers more especially, with the varying temperatures, density, and electricity of the atmosphere, will probably now obtain a fuller investigation, and with a better prospect of success, than heretofore.[102]

Thunderstorms and spectacular phenomena like the Aurora Borealis had, of course, always attracted attention, but it was only with writers like Howard and Dalton in England and Friedrich Heinrich Alexander, Baron von Humboldt (1769–1859), in Germany that attempts were made to explain them in relation to other atmospheric occurrences.

It seems, however, as if Varley's own interest in meteorology was stimulated directly by the close attention he paid to atmospheric phenomena while sketching outdoors. His autobiography contains an account of two such observations, one of the Aurora Borealis and the other of the occurrence of a sudden thunderstorm. Both were made during his travels in north Wales: the first in 1803 with Havell and Cristall, and the second when he was on his own in 1805. This must have triggered his interest in making a more systematic investigation. He opens the first article as follows:

I believe few will contend that any of the hypotheses which have yet been offered respecting atmospheric phaenomena are perfectly satisfactory. I shall therefore be deemed the less presumptuous in offering the present hints; in the hope that they may prove useful to meteorologists, and assist in forming a more correct theory on this intricate subject than we are yet possessed of. The remarks which I offer are founded on actual observations.[103]

As in geology, the aspiration towards the systematic collection of observations was central to the foundation of meteorology as a science in the early nineteenth century, and Varley's descriptions, which gave close attention to surrounding phenomena like temperature, wind and humidity in the air, fit into this discourse.[104] However, Varley was led by the fact that the phenomena he observed clearly displayed the effects of electricity to a conclusion which was at once correct and false. From his observations and his knowledge of electrical activity, he inferred that 'electricity is the principal suspending cause of clouds'.[105] This contradicts Dalton's explanation in terms of vapour pressure and

was bound to be rejected. But it is not that Varley's observations themselves were wrong; rather, he generalised them too quickly in a fashion which had by that time become suspect. As becomes clear from Thomas Forster's *Researches about Atmospheric Phenomena* (1813), which attempted to summarise the specialist discussion of the first decade of the century, the contemporary approach was to allow different causal explanations for different phenomena.[106] Indeed, even today, meteorology has difficulty in bringing all the different causes of an occurrence into a reliable, integrated system. Thus Varley, although his observations reflect the new approach, falls back into a conception of explanation which looks speculatively for a single principle. To claim electricity (which he clearly understands as an electric fluid)[107] to be the sole agent behind atmospheric phenomena reflects a form of mono-causal thinking which was about to be abandoned in the early nineteenth century with the rise of phenomenalism.

Constable's cloud studies have long been cited as a sign of the new interest emerging at that time in the transient, ever-changing aspects of nature[108] (although, as Louis Hawes has rightly pointed out, cloud studies have a much longer tradition).[109] Cornelius Varley's cloud studies[110] and the accompanying engraving to his article of 1809 predate Constable's work by some years.[111] In his book *John Constable's Clouds*, Kurt Badt linked Constable's interest in clouds to the growing interest in meteorology and, in particular, to Luke Howard. Hawes, on the other hand, denied that meteorology was an important influence. In any case, what determined discussion in early nineteenth-century British meteorology was less the classificatory approach than the attempt to link previously isolated phenomena with one another – classification, after all, was only a by-product of Howard's enterprise, produced by his need for a scientific language to communicate his observations. To depict the links between a variety of phenomena, rather than to individuate and classify them, is also the attitude manifest in Cornelius' artistic work. In his sketches, Varley is often apparently able to concentrate on only a single, detailed observation; yet he complements this with other sketches of different phenomena. In this way, Varley seems to have proceeded in his art practice as if he had been observing different phenomena for scientific purposes. In the scientific discourse of meteorology Varley found the practice of learning from the close observation of nature elevated into a method. But, just as Varley tried to identify a single governing principle in his writings on the atmosphere, so too (apart from the short period around 1805 in which his sketches and finished works came close to one another) his exhibited art increasingly moves towards the reintroduction of eighteenth-century pictorial formulae.

The elevation into an artistic method of the scientific ideal of close observation in the study of natural phenomena is what Cornelius appears to have brought to the circle at his brother's house. Linnell reports that when he was living with John Varley: 'Cornelius was often there and was full of scientific schemes and chemical experiments as he has been ever since'.[112] John Varley's teaching at that stage was still fairly loose: Linnell states in his autobiography that he 'might be said to be under [Mulready's] influence far more than [John] Varley's';[113] Hunt's account of open-air sketching sessions with Linnell and Mulready does not mention John.[114] Nor did Varley claim exclusive control of his students. Mulready had joined the Royal Academy Schools in 1800 and he must obviously have encouraged Varley's other students to enrol as well, for, first Linnell, then Cornelius, and, finally, Hunt registered with the Academy in 1805, 1807 and 1808 respectively.[115] Here they encountered the traditional artistic education, confined to drawing and the copying of the human figure, first from antique casts and later from a living model. Certainly, all of them must have come into contact with Dr Monro through John Varley and were able to copy from his landscape watercolour collection. So it is clear that Varley's teaching practice was above all an open system, bringing his students under a variety of different influences, and there does not seem to have been any pressure for the group to develop a common methodological or doctrinal identity. Linnell refers to it as a society, which was 'interesting and full of instruction from its variety',[116] and Hunt relates that, in fact, he never received any systematic education at all.[117]

This open structure explains why it would have been possible for Cornelius to make a strong impact on his brother's pupils. John's most naturalistic watercolours seem to have been made in conjunction with his brother[118] and so it appears more than likely that it was Cornelius and the example of his career which gave John the belief that the first step in the training of an artist was to work informally from nature. This also explains why there are so few informal coloured outdoor sketches among John Varley's own work. As Cornelius' oeuvre makes clear, the practice of outdoor sketching was not a conscious attempt to eliminate the distinction between open-air works and exhibition pieces. We have seen that it was only briefly, in 1805, that Cornelius Varley's extensive sketching carried over into his exhibition work. By and large sketching seems to have been regarded as merely a pedagogical starting-point, and it is unlikely that John Varley would have considered it to be a necessary study for himself.

Only in 1811, when Linnell started his journal, is there written evidence which testifies to the existence of close contacts between Linnell and Cornelius Varley.[119] Throughout 1811 they met frequently, sometimes every other day, and it has long been known that it was Cornelius who introduced Linnell to the Baptist Church, although he did not join himself.[120] Varley himself, in fact, later joined briefly the Sandemanian Sect (from 1844 to 1847) to which, famously, Faraday belonged.[121] Both Linnell's move away from 'formal compositions and picturesque detail towards less contrived depictions of large stretches of open countryside',[122] which took place around 1811, and his abandonment of open-air sketching in oil for watercolour have been linked to his contacts with Cornelius Varley.[123] However Linnell's earlier sketches already show Cornelius' influence. Linnell first mentions Cornelius Varley on 15 May 1811, his journal entry for that day stating that he borrowed from 'Mr. Varley a scetch [sic] from Nature by me – in Black Chalk'.[124] This demonstrates that Cornelius had taken an interest in these earlier sketches. Linnell prepared a series of such sketches in the first decade of the century. Like his oil sketches, they mostly depict an almost arbitrary segment of nature, typically showing not a scene but an everyday activity. For example, the drawings inscribed 'Russell Square 1806 – J. Linnell' represent the building work then taking place in Russell Square.[125] Another pencil drawing on blue paper, entitled *Fields where Gower Street now Stands, Bedford Square* of 1808 (plate 91), shows a single workman, cows and a cart in front of an irregular, tall fence on rough ground. Their relationship is not elaborated in the drawing and the purpose of their being there thus remains obscure. These early drawings by Linnell have something of the character of snapshots: the workmen shown are not engaged in any significant action but form part of the arbitrary registration of phenomenal structure. These sketches display

91   John Linnell, *Fields where Gower Street now Stands, Bedford Square*, 1808, graphite and white chalk on blue paper, 162 × 225, by courtesy of the Trustees of the British Museum, London.

the same attitude as Cornelius Varley had developed in the early years of the nineteenth century: a vision which does not search for the spectacular or picturesque but endeavours to register everyday appearances as conscientiously and meticulously as possible.[126]

However, though it seems to have been Cornelius Varley who transmitted this vision to the artists associated with his brother, it was Linnell who first managed to translate it into a pictorial language. I have argued that, as a result of his attitude towards nature, Cornelius Varley only infrequently succeeded in transforming his transcriptions of natural appearances into a pictorial composition. Varley's pictures are directed towards the representation of the interplay of natural phenomena, such as earth formations, sky, trees and water, within a

given scene, rather than the identification of specifically pictorial or aesthetic phenomena. Linnell, on the other hand, seems to have organised his observing gaze from a pictorial point of view and is more successful in the arrangement of the pictorial space as a whole. For example, the drawing *Bayswater* (plate 92) of 1811 displays a rough textured road in the foreground which leads across a rather empty and unspectacular stretch of landscape.[127] A haystack, devoid of picturesque texture, marks the middle ground to the right. A fence follows the line of the road. Only in the interaction of their different structures, forms and colours, as traced by the pencil and brush, do these features form an interesting ensemble.

Linnell was later able to translate this compositional

92   John Linnell, *Bayswater*, 1811, black chalk and watercolour, heightened with white on blue-grey paper, 221 × 534, private collection, reproduced with the kind permission of the owners.

achievement into a finished oil painting, *Kensington Gravel Pits* (plate 93). In this painting, the dominant structural feature is the earth, which several workers are shown digging. Its irregular texture and surface are highlighted by realistic lighting. The rich red-brown of the foreground is in contrast with the overgrown mound at the right-hand side of the background. Details of the tools in use are clearly delineated and the workmen themselves can be seen engaged in their characteristic activities. In this way the picture with its decentralised composition and everyday subject-matter succeeds in translating into a finished oil painting the instantaneous character of Linnell's sketches. The intricate play of colour texture is emphasised, however, and the workers' movements somewhat idealised. They are given a classicising anatomical depiction, being shown in an attitude which is, as Crouan has observed, repeated three times within the picture.[128]

Although Cornelius Varley had attempted six years previously to turn his sketches into finished work, this clearly posed a problem for him. On the one hand, the observing subject must be eliminated as far as possible, in order to make way for the objective transcription of what is observed at any particular moment; on the other hand, one suspects that it was the very clarity of Varley's observation, purged of any organising subjectivity, which inhibited the production of a successful pictorial conception. After 1805, however, a development took place in Varley's activity through which a separation was introduced between creative artistic subjectivity and the registration of natural phenomena.

The Proto-Photographic Gaze

Cornelius Varley's phenomenalism was, I have argued, influenced by his scientific activities. This approach, on the other hand, and Varley's obvious inability to translate it into finished drawings, seem in turn to have given direction to his scientific activity – a good example of how an aesthetic need can determine the development of technology, rather than solely vice versa, as histories of art and technology often suppose.

In 1809 Cornelius Varley developed his Graphic Telescope, a drawing instrument (plate 94).[129] It was a descendant of the *camera obscura*, the oldest of the more elaborate drawing aids. The most common *camera obscura*, as illustrated here (plate 95, fig. right), consists of a box with an aperture on one end where a sliding convex lens is placed, allowing for focusing. The rays which pass through the lens are than reflected at the other end of the box by a mirror, set at an angle of 45 degrees, onto a screen on top where it can be traced (because of the mirror reflection the image is re-

93   John Linnell, *Kensington Gravel Pits*, exh. 1813, oil on canvas, 700 × 1050, Tate Gallery, London.

inverted on the horizontal axis, but still remains reversed right to left). This screen is shielded from light on three sides so that the image can become adequately visible in light levels lower than those around the object, a fact which gave the *camera obscura* its name – 'dark chamber'. For artistic purposes a type of *camera obscura* which, when collapsed and packed, resembled a book, was more suitable (plate 95, fig. left). While in the reflex *camera obscura* the artist traced a relatively small image on transparent paper, the pyramidal *camera obscura* reflected the image straight onto a larger piece of paper at the bottom, where it could be traced, albeit with the artist's hands moving in the dark. Joshua Reynolds owned a *camera obscura* of this type, but there is no evidence that he used it except for amusement.[130] In fact, there is very little documentation to identify which eighteenth-century artists used the *camera obscura*, but it was certainly very popular. It is known that Paul

Sandby's brother Thomas used it, following Canaletto's example, and also that William Daniell employed it on his tour in India with his uncle between 1784 and 1794.[131] Thus Daniell might very well have also used the device for some of his numerous drawings for the *Voyage round Great Britain*.

Varley's Graphic Telescope was based more directly on William Hyde Wollaston's *camera lucida*, patented in 1806.[132] This instrument had an advantage over the *camera obscura* in that it allowed the viewer to observe scenery, and, at the same time, to draw an image of it. The light from the object is reflected twice within a prism with two reflecting surfaces, and the artist observes the reflection through one half of the eye and the drawing paper with the other half. The Graphic Telescope combined this technology with the greater portability of a *camera obscura*, making it suitable for landscape drawings. Two mirrors, a vertical one in front

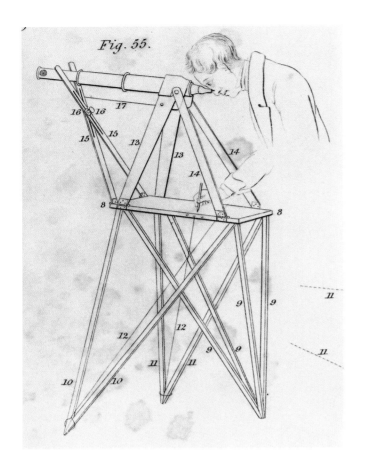

of the Telescope and a horizontal one at the eyepiece, are each set at a 45 degree angle to the axis of the instrument in order to correct the image left-to-right and reverse it. To match the observed image in the eyepiece mirror to the distance of the paper, the eyepiece can be moved in and out and the size of the drawing altered by having the paper closer to or further from the eyepiece.[133] Considerable training, however, is required to divide attention between the refracted image and the pencil tracing, and, as with the *camera obscura*, substantial skill is still needed to transform such an image into an effective painting. But the Graphic Telescope was not just a more convenient device for landscape artists than its predecessors. Its much improved lens system reflected Varley's own interest in the representation of landscape. In his *Treatise on Optical Drawing Instruments* Varley places the emphasis on the

94 (left)   Cornelius Varley, *The Graphic Telescope*, 1845, engraving (H. Adlard) from C. Varley *A Treatise on Optical Drawing Instruments* (1845), private collection, photo by the author.

95 (below)   J. Farey, *Camera Obscura*, 1817, engraving (Lowry), collection Dr Michael Pidgley, photo by the author.

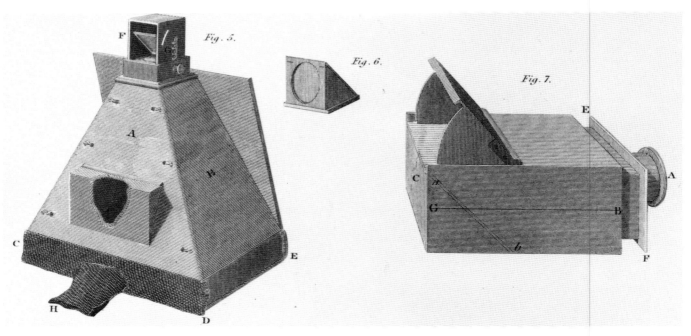

development of lenses to rectify the lack of lateral definition of older drawing aids and the achievement of an achromatic representation.[134] These problems arose from the failure of the lenses available at that time to provide a brightly illuminated and properly focused image across the whole field. Achromatic lenses corrected chromatic aberrations (the inability to bring light rays of different wavelengths into focus at the same point) and thus made the development of larger (and hence brighter) lenses possible. Such developments were not new when Varley invented the Graphic Telescope, and, theoretically, could also have been used in a *camera obscura*. According to Varley, however, they had simply not been applied. It seems that from within a picturesque aesthetic, with its concentration on a single central feature given in monochrome tints, these imperfections did not matter.

What is most strikingly new, however, in Varley's drawing aid is its combination of these features with a telescopic effect. The Graphic Telescope came with a number of additional eyepieces which allowed for the alteration of the original low-power magnification.[135] Again, telescopes of much higher magnification had existed throughout the eighteenth century, but no attempt was made to use them as part of a drawing device. The telescopic perspective not only allows the production of correctly aligned, enlarged (or, if necessary, reduced) images, it also permits the depiction of objects at a greater distance, drawing together background, middle ground and foreground. This is the very effect which Varley had attempted to achieve in his earlier sketches. But, without a technical aid, he was able to concentrate on only one phenomenon in detail at a time.

From 1808 one finds more and more drawings which indicate that he was experimenting with the Graphic Telescope.[136] A faintly coloured sketch, *View from Ferry Bridge Yorkshire* (plate 96), shows the tightly delineated and highly individuated buildings of a village in a crisp light in a wide green setting, next to which a river runs. The bridge in the foreground with a rider on it is sketched in outline. Since the drawing is not fully finished, and yet coloured in various places, it is likely that it is an example of the advantage which the Graphic Telescope offered: the possibility of applying the local colours immediately while tracing through the instrument. Varley patented the Telescope in 1811 and from then on used the initials P.G.T. (Patented Graphic

Telescope) to indicate its use for a drawing, as was the case in the *View from Ferry Bridge*.[137] But, according to his autobiography, manufacturers were not equipped to produce the lenses required, so it did not achieve widespread use. Only forty years later did Varley receive public recognition for his invention, in the form of a prize medal from the jury of the Great Exhibition.[138]

The pamphlet on Cornelius Varley, published anonymously in 1874, records the names of the places Varley drew with his Telescope from 1809 onwards.[139] These were clearly works done on commission from the owners of the properties depicted, a task of topographical recording for which Varley's drawing aid was eminently suitable. The subjects were mainly the residences of the gentry, such as Sir George Pigott's Patshul, Staffordshire (plate 97), which is dated 26 August 1820. It displays the rather flat appearance and the somewhat edgy but unbroken outline which is peculiar to the Graphic Telescope depictions. Other commissions included Newstead Abbey, then the property of Colonel Wildeman. But there are also places such as the Tiverton Lace Factory (owned by Varley's friend and employer John Heathcote), Keyhaven, Isle of Wight, and the Valley of the Exe. From these subjects it becomes clear that a large proportion of Varley's work with topographical titles, exhibited after 1809 at the Royal Academy or the Water-Colour Society, was either executed with the Graphic Telescope or based on drawings done with it.

The exhibition titles of Varley's post-1809 pictures show that the split in his work which was apparent from 1805, the unbridged gap between composed works bearing poetic titles and landscapes drawn with the telescope, was reinforced through the invention of the Graphic Telescope. But, unfortunately, it is only rarely possible to identify exhibited works from those years with pictures now known. One such case is the water-colour *Ruins of Kerry Castle* (plate 98) which is probably Varley's exhibited work of either 1830 or 1842 in the Royal Academy.[140] It bears the inscription 'Painted in 1830 from a sketch made on the spot in 1808' and completely departs from Varley's earlier drawings. It is executed in bodycolours and shows cows and water in the foreground with sparkling white highlights, while the dark ruins recede into the glowing orange and purple colours of a setting sun. In contrast to his earlier works, this drawing marks an attempt to evoke atmosphere and mood, rather than to depict the structural

96 (above) Cornelius Varley, *View from Ferry Bridge Yorkshire*, graphite and watercolour, 356 × 521, by courtesy of the Trustees of the British Museum, London.

97 (left) Cornelius Varley, *Patshul Staffordshire*, 1820, graphite, 346 × 544, by courtesy of the Trustees of the British Museum, London.

98 Cornelius Varley, *Ruins of Kerry Castle*, exh. 1830 or 1842?, watercolour and bodycolour, 371 × 591, by courtesy of the Board of Trustees of the Victoria and Albert Museum, London.

interplay of a given scene. It testifies to Varley's shift towards works of the imagination, indicated in other cases by the use of poetic titles. As seen at the end of the last chapter, this same shift was apparent on a wider scale in the work of other artists. Simultaneously, however, Varley was trying to achieve self-distancing scientific objectivity in the pictures made with the help of the Graphic Telescope.[141]

Phenomenalism and the Retreat from Social Conflict

When one looks through the surviving early work of the members of the Varley circle, one is struck by the recurrence of one subject treated by all of them. Both Varleys, as well as Mulready, Hunt and Linnell, repeatedly depicted cottages and street scenes – a subject which would traditionally fall within the category of the picturesque. But when they depicted such scenes in the first years of the nineteenth century they did so in a way which was in keeping with Monro's encouragement to depict 'insignificant' subject-matter: with their realistic lighting and meticulousness in the representation of detail these pictures abandon topographical or picturesque styles. The graphite and grey wash sketch by Cornelius Varley *View of a Farmyard* (plate 99) is an example of this. Here Varley has chosen a rather unspectacular viewpoint into the yard of a cottage. No framing scenery encloses the view; only a section of the courtyard is shown and its dimensions are not clearly to be grasped from the drawing. This is partly due to the

99 Cornelius Varley, *View of a Farmyard*, graphite and grey wash, 205 × 269, Yale Center for British Art, Paul Mellon Collection, New Haven.

100 After John Crome, *Blacksmith's Shop near Hingham, Norfolk*, c.1808, oil on canvas, 1540 × 1219, Philadelphia Museum of Art, John McFadden Collection.

fact that the left-hand side of the sketch remains unfinished. Nevertheless, enough is visible to make it clear that parts of the buildings belonging to the farm continue beyond the picture space. The subject-matter is a ramshackle shed. But its timber and brick construction, and the tools in the foreground, are too realistically delineated to evoke the ideal of picturesque poverty. As an example of the latter one may take the oil painting *Blacksmith's Shop near Hingham, Norfolk* (plate 100) of c.1808 after an etching by John Crome (1768–1821). In this painting the main scene also shows a building in a ramshackle state, but it is depicted with a broader, less tight brushstroke, so that it melts into its surroundings. A glowing hypernatural light envelops this scene and suggests that even states of poverty are part of and can be safely contained within a harmonious order.[142]

A yet more striking contrast to such paintings is Linnell's fragmentary oil sketch *Study of Buildings* (plate 101) of 1806. Here only the gable ends of the houses are depicted. The dilapidated state of the house in the middle is delineated in such meticulous detail that it appears fragile and almost insubstantial. The same sense of realism is found in a finished oil painting in Mulready's *Cottages and Figures* (plate 102) of 1806–7. This picture is still for the most part in keeping with the formulae of the picturesque. The main object is located in a spotlight in the centre, while the surrounding water and St Albans tower in the background are blurred in

the overall chiaroscuro. The brick, fractured plaster and tile of the cottage are so clearly depicted, and its walls appear so thin, that it seems to be on the verge of falling apart. The comment has been made that these paintings are cast in 'a morbidly Romantic mood'[143] or, more precisely, that they are in a state of suspense between the realistic depiction of the construction work and the 'impossibility of "reading" the remainder'.[144] Compared with the oil painting after John Crome, it seems to be just this realism, drawn from the precise observations made in sketches inserted into a more traditional formula, which gives Mulready's cottage scenes their vague and even disquieting character.[145]

It was realised at the time that such depictions of cottages departed from tradition. Between 1808 and 1815 the artist Francis Stevens (1781–1823) published a series of etchings of *Views of Cottages and Farm-Houses in*

101   John Linnell, *Study of Buildings*, 1806, oil on board, 165 × 254, Tate Gallery, London.

England and Wales from drawings by the two Varleys, Munn (his own teacher), Prout, Wilson, Hill, Pyne, Stevens himself and others.[146] Most of the artists were friends from the Sketching Society, which Stevens re-formed in 1808, or members of the Water-Colour Society of which he had been an Associate from the beginning and of which he became a full member in 1809.[147] The publication advocated the new practice of colouring on the spot as an essential requirement in the depiction of landscapes and argues that it was 'those artists who [made] studies of colour upon the spot' that elevated watercolour painting to a new height.[148]

Stevens' introduction, however, gives more specific reasons for the publication: it was intended to 'yield instruction to the amateur of painting, and amusement to those who delight in contemplating the rural beauties of our isle'. Stevens recommended the contemplation of cottage scenes because, although they might have no architectural beauty, they evoke an atmosphere of comfort. This comfort, he says, arises out of the fact that they are usually inhabited 'by the proprietor of a small farm, whose industrious and frugal family live well on the produce of their own little domain'.[149]

This dearly held myth about rural society was, in fact becoming less and less true.[150] Although not as drastically affected by agricultural change as some other groups, the comfortable existence of such small yeomen was far from being a reassuring reality. The extent of the social consequences of enclosure by statute was publicly recognised. After considerable complaints about the injustices caused by it the House of Commons had, at the height of parliamentary enclosure in the 1770s, set out some regulations for protection. Although its main concern was the rights of the proprietors, as Langford has pointed out, some '(generally ineffectual) attempts were made to protect small yeomen, whose want of capital made it difficult for them either to fight enclosure before the event or benefit by it afterwards'.[151] Cottage scenes like those advocated by Stevens were, however, still the predominant subject in the depiction of rural landscape. They continued to present the rural community as if it were made up of small domestic economic entities, at a time when many of its members had in fact been reduced to dependent wage-earners, employed on a casual basis.[152] Stevens talks about the small rural habitations as if they still existed as secure units among the interrelated parts of the rural economy: 'Humble as the class of subjects which form this work may appear, yet the general study of landscape embraces domestic architecture among the various ramifications of rural economy'.[153]

Four of the engravings taken from drawings by Cornelius Varley are not noticeably out of keeping with the style of the other depictions, partly perhaps because all of them were etched by Stevens and thus have a character which their originals might not display.[154] These etchings, like most of the others, give a clear depiction of picturesque detail, as explained by Stevens:

> The cottage which has been selected for this county, is congenial to the artist's taste: every part is warped by age; and the surfaces of the walls are of various texture, from the dilapidation of time [. . .] offering sufficient material for a graphic imitation.[155]

But one picture by Varley, *Caenarvonshire Conway*, shows features in a more realistic light than the rest. Here the overall chiaroscuro is less marked and therefore its features are less integrated into an aesthetically satisfying interplay of texture and structure. In the accompanying text Stevens argues that the depiction of 'the fewest parts and the rudest lines' is nevertheless legitimate: 'the reflex shadow on the side of the projecting front prevents the abruptness which such a form would produce were the shadows less harmoniously managed'.[156] In other words, Stevens is conceding that Varley has depicted 'unpicturesque' features but argues that the drawing is acceptable because they are shown in a realistic light and shadow distribution. Because the depiction is represented as the registration of a fleeting moment, rather than a documentary comment on the state of the rural society or an evocation of the picturesque ideal, it avoids taking up a position in relation to a subject which had become politically loaded.

The phenomenalism of the Varley circle was not restricted to cottage scenes. The streets of London were a repeated subject in all of their work. The area around Millbank and Westminster was the location for most of John Varley's drawings which are marked as 'sketch' or 'study from nature'. It was here, too, that Linnell, as he recalls in his autobiography, went with Mulready and Hunt for their outdoor sketching practice. This area was at the front of London's transformation from a large town to a modern 'urban environment' with its characteristic problems. City merchants were starting to live away from their commercial operations in Westminster, 'leaving behind them a deteriorating housing stock and a rash of cheap, speculative infill building. Dilapidated and overcrowded tenements and lodgings became warrens of disease'.[157] At the beginning of the nineteenth century, Millbank was a fashionable resort. The landscape was rural. As Edward Walford described it at the turn of the century, 'the bank of the river was edged with pollard oaks, presenting a view almost as rural as that which we now see at Fullham or Putney'.[158] The area had been the subject of picturesque and topographical depictions which concentrated (as does John Varley's work, for the most part) on views along the river.[159] However, there had also been depictions of the Tothill Field Alms and Pest Houses.[160] Such buildings (also shown in one of John Varley's Millbank watercolours probably dating from 1816–17)[161] might be thought to be a conspicuous sign of the presence of poverty in an otherwise fashionable recreational area. They were, however, if we are to follow Redgrave's description, seen as emblems of picturesqueness, part of the image of a rural outpost in the heart of the city:

> a narrow causeway ran through the district to what was then truly Tothill fields, with here and there a few straggling cottages, such as 'The Pest House'. In these fields old Dame Warner kept her geese and sucking-pigs, and here we children used to go with our nurse on our high-days and holidays.[162]

But there are drawings among the Varleys' street scenes, as with their cottage views, which go beyond the mere depiction of delightful picturesque scenery. Cornelius Varley's *Holland Street, Blackfriars Bridge* (plate 103) shows a building with an open wall in a state of dilapidation on the right-hand side. The left part of the sketch contains a façade in reasonable condition with a woman looking out of a window adorned by flowers on the second floor. The drawing thus captures something

102 William Mulready, *Cottage and Figures*, 1806–7, oil on paper laid on board, 397 × 333, Tate Gallery, London.

103 Cornelius Varley, *Holland Street, Blackfriars Bridge*, graphite and watercolour, 226 × 309, by courtesy of the Trustees of the British Museum, London.

of the character of an area in transition from a flourishing residential quarter to a state of delapidation, neglect and speculation. A wonderfully sketchy and colourful watercolour with a rough and wet-washed appearance of a much later date (1830) by John Varley carries the title *Pulling down Old Houses in Crooked Lane for Approach to London* (plate 105). Here the second house on the left-hand side of the street appears as a ruin, not in its picturesque ramshackle state, but as a bare fragment surrounded by scaffolding and in the process of being pulled down. In an area where merchants increasingly lived away from their work, commuter access was essential. These drawings show that the transformation of the city of London from an area where work and life were combined to a speculative space of office building set alongside neglected tenements did not go completely unnoticed by those artists who worked there, although other Millbank drawings of John Varley's might lead one to think so. In these, of which *The Thames near the Penitentiary* (plate 104) of 1816 is an example, Varley is following his usual strategy: although generalising in his treatment, he applies formal compositional precepts to give structural coherence.

But none of the more phenomenalist depictions of cottage and street scenes takes up a clear position with regard to their subject-matter. The street scenes by the Varleys testify to the change of London, but stay well clear of a comment to what they witness. There are no suggestions of a critique of the rash of cheap speculative building projects, such as were the subject of a caricature by George Cruikshank (1792–1878) in his *London Going out of Town – or – The March of Bricks & Mortar* of 1829.[163] It was precisely the phenomenalist attitude taken up by the Varley circle which allowed them to depict cottage and urban street scenes at a time when both were focuses of social conflict rather than social harmony. In order to understand why the artists associated with the Varleys should have developed the strategy of phenomenalism as a retreat from social conflict, we need to map out more fully the social circles and institutions they encountered and moved in during the first decade of the nineteenth century.

At the beginning of their careers, the two Varleys, through Monro, came under the patronage of the Earl of Essex and Edward Lascelles, two of the most substantial benefactors of the arts at the beginning of the nineteenth century. It seems that Lascelles (and, in all likelihood, his close friend the Earl of Essex, too) were committed to a reinvigoration of paternalism during the social crises of the 1790s.[164] Instead of drawing class boundaries more sharply, they, like Uvedale Price, emphasised the gentry's responsibility for the care of the poor. It was said of Lascelles that:

> the whole parish regarded him as their father and their friend; and Edward carried on a tradition of

104 John Varley, *The Thames near the Penitentiary, Millbank, London*, 1816, graphite and watercolour, 292 × 408, Yale Center for British Art, Paul Mellon Collection, New Haven.

105   John Varley, *Pulling down Old Houses in Crooked Lane for Approach to London*, 1830, graphite and watercolour, 275 × 290, by courtesy of the Trustees of the British Museum, London.

enlightened management by providing good accom-modation for his workforce, even going so far as to rebuild the village for them.[165]

Essex and Lascelles belonged to that stratum of genteel society which saw in the application of scientific knowledge the means to alleviate the misery of the poor and so to meet the establishment's fear of a violent alteration in the social structure. These interests were also behind the foundation of such institutions as the Society for Bettering the Conditions of the Poor and the Board of Agriculture, two of the forerunners of the Royal Institution.[166] At its very beginning, one of the Royal Institution's major tasks was to instruct the general public (including the poor) in science. In so far as science conveyed a sense of the unchanging order of nature, it was held to be suitable for promoting social tranquillity.[167] Yet after the turn of the century such paternalist economic and philanthropic schemes be-came problematic. The war with France had instilled a fear of the self-assertive worker. One of the proprietors of the Royal Institution, the religio-moral reformer and philanthropist, William Wilberforce (1759–1833), fa-mous for his anti-slavery campaigns, for example, spon-sored the Combination Acts, which made workers' organisations illegal.[168]

Cornelius and John Varley encountered this new fear of the labouring classes directly when they embarked on their first tour to Wales with Thomas Webster. Webster had been commissioned to build a lecture hall for the Royal Institution which he hoped would bring scien-tific education to a broader public. But in 1802 the Managers of the Royal Institution cancelled the plan and Webster reports that: 'I was asked rudely what I meant by instructing the lower classes in science [. . .; this] was thought to have a political tendency'.[169] Im-mediately after he had left his employment at the Royal Institution, Webster left for north Wales with the Varleys.[170] Working people do not feature in Mulready's or John Varley's depictions, but they do occur in Linnell's, Hunt's and Cornelius Varley's work in an unusually conspicuous way – one, however, which was to be influential for the depiction of the labourers in the second decade of the nineteenth century.[171] The workers are not represented as ostenta-tiously happily pursuing their allotted task, continuing an image of a plentiful and peaceful, stable and paternal-istic society.[172] Nor are they 'tokens of human pres-ence'.[173] In John Linnell's *Kensington Gravel Pits* (plate 93), discussed earlier, the workmen are clearly depicted in the pursuit of their particular tasks. Although they are wearing clean white shirts and their postures are some-what idealised, they do not represent a contented, georgic ideal; they are not agricultural workers but part of a London workforce which would not enjoy the security of a traditional, paternalistic rural society. They do not completely dissolve into their environment, but nor are they the primary focus of attention, for the texture and colour of the earth on which they are working is an equally important element in the subject-matter. The realistic distribution of light and shadow shows them in their everyday labour at a time which has been, apparently, chosen at random. What makes this picture so unusual is that the work on which the labourers are engaged is not made part of a wider narrative context.

Two sawyers depicted by Cornelius Varley are simi-larly unindividuated, although their activity is specific (plate 106): judging by its subject-matter, this is prob-ably the watercolour with the title *Sawyers Clearing Timber from its Knots*, exhibited at the Water-Colour Society in 1806. The two workers are shown sawing at a piece of timber in the foreground to the left. A rough path leads into the wood in the background, where there are more buildings and other figures. Like the realistic depiction of cottages and street scenes, these images of labour seem consciously to steer clear of

106   Cornelius Varley, *Sawyers Clearing Timber from its Knots*, exh. 1806?, 304 × 406, formerly V. Rienaecker Collection, London.

107   Cornelius Varley, *River Wye*, 1803, graphite, 233 × 359, by courtesy of the Trustees of the British Museum, London.

ideological implications. Linnell's black chalk sketches of workmen in Russell Square, mentioned earlier, depict the workers unheroically next to their tools and working material. The figures are neither unemphasised nor less detailed than the surrounding environment. In his drawing entitled *River Wye* (plate 107), dated 12 July 1803, Cornelius Varley typically attempts to capture as many structural appearances as possible in the middle ground while the foreground remains empty. It carries a note in which Varley reminds himself of another aspect of the scene: 'a woman crossed here & back in a washing Tab [sic] with an iron fire shovel for a paddle which twirled her to the right & then to the left'.[174] The fact that the woman – an obvious candidate for picturesque staffage, it would seem – does not appear in the drawing itself makes clear that, for Varley, the accurate delineation of the observed scene took priority over everything else.

The Varleys and their circle encountered some of the social conflict that surrounded their subject-matter through personal associations. Through Essex and Lascelles, the Varley brothers would have been aware of the threats to a stable rural society. Through their friendship with Thomas Webster, they would have encountered the fear of the labouring classes in the aftermath of the French Revolution. Because of Cornelius Varley's involvement, they would have also experienced the widespread caution in scientific institutions, such as the Royal Institution and the Society of Arts, in the first decade of the nineteenth century, against adopting explicitly an ideology associated with a single interest group. The concern with nature or society in its individual appearances enabled them (as was also the case for the founders of scientific geology) to avoid committing themselves to any general doctrine or theory which might have carried political implications. But at the same time it was a position which allowed for a certain flexibility, even eclecticism of approach. So,

143

for instance, the fieldwork geologists accepted without inconsistency vulcanist explanations for one locale and completely different causes for another. Similarly, it was possible for Cornelius Varley to produce a painting of a wood scene entirely in the Dutch picturesque tradition, such as *Stacking Hay* (plate 108; perhaps one of his earliest exhibition pieces),[175] now in the Baroda Museum, Gujarat, while, at the same time, trying to produce phenomenalist depictions of landscape.

One project which was clearly connected to a specific social interest was Cornelius Varley's series of etchings and lithographs entitled *Shipping, Barges, Fishing Boats, and other Vessels, Commonly Met with on the British Coasts, Rivers and Canals*, published in 1809.[176] Drawings by Linnell,[177] Hunt[178] and John Varley[179] show that the depiction of boats was a shared interest among the group, not purely undertaken to gather picturesque staffage material, but from a desire to register visually and document the industrial activities of river navigation. In the introduction to his publication Cornelius Varley emphasises the 'fidelity with which

108 Cornelius Varley, *Stacking Hay*, oil on canvas, 780 × 725, Baroda Museum, Gujarat, India. Courtesy of the Department of Museums, Museum & Picture Gallery, Baroda.

the accompaniments will be adapted to the principal objects in each plate' and he recommends it to the public 'as a work of useful reference, even to others besides the professional and amateur Artist'. Here phenomenalism is clearly – and consciously – linked to the massive investments being undertaken in the early nineteenth century in river and canal transportation, both by industrialists and improving aristocrats like Francis Egerton, 3rd Duke of Bridgewater, and Sir George O'Brien, 3rd Earl of Egremont.[180]

While the *Shipping* publication is linked to the interests of industrialists and improving aristocrats, there is evidence that the Varley circle also moved in radical circles. Mulready, whose cottage scenes of the first decade are more in conformity with established picturesque formulae than Cornelius Varley's or Linnell's, was at that time closely associated with the radical rationalist William Godwin and must have been familiar with his criticisms of the paternalistic conception of society which such picturesque formulae perpetuated. Godwin himself, at that time, like many political radicals, had become discouraged with political activity and had withdrawn into his educational projects. Nevertheless, his house was still a forum for more active radicals, such as Hazlitt and Burdett. However, Godwin's diary for the early years of the nineteenth century shows that he socialised with establishment figures from the Royal Academy, people with such diverse political attitudes as Fuseli, Opie and Shee, Beaumont and Lawrence.[181] Mulready brought 'Varley' (quite certainly John)[182] to Godwin's, ten days after being recorded in the diary for the first time. Sir George Beaumont and Northcote are mentioned on the same occasion (15 March 1805). Linnell's name occurs for the first time on 24 January 1808, although it is likely that he had come to know Godwin earlier through his close friend Mulready. From the late 1810s onwards Linnell and John Varley were also close friends of another radical, William Blake (1757–1827),[183] and yet there is no indication that they shared his political opinions. By this time all the artists in the group had abandoned their pictorial phenomenalism. In any case, phenomenalism was far less a conscious programme for them than it had been for the fieldwork geologists or the philosophers of the Scottish Common Sense School. It was never a fully articulated programme and its most clear expression came practically, in the sketches made outdoors.

★   ★   ★

The End of Phenomenalism

Cornelius Varley seems to embody in a single person a split which was encountered at the end of the last chapter: the gap between what is considered to be the realm of objectivity in science and the more individualistic responses of the artist. His scientific activity was directed mainly towards the development of microscope technology. To devise equipment which makes visible what would otherwise go beyond the human visual capacity places a (supposedly) objectifying medium between observer and observed; in this way it is an attempt to reduce the subjective factors in an experiment to a minimum. Subjectivity, which had no place in Varley's scientific practice, became a strong motive factor in his art, which was itself relegated to

what he described at the end of his autobiography as 'a useful digression'.

Varley's brother John, on the other hand, was an adherent throughout his life of a form of astrology which believed in the visible and palpable effects of the zodiac on human beings.[184] In 1828 he published *A Treatise on Zodiacal Physiognomy*, in which he explained and illustrated the physiognomical typology of the different star signs.[185] Varley justified his belief in astrology in apparently empiricist terms; it was, he claimed, based on nothing more than 'experience and observation'.[186] But, in fact, John Varley's astrology was scientific only in an eighteenth-century sense, in which the explanatory framework extends to principles beyond the realm of secondary causes.

All the other artists moved to a mode of depiction in

109   John Linnell, *River Kennet, near Newbury*, 1815, oil on canvas on wood, 451 × 652, by permission of the Syndics of the Fitzwilliam Museum, Cambridge.

which the subject-matter became the mirror for subjective reflections, similar to the developments discussed in the last chapter. Mulready abandoned landscape painting almost completely after 1813, devoting himself to highly wrought genre paintings endowed with moral, lyrical and often nostalgic qualities. Linnell, as I have shown, carried the spirit of phenomenalism furthest in the exhibited oil painting of *Kensington Gravel Pit* (plate 93). However, he painted another landscape in oil in 1815, *River Kennet, near Newbury* (plate 109), which, although retaining the decentralisation characteristic of the earlier work, clearly departs from phenomenalism in favour of a more emotionally poignant scene. The groups of figures are related to one another in order to create a narrative (a man is fishing in the foreground while, behind him, a dog prepares to steal his lunch) and the light has taken on a glow which elevates the atmosphere beyond the everyday scenes of Linnell's early pictures. In fact, in his journal for 1811, Linnell appears as someone in search of an anchoring framework, not only for his life, but also for his approach to landscape. He borrowed a copy of William Paley's *Evidences of Christianity* (1794) from Cornelius Varley and it was Varley who introduced him to the Baptist Church,[187] which, as Linnell states, gave him 'some hopes and comfort'.[188] It seems to have been the endowment of nature with meaning and the possibility of its unmediated revelation to the individual which Linnell was looking for when reading Paley, so it is not surprising that he was attracted to the Dissenters, with their emphasis on individual faith, and that he converted eventually to the Baptist Church. About two years after his religious conversion Linnell first consciously experienced landscape as an expression of religious faith, in keeping with his new belief. He recalled in his autobiography that during his trip to north Wales in 1813 he experienced landscape as a kind of biblical renewal:

> so thoroughly did some of the valleys near Snowdon carry me away from all former associations with modern Art that I could almost fancy myself living in the times of Jacob and Esau and might expect to meet their flocks.[189]

It is in the sketches made during this trip that one first notices the hyperrealistic sharpness and clarity which give his landscape paintings from then on a visionary quality, endowing them with a meaning beyond the actuality of the landscape's appearance. We can see here the beginning of that attempt to use a hyperrealistic technique to give a transcendental characteristic to landscape depiction that was later to find expression in the Pre-Raphaelite style.

In 1863 Hunt, who had by that time made his reputation by painting close-ups of fruit, minutely worked, richly textured, stippled and highly coloured, recommended outdoor painting to a friend's son, claiming that in this 'more originality might be acquired than in any other branch of Art'.[190] Spontaneity, freshness and attention to detail, characteristics which were a by-product of the phenomenalism of the Varley circle, are given independent meaning. The value of the sketch was now seen either in promoting the expression of subjectivity, or, as in Ruskin, in conveying a moral message through the act of humbly and faithfully tracing God's creation. The emphasis had shifted away from the endeavour to represent landscape as it appeared at the moment of encounter to a stance which valued above all the presence of personal vision.

CONCLUSION

There is no simple explanation for the emergence of phenomenalism. Phenomenalism was not a single, coordinated movement; it was adopted variously by philosophers, scientists and artists for different reasons in different contexts and locations, from Edinburgh to London. Nevertheless, it had one significant consequence wherever it appeared. The French Revolution sent shock waves through British intellectual life. Theoretical approaches that could be associated with scepticism or materialism were suddenly extremely suspect and those who put them forward found themselves subject to public disfavour or even active repression. Phenomenalism was not a conservative political stance; but it did create a space of discourse or mode of depiction within which such material could be dealt with in relative independence and without presenting a threat to the established order. Thus Dugald Stewart was able to sustain his intellectual liberalism at a time when a very reactionary Tory regime had come into power in the town councils in Scotland. The Geological Society's phenomenalism allowed dissociation from theories such as those of Hutton, whose postulation of regular violent upheavals in the earth's history was felt to be dangerously close to current threats to the social order and to present geology as an independent science, above factional interests. The subject-matter treated by the Varley circle was not itself politically suspect, but the conventions within which it had previously been depicted formed part of a pictorial tradition which by that time was badly at odds with contemporary social reality.[1]

Phenomenalism, as I have pointed out throughout this book, was an inherently unstable position. Characteristic of phenomenalist depictions is that each part of the picture is of equal weight – each element is given significance, not by an intrinsic order within the sub-

ject-matter, but by its relation to something outside itself, the observing subject. Constable's work is at its most phenomenalist around 1815. At that time his intense engagement with his surroundings in his native Suffolk led him to search for a mode of depicting the landscape that would be inclusive and non-hierarchical. To that extent, Constable's phenomenalism is already tilted towards subjectivism. When Turner came to depict Staffa he did so in a way which went beyond the phenomenalists' prohibition on general theory. Although the elements of the painting cohere together as an observable scene, the depiction of nature in process and the dynamic character of Turner's treatment of it implies a conception of the order of nature which goes beyond strict phenomenalism. Even within the Geological Society, strict phenomenalism was only a transitional phase. By the mid-nineteenth century, conjectural and imaginative elements in scientific thinking were generally being positively reappraised as an essential part of scientific procedure.[2] This was not, however, a return to eighteenth-century metaphysics, but an acceptance of the need to construct theory in advance of the evidence against which it would be tested.

The evolution of phenomenalism in art also owed a great deal, I am convinced, to the new fashion for panoramas in the first decades of the nineteenth century. The numerous panoramas which sprang into existence after Robert Barker (1739–1806) had erected London's first purpose-built rotunda in Leicester Square in 1793 popularised unselective 360-degree painted views. As in phenomenalism, panoramic depiction emphasised inclusiveness rather than the selection of salient particulars as academic art theory had advocated. In attempting to provide viewers with the impression that they were witnessing a real scene rather than just a painted reproduction of one, panoramas employed the same strategy that phenomenalist depictions had developed: a pictorial presentation in which each part is given equal significance in relation to the observing subject.[3] Their huge success lay in showing such views (mostly of city-scapes) along with representations of events of national pride and glory – in particular the naval successes of the British Fleet – which were likewise presented as if they were being witnessed unmediatedly by the spectators (an early example of the ideological fallacies of photo-journalism). Soon, however, panoramas came to be criticised for their lack of moral content, particularly by artists, who, ever since the foundation of the Royal Academy, had laboured to advance their status based on the intellectual value of their work, not just their capacity for mimetic fidelity.[4] Such criticism was, of course, rather superficial, picking on the overt empiricism of the panoramas' presentation, but paying no attention to their heady mixture of themes, potently designed to arouse feelings of national greatness in their audience.[5]

By the time that the heyday of the panorama was over, in the 1830s, the priority of the empirical had become a widespread cliché in the evaluation of art. Nevertheless, the fact that they painted in the open air did not prevent the Pre-Raphaelites in the next decade from loading their depictions of nature with a heavy transcendental dimension. Their attention to detail, clarity of light and meticulousness of brushstroke depict hypersensitively perceived scenes that are consciously poised on the threshold that points beyond profane appearances. No one had a greater effect upon the Victorian view of art than John Ruskin (a great enthusiast of panoramas, incidentally); it was he who was the principal advocate of the extension of realistic depiction into the finest detail. And yet faithful representation was nothing for Ruskin if it was not endowed with imagination. In *The Eagle's Nest: Ten Lectures on the Relation of Natural Science to Art*, given to the University of Oxford in 1872, Ruskin advised:

> Having learned to represent actual appearances faithfully, if you have any human faculty of your own, visionary appearances will take place to you which will be nobler and more true than any actual or material appearances; and the realization of these is the function of every fine art, which is founded absolutely, therefore, in truth, and consists absolutely in imagination.[6]

The combination of these two elements – fidelity to nature and the need for landscape art to rise above it – are plainly apparent in a famous oil painting by William Dyce (1806–1864), *Pegwell Bay, Kent – A Recollection of October 5th 1858* (plate 110). Dyce carefully depicts the traces of time on the strata of the chalk cliffs, marking with pristine pictorial clarity every point in the field of vision in a way which goes far beyond the *coup d'oeil* approach of earlier landscape artists. The oil painting is based on a watercolour which Dyce painted during a family holiday at Ramsgate in October 1857.[7] In the oil, the line of the cliffs is made more pronounced, the light more poised on the threshold of night; members of Dyce's family are placed prominently in the foreground, and there are more figures in front of the cliff, all pursuing specific interests or tasks. While, for example, the aritist's family is engaged in the collection of shells or fossils, a man on the right with artists' materials (perhaps Dyce himself) is obviously looking for a suitable spot at which to paint, and another man further down is leading three donkeys. Everybody is absorbed in his or her narrow activity, seemingly ignorant of the larger event which motivates the picture. In the oil painting Dyce shows Donati's Comet in the sky. The comet appeared a year after his visit to Pegwell Bay and so was not part of his original observation on the spot. In this way Dyce conveys a moment of intense vision whose moral content is the insignificance of human beings and their concerns beside the vastness of earth's history and cosmic time and space.[8] *Pegwell Bay* resembles a scene taken from observation (so much so that, when it was exhibited in 1860, Dyce was accused of painting from photographs) but this observation serves a vision beyond appearance, just as Ruskin had demanded.

Even before Ruskin asserted the primacy of the scientific ideal of observation for art, John Constable had famously told his audience at the Royal Institution that 'Painting is a science, and should be pursued as an inquiry into the laws of nature'.[9] Like Ruskin, Constable was here giving expression to the idea that art and science are equal partners and share a single method of investigation. Yet, by the time of Constable's lecture, June 1836, the objects of investigation of science and art were in fact diverging rapidly. In the 1830s much scientific activity had shifted away from the observation of phenomena in nature to laboratory work, and large areas of the most prestigious branch of science, the

110   William Dyce, *Pegwell Bay, Kent – A Recollection of October 5th 1858*, exh. 1860, oil on canvas, 635 × 889, Tate Gallery, London.

physical sciences – most noticeably optics, electricity and the theory of heat – were being conducted in the ever more abstract language of mathematics.

Of course, art and science are part of a wider culture and so it will always be fruitful to explore the avenues through which they are connected. Nevertheless, the relationship between art and science in the early nineteenth century was exceptional. Phenomenalism, in its concentration on the observable, produced a convergence between the object of scientific knowledge and the subject-matter of artistic depiction. The interaction of art and science later in the century was quite different. When the Impressionists turned to science, for instance, they did so precisely because the science of the visual had by this stage passed beyond the realm of what was itself directly observable. In this way, the scientist becomes a source of theoretical knowledge that the artist can apply in the service of representation. Thus the distinction made by the scientists between additive and subtractive mixtures of colour led Seurat to try to create his pictures by juxtaposing those coloured constituents of light which fuse optically (an attempt which was doomed to failure, because different hues in fact fuse at different distances, something which does not seem to have bothered Seurat).[10] From the point of view of phenomenalism, on the other hand, both the scientist and the artist must restrict themselves to what is given. This is the common factor running through Constable's *Flatford Mill*, William Daniell's engravings for the *Voyage round Great Britain* and Cornelius Varley's sketches of north Wales.

★   ★   ★

When I started research on the subject of this book in the late 1980s, my interest in the perception and depiction of nature was – more or less consciously – motivated by the new urgency with which questions concerning our relationship to nature had returned to the political agenda. For many of my generation, who grew up in the 1970s and 1980s in Germany, the seriousness of our ecological predicament was at the core of our political thinking. The general understanding in the ecological movement was that centuries of technological exploitation of nature and the recklessly selfish abuse of vital resources had led us to the threshold of a major catastrophe whose bleak result would be extinction. This account implies a fixed antithesis between advanced Western culture and nature, with the consequence either that we are doomed, for we cannot escape from our culture, or that there is a prospect of redemption only if we abandon culture in favour of the primitive parts of ourselves. Both attitudes seemed deeply suspicious to me, the first for its blanket pessimism, the second because it invests nature with sacred, mythic qualities which appear to be just another projection of our own human desires and obsessions.

This book was written because, perhaps naively, I wanted to see if history could not offer an alternative to this rigid binary perspective, and no other period and country seemed to offer itself more than Britain in the age of the Industrial Revolution, which was also the great age of British landscape art. But history does not offer answers to today's question so easily. I was struck by the assumption I found in the eighteenth-century treatises I read that there must be a direct physical link, a shared property between ourselves and nature, not only for us to be human beings, but human beings capable of cultural progress. This is an understanding of a relationship with nature quite different from the culture–nature opposition which dominates contemporary thinking. Yet the eighteenth century was without doubt also the century in which the most widespread and intensive exploitation of natural resources was established. Phenomenalism, in my account, represented the demise of an understanding which saw the mediation between subject and nature as a direct physical link, and could thus perhaps be seen as initiating the most alienated phase of our relationship to the natural world. From one point of view, phenomenalism can, of course, appear to be another attempt to objectify nature by making observation scientific and in this way

amenable to domination – a precarious attempt in this particular case which was doomed to failure. But in the course of my research I came to think that there was more to phenomenalism; that it was a means of expression which, precisely because of its unstable nature, was able to mediate the otherwise harsh opposition between subject and nature. Of course, the mere suggestion that at some point in the past an attitude appears to have manifested itself which transcended the nature–culture opposition will do nothing to restore the balance between human beings and their environment so urgently needed today. All such reflection can do is to point towards wider horizons and question narrow oppositions.

As I pointed out in the Introduction, one attempt to prevent the exploitation and subordination of nature – practically and theoretically – is Theodor Adorno's prohibition in his *Ästhetische Theorie* of discourse about nature in positive terms. Any such conceptual appropriation, Adorno argues, must violate the 'non-identity' of nature as the epitome of the non-human. Adorno's position that all our acts of mapping the world are always already culturally mediated has become very much the orthodox position among so-called postmodernist writers. A typical recent example of this is *Landscape and Power*, edited by W.J.T. Mitchell.[11] For Mitchell, nature has all but disappeared, making landscape into an artefact of culture: 'landscape is best understood as a medium of cultural expression, not a genre of painting or fine art [. . .]. Landscape is already artifice in the moment of its beholding, long before it becomes the subject of pictorial representation'.[12] Mitchell turns the screw even further. According to him, the interpretation of landscape requires not only the deciphering of the cultural meanings encoded within it, as other recent works have set out to do; it also has to show how such encodings affect us in turn: 'it has to trace the process by which landscape effaces its own readability and naturalizes itself [. . .]. What we have done and are doing to our environment, what the environment in turn does to us'.[13] From this viewpoint, phenomenalism might be judged to be merely naive, a fetishism of the given. But this would be to oversimplify its endeavour. In my view, phenomenalism is best understood not as a fantasy of the recovery of lost innocence, but, at its best, as a critical reflection on – and against – the inevitably mediated nature of perception.

What I have in mind is captured by Walter Benjamin's (admittedly highly theological and utopian) conception of the *Augenblick*: the idea that a moment of experience may become so highly charged that it can transcend the sphere of the subject and provide a channel or window for the epiphany of what is experienced – the non-subject.[14] In this experiential showing forth (*Aufscheinen*) the subject endeavours to escape from its own subjective attitude without thereby returning to a naive realism. If there are such experiences, they must be momentary: as soon as the attempt is made to fix such a vision by means of a language (whether verbal or pictorial) the fluid element in experience which transcends the structures of the subject – the non-identical – is lost.

A sketch such as Cornelius Varley's *Near Ross* (plate 111) represents an encounter whose turbulent character threatens to burst the pictorial resources available to the two-dimensional medium of drawing. At the same time, just because it stretches a mode of depiction to its utmost limits, this sketch, for me, can convey a tension whose force cannot be expressed in words. It is here that its phenomenalism has a utopian dimension. In experiencing it, the subject may recognise, however briefly, a point of integration beyond the subject–object division.

111   Cornelius Varley, *Near Ross*, 1803, graphite and watercolour,
367 × 235, sold Colnaghi's, London,
21 February–16 March 1973,
photo Dr Michael Pidgley.

NOTES

INTRODUCTION

1 The term 'science' here and elsewhere in the book should not be understood in the modern sense, as implying a set of separate, specialised disciplines aimed at the 'study of the material or external world from the standpoint of a neutral, methodical observer' conducted by professionals (William F. Bynum, E.J. Browne and Roy Porter, eds., *Macmillan Dictionary of the History of Science*, London, 1981: 287). For the changes in the meaning of the word 'science', see S. Ross, 'Scientist: The Story of the Word', *Annals of Science* 18 (1962): 65–85. During the period I am considering here, science or natural philosophy was a pursuit carried on by men of independent means that encompassed a wide range of inquiries from mineralogy to the studies of antiquities, all of which were seen as interconnected. It was only through the institutional and social changes that took place in the 1830s that the professionalisation and specialisation of science started to emerge. It was at this time that the term 'scientist' was coined by Whewell (Roy M. MacLeod, 'Whigs and Savants: Reflections on the Reform Movement in the Royal Society, 1830–48', in Ian Inkster and Jack Morrell, eds., *Metropolis and Province: Science in British Culture, 1780–1850*, London, 1983: 55–90; see also, in the same publication, J.N. Hays, 'The London Lecturing Empire: 1800–50': 91–119).

2 Kenneth Clark, *Landscape into Art*, 1949, 6th ed. (London, 1991). It was repeated as recently as 1991 by Leslie Parris and Ian Fleming-Williams (*Constable*, exhib. cat. Tate Gallery, London, 1991: 58).

3 Clark, 1991: 147.

4 Clark, 1991: 150. Constable believed, according to Clark: 'that there was something in trees, flowers, meadows and mountains which was so full of the divine that if it was contemplated with sufficient devotion it would reveal a moral and spiritual quality of its own' (p. 151).

5 Ernst Gombrich, *Art and Illusion: A Study in the Psychology of Pictorial Representation*, 1960 (Oxford, 1991).

6 Gombrich, 1991: 44.

7 Gombrich, 1991: 268.

8 Gombrich, 1991: 271.

9 Gombrich, it should be remembered, formed his account of 'revision [. . .] in the story of visual discoveries' on the model of Karl Popper's trial-and-error theory of scientific discovery (1991: 271).

10 An extensive critical account of Gombrich's position is presented in W.J.T. Mitchell, *Iconology: Image, Text, Ideology* (Chicago, 1986): 75–94. Gombrich's distinction between images as natural signs with a privileged access to the way things are and texts as wholly conventional signs is here set off against the radical nominalism of Nelson Goodman, who reduces perceptions and representations, be they visual or textual, to culturally relative constructions or interpretations (pp. 53–74). Mitchell, who comes down on Goodman's side, but seeks to provide Goodman's analysis with a historical dimension it facilitates but lacks, provides some insights into Gombrich's theory. He seems to miss the subtlety of Gombrich's argument about experimentation and approximation, however, when he charges Gombrich's central distinction between nature and convention with incoherence (p. 89).

11 John Berger, *Ways of Seeing* (London, 1972): 104–8.

12 Norman Bryson, *Vision and Painting: The Logic of the Gaze* (London, 1983): 6.

13 The most notable publications which are conceived along those lines with regard to landscape art are: Denis Cosgrove and Stephen Daniels, eds., *The Iconography of Landscape* (Cambridge, 1988); Simon Pugh, ed., *Reading Landscape: Country-City-Capital* (Manchester, 1990); W.J.T. Mitchell, ed., *Landscape and Power* (Chicago, 1994).

14 Among Adorno's works *Die Dialektik der Aufklärung*, 1947 (Frankfurt am Main, 1969), written with Max Horkheimer, and *Ästhetische Theorie* 1970 (Frankfurt am Main, 1973) are especially relevant here, as is Walter Benjamin's 'Geschichtsphilosophische Thesen' (1942), in *Illuminationen: Ausgewählte Schriften* (Frankfurt am Main, 1961): 268–79.

15 See, for example, Conrad H. Waddington, *Behind Appearance: A Study of the Relations between Painting and the Natural Sciences in this Century* (Edinburgh, 1969); Robert S. Root-Bernstein, 'On Paradigms and Revolutions in Science and Art: The Challenge of Interpretation', *Art Journal* 44 (1984): 109–18; and Gordon Fyfe and John Law, eds., *Picturing Power: Visual Depiction and Social Relations* (London, 1988). Gombrich, though his art history is modelled on Popper's philosophy of science, insists however

16 Timothy F. Mitchell, *Art and Science in German Landscape Painting 1770–1840* (New York, 1993).

17 See, for example, Martin Pollock, ed., *Common Denominators in Art and Science* (Aberdeen, 1983); and Martin Kemp, *The Science of Art: Optical Themes in Western Art from Brunelleschi to Seurat* (New Haven, 1990).

18 Barbara Maria Stafford, *Voyage into Substance: Art, Science, and the Illustrated Travel Account, 1760–1840* (Cambridge, Mass., 1984).

19 Stafford, 1984: 486.

20 Stafford, 1984: 439.

21 See with regard to the changes of landscape and depiction in the age of industrialisation: Francis Klingender, *Art and the Industrial Revolution* (London, 1947); Monika Wagner, *Die Industrielandschaft in der Englischen Malerei und Grafik, 1770–1830* (Frankfurt am Main, 1979); with emphasis on the depiction of labour: John Barrell, *The Dark Side of Landscape: The Rural Poor in English Painting 1730–1840* (Cambridge, 1980) and *The Birth of Pandora and the Division of Knowledge* (London, 1992); with emphasis on agrarian change: Michael Rosenthal, *British Landscape Painting* (Oxford, 1982); Hugh Prince, 'Art and Agrarian Change, 1710–1815', in Cosgrove and Daniels, eds., pp. 98–118; Christiana Payne, *Toil and Plenty: Images of the Agricultural Landscape in England 1780–1890*, exhib. cat. Yale Center for British Art (New Haven, 1993). Ann Bermingham's *Landscape and Ideology: The English Rustic Tradition 1740–1840* (London, 1987) also deals with agrarian changes, but the second part of her book takes a distinctly psychoanalytical approach, also adopted by Ronald Paulson in *Emblem and Expression: Meaning in English Art of the Eighteenth Century* (London, 1978). For an analysis of class interests and landscape art, see Andrew Hemingway, *Landscape Imagery & Urban Culture in Early Nineteenth-Century Britain* (Cambridge, 1992).

22 Michel Foucault, *Les mots et les choses: Une archéologie des sciences humaines* (Paris, 1966). I am quoting from the English edition *The Order of Things: An Archaeology of the Human Sciences*, 1970 (London, 1991).

23 Foucault, 1991: xxiii.

24 Foucault, 1991: 217.

25 Within the analysis of his finiteness, man remains, in Foucault's most famous phrase, 'a strange empirico-transcendental doublet' (*un étrange doublet empirico-transcendantal*) (1991: 318).

26 Foucault, 1991: 387.

27 For a critique of this methodology, as well as for a discussion of other, related issues, see David Couzens Hoy, ed., *Foucault: A Critical Reader* (Oxford, 1986).

28 Foucault, 1991: 217.

29 I believe that such developments are not confined to the particular examples chosen for this book and could be extended. A study of early nineteenth-century colour theory and art from this angle, for example, might yield similar results. In 1801–2 Thomas Young proposed a wave theory of light. This supposed light to consist in longitudinal (instead of, as would come to be accepted later, transverse) undulations in an etherial medium and it took colours to be the product of interference in the light waves. A theory such as Young's proved problematic for those scientists who were influenced by phenomenalism. What troubled them was the assumption that the æther amounted to more than a useful hypothesis. David Brewster, a student of Dugald Stewart, took up a clearly phenomenalist stance in this debate. Brewster's interest in optical phenomena brought him into contact with artists. J.M.W. Turner had the chance to discuss optical phenomena with him when he toured Scotland, and Brewster's observations on the kaleidoscope became influential for discussions of non-representational colour in the nineteenth century (John Gage, *Colour and Culture: Practice and Meaning from Antiquity to Abstraction*, London, 1993: 298, fn. 74). Equally, the discussion of the interaction between artists and geologists in Chapter III could be extended to other locations in England. So, for example, a very similar story could be told for the Isle of Wight, one of the few places where a natural formation of the coastline aroused the attention of picturesque travellers. Very early in the nineteenth century it was made the subject of scientific examination by one of the phenomenalist geologists, Thomas Webster, whose drawings influenced Peter DeWint's illustrations for George and William Cooke's *Picturesque Views on the Southern Coast of England* (London, 1826). Finally, the discussion of the work of the Varley circle in the last chapter could, I am convinced, be fruitfully extended to other artists who participated in the phenomenalist tendencies of the period, for example George Robert Lewis, William Havell, William Dixon and Augustus Wall Callcott.

I AESTHETICS, PHILOSOPHY AND PHYSIOLOGY: THE ROAD TO PHENOMENALISM

1 Quoted in Malcolm Andrews, *The Search for the Picturesque: Landscape Aesthetics and Tourism in Britain, 1760–1800* (Aldershot, 1989): 39.

2 Andrews, 1989: 39.

3 Joshua Reynolds, *Discourses on Art*, ed. Robert R. Wark (New Haven, 1981): 255.

4 Most research on the picturesque includes discussion of Gilpin. The two monographs on him are: Carl P. Barbier, *William Gilpin: His Drawings, Teaching, and Theory of the Picturesque* (Oxford, 1963) and William D. Templeman, *The Life and Work of William Gilpin*, Illinois Studies in Language and Literature 24 (Urbana, 1939).

5 William Gilpin, *Three Essays: On Picturesque Beauty; On Picturesque Travel; and On Sketching Landscape: to which is Added a Poem, On Landscape Painting*, 1792, 2nd ed. (London, 1794). Gilpin had earlier sent the first of these

essays to Reynolds, hoping for his imprimatur, and reprinted Reynolds' comments and his own reply to them at the end of the essay. Reynolds responded in 1791 with patrician generosity, but cautiously: 'Without opposing any of your sentiments, it has suggested an idea, that may be worth consideration – whether the epithet *picturesque* is not applicable to the excellences of the inferior schools, rather than to the higher' (1794: 34). In Reynolds' view, the picturesque was incompatible with the Grand Style: while 'variety of tints and forms is picturesque; [. . .] the reverse of this – (uniformity of colour, and a long continuation of lines,) produces grandeur' (p. 35). Gilpin saw no objection to his own views in Reynolds' reservations about the picturesque, for he himself, he states, had always used the term 'merely to denote *such objects, as are proper subjects for painting*: so that according to *my definition*, one of the cartoons, and a flower piece are equally picturesque' (pp. 36–7).

6 Samuel H. Monk (*The Sublime: A Study of Critical Theories in XVIII-Century England*, New York, 1935) presents an account of eighteenth-century aesthetics in which each successive thinker is part of an internally developing dialectic with a single author as its culmination (for Monk, that point lies beyond the boundaries of Britain itself in Immanuel Kant). Walter J. Hipple (*The Beautiful, the Sublime, and the Picturesque in Eighteenth-Century British Aesthetic Theory*, Carbondale, 1957) strongly criticises Monk's approach; nevertheless, he too represents the Scottish aesthetic theorists, Alison and Stewart, as successive approaches to an ideal of inductive method which he finds in John Stuart Mill.

Typically, historians who concentrate on philosophy and aesthetics have taken Locke's sensualist epistemology as their point of departure. Apart from Monk and Hipple, the major general studies of this kind are: Howard C. Warren, *A History of the Association Psychology* (London, 1921); Christopher Hussey, *The Picturesque: Studies in a Point of View* (London, 1927); Gordon McKenzie, *Critical Responsiveness: A Study of the Psychological Current in Later Eighteenth-Century Criticism* (Berkeley, 1949); also Jerome Stolnitz, 'On the Origins of Aesthetic Disinterestedness', *Journal of Aesthetics and Art Criticism* 20 (1961): 121–32 and 'Beauty: Some Stages in the History of an Idea', *Journal of the History of Ideas* 22 (1961): 185–204; Robert Hoeldtke, 'The History of Associationism and British Medical Psychology', *Medical History* 11 (1967): 46–65; Martin Kallich, *The Association of Ideas and Critical Theory in Eighteenth Century England* (The Hague, 1970) (though he also points to Hobbes); Johannes Dobai, *Die Kunstliteratur des Klassizismus und der Romantik in England 1700–1840*, 3 vols. (Berne, 1974–7); Donald B. Doe, *The Sublime as an Aesthetic Correlative: A Study of Late Eighteenth Century English Aesthetic Theory, Landscape Painting and Gothic Drama*, diss. Ohio University, 1977 (UMI, 1980, 48106).

Historians of science, on the other hand, generally focus on Newton. An example which relates to neurophysiology is Robert E. Schofield's *Mechanism and*

Materialism: British Natural Philosophy in an Age of Reason (Princeton, 1970). For a critique of the prevalent Newtonianism in histories of science, see Simon Schaffer, 'Natural Philosophy', in G.S. Rousseau and Roy Porter, eds., *The Ferment of Knowledge* (Cambridge, 1980): 55–91. The main bulk of work on the emerging science of neurology, however, is restricted to a straightforward account of the development of different concepts from the time of Galen, seen from the point of view of their contribution to our contemporary understanding of neurophysiology. The main works are: Lester S. King, *The Medical World of the Eighteenth Century* (Chicago, 1958): 193–226; Edwin S. Clarke and C.D. O'Malley, *The Human Brain and Spinal Cord* (Berkeley, 1968); Eric T. Carlson and Meribeth M. Simpson, 'Models of the Nervous System in Eighteenth-Century Psychiatry', *Bulletin of the History of Medicine* 43 (1969): 101–15; Stanley W. Jackson, 'Force and Kindred Notions in Eighteenth-Century Neurophysiology and Medical Psychology', *Bulletin of the History of Medicine* 44 (1970): 397–410, 539–54; John Spillane, *The Doctrine of the Nerves: Chapters in the History of Neurology* (Oxford, 1981).

More recent research has been directed towards locating the underlying causes of intellectual developments in the structures of social life. For neurophysiology in Scotland, see, for example, Christopher Lawrence, 'The Nervous System and Society in the Scottish Enlightenment', in Barry Barnes and Steven Shapin, eds., *Natural Order: Historical Studies of Scientific Culture* (London, 1979): 19–40. In the same publication see also Steven Shapin, 'Homo Phrenologicus: Anthropological Perspectives on an Historical Problem', pp. 41–71. For aesthetics, also in Scotland, see Andrew Hemingway, 'The "Sociology" of Taste in the Scottish Enlightenment', *Oxford Art Journal*, 12 (1989): 3–35, and for England, Nigel H. Everett, *The Tory View of Landscape* (New Haven, 1994) and Bermingham, 1987: 63–83.

7 Stolnitz, 'Beauty', 1961: 201.

8 Hussey, one of the pioneers of historical writing on aesthetics, set the tone when he described the aesthetic of the picturesque as a 'prelude to romanticism', and emphasised what he saw as its emancipation of the imagination (1927: 4). Hipple is an exception to this generalisation in that he does not investigate the texts with regard to the development of subjectivity. However, his account (1957) shows a different kind of teleology (see n. 6 above). More recently, literary critics, informed by Lacan, have concentrated on the sublime: see Thomas Weiskel, *The Romantic Sublime: Studies in the Structure and Psychology of Transcendence* (Baltimore, 1976); and Peter De Bolla, *The Discourse of the Sublime: Readings in History, Aesthetics and the Subject* (Oxford, 1989). While his concerns and methodology are very different from those of his predecessors, Weiskel nevertheless presents his account in the form of a teleological development towards subjectivity. De Bolla, in my view correctly, criticises Weiskel by pointing out that the eighteenth-century theorists did not assume a unified

subject. His own analysis, however, focuses solely on the subject and the generation of what he calls the 'subject surplus' which changes character at the turn of the century.

9 Such a position was by no means confined to Scotland, though there it was particularly prominent. It can be seen at the end of the eighteenth century in England in Erasmus Darwin's *Zoonomia: Or, the Laws of Organic Life*, 2 vols. (London, 1794–6). Darwin seeks on the one hand to explain the motions in living matter by recourse to the various physical and chemical processes; yet, on the other hand, he assumes the mediating substance in the nervous system to be something entirely peculiar to living organisms. For the concept of vitalism in England see Theodore M. Brown, 'From Mechanism to Vitalism in Eighteenth-Century English Physiology', *Journal of the History of Biology* 7 (1974): 179–216.

10 See Michael Clarke and Nicholas Penny, *The Arrogant Connoisseur: Richard Payne Knight 1751–1824*, exhib. cat. Whitworth Art Gallery (Manchester, 1982): 10. Although the dispute between Knight and Price is mentioned in most discussions of the picturesque, it is discussed at length by Hipple (1957: 238–83) and, from a different, more political, less philosophical, angle in Sidney K. Robinson, *Inquiry into the Picturesque* (Chicago, 1991).

11 Schofield, 1970, part 2.

12 David Hartley, *Observations on Man, his Frame, his Duty, and his Expectations*, 2 vols. (London, 1749). On Locke and Hartley, see Kallich, 1970: 11.

13 See John P. Wright, *The Sceptical Realism of David Hume* (Manchester, 1983): ch. 5.

14 Hartley, 1749, vol. 1, p. 21.

15 Hartley, 1749, vol. 1, p. 56.

16 Hartley, 1749, vol. 1, p. 79.

17 Hartley, 1749, vol. 1, p. 80.

18 Hartley, 1749, vol. 1, p. 203.

19 Hartley, 1749, vol. 1, p. 58.

20 Hartley distinguishes between the perception of colour and light and shade. The seven primary colours, he explains, 'estimated both from their limits, and their middle points, exceed vibrations, which are to each other in the simplest ratios that are consistent with each other' (Hartley, 1749, vol. 1, p. 193). They 'leave distinct ideas of themselves' (p. 220), distinct from those of distance, magnitude, motion, figure and position. Hartley assumes that these latter features, once such images are 'stored' and associated in 'vibratiuncles', come to our mind involuntarily, while colours need the exertion of the voluntary power of the will. Hartley's separation between colour and chiaroscuro, like Locke's earlier distinction between primary and secondary qualities, although it endorses theoretically the eighteenth-century mode of painting which separates the distribution of light and shade from the introduction of colour, is, of course, grounded in much earlier practice (see Gage, 1993, ch. 7).

21 An interpretation apparently initiated by Elie Halévy, *The Growth of Philosophic Radicalism* (London, 1928): 17.

22 Hartley, 1749, vol. 1, p. 83.

23 Joseph Priestley, *Hartley's Theory of the Human Mind: On the Principle of the Association of Ideas* (London, 1775).

24 Hartley, 1749, vol. 2, p. 404. Margaret Leslie ('Mysticism Misunderstood: David Hartley and the Idea of Progress', *Journal of the History of Ideas* 33, 1972: 625–32) took issue with those interpretations which claim that Hartley's writing contains a progressive view of society. His aim, on her account, is rather man's spiritual perfection. She states that, in Hartley's view, all governments of the world were degenerate and that little could be done 'to salvage a world so hopelessly corrupt, and the duty of the Christian was rather to dissociate himself from it' (p. 628).

25 Leslie, 1972: 629. A similar argument was used by Noam Chomsky against a modern version of associationism: B.F. Skinner's behaviourist psychology. It would be impossible, according to Chomsky, to acquire the complex knowledge involved in linguistic behaviour simply by the gradual accumulation of experience.

26 Hartley, 1749, vol. 2, p. 229.

27 This, as we shall see, was left to later writers like Priestley and Godwin.

28 This is summed up in the following passage: 'Most of the ideas which are capable of making a powerful impression on the mind, whether simply of Pain or Pleasure, or of the modification of those, may be reduced very nearly to these two heads, *self-preservation* and *society*; to the ends of one or the other of which all our passions are calculated to answer. The passions which concern self-preservation, turn mostly on *pain* or *danger*. The ideas of *pain, sickness*, and *death*, fill the mind with strong emotions of horror; but *life* and *health*, though they put us in a capacity of being affected with pleasure, they make no such impression by the simple enjoyment. The passions therefore which are conversant about the preservation of the individual, turn chiefly on *pain* and *danger*, and they are the most powerful of all the passions' (Edmund Burke, *A Philosophical Enquiry into the Origin of our Ideas of the Sublime and Beautiful, with an Introductory Discourse Concerning Taste*, 1757, 2nd ed. 1758, ed. J.T. Boulton, London, 1958: 38).

29 Burke, ed. 1958: 39.

30 Burke, ed. 1958: 39.

31 Burke, ed. 1958: 91.

32 Scottish writers on aesthetics, on the other hand, saw the sublime and the beautiful as categories of the mind for which the correlative qualities in objects acted as triggers (see, for example, Alexander Gerard's first *Essay on Taste* (London, 1759), which appeared two years after Burke's publication, and Henry Home's *Elements of Criticism*, 3 vols. (Edinburgh, 1762). From Hutcheson on, the Scottish aestheticians had argued that knowledge of the expressions of nature is implanted in human beings by nature. For Burke such knowledge is only created in response to outer stimuli. It might seem that, if aesthetic appreciation is not explained with reference to an innate sense, a theory of association of the sort developed by Hartley would serve best as the basis for aesthetic theory. Consequently, it has

puzzled later commentators that Burke should have opposed the use of the theory of association as the foundation for an account of aesthetic appreciation (Hipple, 1957: 91; Kallich, 1970: 134). In fact, Burke does not reject association as a principle altogether. The sublime and the beautiful are emotions which are initiated not just by their own particular objects, but also by those which are merely suggestive of terror or love. Thus Burke does have recourse to the theory of association, albeit in a secondary role (ed. 1958: 130–1).

33 As Jackson puts it, 'the lack of a grossly apparent elasticity seems to have been enough to put this idea to rest in the first half of the 18th century' (1970: 404).

34 Burke, ed. 1958: 130. This is perhaps the reason why Burke could not take account of Hartley's theory.

35 Burke, ed. 1958: 132.

36 Burke, ed. 1958: 150.

37 Burke, ed. 1958: 132.

38 Burke, ed. 1958: 134.

39 Burke, ed. 1958: 136.

40 Burke, ed. 1958: 136. Hipple, the only author known to me who tackles Burke's physiology in any detail, clearly misses this point when he writes: 'Already difficulties crowd upon us. The sublime should be, by this account, simply a weaker degree of terror – enough to tone up but not to overstretch the nerves. But this is not conformable to experience, for an emotion of the sublime may be far stronger than a faint emotion of terror' (1957: 91–2).

For reasons which will, I hope, have become clear, the Burkeian sublime does not fit into the currently fashionable discussion of the sublime, which does not sufficiently acknowledge the physiological basis for his theory (see, for example, De Bolla, 1989; and Christine Pries, ed., *Das Erhabene: Zwischen Grenzerfahrung und Grössenwahn*, Weinheim, 1989). Jean-François Lyotard's use of the Kantian sublime (*Le différend*, Paris, 1983; Eng. trans. as *The Differend: Phrases in Dispute*, Manchester, 1988) is at the centre of this modern discussion. For Kant (in *Die Kritik der Urteilskraft*, Zweites Buch: Analytik des Erhabenen, 1790, ed. Wilhelm Weischedel, Wiesbaden, 1957) the sublime is that which exceeds all powers of determinate representation. It is an experience which does not fit either a sensuous or a conceptual mode of apprehension. What gives the sublime meaning is the activation of a responsive capacity in us which is suprasensible (non-phenomenal), the realm of pure ideas and judgements. Kant's emphasis on the sublime as an experience beyond the domain of phenomenal cognition is thus entirely different from Burke. This conception of the sublime as a means of expressing what is beyond the realm of phenomenal experience and cognitive concepts is taken up by Lyotard. But while, for Kant, the sublime functions as an analogical expression for the realm of practical reason, for Lyotard it is an index for the radically disjunct or heterogeneous character of ethical positions and judgements; in his terms, for the uncommunicability of different phrase-regimes and language-games.

41 Burke, ed. 1958: 137.

42 Burke, ed. 1958: 137. Hipple quotes Richard Payne Knight's sarcastic criticism that such a theory means that one's pen a foot away makes a greater impression on the retina than Salisbury steeple a mile away. He also states that Burke's physiological explanation of the effect of darkness on the eye was 'reckoned an absurdity even in the eighteenth century' (1957: 92).

43 Burke, ed. 1958: 155.

44 Burke, ed. 1958: 155.

45 Burke, ed. 1958: 16.

46 John Barrell, *The Political Theory of Painting from Reynolds to Hazlitt: The Body of the Public* (New Haven, 1986). See also Barrell, 1992: 41; for the Scottish context see Hemingway, 1989.

47 Burke, ed. 1958: 24.

48 Burke, ed. 1958: 24.

49 Burke, ed. 1958: 24–5. If the capacity for judgement is the qualification for exercising political authority, it follows that power should be distributed in the same way as sensibility, unequally.

50 Burke, ed. 1958: 24.

51 Burke, ed. 1958: 24.

52 This theme resurfaces in his *Letter to a Noble Lord* in the 1790s (UEA English Studies Group, 'Strategies for Representing Revolution', in Francis Barker et al., eds., *1789: Reading Writing Revolution: Proceedings of the Essex Conference on the Sociology of Literature*, Essex, 1982: 90).

53 Peter H. Melvin, 'Burke on Theatricality and Revolution', *Journal of the History of Ideas* 36 (1975): 460.

54 See Michael Freeman, *Edmund Burke and the Critique of Political Radicalism* (Oxford, 1980): 111–14.

55 Simon Schaffer, 'States of Mind: Enlightenment and Natural Philosophy', in G.S. Rousseau, ed., *The Languages of Psyche, Mind and Body in Enlightenment Thought* (Berkeley, 1990): 250. See also Melvin, 1975.

56 Edmund Burke, *Reflections on the Revolution in France*, 1790, ed. Conor Cruise O'Brien (London, 1968). See L.G. Mitchell's introduction to *The Writings and Speeches of Edmund Burke*, gen. ed. Paul Langford, vol. 8, *The French Revolution 1790–1794*, ed. L.G. Mitchell (Oxford, 1989): 12.

57 For a discussion of the circle, see Schaffer, 1990: 252.

58 According to Mitchell (1989: 10), Burke held that Shelburne had destroyed the Rockingham Administration of 1782 by intrigue.

59 *The Writings and Speeches of Edmund Burke*, gen. ed. Paul Langford, vol. 2, *Party, Parliament, and the American Crisis, 1766–74*, ed. Paul Langford (Oxford, 1981): 364.

60 Burke, ed. 1958: 107–8.

61 Joseph Priestley, *An Examination of Dr. Reid's Inquiry into the Human Mind on the Principles of Common Sense, Dr. Beattie's Essay on the Nature and Immutability of Truth and Dr. Oswald's Appeal to Common Sense on Behalf of Religion*, 1774, 2nd ed. (London, 1775) and *Hartley's Theory*.

62 Priestley, 2/1775: 200–1.

63 Jack Fruchtman, 'Common Sense and the Association of

Ideas: The Reid–Priestley Controversy', in Melvin Dalgarno and Eric Matthews, eds., *The Philosophy of Thomas Reid*, Philosophical Studies Series 42 (Dordrecht, 1989): 425–6. In this otherwise illuminating article, Fruchtman, like most writers on Hartley and Priestley, ignores the important differences between the two.

64 Fruchtman, 1989: 426.

65 Isaac Kramnick, *Republicanism and Bourgeois Radicalism: Political Ideology in Late Eighteenth-Century England and America* (New York, 1990): 17. Priestley responded by publishing his *Letters to the Right Honourable Edmund Burke* (Birmingham, 1791); I had access only to the French translation, *Lettres au très-honorable Edmund Burke, Au sujet de ses réflexions sur la Révolution de France* (Paris, 1791).

66 Letter to Charles James Fox, 9 September 1789 (*The Correspondence of Edmund Burke*, eds. Alfred Cobban and Robert A. Smith, vol. 6, Cambridge, 1967: 15).

67 Burke had subscribed to Priestley's *History and Present State of Discoveries Relating to Vision, Light, and Colours* (1772) and visited his laboratory in Birmingham in 1782. Priestley wrote to Burke on 11 December 1782, describing an experiment (*The Correspondence of Edmund Burke*, eds. Holden Furber and P.J. Marshall, vol. 5, Cambridge, 1965: 53–4).

68 Schaffer, 1990: 250.

69 Mrs Crewe reports a table conversation with Burke at Crewe Hall after Price's and Knight's treatises on the picturesque had appeared in 1794: Burke 'admired many parts of Mr. Price's book, and thought both he and Mr Knight often discovered much genius in their observations, though like most system-mongers they had pursued their theories to a dangerous length' (quoted in Messmann, 1974: 66). Burke wrote to Price to thank him for sending his book and expressed his admiration (*The Correspondence of Edmund Burke*, eds. P.J. Marshall and John A. Woods, vol. 7, Cambridge, 1968: 547–8).

70 Priestley, 1775: iii.

71 Hartley, 1749, vol. 1, p. 83.

72 Priestley, 1775: xxxii.

73 Priestley, 1775: xliii–iv.

74 Hartley, 1749, vol. 1, p. i.

75 Priestley, 1775: xx.

76 Priestley, 1775: vii–viii.

77 Schofield, 1970: 264. From a different angle: Robert E. Schofield, 'Joseph Priestley: Eighteenth-Century British Neoplatonism, and S.T. Coleridge', in Everett Mendelsohn, ed., *Transformation and Tradition in the Sciences: Essays in Honor of I. Bernard Cohen* (Cambridge, 1984): 237–54.

78 Priestley, 1775: xx.

79 Kramnick, 1990: 86. Unfortunately, Kramnick also argues for a direct lineage from Hartley to Priestley, Bentham and Mill, thus missing the crucial differences in their respective theories.

80 Kramnick, 1990: 91.

81 On the use of language by both the radical dissenters and their opponents to discredit each other as insane, speculative or theatrical, see Schaffer, 1990.

82 Just as Priestley retains some fundamental traditional assumptions in his natural philosophy, he does not argue for a radical, Benthamite utilitarianism in his politics, as is often wrongly assumed. Instead, Priestley advocates a utilitarianism which is modified by the traditional view of natural law. See Margaret Canovan, 'The Un-Benthamite Utilitarianism of Joseph Priestley', *Journal of the History of Ideas* 45 (1984): 435–50.

83 On the closely knit world of the élite in private clubs, societies and universities, see Nicholas T. Phillipson, 'Culture and Society in the Eighteenth Century Province: The Case of Edinburgh and the Scottish Enlightenment', in Laurence Stone, ed., *The University in Society*, vol. 2 (Princeton, 1975): 407–48. On Scottish culture and science, see J.B. Morrell, 'The University of Edinburgh in the Late Eighteenth Century: Its Scientific Eminence and Academic Structure', *ISIS* 62 (1971): 158–71; J.B. Morrell, 'Science and Scottish University Reform: Edinburgh in 1826', *British Journal for the History of Science* 6 (1972): 39–56; John R.R. Christie, 'The Rise and Fall of Scottish Science', in Maurice P. Crosland, ed., *The Emergence of Science in Western Europe* (London, 1975): 111–26; John R.R. Christie, 'Ideology and Representation in Eighteenth-Century Natural History', *Oxford Art Journal* 13 (1990): 3–10; John R.R. Christie, 'Origins and Development of the Scottish Scientific Community, 1680–1760', *History of Science* 12 (1974): 122–40; and Lawrence, 1979.

84 L.S. Jacyna, *Philosophic Whigs: Medicine, Science and Citizenship in Edinburgh, 1789–1848* (London, 1994).

85 Lawrence has argued that through a 'theory of sensibility, physiology served to sanction the introduction of new economic and associated cultural forms by identifying the landed minority as the custodians of civilization, and therefore the natural governors, in a backward society. A related theory of sympathy expressed and moulded their social solidarity' (1979: 20). Lawrence's article was designed 'to explicate the concatenation of vitalistic theory [. . .], mental and social philosophy, and social legitimation' which was found to such an extent only in Scotland (1979: 34). Hume, whose social doctrines were at the heart of this concatenation, had recourse to the physical mechanism of Descartes and Malebranche (see Wright, 1983: ch. 5). It seems, therefore, that it was less the vitalist aspects of Scottish physiology than the centrality of the reactive capacity of the nervous system as such which was important for contemporary social and political discourse.

86 Roger K. French, *Robert Whytt: The Soul, and Medicine* (London, 1969).

87 Robert Whytt, *An Essay on the Vital and other Involuntary Motions of Animals* (Edinburgh, 1751): 324–5.

88 Lawrence, 1979: 25. However, Whytt's theory is distinct from Georg Ernst Stahl's vitalism, which was enjoying great popularity in France and Germany at the time. Vitalism, as employed by Stahl, was based on the notion of the 'anima' or soul, an immaterial factor which, diffused

through the body, created activity in passive matter; it caused and controlled physiological functions, mediating such effects through corpuscular motion; and it operated only in and by means of the body. Whytt, though he shared Stahl's basic assumptions, nevertheless criticised him for having gone 'too far' (1751: 267). In contrast to Stahl, Whytt did not assume the soul to act freely and consciously but to be bound by laws in its action, and quite unconscious (French, 1969: 139).

89 Whytt, 1751: 9.

90 In fact, for Whytt the sentient principle was part of the mind, which he divided in an almost medieval fashion into four souls: 'a rational, a reminiscent, an active, and a sentient one' (1751: 284).

91 French, 1969: 108.

92 Robert Whytt, *Observations on the Nature, Causes, and Cure of those Disorders which have been Commonly Called Nervous, Hypochondriac, or Hysteric*, 1765, 2nd corrected ed. (Edinburgh, 1765): iv.

93 So for example: 'Epileptic fits have been cured by whipping; – Convulsions from the toothach [sic] are removed by blisters; – vomitting has been stopt by putting the hands suddenly in cold water' (Whytt, 2/1765: 438).

94 Lawrence, 1979: 26.

95 William Cullen, *A Treatise of the Materia Medica*, vol. 1 (Edinburgh, 1789): 57.

96 Cullen, 1789, vol. 1, p. 91.

97 Cullen, 1789, vol. 1, p. 59. But Cullen could not agree with Whytt's view of it as *co-extensive* with the soul. For him, the soul is seated in the brain and only there is it capable of sensation.

98 Lawrence, 1979: 26.

99 Home, 1762, vol. 2, p. 355.

100 Home, 1762, vol. 3, p. 373.

101 For Home, *good* taste was the outcome of cultivation and needed the capacity for abstract thinking. This in turn required education and that position in the social order which could afford it. He writes: 'The exclusion of classes so many and various, reduces within a narrow compass those who are qualified to be judges in the fine arts. Many circumstances are necessary to form a judge of this sort' (1762, vol. 3, p. 371).

102 Gerard, 1759: 181.

103 Gerard, 1759: 104.

104 Home, 1762, vol. 1, p. 6.

105 Home, 1762, vol. 3, p. 371.

106 Home, 1762, vol. 1, p. 7.

107 Hemingway (1989) has shown that Scottish writers on aesthetics like Gerard and Home struggled to incorporate the existence of change and progress without compromising the universality of their perspective. According to Ronald L. Meek (*Social Science and the Ignoble Savage*, Cambridge, 1976) the Scottish writers shared this understanding of social progress taking place in stages with contemporary French authors.

108 Anand C. Chitnis, *The Scottish Enlightenment: A Social History* (London, 1976): 239.

109 George E. Davie, *The Scottish Enlightenment*, The Historical Association's General Series 99 (London, 1981): 19.

110 Richard Olson, *Scottish Philosophy and British Physics 1750 – 1880: A Study in the Foundations of the Victorian Scientific Style* (Princeton, 1975): 27.

111 Reid left Aberdeen in 1764 to become Adam Smith's successor as Professor of Moral Philosophy at Glasgow.

112 Davie, 1981: 18.

113 Davie, 1981: 18.

114 Davie, 1981: 18.

115 Reid's theory is of course descended from those Scottish writers, like Hutcheson, who assumed the existence of an innate sense. But it is different in rejecting any form of the empiricist theory of ideas.

116 Thomas Reid, *An Inquiry into the Human Mind: On the Principle of Common Sense* (Edinburgh, 1764): 489.

117 L.L. Laudan, 'Thomas Reid and the Newtonian Turn of British Methodological Thought', in R.E. Butts and John W. Davis, eds., *The Methodological Heritage of Newton* (Oxford, 1970): 125–9.

118 Reid, 1764: 14.

119 Reid, 1764: 430–1.

120 As summarised in Laudan, 1970: 129.

121 Michel Malherbe, 'Thomas Reid on the Five Senses', in Melvin Dalgarno and Eric Matthews, eds., *The Philosophy of Thomas Reid*, Philosophical Studies Series 42 (Dordrecht, 1989): 108.

122 Malherbe, 1989: 108.

123 Reid, 1764: 146.

124 Unknown, because in colour we perceive only the effect, not what causes the phenomena. Since effect and cause are not the same, reasoning about the latter would be mere speculation.

125 Malherbe, 1989: 109.

126 Thomas Reid, *Essays on the Intellectual Powers of Man* (Edinburgh, 1785).

127 Malherbe, 1989: 114.

128 Archibald Alison, *Essays on the Nature and Principles of Taste* (Edinburgh, 1790); Dugald Stewart, *Elements of the Human Mind*, 3 vols. (London and Edinburgh, 1792–1827).

129 Alison, 1790: 411; Stewart, 1792–1827, vol. 1, dedication and introduction.

130 Hipple, 1957: 158.

131 Hipple, 1957: 162.

132 For the story of the reception see Hipple, 1957: 158; Hemingway, 1989: 35, n. 177.

133 Alison, 1790: 410.

134 Alison, 1790: 5.

135 Monk, 1935: 148; McKenzie, 1949: 46; Kallich, 1970: 250. This has been criticised by Hipple, 1957: 168–9.

136 Alison, 1790: 2.

137 For example, Hussey, 1927: 15.

138 Alison, 1790: 62.

139 Alison, 1790: 26.

140 Alison, 1790: 11–12.

141 Alison, 1790: 62.

142 Barrell, 1986: introduction.

143 Paul Langford, *Public Life and the Propertied Englishman 1689–1798* (Oxford, 1994).

144 Alison, 1790: 63.

145 The three volumes of this publication display a highly professionalised philosophical language, which may be the reason why they have been largely neglected by those few authors who mention Stewart (Monk, 1935; Hipple, 1957; Stolnitz, 'Beauty', 1961; Kallich, 1970; Doe, 1977; Hemingway, 1989).

146 Stewart, 1792–1827, vol. 1, pp. 68–9.

147 Stewart, 1792–1827, vol. 1, p. 71.

148 Stewart, 1792–1827, vol. 1, pp. 10–11.

149 A detailed discussion of this account in connection with Richard Payne Knight is in Clarke and Penny, 1982: 86.

150 Stewart, 1792–1827, vol. 1, p. 146.

151 Stewart, 1792–1827, vol. 1, p. 130.

152 Stewart, 1792–1827, vol. 1, p. 131.

153 'Essay First: On the Beautiful' and 'Essay Second: On the Sublime', in William Hamilton, ed., *The Collected Works of Dugald Stewart*, vol. 5 (Edinburgh, 1855): 189–329.

154 Stewart, ed. 1855, 'Essay First', pp. 195–6.

155 Stewart, ed. 1855, 'Essay First', p. 196. A term which Stewart, incidentally, adopted from Richard Payne Knight's *An Analytical Inquiry into the Principles of Taste* (London, 1805): 11.

156 Stewart, ed. 1855, 'Essay Second', p. 322.

157 As L.S. Jacyna's account (1994) of the diverse careers of John Allen and John Thomson makes clear, both of these had to struggle with this charge.

158 Steven Shapin, 'The Politics of Observation: Cerebral Anatomy and Social Interests in the Edinburgh Phrenology Disputes', in Harry M. Collins, ed., *Sociology of Scientific Knowledge: A Source Book* (Bath, 1982): 108. Also Shapin, 1979: 41–71.

159 A challenge to the dominance of the Common Sense philosophy came from outside the academy with the rise of a new approach to the study of the mind – phrenology. Phrenology, according to Shapin (1982: 108–9), was an attempt by 'outsider intellectuals and their audience of superior working-class and petty-bourgeois groups' to establish themselves on the Edinburgh political and intellectual scene and Stewart's disciples mounted a fierce defence against it. Yet phrenology also contains significant similarities to Stewart's philosophy of mind, in so far as the latter was distinct from the eighteenth-century School of Common Sense: both emphasised the distinctiveness of the mental capacities of every individual, not in order to justify the social differentiation characteristic of a patrician society but to emphasise the possibility of developing an individual's endowments, once these had been scientifically identified. Neither discipline, however, endorsed an egalitarian view of society, and it was this which set them both in opposition to the more radically inclined intellectual movements of the 1830s (for Stewart, see Hemingway, 1989: 27–9; for the phrenologists, and particularly Combe's anti-egalitarianism, see Shapin, 1979: 59–60).

160 This was Thomas Young's assumption, when he proposed a wave theory of light in 1801–2, based on the supposition that light consists in longitudinal undulations in an etherial medium. Richard Olson (*Scottish Philosophy and British Physics 1750–1880*, Princeton, 1975) notes, regarding Dugald Stewart's student, Brewster: 'Brewster's attitude toward the etherial undulatory theory of light is particularly interesting because of its constant emphasis on the great utility and value which may accrue to the hypothesis even if it is incorrect in some absolute sense – *so long as one recognizes that it is merely a hypothesis*. In this vein he clearly developed and extended the arguments made by Stewart' (pp. 178–9).

161 Olson, 1975: 194.

162 Gilpin, 2/1794: 4.

163 Uvedale Price, *An Essay on the Picturesque, as compared with the Sublime and the Beautiful*, 2nd ed. (London, 1796).

164 Price, 2/1796: 49.

165 Price, 2/1796: 76.

166 Price, 2/1796: 103.

167 Price, 2/1796: 105.

168 Hipple, 1957: 206.

169 Price, 2/1796: 139.

170 Richard P. Knight, *The Landscape: A Didactic Poem* (London, 1794, 2nd ed., London, 1795). For the contemporary response to Price's and Knight's texts, see Frank J. Messmann, *Richard Payne Knight: The Twilight of Virtuosity*, Studies in English Literature 89 (The Hague, 1974): 63.

171 Knight, 2/1795: 19–24.

172 Uvedale Price, *A Dialogue on the Distinct Characters of the Picturesque and the Beautiful: In Answer to the Objections of Mr. Knight* (Hereford, 1801).

173 Letter to Lord Aberdeen, quoted in Clarke and Penny, 1982: 89.

174 According to Nicholas Penny, 'in the debate between them Price showed more common sense and far more agreeable polemical manners but Knight a profounder grasp of aesthetics and psychology' (Clarke and Penny, 1982: 49).

175 Bermingham, 1987: 83.

176 Andrew Ballantyne, 'Turbulence and Repression: Re-reading "The Landscape"', in Stephen Daniels and Charles Watkins, eds., *The Picturesque Landscape: Visions of Georgian Herefordshire*, exhib. cat. University Art Gallery Nottingham (Nottingham, 1994): 74.

177 Sidney K. Robinson (1991) sees no difference in the political implications of the theoretical writings of Price and Knight. For him the picturesque is an aesthetic of contemporary liberalism connected to the politics of Charles James Fox. Their differences are, in Robinson's opinion, just part of the suspicion of systems symptomatic of aesthetics of the picturesque: 'Price and Knight, suspicious of system, cast a wary eye on each other, as well' (p. 121). Most recent writing on the picturesque, however, emphasise, as I do, the variousness of the political implications of the aesthetic. The contributors to Stephen Copley and Peter Garside, eds., *The Politics of the Picturesque*

178 Knight, 1805: 61.

179 Knight, 1805: 62.

180 Knight was certainly not advocating, as he has been made out to do, the high key-note in colour which dominated painting after the 1820s (Cara D. Denison, Evelyn J. Phimister and Stephanie Wiles, *Gainsborough to Ruskin: British Landscape Drawings & Watercolors from the Morgan Library*, New York, 1994: 30).

181 Knight, 1805: 71.

182 Knight, 2/1795: 18; Price, 1801: 94–5.

183 Knight, 2/1795: 19.

184 See Clarke and Penny, 1982: 83.

185 Knight, 1805: 71.

186 Knight's position as a connoisseur in the controversy between artists and connoisseurs is discussed by Peter D. Funnell, *Richard Payne Knight 1751–1824: Aspects of Antiquarianism, Aesthetic and Art Criticism in England in the Late Eighteenth and Early Nineteenth Centuries*, D.Phil. Thesis (Oxford University, 1985).

187 The latter is set out in Knight's *The Progress of Civil Society: A Didactic Poem in Six Books* (London, 1796).

188 See Albert O. Hirschman, *The Passions and the Interests: Political Arguments for Capitalism before its Triumph* (Princeton, 1992) and Meek, 1976.

189 Knight, 1796: 13.

190 Knight, 1805: 1–2.

191 This pessimistic view is in contrast to the Scottish thinkers' more or less whole-hearted belief in progress.

192 Knight, 1796: 152.

193 Knight, 1796: 12.

194 Knight, 1796: 142.

195 Knight, 1805: 287.

196 Knight, 1805: 287.

197 On Knight's view of progress in the arts, see particularly his review of Northcote's *Life of Sir Joshua Reynolds, Edinburgh Review* 23 (1814): 263–92.

198 Knight, 1805: 145–6.

199 Knight, 1805: 300.

200 Knight, 1805: 180.

201 Knight, 1805: 454.

202 Knight, 1805: 256.

203 Richard P. Knight, *A Monody on the Death of the Rt. Hn. Charles James Fox* (London, 1807).

204 For Walpole and other critics, see Messmann, 1974: 83.

205 Knight, 2/1795: 91–2.

206 Knight, 2/1795: 94–5.

207 'All that I entreat is, that they will not at this time, when men's minds are so full of plots and conspiracies, endeavour to find analogies between picturesque compositions and political confusion' (Knight, 2/1795: 104).

208 Quoted by Claudia Stumpf, 'The Expedition into Sicily', in Clarke and Penny, 1982: 29.

209 Robert Hole, *Pulpits, Politics and Public Order in England 1760–1832* (Cambridge, 1989): 19.

210 Clarke and Penny, 1982: 16.

211 Knight, 1796: 145.

212 Knight, 1796: 483.

213 K.D.M. Snell, *Annals of the Labouring Poor: Social Change and Agrarian England 1660–1900* (London, 1985).

214 Stephen Daniels and Charles Watkins, 'Picturesque Landscaping and Estate Management: Uvedale Price and Nathaniel Kent at Foxley', in Copley and Garside, eds., 1994: 13–41.

215 Price, 2/1796: 379–80.

216 Uvedale Price, *Thoughts on the Defence of Property* (Hereford, 1797).

217 Price, 1797: 17.

218 Price, 1797: 27.

219 Price, 1797: 20.

220 Daniels and Watkins, 1994: 13–41.

221 Price, 1797: 19.

222 Langford, 1994: 367.

223 Langford, 1994: 367–436.

224 Knight, 2/1795: 36.

II THE TEMPLE OF FLORA

1 Robert John Thornton, *A New Illustration of the Sexual System of Carolus von Linnaeus* (London, 1807): n. pag. An edition of *A New Illustration* without *The Temple of Flora* and smaller, uncoloured engravings seems to have been the first to be issued in 1799. The copy in the University Library, Cambridge, however, contains prints which were printed as late as 1810.

2 Georg D. Ehret, *Trew's Plantae Selectae* (Norimbergae [Nuremberg], 1750–73). Ehret's original drawings have recently been rediscovered and are described by Heidrun Ludwig in her article 'Rediscovery of the Original Drawings of Georg Dionysius Ehret for the *Plantae Selectae*', *Archives of Natural History* 20 (1993): 381–90.

3 An example of this is John Edwards' *A Collection of Flowers, Drawn after Nature, and Disposed in an Ornamental and Picturesque Manner* (London, 1801), whose title already indicates the new importance.

4 Robert John Thornton, *Advertisement to the New Illustration of the Sexual System of Linnaeus by Robert John Thornton, M.D. Late of Trinity College, Cambridge; Fellow of the Linnaean Society, &c.&c.* 1 January 1797; a copy is in the British Library, London.

5 So far commentaries on *The Temple of Flora* have concentrated on the genesis of the publication, rather than on the interpretation of its imagery. I shall take advantage of this and omit detailed discussion of the prints, their engravers, techniques and editions. Treatment of these issues is to be found in Geoffrey Grigson and Handasyde Buchanan, *Thornton's Temple of Flora with the Plates Faithfully Reproduced from the Original Engravings*, 1951 (London, 1972) and in Ronald King, *The Temple of Flora by Robert Thornton* (London, 1981). Thornton is mentioned in relation to

other botanical publications by Gordon Dunthorne (*Flower and Fruit Prints of the Eighteenth and Early Nineteenth Centuries*, London, 1938: 37–40), who also produced what appears to be the first extensive description of the prints and their states and editions (nos. 243–56), and by Wilfrid Blunt (*The Art of Botanical Illustrations*, London, 1950: ch. 18). A brief botanical commentary was made by F.M.G. Cardew, 'Dr. Thornton and "The New Illustration" 1799–1807', *Journal of the Royal Horticultural Society* 72 (1947): 281–5, 450–3. Clive Bush's article 'Erasmus Darwin, Robert John Thornton, and Linnaeus' Sexual System', *Eighteenth-Century Studies* 7 (1974): 295–320, is unusual in trying to interpret the landscape backgrounds and to set them in relation to influences on Thornton, such as Erasmus Darwin's *The Botanic Garden* (London, 1789–91). As will become clear, my interpretation differs from Bush's.

6 Even after this project, Thornton entertained strong links with artists. He was doctor to John Linnell's family and, in 1820, in his third edition of the *Pastorals of Virgil* employed William Blake for the illustrations.

7 Lance Bertelsen, *The Nonsense Club: Literature and Popular Culture, 1749–1769* (Oxford, 1986).

8 Ronald Paulson, *Hogarth*, vol. 3: *Art and Politics, 1750–1764*, 1971, 2nd ed. (Cambridge, 1993): 336–61.

9 John Pye, *Patronage of British Art: A Historical Sketch* (London, 1845): 113.

10 Dorothy A. Stansfield and Ronald G. Stansfield, 'Dr. Thomas Beddoes and James Watt: Preparatory Work 1794–96 for the Bristol Pneumatic Institute', *Medical History* 30 (1986): 295.

11 Brunonianism was a system of medicine named after John Brown (1735–88). Central to Brown's teaching was the irritability and sensibility of the nervous system. Brown held that health was the effect of an equilibrium between outside stimulation and body excitability, and that diseases therefore fell into two groups, those in which insufficient stimulation caused a lack of excitement and a surfeit of unused excitablility, and those in which too much stimulation led to just the opposite. The first group – asthenic diseases – was by far the most commonly diagnosed and was mostly treated with ingestions of opium and alcohol, a fact which made Brunonianism suspect in England. In France and Germany, however, a modified form of Brown's medical system enjoyed a widespread vogue.

12 Roy Porter, *Doctor of Society: Thomas Beddoes and the Sicktrade in Late-Enlightenment England* (London, 1992).

13 Stansfield and Stansfield, 1986: 295.

14 [Robert John Thornton], *The Politician's Creed, Being the Great Outline of Political Science: From the Writings of Montesquieu, Hume, Gibbon, Paley, Townsend, &c. &c. by an Independent* (London, 1795). Although published anonymously it is identifiable as being by Thornton, because he cites himself as its author in the subtitle of his later publications (it also includes passages which are identical with part of *The Philosophy of Medicine*).

15 Thornton, 1795: 26 and 137.

16 Thornton, 1795: 35.

17 Thornton, 1795: 179.

18 This quotation comes from what is, according to the title-page, the fifth edition of *The Philosophy of Medicine: Or, Medical Extracts on the Nature of Health and Disease*, 5th ed., vol. 1 (London, 1813): 469. Yet there is something dubious about this publication. Given that it is supposed to have had so many editions, it is surprising that the four earlier editions are not widely available in public libraries today. The Bodleian Library, Oxford, contains a publication described as 'A New edition' dated 1796–7 (*Medical Extracts: On the Nature of Health: With Practical Observations, And the Laws of the Nervous and Fibrous Systems*, new ed., 4 vols., 1796–7). It also holds a fourth edition (5 vols.) from 1799–1800, which has the same title as the 1813 edition. Both earlier versions were published anonymously ('by a Friend to Improvements'). However, I believe that neither earlier version was published before 1804: many of the plates in the first two volumes, said to have been published in 1799, bear a later date (1800 or 1801); moreover, they contain a reference to an allegorical painting by Russell, *Cupid Presenting the Night-Blowing Cereus to Hymen*, which states that '[t]his picture was painted for Dr. Thornton's New Illustration of the Sexual System of Linnaeus and was in the Exhibition' (new ed., vol. 4, 1797: 853; 4th ed., vol. 3, 1800: 238). Such a painting was indeed listed in the catalogue to the exhibition, although it never appeared in *A New Illustration*. But the exhibition itself was not staged until 1804! It is possible that Thornton published the work around that time because the exhibition catalogue refers to him as the author of *The Philosophy of Medicine*. (That the painting was not included in the 1807 edition of *A New Illustration* seems to indicate that the latter had not appeared when the two earlier versions of *The Philosophy* were published, so 1807 may be taken as a date *ante quem* for the latter.) This confusion of dates seems to be an indication of Thornton's unscrupulous attempts to claim more success for himself than he actually enjoyed (for example, he made unsuccessful attempts in 1800 and 1812 to offer gratuitous lectures in the Royal Institution, *The Archives of the Royal Institution of Great Britain: In Facsimile Minutes of Managers' Meetings 1799–1900*, eds. Frank Greenway et al., vol. 2, London, 1971: 39; vol. 5, London, 1975: 283).

19 Thornton, *The Philosophy of Medicine*, 4th ed., vol. 2 (1799): 163–4.

20 See Robert E. Schofield, *The Lunar Society of Birmingham* (Oxford, 1963).

21 Darwin has been studied most comprehensively by Desmond King-Hele (*Erasmus Darwin*, London, 1963; *The Essential Writings of Erasmus Darwin*, London, 1968; *Doctor of Revolution: The Life and Genius of Erasmus Darwin*, London, 1977; *The Letters of Erasmus Darwin*, Cambridge, 1981; 'Erasmus Darwin. Master of Interdisciplinary Science', *Interdisciplinary Science Reviews* 10, 1985: 170–91; *Erasmus Darwin and the Romantic Poets*, London, 1986). The most recent publication on Darwin is Maureen

McNeil's excellent *Under the Banner of Science: Erasmus Darwin and his Age* (Manchester, 1987).

22   It is not surprising that the first subject that Thornton announced as part of a separate portrait publication (entitled *Portraits of Eminent Authors, either to Frame for the Study, or Affix to their Respective Works*) was Darwin. This did not materialise. In the advertisement for this publication in the *Morning Chronicle* of 18 February 1804 Thornton states: 'The first Portrait is the head of Dr. Darwin painted but a week before his death, and is acknowledged by Mrs. Darwin, and the rest of his family and friends, to be a very striking likeness of that celebrated poet, physician, and philosopher; and the only picture extant that the Doctor regularly sat for; and therefore, the only one that can represent correctly the feature of this great man'. It was painted by Rawlinson. Of the thirty plants commissioned by Thornton for *The Temple of Flora* (including the Egg-Plant, not published in the 1807 edition) only twelve were not mentioned by Darwin in the *Botanic Garden* (the hyacinths, the roses, the auriculas, the Queen, the aloe, the renealmia, the begonia, the passion flower, the stapelia, rhododendron, kalmia and limodron). In 1803 Darwin's last work, *The Temple of Nature* was published; *The Botanic Garden* and *The Temple of Nature* seem to have inspired Thornton's calling the last part of *A New Illustration* on its publication in 1807 *The Temple of Flora: Or, Garden of Nature*.

23   Erasmus Darwin, *Phytologia: Or, the Philosophy of Agriculture and Gardening* (London, 1800): 133.

24   Darwin, 1800: 139.

25   Darwin, 1800: 103.

26   Darwin, 1800: 115.

27   Darwin, 1789: 25.

28   Darwin, 1789: 152–3.

29   Thornton, *The Philosophy of Medicine*, 4th ed., vol. 1, p. 66.

30   Darwin, 1794–6, vol. 1, p. 6.

31   He excepts the soul, which is said to be in the brain and to be 'a substance [. . .] indifferent to motion and rest', but 'related to a substance that thinks, and though unagitated by external impressions can generally at will regain the former connexion' (*The Philosophy of Medicine*, 4th ed., vol. 2, p. 186).

32   Darwin, 1791: 120; 1794–6, vol. 1, pp. 478–533.

33   King-Hele, 1985: 174.

34   Darwin, 1794–6, vol. 1, p. 505.

35   Darwin, 1794–6, vol. 1, p. 505.

36   See McNeil, 1987.

37   Thornton, 1795: 34.

38   Norton Garfinkel, 'Science and Religion in England 1790–1800: The Critical Response to the Work of Erasmus Darwin', *Journal of the History of Ideas* 16 (1955): 376–88.

39   In *The Philosophy of Medicine* he writes, '[t]here are two great tyrannies, the tyranny of a despot and that of a multitude. Of these the most dreadful is republican tyranny' (4th ed., vol. 2, p. 246). And yet this publication celebrates the scientific achievements of a political radical like Thomas Beddoes.

40   Given Darwin's political associations, it was only to be expected that, after the outbreak of the French Revolution, the conservative press should react badly to his writings. But, as Garfinkel argues, 'what is striking is that the reviews which had formerly praised Darwin [including the Whiggian *Monthly Review*] were now almost unanimous in condemning this new work' (1955: 386). According to King-Hele, the 'most effective attack on Darwin in 1798 which transformed him from a fashionable author almost to a laughing-stock within a few weeks, was government-inspired, the originator being George Canning, Under-Secretary for Foreign Affairs in Pitt's Government' (1977: 264). Canning published a parody in *The Anti-Jacobin* periodical with the title 'The Loves of the Triangles'.

41   Thornton advertised this exhibition eight times in the *Morning Chronicle* between 9 May 1804 and 25 June 1804, when he announced its last week. He gave it the title *Botanical Exhibition* and promised 'a catalogue descriptive and poetic'. A copy of the catalogue is in the British Library, London, and entitled *Dr. Thornton's Exhibition of Botanical Paintings. Now Open at No. 49 Bond Street: With the Poetic Compositives made on the Different Subjects, and Explanatory Notes* (London, 1804). The catalogue was later elaborated to form the text accompanying the plates in the 1807 edition of *A New Illustration*. Apparently he had to raise the price of the catalogue from 6d to 1s within the first week of the opening. Obviously his calculation of demand did not meet his own expenditure.

42   Apart from Philip Reinagle's *The Superb Lily* and *Cupid Inspiring Plants with Love*, now in the Fitzwilliam Museum, Cambridge, I have been unable to trace any of the other paintings. Nor do any of them seem to have appeared on the art market.

43   In 1812 Thornton produced a second edition of the plates, known as the *Quarto Edition*. Presumably it was specifically intended to serve as the third prize for the Lottery. A much smaller and inferior production, consisting only of *The Temple of Flora*, the last part of *A New Illustration*, it included engravings of paintings which did not appear in the 1807 edition but in the catalogue of 1804.

44   He had become a Royal Academician in 1788 and a year later was made a court painter.

45   King, 1981: 38.

46   His paintings are rare in public collections, but some are in Bath, Cambridge and Dublin. Drawings by Reinagle are in the British Museum and the Victoria and Albert Museum, London. Reinagle was born in 1749, the son of a Hungarian musician. Trained as a portrait painter under Allan Ramsay at the Royal Academy Schools, he was subsequently engaged by Ramsay to make a series of painstaking copies of royal portraits, including portraits of George III and Queen Charlotte. As a result he exhibited only portraits at the Royal Academy from 1773 to 1785. By the time he was employed by Thornton, however, he

had changed genres, turning first to animal painting and sporting subjects, and then, from 1794, chiefly to landscape painting. He did this probably in order to escape the 'sporting stigma' which he might have held responsible for his failure at Royal Academy elections (Stephen Deuchar, *Sporting Art in Eighteenth-Century England*, London and New Haven, 1988: 135). Reinagle had become an ARA in 1787, but only in 1812 was he elected RA. He appears always to have been short of money and in 1798 appealed to the Royal Academy for one hundred and fifty pounds to save himself and his family from ruin. This might also be the reason for his agreeing to work for Thornton. (Samuel Redgrave, *A Dictionary of Artists of the English School*, London, 1874: 334; Michael Bryan, *Dictionary of Painters and Engravers*, vol. 4, London, 1904: 207; Ulrich Thieme and Felix Becker, *Allgemeines Lexikon der Bildenden Künstler von der Antike bis zur Gegenwart*, vol. 28, Leipzig, 1934: 116; Maurice H. Grant, *A Dictionary of British Landscape Painters from the 16th to the 20th Century*, Leigh-on-Sea, 1952: 152; Ellis K. Waterhouse, *The Dictionary of British Eighteenth-Century Painters in Oils and Crayon*, Woodbridge, 1981: 298.)

47 Algernon Graves, *The Royal Academy of Arts: A Complete Dictionary of Contributors and their Work from its Foundation in 1769 to 1904*, vol. 6 (London, 1905): 258–60. This catalogue shows that between 1797 and 1800 Reinagle exhibited in the Royal Academy seven of the oil paintings Thornton had commissioned (*A Sensitive Plant*, 1797; *Tournefort's System*, 1798; *Cupid Inspiring Plants with Love*, *The American Aloe* and *The Begonia*, all 1799; and *The Blue Passion Flower* and *The Night-Blowing Cereus*, both 1800). The painting with the title *The American Aloe* must have been the one which was later published as *The Aloe*. The plant shown is in fact an agave. As Ronald King points out, 'agaves, though similar in appearance, are inhabitants of the New World. Neither is found wild in the other's territory' (1981: 70). King speculates that Thornton realised his mistake 'and named a second picture of the same plant published later "The American Aloe"' (p. 70). However, it is very likely that the painting *The American Aloe* shown in the Royal Academy Exhibition in 1799 was the original, now given its correct title, since Thornton showed all the existing paintings in an exhibition in 1804 and *The Aloe* was shown in only one version (albeit once again with the incorrect name, while the text to the first plate of the 1807 edition of *A New Illustration* correctly titles it: *American Aloe, Or Agave Americana*).

48 William Curtis, who published the first successful botanical periodical in Britain, the *Botanical Magazine: Or, Flower-Garden Displayed*, took Edwards on at the outset of his career, and, from the second volume (1788) of the *Botanical Magazine* onwards, almost all the drawings in it were executed by Edwards. In 1809 he had already successfully published his *Representation of 150 Rare and Curious Ornamental Plants* in London, so that in 1815, when he fell out with Curtis, he was in a position to start his own rival

venture, the *Botanical Register, New Flora Britannica*. He also produced drawings of dogs and horses for *Cynographia Britannica* (1800–5), Rees' *Encyclopedia* and *The Sportman's Magazine*. (See Redgrave, 1874: 138–9; Grant, 1952: 62; Thieme and Becker, vol. 10, 1914: 352; Robert B. Burbidge, *A Dictionary of British Flower, Fruit and Still Life Painters*, vol. 1, Leigh-on-Sea, 1974: 18.)

49 Graves, 1905–6, vol. 3, p. 28.

50 Sotheby's sold an oil painting of 1810 on 18 November 1987 with the title *Fowl and Chicks in a Landscape*. Here the animals are set in front of a dark mountain, which is part of a chain leading into the background. The cloudy sky reveals patches of sun. The atmosphere of the whole composition displays a fairly generalised sublime mood. A very similar undetailed mountainous landscape also forms the background to another oil painting, which was on sale at Christie's, 13 October 1989. But *Mares and a Fowl in a Wooded Landscape*, dated 1798, conveys a much more picturesque impression. The foreground shows rather feathery trees and far more texture than the *Fowl and Chicks* painting. Drawings by Sydenham Teak Edwards are in the British Museum and the Victoria and Albert Museum.

51 Redgrave, 1874: 134. Presumably his connection with William Curtis was an additional source of recommendation. Thornton wrote a short biography of Curtis in 1805. ('Sketch of the Life and Writings of the late Mr. William Curtis by Dr. Thornton', preface to William Curtis, *Lectures on Botany, as Delivered in the Botanic Garden at Lambeth. By the Late William Curtis, F.L.S.*, ed. Samuel Curtis, vol. 1, London, 1805.)

52 Abraham Pether was born at Chichester in 1756. There he became a pupil of George Smith. He exhibited 'small landscapes' with the Incorporated Society of Artists from 1773 until 1791 (Algernon Graves, *The Society of Artists of Great Britain 1760–1791, The Free Society of Artists 1761–1783: A Complete Dictionary of Contributors and their Work from the Foundation of the Societies to 1791*, London, 1907: 195–6). By the time Pether showed work at the Royal Academy (1784–1811) he had chiefly turned to highly charged sublime landscapes of moonlight scenes, volcanoes, ruins and scenes with titles like 'Effect of the sun just before a shower' (1796) (Graves, 1905–6, vol. 6, p. 113). He also lectured on philosophy and mathematics, illustrating his talks with his own inventions of telescopes, microscopes and electrical gadgets. (See Redgrave, 1874: 313; and Bryan, 1903–4, vol. 4, pp. 102–3; see also Thieme and Becker, vol. 26, 1932: 488; Grant, 1952: 148; and Waterhouse, 1981: 278.)

53 Besides drawings in the British Museum and the Victoria and Albert Museum, there are two paintings in the Manchester City Art Gallery, and one is owned by the Corporation of London collections. An indication of the character of Pether's work can be gleaned from the titles of those that have appeared on the art market, for example, Sotheby's: *An Evening Landscape*, 1795 (18 November 1981); *A Village Church Burning in a Moonlit River Landscape*

(17 March 1982); *Wooded Landscape with a Rustic and Cattle and Sheep by a Farm*, 1783 (21 November 1984); *View of God's House and the Quay, South Hampton by Moonlight with Gentlemen* (8 March 1989); *An Extensive Italianate Landscape with Sheep* (13 July 1984); *An Extensive Wooded River Landscape* (13 July 1984; also at Christie's, 26 March 1976); *A River Landscape at Evening* (27 May 1983); *The Eruption of Vesuvius by Moonlight*, 1800 (27 May 1983; also at Christie's, 16 April 1982); *A View of Rome* (21 November 1979); and *A Moonlit River Landscape* (29 January 1988).

54 *The Works of the Late Edward Dayes*, ed. Mrs. E. Dayes (London, 1805): 343.

55 Redgrave, 1874: 313.

56 This point was made by Cardew, 1947: 284.

57 Bush (1974: 295) cites as a recent example the following lines of the poem *The Midnite Show* (1960) by the American author Jonathan Williams:

> I remember the NIGHT-BLOOMING
> CEREUS, by Dr. Thornton, . . .
> . . . , it
>   hangs in the hall outside the bedroom
> swaying hungrily like these
>   giant white goddesses of the dark grotto.

58 Robert John Thornton, *The Religious Use of Botany: Being an Introduction to the Science* (London, 1824): 24.

59 Thornton, *The Temple of Flora*, 'Explanation to the Picturesque Plates'.

60 Curtis, *Botanical Magazine* 2 (1788): no. 44; William T. Stearn, 'Botanical Notes', in Grigson and Buchanan, 1972: 66.

61 Graves, 1905–6, vol. 4, pp. 67–8. It should be pointed out that, judging by the extremely high numbers in the catalogue, none of the paintings commissioned by Thornton was hung prominently at the Royal Academy. This is, of course, not surprising, given that they were flower pieces.

62 After the period of his work for *A New Illustration* Henderson continued to exhibit flower and fruit pieces as well as portraiture at the British Institution and the Royal Academy. In 1806 he published his own botanical treatise (with drawing manual), *The Seasons or Flower-Garden* (London, 1806), and two years later a work on fruits, *Pomona* (London, 1808); see Dunthorne, 1938: 46, no. 206. From 1812 he seems to have turned to historical and allegorical subjects, in order to establish his reputation. But none of his paintings is known today, nor anything about his life (Thieme and Becker, vol. 16, 1923: 378; Burbidge, 1974: 22).

63 An exception to some extent is Reinagle. He painted three other plants before 1804 (*Pitcher Plant*, published in 1803; *The Narrow-leaved Kalmia*, published in 1804; and *American Bog-Plants*, published in 1806 but evidently finished by 1804, since it appeared in the exhibition).

In 1807 Thornton must have approached Reinagle once again, this time not for a new commission but for the repainting of Henderson's *A Group of Four Auriculas* and Reinagle's own *The Aloe* (for a more extensive discussion of this and other aspects of the genesis of the work, see the Appendix to my thesis, *Science and the Perception of Nature: British Landscape Art in the Late Eighteenth and Early Nineteenth Centuries*, Ph.D. Thesis, University of Cambridge, 1992). Although Thornton did not commission new artists after 1804 he nevertheless states in the exhibition catalogue that he has engaged the following fifteen 'eminent artists': Sir William Beechy, RA; Russel, RA; Opie, RA; Reinagle, ARA; Harlow; Pether; Henderson; Raeburn; Sidney Edwards; Thomson; Corbould; Burney; Dayes; Girten; and Rawlinson. For a discussion of these names in relation to Thornton's project, see also my thesis (pp. 83–5). Here, let it suffice to say that Thornton was not above boasting. He was, for example, rejected as a Fellow of the Linnean Society (according to Alexander McLeay in a letter to James Edward Smith, the President of the Society) 'because he was considered a Quack in Botany as well as in Medicine and chiefly because he published himself as F.L.S. before he was even proposed to the Society, as if his Election were a mere matter of course' (quoted in A.T. Gage and W.T. Stearn, *A Bicentenary History of the Linnean Society of London*, London, 1988: 141). Thornton's misuse of the title F.L.S. is evident in the subtitle of his *Advertisement* of 1797. In *A New Illustration* Thornton was more careful, claiming generally to be a member of several societies.

64 A fact which surely casts doubt on Ronald King's view: 'So attractive is the picture, so superbly engraved, and, in the best specimens, so well coloured, that it is legitimate to ask why Thornton did not use more of his own work. Those who accuse him of vanity are hard put to it to explain this away' (1981: 36). Nevertheless, Thornton's description is puzzling. The sunrise is characterised allegorically and no 'Zephyr crowning Spring with roses' is visible as such in the plate. The allegorical description of the sunrise, is, however, not as far fetched as it might seem in relation to Dayes' topographical work. Dayes had been trying to make his name as a painter of allegorical subjects.

65 I am not convinced by Clive Bush's theatrical metaphor in his description of the plates. As he describes it, one perceives 'the near object of the flower and the far background of the landscape from two different viewpoints simultaneously, and simultaneously in focus', from which he concludes that the result is 'a strange new world' (1974: 314). In this way, he thinks, a self-contained space is created in the pictures, although one which is visionary rather than real. I cannot share this conclusion; I do not see the creation of a unified space (however 'unreal') so much as two independent levels in the background and foreground which function as reflections of one another.

66 None of the plants shown resembles its depiction in Curtis' *Botanical Magazine*, although the following could have formed models since they appeared there earlier: *The American Cowslip*, *The Blue Passion Flower*, 1 (1787); *The Persian Cyclamen* and *The Winged Passion Flower*, 2 (1788); *The Queen*, 4 (1790); *The White Lily*, 8 (1794); *The Narrow-leaved Kalmia*, 10 (1796); *Indian Reed*, 13 (1799); and *The*

Blue Egyptian Water-Lily, 16 (1802). During these years depicting after real models became popular and Sydenham Teak Edwards achieved fame for his ability to draw after nature. Only one drawing by Georg Dionysius Ehret in his *Trew's Plantae Selectae* shows a close similarity to Thornton's engravings and could have functioned as a model: the cereus (Tab. 31) has a similar arrangement of its stem, although the inside of the flower is more detailed in Thornton's version. However the following depiction in Ehret (Tab. 32) shows a detailed illustration of the inside of the plant, which resembles Thornton's. But *The Superb Lily* (Tab. 11), *The Arum* (Tab. 56) and *The Rhododendron* (Tab. 66) as well as *The Mimosa* (Tab. 45) show different species, while *The Meadia* (Tab. 12) is different in conception altogether.

67 It could not have been drawn there by Reinagle, who started working for Thornton in 1797 and exhibited a painting of that plant in 1799. Thornton must have come to know about this plant when he was a student at Guy's Hospital, where Sir James Edward Smith (later the President of the Linnean Society) was lecturing on medical botany. But he would not have witnessed its flowering in 1790, because he did not arrive there until three years later.

68 This letter was written in self-defence by Thornton in response to a scathingly hostile notice of *A New Illustration* published in the *Annual Review* (*Philosophical Magazine* 19, 1804: 145).

69 Thornton, *Advertisement*, 1797.

70 Altogether Thornton offers eighteen poems on the subject of the rose!

71 Bush, 1974: 318.

72 Cardew, 1947: 284.

73 Thornton had, of course, a strong interest in portraiture and intended to produce, as mentioned earlier, a separate portrait publication. His exhibition catalogue of 1804 makes it clear that he owned some portraits himself. The portraits published in the first parts of *A New Illustration*, however, in contrast to the flower plates, are mostly half-length vignettes without background (the exception is an interior portrait of Linnaeus in Lapp costume).

74 Marcia Pointon, 'Portrait-Painting as a Business Enterprise in London in the 1780s', *Art History* 7 (1984): 187–205.

75 The tradition of portraits which clearly define and demarcate the sitter against their background was given up by Gainsborough in his later paintings. The more his understanding of nature gained a subjective quality, the more he allowed himself to merge his sitters into it (Paulson, 1978: 218; Bermingham, 1987: 58).

76 James Northcote, *Memoirs of Sir Joshua Reynolds, Knt* (London, 1813): 36–7.

77 Deuchar, 1988: 30.

78 Thornton, 1824: 21.

79 Thornton, 1795: 26.

80 Thus it was not 'passion, sexuality, and madness' which 'continually threatened the security of the fixed point of view in which everything appeared in just proportion and harmony', as Clive Bush (1974: 314) concluded in his discussion of Thornton's *Temple of Flora*, but rather individual aspirations which were not in accordance with the pre-established order.

81 Darwin changed his ideas about how variety was created and the contribution made by each partner to its progeny. In the *Zoonomia* (1794–6) he saw, according to Janet Browne, only the male partner as a formative influence, while in the *Phytologia* (1800) both partners were influential; towards the end of his life he attributed different, but complementary, qualities to males and females (Janet Browne, 'Botany for Gentlemen: Erasmus Darwin and "The Loves of the Plants"', *ISIS* 80, 1989: 603).

82 In *The Philosophy of Medicine*, 4th ed., vol. 4, p. 135, Thornton writes that 'without irritability there is neither sensation nor life'.

83 *The Philosophy of Medicine*, 4th ed., vol. 3 (1800): 238–9. How closely Pether must have followed Joseph Wright of Derby becomes clear from this account. The described paintings must be the following exhibited at the Royal Academy and Society of Artists: *A Fire; By Moonlight* (elected F.S.A.), Society of Artists, 1790; *An Iron Foundry by Moonlight*, Royal Academy, 1796; *The Eruption of Mount Vesuvius as Seen in 1802*, Royal Academy, 1811 (Graves, 1905–6, vol. 6, p. 113; Graves, 1907: 195–6).

84 *The Philosophy of Medicine*, 5th ed., vol. 1, p. 469. Thornton adds in a footnote to the text of *The Dragon Arum* in *The Temple of Flora* that the roots can be used for medicinal purposes, thus justifying his belief that there is no evil that does not also contain some good.

85 *The Philosophy of Medicine*, 5th ed., vol. 1, p. 469.

86 I hypothesise that the hanging in that exhibition (assuming that it corresponded to the order in the catalogue, i.e. starting with Reinagle's paintings of *The Aloe*, then *The Night-Blowing Cereus*, *Large Flowering Sensitive Plant*, *The Oblique-leaved Begonia* and *The Blue Passion Flower*) came closer to the order of commission than did the final arrangement of the prints. It is worth noting that these are the plants which correspond most clearly to Darwin's analogical way of thinking (the begonia stands as an example for the conspicuous differentiation between male and female flowers, which, though they differ in appearance, are nevertheless found on the same plant). After Reinagle's painting of the passion flower, Thornton displayed the two other versions done by Henderson. The two paintings by Pether, which later formed the beginning of *A New Illustration*, were placed next, followed by Edwards' *Hyacinths* and one of Reinagle's earlier paintings, *Tulips*. Thornton also placed two of Reinagle's other early paintings later. *The Narrow-leaved Kalmia* and *The Superb Lily* appear before Henderson's *The White Lily*. The last item in the exhibition, following the painting of *The Sacred Egyptian Bean*, was Thornton's own painting, *Roses*. Both paintings are accompanied by the most extensive mythological commentary.

87 Robert Furber, *Twelve Months of Flowers and the Flower Garden Display'd* (London, 1732). Although Furber took pride in the fact that the plants were delineated and

88 Darwin, 1791: 154.

89 Thornton makes this particularly explicit in his later publication *The Religious Use of Botany* (1824: 24).

90 Clive Emsley, *British Society and the French Wars 1793–1815* (London, 1979): 115.

91 Thornton, 1824: 24.

92 On Darwin and his use of mythology, see Irwin Primer, 'Erasmus Darwin's Temple of Nature: Progress, Evolution, and the Eleusinian Mysteries', *Journal of the History of Ideas* 25 (1964): 58–76; see also R.N. Ross, '"To Charm the Curious Eye": Erasmus Darwin's Poetry at the Vestibule of Knowledge', *Journal of the History of Ideas* 32 (1971): 379–94. In the dedication of *A New Illustration* to the Queen, Thornton too speaks of the improvements of 'useful and ornamental Sciences' (by which he means the Arts) and he praises the 'unbounded protection' of the King and Queen for having made such progress possible. Thus the reference to mythology serves here, as in Darwin's writing, merely to confirm the eternal validity of Divine laws, now (particularly since Linnaeus) more thoroughly understood by modern science.

93 Thornton, 1824: 43.

94 Thornton, 1824: 41.

95 Thornton, 1824: 33.

96 Anonymous, *Monthly Magazine, or British Register* 17 (1804): 647.

97 *Monthly Magazine* 17 (1804): 346.

98 An even longer and more scathing anonymous review appeared in the *Annual Review, and History of Literature, for 1803* 11 (1804): 873–82. It concluded: 'The patience of the public must soon be exhausted. [. . .] and [*A New Illustration*] instead of a national honour, may more justly be deemed a national disgrace' (p. 882). Thornton reacted fiercely to this review in several letters to the *Philosophical Magazine* 18 (1804): 326–32; 19 (1804): 141–6, 218–60, 360–3). Both the editor of the *Annual Review*, Aikin (who distanced himself from the review), and the anonymous critic replied to Thornton's first letter in the *Philosophical Magazine* 19 (1804): 39–41.

99 Thornton was clearly trying to copy the example of John Boydell, who (having first obtained special parliamentary permission) successfully disposed of the pictures from his Shakespeare Gallery by a lottery in 1805.

100 Grigson and Buchanan, 1972: 6.

101 Thornton announced the drawing of the lottery in the *London Gazette* between 13 March 1813 (p. 535) and 16 March.

102 *Annual Register: Or, A View of the History, Politics, and Literature, of the Year 1837*, 79 (1838): 171–2.

103 L.D. Schwarz, *London in the Age of Industrializations: Entrepreneurs, Labour Force and Living Conditions, 1700–1850* (Cambridge, 1992).

104 Langford, 1994: 455.

105 *Monthly Magazine* 17 (1804): 647.

106 Keith Maslen, 'Printing for the Author: From Bowyer Printing Ledgers, 1710–1775', *The Library*, Fifth Series, 27 (1972): 302–9.

107 Schaffer, 1990.

108 Thornton writes: 'The brain may therefore be compared to a *carte blanche*, receiving every impression; and to a cabinet, wherein the different portions of the universe are painted in miniature, and may be drawn out at pleasure' (*The Philosophy of Medicine*, 4th ed., vol. 2, p. 186). For Darwin and the Lockean notion, see McNeil, 1987: 173.

109 *Annual Review* 11 (1804): 878.

III FROM PICTURESQUE TRAVEL TO SCIENTIFIC OBSERVATION

1 William Daniell, *Interesting Selections from Animated Nature with Illustrative Scenery*, 2 vols. (London [1812?]) n. pag. The publication date of this book is not entirely clear. Judging by the dates on the plates, Daniell must have finished it around 1812.

2 60 of the 120 engravings in Daniell (1812?) had already appeared in William Wood's *Zoography: Or the Beauties of Nature Displayed*, 3 vols. (London, 1807). Wood employed Daniell for the design and execution of the prints in this work. Since Daniell states in the preface to the *Interesting Selections* that Wood's *Zoography* had appeared in the previous year, it can be inferred that he started his own project in 1808. The second volume consists almost entirely of images printed in 1809. All of these refer to subjects in Wood's publication and could well have been drawn for it but then not published. It seems that Daniell prepared a final eleven pictures for his own edition in 1812 in order to make 120. The subjects for these engravings are all taken from reference books noted by Wood, quite often with plate numbers.

3 William Daniell, *A Voyage round Great Britain*, 8 vols. (London, 1814–25). Richard Ayton provided the text for volumes 1 and 2, while from volume 3 onwards, Daniell carried out the project on his own. A brief attempt to throw light on Daniell's publication contract has been undertaken by Ian Bain, *William Daniell's A Voyage round Great Britain, 1814–1825: A Note on its Production and the Subsequent History of the Aquatint Plates Now Owned by Nattali & Maurice* (London, 1966). See also Thomas Sutton, *The Daniells: Artists and Travellers* (London, 1954); Sarah T. Prideaux, *Aquatint Engravings: A Chapter in the History of Book Illustration* (London, 1909); Martin Hardie and Muriel Clayton, 'Thomas Daniell, R.A., William Daniell, R.A.', *Walker's Quarterly* 35–6 (1932): 1–106.

4 Daniell, 1814–25, vol. 3, pp. 35–48. In the same year Daniell also published the set of nine Staffa views separately in a folio edition called *Illustrations of the Island of Staffa in a Series of Views: Accompanied by Topographical and Geological Description* (London, 1818).

5 Daniell, 1814–25, vol. 3, pp. 35–6.

6 Daniell, 1814–25, vol. 3, p. 37.

7   On the foundation and development of the Geological Society of London, see Martin J.S. Rudwick, 'The Foundation of the Geological Society of London: Its Scheme for Co-operative Research and its Struggle for Independence', *British Journal for the History of Science* 1 (1963): 325–55; Paul J. Weindling, 'Geological Controversy and its Historiography: The Prehistory of the Geological Society of London', in Ludmilla J. Jordanova and Roy Porter, eds., *Images of the Earth: Essays in the History of Environmental Sciences* (Chalfont St Giles, 1979): 249–71; Martin J.S. Rudwick, *The Great Devonian Controversy: The Shaping of Scientific Knowledge among Gentlemanly Specialists* (Chicago, 1985): 18–27.

8   His longstanding work for the Ordnance Survey in Scotland did not pass without severe disputes. He was accused of submitting enormous bills and subsequently was described as 'a blackguard, a thief and "the last high priest of a supplanted religion"' (Archibald Geikie, quoted after David A. Cumming, 'John MacCulloch, Blackguard, Thief and High Priest, Reassessed', in Alwyne Wheeler and James H. Price, eds., *From Linnaeus to Darwin: Commentaries on the History of Biology and Geology. Papers from the Fifth Easter Meeting of the Society for the History of Natural History 28–31 March*, London, 1985: 77). However, Cumming argues that the epithets were unjustified: 'He was one of the earliest truly professional geologists in Britain [. . .]. MacCulloch's Scottish surveys extended rather than plagiarised existing work, but brought on him the wrath of a jealous rival [Robert Jameson, a former friend]' (p. 85).

9   John MacCulloch, 'On Staffa', *Transactions of the Geological Society of London* 2 (1814): 501–9.

10 Daniell, 1814–25, vol. 3, p. 37.

11 Daniell, 1812?, vol. 1.

12 Thornton was also an Annual Subscriber to the British School, in which Daniell was an exhibitor. See John Gage, *George Field and his Circle: From Romanticism to the Pre-Raphaelite Brotherhood*, exhib. cat. Fitzwilliam Museum, Cambridge (London, 1989): 13, 26.

13 Daniell, 1812?, vol. 1.

14 Daniell, 1812?, vol. 2.

15 They are, in fact, brief versions of Wood's descriptions.

16 These images had already appeared in Wood's short section on minerals. Barbara M. Stafford ('Rude Sublime: The Taste for Nature's Colossi during the Late Eighteenth and Early Nineteenth Centuries', *Gazette des Beaux-Arts* 1287, 1976: 113–26) discusses the non-distinction between artefacts and natural phenomena in pictorial material during the second half of the eighteenth century and uses three of these illustrations as examples (pp. 119–20). In her later *Voyage into Substance* (1984) she mainly concentrates on Daniell's earlier enterprise, the *Oriental Sceneries*, but nevertheless shows the four prints of his *Interesting Selections* (pp. 71, 72, 76, 343). (In her article Stafford mistakenly states that the book was published in 1807, and in *Voyage into Substance* she also wrongly names Thomas Daniell as responsible for the publication.)

17 Daniell, 1812?, vol. 1.

18 John Challinor, *The History of British Geology: A Bibliographical Study* (Newton Abbot, 1971): 88.

19 Martin J.S. Rudwick, 'The Emergence of a Visual Language for Geological Science 1760–1840', *History of Science* 14 (1976): 149–95. My research for this chapter is not only greatly indebted to this article, but also to Rudwick's perceptive comments on the version which appeared in my thesis.

20 Rudwick, 1976: 175.

21 Duncan Macmillan, *Painting in Scotland: The Golden Age* (Oxford, 1986); James Holloway and Lindsay Errington, *The Discovery of Scotland: The Appreciation of Scottish Scenery through Two Centuries of Painting*, exhib. cat. National Gallery of Scotland (Edinburgh, 1978).

22 Thomas Pennant, *A Tour in Scotland* (Chester, 1771).

23 Paul Sandby, *The Virtuosi's Museum; Containing Select Views, in England, Scotland, and Ireland* (London, 1778).

24 Julian Faigan, *Paul Sandby Drawings*, exhib. cat. City of Hamilton Art Gallery (Sydney, 1981); Luke Herrmann, *Paul and Thomas Sandby* (London, 1986); Bruce Robertson, *The Art of Paul Sandby*, exhib. cat. Yale Center for British Art (New Haven, 1985).

25 Jessica Christian, 'Paul Sandby and the Military Survey of Scotland', in Nicholas Alfrey and Stephen Daniels, eds., *Mapping the Landscape: Essays on Art and Cartography*, exhib. cat. University Art Gallery, Nottingham (Nottingham, 1990): 18–22.

26 Sandby etched this view after his return from Scotland, issuing it together with other Scottish depictions in 1751.

27 Notebooks for Farington's Scotland Tour in 1788 are divided between the British Museum and the Edinburgh Public Library. Notebooks for the tour in 1792 are in the Edinburgh Public Library. I have consulted the material in the British Museum, which also includes the sketchbooks for both journeys.

28 Farington, quoted in Holloway and Errington, 1978: 87.

29 William Gilpin, *Observations Relative Chiefly to Picturesque Beauty: Made in the Year 1776, on Several Parts of Great Britain, particularly the High-lands of Scotland*, 2 vols. (London, 1789).

30 Gilpin, 1789, vol. 2, p. 122.

31 *The Diary of Joseph Farington*, vol. 5, eds. Kenneth Garlick and Angus Macintyre (New Haven, 1979): 1655, 10 October 1801.

32 Farington, ed. 1979, vol. 5, p. 1664, 15 October 1801.

33 Peter Howard, 'Painter's Preferred Places', *Journal of Historical Geography* 11 (1985): 139. See also Christopher Smout, 'Tours in the Scottish Highlands from the Eighteenth to the Twentieth Centuries', *Northern Scotland* 5 (1982): 99–121.

34 Graves, 1905–6.

35 W.D. MacKay and Frank Rinder, *The Royal Scottish Academy, 1826–1916* (Glasgow, 1917).

36 Francina Irwin, *Turner in Scotland*, exhib. cat. Aberdeen Art Gallery (London, 1982): 7.

37 In my view Malcolm Andrews (1989) does not sufficiently distinguish between naturalist travellers and artists when he writes in his otherwise informative chapter 'The Highlands Tour and the Ossianic Sublime' that: 'There were two Scottish tours recognised over this period [the second half of the eighteenth century]. What might be called the "Long Tour" followed the north-eastern coastline up to Aberdeen and round to Inverness, then down by Loch Ness and Ben Nevis with perhaps an excursion to the Western Islands, especially Iona and Staffa, and then back to Glasgow [. . .]. The other tour was undertaken by those who came to Edinburgh for reasons of health or amusement: [they] generally visit Glasgow, Loch Lomond, and Inverary, on the West; or Perth, Dunkeld, Blair, and Taymouth, on the North' (p. 206). It seems that only the short tour was taken by the majority of eighteenth-century artists. Arthur Mitchell's list of travels to Scotland seems to be fairly complete and has proved enormously helpful for my research: 'A List of Travels, Tours, Journeys, Voyages, Cruises, Excursions, Wanderings, Rambles, Visits, etc., Relating to Scotland', *Proceedings of the Society of Antiquaries of Scotland* 11 (1900–1): 431–638.

38 I am grateful to Richard Sharpe for lending me the manuscript of his forthcoming publication, an annotated list of works relating to Iona and St Columba including the neighbouring island of Staffa, which has saved me from some bibliographical errors.

39 Banks published a short notice of his 1772 voyage, when he was on his way back, in the *Scots Magazine* 34 (1772): 637 and the *Gentleman's Magazine* 42 (1772): 540, announcing the sights of Staffa to be the 'greatest natural curiosities in the world'. The journal of this voyage is reprinted in Roy A. Rauschenberg, 'The Journals of Joseph Banks' Voyage up Great Britain's West Coast to Iceland and to the Orkney Isles, July to October 1772', *Proceedings of the American Philosophical Society* 117 (1973): 186–226.

40 There is some confusion in the secondary literature about the dates of Pennant's publications. The following seems to me to be the right order: Pennant's account of his tour on the mainland in 1769 appeared with illustrations mainly by Tomkins, but also by Paul Sandby, for the first time in Chester and London in 1771. In 1772 Pennant undertook his journey to the Hebrides, apparently, as he states, at the same time as Banks. He then published two volumes, consisting of two parts with illustrations mainly by his companion, Moses Griffiths, but with further engravings by Sandby. The first volume appeared in 1774 and contains an account of a second tour on the mainland, this time more towards the west of the country, and the beginning of his account of travel to the Hebrides, which forms the contents of the second volume, published in 1776. Banks' account appears in the second volume, pp. 299–309. Pennant's entire tour of Scotland had also appeared as a whole without illustrations in two volumes the previous year (Dublin, 1775).

41 Martin Martin, *A Description of the Western Islands of Scotland* (London, 1703).

42 Pennant, 1774–6, vol. 2, pp. 300–1.

43 Pennant, 1774–6, vol. 2, facing p. 299.

44 The original sketches executed on Banks' voyage to the Hebrides, Orkneys and Iceland in 1772 and the preparatory copies for the engravings in Pennant's publication were left by Banks to the British Museum (BL Add. 15509-12). The drawings and coloured fair copies of Staffa are in the second volume (Add. 15510, nos. 20–43). Among them are drawings copied from the originals in 1774 by an artist whose name I was unable to decipher (Ruotta?).

45 Strikingly, the sketch in the British Library (Add. 15510, no. 40) does not display this regularity, nor does it show any accompanying figures, except for a single boat deep inside the cave.

46 This date becomes apparent from Banks' correspondence in which Faujas de Saint-Fond is mentioned a few times, particularly in the year 1784 with reference to his trip to Staffa (*The Banks Letters: A Calendar of the Manuscript Correspondence*, ed. Warren Dawson, London, 1958: 64–5, 276).

47 Bartélemi Faujas de Saint-Fond, *Voyage en Angleterre, en Écosse, et aux Iles Hébrides*, 2 vols. (Paris, 1797). An English translation appeared in London in 1799.

48 Banks, ed. 1958: 321. Faujas de Saint-Fond (1797, vol. 1) describes calling on Banks in London before he set off to Scotland.

49 Faujas de Saint-Fond, 1797, vol. 2, p. 55, fn.

50 Banks, ed. 1958: 276.

51 Banks, ed. 1958: 65.

52 Banks, ed. 1958: 493.

53 Thomas Garnett, *Observations on a Tour through the Highlands and Part of the Western Isles of Scotland, particularly Staffa and Icolmkill*, 2 vols. (London, 1800). The three plates of Staffa appeared in vol. 1, facing pp. 219, 221, 224.

54 Louis A. Necker de Saussure, *Voyage en Écosse et aux Isles Hébrides*, 3 vols. (Geneva, 1821). I consulted the second editon of the translation which appeared in London in 1822 (the first, in 1821, was without plates): *A Voyage to the Hebrides or Western Isles of Scotland* (London, 1822).

55 Hugh S. Torrens, 'Patronage and Problems: Banks and the Earth Sciences', in R.E.R. Banks et al., eds., *Sir Joseph Banks: A Global Perspective* (Kew, 1974): 52.

56 Torrens, 1974: 52.

57 Pennant, 1774–6, vol. 2, p. 306.

58 William Hamilton, 'An Account of the Late Eruption of Mount Vesuvius', *Philosophical Transactions of the Royal Society of London* 85 (1795): 73–116 (Tab. 5–11). Hamilton first published his extensive observations in the form of letters to the Royal Society in English and French in Naples in 1776 (*Campi Phlegraei. Observations on the Volcanos of the Two Sicilies*, 2 vols., Naples, 1776), adding a supplement with illustrations in 1779. All three parts are bound in one volume in the copy in the Bodleian Library, Oxford (a second copy does not contain the supplement).

59 Robert Jameson, *A Mineralogy of the Scottish Isles*, 2 vols. (Edinburgh, 1800).

60 Daniell, 1812?, vol. 1.

61 Daniell, 1812?, vol. 1.

62 See Roy Porter, *The Making of Geology: Earth Science in Britain 1660–1815* (Cambridge, 1977).

63 Archibald Geikie, *The Scottish School of Geology* (Edinburgh, 1871): 21.

64 Rachel Laudan, *From Mineralogy to Geology: The Foundations of a Science, 1650–1830* (Chicago and London, 1987): 108.

65 John Playfair, *Illustrations of the Huttonian Theory of the Earth* (Edinburgh, 1802).

66 James Hutton, 'Theory of the Earth: Or an Investigation of the Laws Observable in the Composition, Dissolution, and Restoration of Land upon the Globe', *Transactions of the Royal Society of Edinburgh* 1 (1788): 209–304.

67 James Hutton, *Theory of the Earth with Proofs and Illustrations*, 2 vols. (Edinburgh, 1795). Geikie published a third volume in 1899 which was made up of Hutton's unpublished notes.

68 Stephen J. Gould (*Time's Arrow, Time's Cycle: Myth and Metaphor in the Discovery of Geological Time*, London, 1988: 61) notes that 'Lyell admitted that he had never managed to read it all. Even Kirwan, Hutton's dogged, almost frantic critic [. . .] never read all of both volumes – for many pages of his personal copy are uncut' (p. 93).

69 Hutton (1795) himself talks of 'junction'. Thus he writes that 'at Siccar point we found a beautiful picture of junction marked bare by sea' (vol. 1, p. 458).

70 Hutton, 1788: 304.

71 Hutton, 1788: 304.

72 Porter, 1977: 196. For Kirwan and de Luc, see Richard Kirwan, *Geological Essays* (London, 1799) and Jean André de Luc, *Letters on the Physical History of the Earth* (London, 1831).

73 Hutton, 1795, vol. 1, p. 453.

74 Laudan, 1987: 129–30.

75 Subsequently published in two papers illustrated with these drawings (James Hall, 'On the Vertical Position and Convolutions of Certain Strata, and their Relations with Granite' and 'On the Revolutions of the Earth's Surface', *Transactions of the Royal Society of Edinburgh* 7 (1815): 79–108 and 139–211).

76 G.Y. Craig, ed., *James Hutton's Theory of the Earth: The Lost Drawings* (Edinburgh, 1978).

77 Craig, 1978: 16.

78 Kirwan, 1799: 483.

79 Porter, 1977: 205.

80 Geological Society of London, *Transactions* 1 (1811): viii–ix.

81 *Transactions* 1 (1811): v.

82 Weindling, 1979.

83 Weindling, 'The British Mineralogical Society: A Case Study in Science and Social Improvement', in Inkster and Morrell, eds., 1983: 120–50.

84 Richard Yeo ('An Idol of the Market-Place: Baconianism in Nineteenth-Century Britain', *History of Science* 23, 1985: 284) explores the shift of meaning in the evocation of Baconian methodology from the eighteenth to the nineteenth centuries. He describes how Bacon was presented in the early nineteenth century as the advocate of theories of induction at the expense of eighteenth-century utilitarian readings of him 'as author of a radical philosophy capable of transforming not only natural knowledge, but established social institutions and values' (p. 288). Yeo uses Baconianism to describe the rhetoric of the Geological Society. His article, however, illustrates the problems of using a label whose meaning is historically variable.

85 Geological Society of London, *Annual Report of the Meeting of the Council and Museum Committee, 1815*. A copy is among the George Bellas Greenough Papers and Correspondence, held in the Manuscript Room, University College Library, London (classmark 5/2, p. 17).

86 James A. Secord, *Controversy in Victorian Geology: The Cambrian-Silurian Dispute* (Princeton, 1986): 20.

87 Greenough's journals kept on this tour are among the Greenough Papers and Correspondence in the Manuscript Room, University College Library, London (classmark 7/11 and 7/12). The two volumes have been examined by Martin Rudwick, 'Hutton and Werner Compared: George Greenough's Geological Tour of Scotland in 1805', *British Journal for the History of Science* 1 (1962): 117.

88 John MacCulloch, *A Description of the Western Isles of Scotland*, 3 vols. (Edinburgh, 1819).

89 Daniell, 1814–25, vol. 3, p. 1.

90 For a brief discussion of Staffa in the eighteenth century see Geoffrey Grigson, 'Fingal's Cave', *Architectural Review* 104 (1948): 51–4. Joseph Rykwert (*On Adam's House in Paradise: The Idea of the Primitive Hut in Architectural History*, New York, 1972) includes a reproduction of a picture by J.M. Gandy in the Sir John Soane Museum, London, with the title *Architecture: Its Natural Model* (facing p. 75). The presence of Fingal's Cave on the right of the picture shows that Staffa had a place in the eighteenth-century search for mankind's 'original home' (I owe this reference to Jim Secord).

91 James Fittler, *Scotia Depicta* (London, 1804). Nattes went to Scotland independently of Fittler in 1799 as the text to the engraving makes clear, and showed the picture of Staffa in the Royal Academy in 1803.

92 In fact, Ozias Humphry refers to Nattes' painting of *Fingal's Cave* at the Royal Academy exhibition in just such terms. He wrote to a friend from Edinburgh that this picture gives a particularly good impression of the Cave of Fingal, which according to him ranks among the wonders of the world. I owe this reference to John Brewer, who quoted it for me from a letter (G. Aust to O.H., 18 September 1804, Edinburgh) in the Ozias Humphry Correspondence in the Royal Academy (HU/1/6).

93 Jameson, 1800, vol. 2, p. 94.

94 Jameson, 1800, vol. 2, p. 46.

95 MacCulloch, 1819. The third volume contains the illustrations, of which most are maps.

96 MacCulloch, 1819, vol. 1, p. xiii.

97 MacCulloch, 1819, vol. 1, p. 509.

98 MacCulloch, 1819, vol. 1, pp. 508–9.

99 MacCulloch, *The Highlands and Western Isles of Scotland*, 4 vols. (London, 1824).

100 MacCulloch, 1824, vol. 3, pp. 476–7.

101 MacCulloch, 1819, vol. 2, p. 1.

102 *John MacCulloch Drawings*, Geological Society of London, ref. LDGSL 400.

103 MacCulloch, 1819, vol. 2, p. 10.

104 MacCulloch, 1814: 501.

105 MacCulloch, 1819, vol. 2, p. 11.

106 MacCulloch, 1814: 508.

107 MacCulloch, 1814: 509.

108 MacCulloch, 1819: vol. 2, p. 15.

109 A similar dualism is still to be found in MacCulloch (1824), in which he claims to give a supposedly objective analysis of the present state of the Highlanders, while launching into a highly subjectivist account of the natural scenery: 'I must, however, trust, that being anxious only to ascertain the truth, my own Highland prejudices and attachments have not materially influenced my judgement; and that, on the other hand when I have differed from those who have engaged in the same subjects, with a laudable, though injudicious, warmth of feeling, and with a partiality to a fictitious and imaginary state of things, I have been only desirous to rest these claims, such as they are, on an unimpeached and inmutable [sic] basis, and thus to give them a firmness and a support, which will be sought in vain in misplaced enthusiasm and in unfounded tradition and belief' (vol. 1, p. 7). He thus entered the highly charged discussion of the Highland tradition. A year after his publication a fierce reply appeared which accused MacCulloch of being willing to white-wash 'the Highland landlords, and to justify the proceedings to which they have had recourse, by representing the native population on their estates as brutalized beyond all hope of regeneration' (J. Browne, *Critical Examination of Dr. MacCulloch's Work on the Highlands and Western Isles of Scotland*, Edinburgh, 1825: 27).

110 The discrepancy between this painting and the topography of Staffa led John Gage ('The Distinctness of Turner', *Journal of the Royal Society for the Encouragement of Arts* 123, 1975: 448), to suggest that the painting was not of the cave but of the opposite side of the island. However, as John Gage has pointed out to me, cleaning has now shown that Turner did indeed depict the cave with the sun setting in the west and thus clearly rearranged the topography for pictorial purposes.

111 Quoted in Martin Butlin and Evelyn Joll, *The Paintings of J.M.W. Turner*, 1977, rev. ed., vol. 1 (New Haven, 1984): 198.

112 *The Complete Poetical Works of Sir Walter Scott*, vol. 10 (Edinburgh, 1834).

113 This viewpoint had, however, some tradition: Garnett (1800, frontispiece), Daniell (1814–25, vol. 3, facing p. 40) and Necker de Saussure (1822, frontispiece) had chosen it before Turner.

114 Gage, 1975: 449.

115 Now in the Tate Gallery, London.

116 There is, of course, a difference in purpose behind an oil painting, such as Turner's, exhibited at the Royal Academy, and topographical drawings, such as Daniell's, produced to be reproduced for the mass market. A landscape painting at the Royal Academy would always demand a more obviously interpretative view. In Turner's case, however, the comparison of an oil painting with book illustrations is justified, I think, because he himself contributed substantially to topographical publications, such as Walter Scott's *The Provincial Antiquities and Picturesque Scenery of Scotland, with Descriptive Illustrations* (2 vols., London, 1826), and this work does not differ in conception from his oil painting. Turner's concentration on the depiction of atmospheric forces in both media indicates a view of nature made up of constantly changing but interlinked appearances.

117 David Philip Miller, 'Method and the "Micropolitics" of Science: The Early Years of the Geological and Astronomical Societies of London', in John A. Schuster and Richard Yeo, eds., *The Politics and Rhetoric of Scientific Method* (Dordrecht, 1986): 227–57.

118 Webster's account of the Isle of Wight appeared first in Henry C. Englefield, *A Description of the Principal Picturesque Beauties, Antiquities, and Geological Phenomena of the Isle of Wight* (London, 1816): 217.

119 Revd W.D. Conybeare and William Phillips, *Outlines of the Geology of England and Wales* (London, 1822): xvi.

120 Charles Lyell, *Principles of Geology: Being an Attempt to Explain the Former Changes of the Earth's Surface by Reference to Causes Now in Operation*, 3 vols. (London, 1830–3).

121 Yeo, 1985: 267.

122 John MacCulloch, *A System of Geology, with a Theory of the Earth* (London, 1831).

123 *Proofs and Illustrations of the Attributes of God, from the Facts and Laws of the Physical Universe: Being the Foundation of Natural and Revealed Religion*, 3 vols. (London, 1837). It was published posthumously.

124 His publication of 1831 brought MacCulloch the accusation that he was a defender of outmoded techniques, particularly so since he refused to accept the evidence of stratigraphical palaeontology, as expounded by Cuvier, which became the major preoccupation of geology in the following decades (Cumming, 1985: 83).

125 W. Daniell, Royal Academy, 1816; G.F. Howman, Royal Academy, 1827 (not traced); J.M.W. Turner, Royal Academy, 1832; W. Nicholson, Royal Scottish Academy, 1841 (not traced); A. Van Dyke Copley Fielding, British Institution, 1853.

126 Daniell, 1818: 2.

127 At first the steamboat ran only from Glasgow via the Crinan Canal to Oban and Fort William, while the tour to Staffa still involved a sailing boat. The steamboat tour to Staffa was included in the second edition of *The Steam Boat Companion; And Stranger's Guide to the Western Islands and Highlands of Scotland*, 2nd ed. (Glasgow, 1825). Daniell was a passenger on the first short steamboat line between

Greenock and Dumbarton and included a steamboat in the accompanying print (1814–25, vol. 3, p. 17).

128 Scott, 1833–4, vol. 10, p. 7, introduction to this poem.

129 Catherine Gordon, 'The Illustration of Sir Walter Scott: Nineteenth-Century Enthusiasm and Adaptation', *Journal of the Warburg and Courtauld Institutes* 34 (1971): 305.

130 Turner's illustrations for Scott's writings are discussed by Gerald Finley, *Landscapes of Memory: Turner as Illustrator to Scott* (London, 1980).

131 Pennant, 1774–6, vol. 2, facing p. 329.

132 John MacCulloch, 'A Sketch of the Mineralogy of Sky', *Transactions of the Geological Society of London* 3 (1816): 1–111; 4 (1817): 156–92.

133 MacCulloch, 1819, vol. 1, p. 281.

134 Scott's 'Vacation 1814: Voyage in the Lighthouse Yacht to Nova Zembla, and the Lord Knows Where' was printed in *Memoirs of the Life of Sir Walter Scott*, ed. John G. Lockhart, vol. 3 (Edinburgh, 1837): 232.

135 MacCulloch, 1816: 2.

136 MacCulloch, 1816: 3.

137 MacCulloch, 1816: 12.

138 Daniell, 1814–25, vol. 4, pp. 24–41.

139 Daniell, 1814–25, vol. 4, p. 25. For the northern parts of the island, Daniell also quotes Jameson (vol. 4, p. 23).

140 Holloway and Errington, 1978: 113.

141 Scott, 1833–4, vol. 10, pp. 109–10, III: 14.

142 Scott, 1833–4, vol. 10, p. 113, III: 17.

143 Two were on sale at Christie's, 18 March 1980, of which one is dated August 1828, therefore the probable date of their production. A large watercolour is in the Victoria and Albert Museum and another in the Tate Gallery.

144 The painting is undated, but must have been produced some time before 1840, when Knox retired to Keswick. He died in 1845.

145 John Ruskin, *Modern Painters*, 1843–60, new ed. 5 vols (New York, 1880–1); see vol. 1 ('On the Inferior Mountains') and vol. 4 ('Resulting Forms: – Secondly, Crests').

146 Ruskin, 1880–1, vol. 4, p. 221.

147 MacCulloch, 1819, vol. 1, p. 385. Scott's verses (1833–4, vol. 10, pp. 111–12, III: 15) emphasised the movements of the clouds and rain around the range of mountains.

148 John Gage, *J.M.W. Turner: A Wonderful Range of Mind* (New Haven, 1987): 220.

149 MacCulloch, 1824, vol. 3, pp. 474–5.

150 MacCulloch, 1816: 74.

151 The drawing is discussed by Finley, 1980: 138. But he sees in the jagged outlines which 'are softened and obscured by the upward sweep of cloud and mist [. . .] a permanent record of the cataclysmic events that shaped the early history of the earth', rather than a depiction of nature as still in change.

152 MacCulloch, 1819, vol. 1, p. 393.

153 William Gilpin, *Observation on the Coast of Hampshire, Sussex, and Kent: Relative Chiefly to Picturesque Beauty; Made in the Summer of the Year 1774* (London, 1804): 3–6.

154 Gilpin, 1804: 77.

155 Francis Grose, *The Antiquities of Scotland*, vol. 1 (London, 1789).

156 Pennant, 1771: 44. Bad weather finally prevented him from visiting the rock.

157 *Sketchbook: 'Tantallon Castle and the Bass Rock' and 'Bass Rock'* (British Museum). A brief description of the Bass Rock is contained in Farington, ed. 1979, vol. 5, p. 1626, 18 September 1801.

158 According to Janet Cooksey (*Alexander Nasmyth HRSA, 1758–1840: A Man of the Scottish Renaissance*, Haddington, 1991: 114) Nasmyth exhibited three views of Tantallon, in 1811, 1826 and 1829, and this version seems to be a fourth. A sketch of 1816 is related to it.

159 Now belonging to the Grosvenor Estates.

160 Now in the Southampton Art Gallery.

161 James Nasmyth, *An Autobiography* (London, 1883): 49.

162 Martin Kemp, 'Alexander Nasmyth and the Style of Graphic Eloquence', *The Connoisseur* 173 (1970): 98.

163 Scott, 1826. It was, according to Finley (1980: 68), 'an unqualified commercial disaster'.

164 The Witt Library, Courtauld Institute, London, has documented five different versions of *Fast Castle* by Thomson.

165 Robert W. Napier (*John Thomson of Duddingston, Landscape Painter: His Life and Work*, Edinburgh, 1919) names eight versions of Tantallon Castle (p. 408). Two paintings are known today: one with the Bass Rock is in a private collection; the other, without the Bass Rock, is now in the Walker Art Gallery, Liverpool, and was exhibited in 1837 in the Royal Scottish Academy.

166 Farington, ed. 1983, vol. 12, p. 4306, 27 February 1813.

IV SKETCHING FROM NATURE: JOHN AND CORNELIUS VARLEY AND THEIR CIRCLE

1 After his returns Daniell appears to have prepared sepia drawings from these sketches in order to determine the various tone strengths achieved in the biting in of the printing process. He will then have prepared a coloured guide on a print for the trade colourists who finished his aquatints (see Bain, 1966).

2 In recent years the practice of sketching has attracted considerable attention from art historians. It is often taken as having opened the door to modern art. An oversimplified form of the argument might run something like this: in leaving the walls of the studio the artist became free from conventions. This, it is in turn argued, led to what is indeed a fundamental feature of modern art: the choice of everyday or apparently intrinsically insignificant subject-matter; and so, in the end, the artist's imagination was 'liberated' by being thrown back upon his or her own subjectivity in the encounter with what was depicted. Until recently, credit for this was usually given to the French Impressionists. In the most recent art historical writing, however, there have been attempts to push the threshold of modernity in this sense back into the late

eighteenth and early nineteenth century (most marked in Werner Hofmann's celebrated series of exhibitions, *Kunst um 1800*, held in 1974–80 at the Kunsthalle, Hamburg). Attention has focused on the practices of *plein-air* artistic activity undertaken in the milieu surrounding the well-documented but highly individual figures of Constable and Turner, e.g.: David Blayney Brown, *Oil Sketches from Nature: Turner and his Contemporaries*, exhib. cat. Tate Gallery (London, 1991). The ground for this exhibition was well prepared, notably by Gage, 1969; Philip Conisbee, 'Pre-Romantic Plein-Air Painting', *Art History* 2 (1979): 413–28; Lawrence Gowing and Philip Conisbee, *Painting from Nature: The Tradition of Open-Air Oil Sketching from the 17th to the 19th Centuries*, exhib. cat. Fitzwilliam Museum (Cambridge, 1980); Paula R. Radisich, 'Eighteenth-Century Plein-Air Painting and the Sketches of P.H. de Valenciennes', *Art Bulletin* 64 (1982): 98–103; Werner Busch, 'Die autonome Ölskizze in der Landschaftsmalerei: Der wahr- und für wahr-genommene Ausschnitt aus Zeit und Raum', *Pantheon* 41 (1983): 126–33; and Malcolm Cormack, *Oil on Water: Oil Sketches by British Watercolourists*, exhib. cat. Yale Center for British Art (New Haven, 1986).

3   Because of this loose structure, I use the term 'circle' in relation to the artists associated with Varley cautiously. It should not imply that they formed a coherent group which shared a common intellectual identity; quite on the contrary as we will see.

4   Alfred Story, *The Life of John Linnell*, vol. 1 (London, 1892): 25.

5   C.M. Kauffmann, *John Varley 1778–1842*, exhib. cat. Victoria and Albert Museum (London, 1984): 37.

6   It is only in Varley's chalk sketches (for example in sketch-books in the Victoria and Albert Museum and British Museum) that one can find traces of a less formalised approach. Anne Lyles ('John Varley's Early Work', *The Old Water-Colour Society's Club* 59, 1984: 1–22) attributes an oil sketch, *Plants at the Edge of a Stream* (Sotheby's, 19 March 1981), to John Varley which would connect him more closely to the artists associated with him. Her attribution is based on the inscription 'Varley' on the verso and on her belief that John but not Cornelius Varley took up oil painting later in their careers, when the gap between sketch and finished work had once again markedly widened (p. 11). But it is much more likely that the sketch was prepared by Cornelius, who had taken up oil painting quite early in the nineteenth century, a fact which brought about his resignation from the Water-colour Society in 1820 when the latter reintroduced a restriction to water-colour exhibits. Although none of the pictures by Cornelius Varley known today can be securely identified as oils, the sale of his remaining works at Christie's (15 July 1875; there is a copy in J.J. Jenkins, *Papers*, Royal Water-colour Society, Bankside Gallery, London, file 'Cornelius Varley') after his death listed eighteen oil paintings, dated from around 1806, 1818, the 1820s and the 1850s. The

inventory prepared by Varley's family for this sale of the remaining work in the studio, excluding the sketches, is in a private collection (Cornelius Varley, *Inventory*, Walker Collection).

7   Until 1805 Mulready gives Varley's address as his own in the Royal Academy exhibition catalogue (Graves, 1905–6, vol. 5, pp. 323–4). Later, Mulready assisted John Varley with his teaching.

8   John Linnell, *Autobiographical Notes*, Redhill, 1864, Linnell Trust, p. 8.

9   Jenkins, file 'William Henry Hunt'. This manuscript formed the source for John L. Roget's *History of the Old Water-Colour Society*, 2 vols. (London, 1891). Jenkins collected letters, transcriptions of conversations with surviving members and similar material in order to write his own history, which was never completed. The existing papers contain Jenkins' material as well as Roget's transcription and show how thoroughly the latter depended upon this source.

10 Now in a private collection; photograph in the Paul Mellon Centre, London.

11 Blayney Brown, 1991: 9.

12 Linnell, 1864: 5.

13 *Memorials of the Late Francis Oliver Finch*, ed. E. Finch (London, 1865). Finch went to Varley in 1813 or 1814 for three years but stayed five.

14 For Varley's later teaching practice see Roget, 1891, vol. 1, p. 315.

15 Jenkins, file 'John Varley'.

16 John Varley, *A Treatise on the Principles of Landscape Design* (London, 1821).

17 Christiana Payne has suggested to me that artists may have been concerned to build up a stock of sketches at the start of their careers. While this is certainly a possibility, I am not convinced that it provides a sufficient explanation for the reduced importance of sketching out of doors in the Varley circle later.

18 *John Constable's Correspondence*, ed. R.B. Beckett, 6 vols. (Ipswich, 1962–8), vol. 2, pp. 31–2.

19 See Michael Rosenthal, *Constable: The Painter and his Landscape* (New Haven, 1983): 31.

20 Rosenthal, 1983: 140.

21 Edward Dayes, 'On Painting', *Philosophical Magazine* 13 (1802): 122–9, 211–19, 348–54; 14 (1803): 31–41, 97–107, 218–28; 15 (1803): 12–15, 115–26; republished in Dayes, 1805: 191–278.

22 Dayes, 1803: 227.

23 Dayes, 1803: 40.

24 Joshua Reynolds, *Discourses on Art*, ed. Robert R. Wark (New Haven, 1981); see 'Discourse II', p. 30.

25 Radisich, 1982: 101; Bermingham, 1987: 64–5.

26 Gilpin, 2/1794: 67.

27 Gilpin, 2/1794: 51.

28 Gilpin, 2/1794: 66.

29 Gilpin, 2/1794: 19.

30 Conisbee, 1979: 425–6. It was only after the turn of the

century that the practice of open-air sketching (often in oil) significantly influenced finished works. John and Cornelius Varley's drawings, and Linnell's and Hunt's oil sketches, are early British examples. Similar developments on the Continent, notably among the international artists' community in Rome, took place rather later (Peter Galassi, *Before Photography: Painting and the Invention of Photography*, exhib. cat. Museum of Modern Art, New York, 1981; see also Galassi, *Corot in Italy*, New Haven, 1991). Open-air sketching also developed in Scandinavia during the same period (Torsten Gunnarsson, *Friluftsmaleri före friluftsmaleriet*, Acta Universitatis Upsaliensis, Ars Suetica 12, Uppsala, 1989).

31 Graves, 1905–6, vol. 3, p. 86. The terms 'study' and 'sketch' seem to be used interchangeably, as can be inferred from the inscriptions on John Varley's work, for example.

32 Radisich (1982: 102) has described a similar coming together of the view and the composed sketch, both in theory and in practice, around 1800 in France.

33 Quoted in Sydney D. Kitson, *The Life of John Sell Cotman* (London, 1937): 79.

34 Quoted in Roget, 1891, vol. 1, p. 95.

35 For a list of works exhibited by Cornelius Varley, see Basil S. Long, 'Cornelius Varley', *The Old Water-Colour Society's Club* 14 (1936–7): 9–10.

36 Gilpin, 2/1794: 87.

37 John Varley has been reassessed by Anne Lyles (1984), an article based on her M.A. Report, *John Varley (1778–1842): A Catalogue of his Watercolours and Drawings in the British Museum*, Courtauld Institute (London, 1980); and by Kauffmann (1984). Both authors include extensive bibliographies and descriptions of his career. Lyles, in particular, proposes a re-evaluation of Varley's early years in the light of his more naturalistic watercolours.

38 Kauffmann, 1984: 94–6.

39 In the British Museum.

40 Sotheby's, 16 March 1978.

41 Lyles, 1984: 3.

42 This decentralised panoramic view has been taken to show the influence Girtin had on Varley through the mediation of Dr Monro (Randall Davies, 'John Varley', *Old Water-Colour Society's Club* 11, 1924–5: 12). But, with some exceptions, Girtin's drawings, unlike Varley's, do not attempt to catch an actual light and colour situation, but use subdued tones and light and shadow in order to convey a mood.

43 Jenkins, file 'John Varley'.

44 F.J.G. Jefferiss, *Dr. Thomas Monro (1759–1833) and the Monro Academy*, exhib. cat. Victoria and Albert Museum (London, 1976) n. pag. Jefferiss draws his information from the diary of Monro's eldest son.

45 Jenkins, file 'John Varley'.

46 See Jefferiss, 1976.

47 In a conversation in 1858, Cornelius Varley related to Jenkins how this Academy was organised (Jenkins, file 'Dr T. Monro'). This account appeared in Roget (1891, vol. 1, p. 79) without the source for the information being given. It is the only relatively detailed account of Monro's Academy. The other reference is to be found in Farington's diary (Farington, ed. 1978, vol. 1, p. 283, 30 December 1794; ed. 1979, vol. 3, p. 1090, 12 November 1798).

48 He moved away from Fetcham in 1805 and took a house in the neighbourhood of Bushey in 1808.

49 John Witt, *William Henry Hunt (1790–1864): Life and Work with a Catalogue* (London, 1982): nos. 14–17.

50 Christie's, 26 June 1833. A copy is in Jenkins, file 'Dr Monro'.

51 Raymond Lister, *The Letters of Samuel Palmer*, vol. 1 (Oxford, 1974): 42.

52 Lister, 1974, vol. 1, p. 44.

53 Jefferiss, 1976.

54 Jane Bayard, *Works of Splendor and Imagination: The Exhibition Watercolor, 1770–1870*, exhib. cat. Yale Center for British Art (New Haven, 1981): 15–24.

55 Charles Newman, *The Evolution of Medical Education in the Nineteenth Century* (London, 1957).

56 Newman, 1957: 28; Roy Porter, *Disease, Medicine and Society in England 1550–1860* (Basingstoke, 1987): 33 [the book includes a characteristically extensive bibliography].

57 Porter, 1987: 35.

58 An obvious indication of the political attitude of the College of Physicians is its donation of £50 in 1792 to the suffering clergy among the French royalist refugees, and a further £100 in 1793 (George Clark, *A History of the Royal College of Physicians of London*, vol. 2, Oxford, 1966: 600).

59 William Munk, *The Roll of the Royal College of Physicians (1701 to 1800)*, 1861, 2nd ed., vol. 2 (London, 1878): 414.

60 Though Bethlem admitted only curable cases (Joan Busfield, *Managing Madness: Changing Ideas and Practice*, London, 1986: 205). Later in his career, Monro must have become directly aware of the structural changes which were going on in his profession. After 1790 Bethlem, along with other lunatic asylums, came under increasingly severe criticism for its barbaric treatment of the mentally ill and for its lack of therapy. Thomas Monro himself was called to give evidence to a parliamentary committee in 1815. At the same time, the understanding of the nature of madness was undergoing a radical change and this affected its treatment. Madness in the eighteenth century was seen as a phenomenon in which both mind and body were implicated. Its causes were sought either in the mind, in the body or in a common substance which was thought to link human beings with the outside world (Michel Foucault, *Historie de la folie*, Paris, 1961). Only after the rise of a phenomenalist approach in the early nineteenth century did madness come to be seen as a disease exclusively of the mind; thus a moral treatment was introduced, which consisted 'in providing an environment that would facilitate this struggle for self-control, an environment that was itself well regulated and disciplined and governed by

moral principles and moral authority. The power of physical coercion was to be replaced by the power of moral authority' (Busfield, 1986: 212).

61 Certainly there were differences: for instance (if we are to follow the testimony of Turner) Monro paid the artists for their copying. Linnell later claimed that Monro sold copies made by Linnell and Hunt as original Girtins and Turners (Linnell, 1864: 21). However, it must be said, against this, that no copies clearly identifiable as being by Linnell or Hunt have appeared on the art market.

62 36 in the Water-Colour Society and 4 in the Royal Academy. Algernon Graves puts the total number of his works exhibited during his life-time at 129, of which 29 were in the Royal Academy (mainly after 1819), 4 in the British Institution (1815, 2 in 1822 and 1840), 29 in Suffolk Street and 8 elsewhere (*A Dictionary of Artists, who have Exhibited Works in the Principal London Exhibitions, from 1760 to 1893*, London, 1901: 286). Adding the 36 pictures exhibited in the Water-Colour Society in the first decade to the 24 shown between 1811 and 1820, I count 130 exhibits.

63 Long (1936–7) was more concerned with Cornelius Varley's role in the foundation of the Water-Colour Society than with his qualities as an artist. He states that 'according to [Varley's] own account, he conceived the idea of a water-colour society' (p. 2). This claim is not correct, although it has occasionally been repeated. Long seems to have based his biographical account largely on Story (1894), who in turn acknowledges a narrative which must have been the anonymously published *Brief Notice of the Life and Labours of the Late Cornelius Varley* (London, [1874]) (preserved as pamphlet 101,K in the Royal Institution; another copy in the Walker Collection). This pamphlet seems to me to be the outcome of a small notice which the Society of Arts published and sent to acquaintances of Cornelius Varley after his death, asking for information about the deceased in order to prepare a 'Varley Testimonial' to be 'issued under the superintendence of the Committee' of the Society of Arts. (A copy, dated December 1873, was sent to Linnell and is now among his *Letters*, Linnell Trust). The pamphlet itself is largely based on the manuscript *Cornelius Varley's Narrative Written by Himself* (Walker Collection; this appears to be a copy by a second hand). Here Varley states only that he 'was one of the party who held the preliminary meetings which decided to form the New Water-Colour Society' (p. 7). The pamphlet, however, claims that he 'originated the idea of the foundation' (p. 6).

64 Story, 1894: 299.

65 Martin Hardie, *Water-Colour Painting in Britain*, 3 vols. (London, 1966–8), vol. 2, p. 108.

66 Iolo A. Williams, *Early English Watercolours* (London, 1952): 227.

67 Gage, 1969: 12.

68 Michael Pidgley, 'Cornelius Varley, Cotman, and the Graphic Telescope', *Burlington Magazine* 114 (1972): 781–6 and 'Introduction', P. & D. Colnaghi, *Exhibition of Drawings and Watercolours by Cornelius Varley*, sales cat. (London, 1973). My own research on Cornelius Varley is not only greatly indebted to these texts, but also to Michael Pidgley's generous sharing of his knowledge of Varley with me.

69 Kauffmann, 1984: 11.

70 C. Varley, *Narrative*, pp. 1–2.

71 Stanhope was known as someone who moved in radical circles (so much so that he was given the nickname 'Citizen'); he was a member of the Revolutionary Society, which met at the London Tavern. He seems to have employed Samuel Varley in order to help him develop his method of stereotyping, a process in which a solid plate of type-metal, cast from a papier-maché or plaster mould taken from the surface of a form of type, is used for printing instead of the form itself.

72 A related drawing was sold at Colnaghi in 1973 (no. 56). Most of Varley's drawings known today are signed and dated in his own hand. This drawing has two inscriptions. I suspect, however, that most were inscribed retrospectively (as was Linnell's practice), since a drawing in the British Museum (*From Harlech Marshes*) is dated '1802 or 3', an obvious sign that it was inscribed later. It seems that at the beginning of his career in 1801–2 Varley signed only with his initials.

73 The tinted watercolour is in the British Museum, another drawing of the same subject was sold at Sotheby's, 13 March 1980, and a third is in a private collection. All of these might have been included in the 1875 sale at Christie's: Lot 62 *Lord Rouse's Seat: Gentlemen's Residences and Churches in Suffolk, 1801, 1807* or Lot 63, *Ditto, Suffolk, 1801, 1807*, and only the last undated one possibly in Lot 69 *Lord Rouse's Park, 1807*.

74 C. Varley, *Narrative*, p. 7.

75 There is, however, a drawing in the British Museum with the inscription *Henham Hall Suffolk Lord Rous*, dated 1801 (perhaps corrected to 1803) which shows an early attempt at a perspectively accurate delineation of the manor house in the middle ground, while the foreground contains lightly sketched-in trees and resting figures. It looks as if Varley might have used a drawing aid, such as the *camera obscura*.

76 Basil Taylor, *Joshua Cristall (1768–1847)*, exhib. cat. Victoria and Albert Museum (London, 1975): 17.

77 Blayney Brown, 1991: 67–8.

78 The same is true for the panoramic view, stretching over several sheets, of Dolgelly and Cader Idris in Varley's sketchbook for the year 1803 (Pierpont Morgan Library, New York, fols.10–16). Although the landscape is more fully sketched in than in the watercolours, only certain patches are executed in detail.

79 Private Collection. Reproduced in Kauffmann, 1984: 27.

80 For example, *After Sunset: North Wales* (Victoria and Albert Museum) or *Sunset over a Wide Plain* (City of Birmingham Museum and Art Gallery).

81 The drawing is inscribed 'Barmouth Vale from the banks of Cader Idris'. Comparable are two watercolours in

public collections: *Near St Albans* (Tate Gallery) of 1804 and *Landscape Near St Albans* (Ashmolean Museum, Oxford).

82 Colnaghi, 1973: no. 54.

83 Quoted in Colnaghi, 1973: no. 54.

84 Graves, 1905–6, vol. 8, p. 74.

85 *Morning Post*, 2 May 1805. Quoted in Long, 1936–7: 9. I have not been able to establish the identity of these sketches.

86 Roget (1891) recounts that the members of the Water-Colour Society estimated the value of their own work for the first exhibitions and distributed the profit accordingly. The prices set in the first exhibition ranged from £2860, set by Shelley, down to 'a modest 44l.12s.6d by Cornelius Varley' (vol. 1, p. 207).

87 An idea of what this work would have been like can be gained from a rather formulaic watercolour *Landscape Composition*, similar to productions by John Varley, which was sold at Sotheby's on 19 March 1981. Interestingly, its provenance is said to have been the artist James Ward. The same provenance is given for the watercolour *Mountainous Landscape* in the Fitzwilliam Museum.

88 Jean Hamilton, *The Sketching Society, 1799–1851*, exhib. cat. Victoria and Albert Museum (London, 1971).

89 Long, 1936–7: 8.

90 Christie's *Catalogue of the Whole of the Remaining Works of Cornelius Varley* (1875) and the Cornelius Varley *Inventory* (Walker Collection) list a drawing (in the category of the more finished work) with the title *Falls Near Devil's Dyke, North Wales* and date 1804, which might well be this one.

91 Rosenthal (1982: 78) uses the watercolour *Landscape in North Wales* (Collection Marchioness of Dufferin and Ava) as an illustration for this statement, but this is quite distinct from Varley's usual work. This watercolour is one of a series of four, which progresses from a pencil sketch and a washed drawing (signed and dated 1805) through to two watercolour versions (all in the same private collection). Each demonstrates a different sky effect and thus it seems to me that this watercolour was executed for teaching purposes and exhibits a far less detailed, more perspectival depiction, in which the topographical elements are subdued in colour so as to produce a more uniform effect.

92 Judging by the work listed in the Christie's catalogue (1875).

93 Roget (1891) judges it probable that the work with the ambitious title *The Vale of Tempe*, exhibited by Varley in his last year of exhibition with the Society, 1820, was the product of that award (vol. 1, p. 407).

94 Jenkins, file 'John Varley'. See also Roget, 1891, vol. 1, p. 172.

95 This was almost certainly the engraver Wilson Lowry and his wife. Lowry had strong links with the scientific community in London and executed many plates for the *Philosophical Magazine* and the *Journal of the Society of Arts*, in both of which Cornelius Varley subsequently published articles. According to the *Dictionary of National Biography* (vol. 13, London, 1890: 213) Lowry 'devised several ingen-

ious instruments', including (around 1790) a 'ruling machine', designed to achieve accuracy of line and evenness of texture in engravings. Such inventions would certainly have been of particular interest to Varley. In 1825 John Varley married Lowry's daughter Delvalle (it was his second marriage). All of this indicates that the encounter in Wales led to a close and lasting connection between Lowry and the Varleys.

96 A. Rupert Hall, 'The Royal Society of Arts: Two Centuries of Progress in Science and Technology', *Journal of the Royal Society of Arts* 122 (1974): 648.

97 Frank A.J.L. James, 'Michael Faraday, the City Philosophical Society and the Society of Arts', *RSA Journal* 140 (1992): 192–9.

98 He later received the Isis Gold Medal from the Society of Arts for improvements in the construction of microscopes (*Transactions of the Society of Arts* 53, 1841: 32), as well as two Silver Medals, for machinery for grinding and polishing specula (49, 1833: 91) and for observations and illustrations of the circulation of the sap in water-plants (48, 1831: 332).

99 Cornelius Varley, 'On Atmospheric Phaenomena: particularly the Formation of Clouds; their Permanence; their Precipitation in Rain, Snow, and Hail; and the consequent Rise of the Barometer', *Philosophical Magazine* 27 (1807): 115–21; and 'Meteorological Observations on a Thunder Storm; with some Remarks on Medical Electricity', *Philosophical Magazine* 34 (1809): 161–3, 201–2.

100 Luke Howard, 'On the Modification of Clouds, and on the Principles of their Production, Suspension, and Destruction', *Philosophical Magazine* 16 (1803): 97.

101 Luke Howard, 'Considerations on Dr. Hutton's Theory of Rain', *Philosophical Magazine* 14 (1803): 55–62.

102 Howard, 16 (1803): 107.

103 C. Varley, 1807: 115.

104 Meteorological debate at that time appears to have taken place mainly in the *Philosophical Magazine*.

105 C. Varley, 1807: 120.

106 Thomas Forster, *Researches about Atmospheric Phenomena* (London, 1813).

107 C. Varley, 34 (1809): 161.

108 Kurt Badt, *John Constable's Clouds* (London, 1950).

109 Louis Hawes, 'Constable's Sky Sketches', *Journal of the Warburg and Courtauld Institutes* 32 (1969): 344–65.

110 A drawing entitled *Mountain Panorama in Wales* (Yale Center for British Art, New Haven) is a good example of these. It bears the inscription at the top right-hand side 'Sun over here. Clouds colour of drawing paper', and at the bottom 'fine weather, wind S.E., clouds coming towards me all the morning, but dissolve into transparent atmosphere as fast as they came so that I had constant blue sky over head. Sun shone yet the hills came forward darker'.

111 They are briefly discussed in Pidgley, 1972: 781.

112 Linnell, 1864: 12.

113 Linnell, 1864: 7. This is also quoted in David Linnell's *Blake, Palmer, Linnell and Co.: The Life of John Linnell*

114 (Lewes, 1994: 10), a book by a descendant, whose account is mainly biographical.

114 I will here omit discussion of William Turner of Oxford, though in 1805–11 he too was a student at John Varley's and participated in the outdoor sketching practice, as the drawing *Trees on a River Bank* in the Victoria and Albert Museum shows. Most of his work is undated and therefore his early works are too uncertain to be included in a sensible way in my discussion. The earliest known dated drawings cannot be clearly linked to open-air sketching practice, unlike Linnell's, Hunt's and Mulready's. (See Martin Hardie, 'William Turner of Oxford', *Old Water-Colour Society's Club* 9, 1932: 1–23; and Christopher Titterington, 'William Turner of Oxford and British Romantic Naturalism', *Old Water-Colour Society's Club* 59, 1984: 23–52; see also A.L. Baldry, 'William Turner of Oxford, Water-Colour Painter, Born 1789, Died 1862', *Walker's Quarterly* 11, 1923: 3–18, which is largely biographical.)

115 Sidney C. Hutchison, 'The Royal Academy Schools, 1768–1830', *Walpole Society* 38 (1962): 123–91. The schools do not seem to have made any great impact on Cornelius Varley, since he does not mention them in his *Narrative*.

116 Linnell, 1864: 14.

117 Jenkins, file 'William Henry Hunt': 'I think I could tell a young one what would be good advice + never having had any myself' (letter to 'Friend Brown', 23 March 1864).

118 In addition to the depictions of subjects at Chester and Conway, mentioned earlier, there is also a graphite and watercolour drawing inscribed verso *View of Millbank-Westminster a Sketch* (Sotheby's, 10 July 1986): signed and dated 1809, this is related to Cornelius' undated drawing *Millbank – Thames* (Tate Gallery), which can be attributed on stylistic grounds to the years around 1804–7. Kauffmann (1984: 39) states that John Varley's 'earliest dated watercolour studies of Lambeth and Millbank are 1816', though he finds evidence to prove that Varley was sketching in this area at least as early as 1809 through the existence of thumbnail sketches in the Cyril Fry Collection (p. 55). The watercolour sold at Sotheby's proves that he was also sketching in colour in this area before 1809.

119 Linnell, *Journals*, 15 vols., 1811–79, Fitzwilliam Museum, Cambridge, on behalf of the Linnell Trust. Unfortunately, volume 2 (1812–17) is missing; according to Christiana Knowles (*John Linnell: His Early Landscapes, to 1830*, M.A. Report, Courtauld Institute, London, 1990: 3), it was already missing in 1863 when Linnell wrote his autobiography.

120 Linnell stated: 'C. Varley who had led me with good arguments to the conviction of its necessity to a true Christian Confession [joining the Baptist Church] never himself followed his own true principle' (Linnell, 1864: 52); also quoted in David Linnell, 1994: 46.

121 Geoffry Cantor, *Michael Faraday, Sandemanian and Scientist: A Study of Science and Religion in the Nineteenth Century* (Basingstoke, 1991), Appendix B, p. 301. Long (1936–7: 5) stated that 'Cornelius Varley and his family belonged to the Sandemanian Sect', although neither Roget (1891) nor Story (1892), on whom Long depended for most of his information, mentions the fact. However, he also drew on oral evidence from an old lady, Miss E.M. Spiller, who lived in Varley's neighbourhood in Kentish Town, London, as well as from a Reverend Roland O. Stafford, either of whom may have provided this information. Varley himself did not mention this in his *Narrative*.

122 Katharine Crouan, *John Linnell: A Centennial Exhibition*, exhib. cat. Fitzwilliam Museum (Cambridge, 1982): xii.

123 Knowles, 1990: 16.

124 Linnell, *Journals*, vol. 1, 15 May 1811.

125 Illustrated in Crouan, 1982: 48–9.

126 The most famous examples for this attitude are the three studies of a *Brick Kiln* (private collection), which show an unpicturesque object under different light effects and from different points of view (Crouan, 1982: nos. 18–20).

127 Crouan, 1982: no. 15.

128 Crouan, 1982: no. 22.

129 For an example of an account of Varley's Graphic Telescope as a mere technical refinement, rather than the product of a shift in nature perception, see Martin Kemp, *The Science of Art: Optical Themes in Western Art from Brunelleschi to Seurat* (New Haven, 1990): 202–3.

130 John H. Hammond, *The Camera Obscura: A Chronicle* (Bristol, 1981): 47.

131 Martin Hardie and Muriel Clayton, 1932: 5.

132 A lengthy account of Varley's Graphic Telescope can be found in John H. Hammond and Jill Austin, *The Camera Lucida in Art and Science* (Bristol, 1987): 57–77, 85. Although it mentions artists who used the device (notably Cotman), the authors do not discuss the interrelation between aesthetics and technology.

133 Hammond and Austin, 1987: 59.

134 Cornelius Varley, *A Treatise on Optical Drawing Instruments: Also, A Method of Preserving Pictures in Oil and in Water Colours* (London, 1845). He first published a version of this treatise in an article in the *Transactions of the Society of Arts* 51 (1837): 189–224.

135 The Science Museum, London, contains several models of the Graphic Telescope, including the one which Varley patented in 1811. It comes with three eyepieces and two lenses, giving a range of magnifications from five to twenty.

136 One of the earliest exercises with the Graphic Telescope seems to be a graphite drawing entitled *Hilly Landscape* (Sir John and Lady Witt Collection).

137 Varley's use of the Graphic Telescope and its use by others is briefly discussed in Pidgley, 1972: 785. The meaning of the initials P.G.T. was first identified by Randall Davies (Long, 1936–7: 5–6).

138 It does not come as a surprise that Cornelius Varley should have welcomed the development of photography (1845: 3). The family published an obituary notice after his death (preserved in a private collection) with a photograph of

Varley which states that it is an engraved portrait from a photograph by Messrs. Varley Brothers, Oakley Street, indicating that the family pursued this new technology. The obituary notice with portrait in the *Illustrated London News* (25 October 1873) seems to be based on this.

139 Anonymous, [1874]: 8.

140 Graves, 1905–6, vol. 8, p. 74. Another example is, possibly, the watercolour, heightened with white, *An Irish Cowshed*, signed and dated 1828 (Christie's, 18 March 1980). It might have been the last picture exhibited in the Royal Academy in 1859 with the title *Cows and Shed, Armagh, Ireland.*

141 An example of such a work could be the drawing *Young Ladies and Children in the Garden of a Country House*, signed and dated 1852 (sold at Sotheby's, 21 January 1982), which might be the exhibit of 1852 in the Royal Academy with the title *The Tower and Part of Gillingham Hall, Norfolk; Taken from the Garden, the Residence of Mrs. Bacon Schutz* (Graves, 1905–6, vol. 8, p. 75).

142 Examples of departures from this formula in the work of William Henry Hunt and John Varley would be Hunt's *Village Scene with Timbered Houses* (Collection Cecil Higgins AG, Bedford) and Varley's *View of Millbank-Westminster a Sketch* of 1809 (Sotheby's, 10 July 1986).

143 Kathryn Moore Heleniak, *William Mulready* (New Haven, 1980): 56.

144 Marcia Pointon, *Mulready*, exhib. cat. Victoria and Albert Museum (London, 1986): 45.

145 For the sketches, see Moore Heleniak, 1980: 54–60.

146 Francis Stevens, *Views of Cottages and Farm-Houses in England and Wales* (London, 1815). According to Roget (1891), two editions were published by Ackermann, dated 1808 and 1815 (vol. 1, pp. 326–7).

147 Roget, 1891, vol. 1, p. 326.

148 Stevens, 1815: 2.

149 Stevens, 1815: 21.

150 For the pervasiveness of this myth and other aspects of rural depictions, see Payne, 1993.

151 Langford, 1994: 370.

152 For a discussion of this, see Barrell, 1980: 73. Harry Mount, however, has put the view to me that it was just the passing of the 'traditional' cottage that made it an 'amusing' subject of depiction. This strikes me as plausible, but, in that case, it is surely remarkable that the Varley circle should have presented this subject-matter with none of the patina of picturesque nostalgia.

153 Stevens, 1815, introduction.

154 The engravings are *Suffolk, Near Brampton* (text in Stevens, 1815: 28), *Surrey, Near Leatherhead* (p. 28), *Merionethshire Dolgelly* (p. 36) and *Caenarvonshire Conway* (p. 33). Dolgelly and Conway were visited by Varley on his tours to Wales. Suffolk was known to Varley from the outset of his career and he also knew the area around Leatherhead through his contact with Dr Monro, who owned a house in the neighbourhood.

155 Stevens, 1815: 36.

156 Stevens, 1815: 33.

157 Edward Royle, *Modern Britain: A Social History 1750–1985* (London, 1987): 23–4.

158 Edward Walford and George W. Thornbury, *Old and New London: A Narrative of its History, its People, and its Places*, 6 vols. (London, 1879–85), vol. 4, p. 4.

159 See Frederick Crace Collection, *Views of London*, portofolio 14, in the British Museum.

160 Crace Collection, portofolio 14.

161 This watercolour in the Victoria and Albert Museum has been identified by Kauffmann (1984: no. 37) as *The Pest Houses, Tothill Fields.*

162 *Richard Redgrave, C.B., R.A.: A Memoir, Compiled from his Diary*, ed. Frances M. Redgrave (London, 1891): 4.

163 In George Cruikshank, *Scraps and Sketches*, vol. 2 (London, 1829): plate 1; reproduced in Richard A. Vogler, *Graphic Works of George Cruikshank* (New York, 1979).

164 David Hill, 'A Taste of the Arts: Turner and the Patronage of Edward Lascelles of Harewood House', *Turner Studies* 4 (1984): 24–33.

165 Quoted in Hill, 1984: 28.

166 Morris Berman, *Social Change and Scientific Organization: The Royal Institution, 1799–1844* (London, 1978): 1–31.

167 Berman, 1978: 7.

168 Berman, 1978: 27.

169 Quoted in Berman, 1978: 25. I was unable to consult the manuscript of Webster's autobiography, because it could not be traced in the archive of the Royal Institution where it is normally kept.

170 Cornelius Varley became involved with the Royal Institution much later. The *Royal Institution Minutes of General Meetings* first record the delivery of a lecture on nature and the Graphic Telescope by Cornelius Varley in 1826 (vol. 3, 6 March). The next references, now on the microscope, are noted in 1832 (vol. 4, 2 July), 1833 (vol. 4, 1 July), 1834 (vol. 4, 7 July), 1836 (vol. 4, 6 June) and 1838 (vol. 5, 2 July) and from then on every year until July 1861 (vols. 5 and 6); see also *Royal Institution Index to Lectures 1799–1929* (7 boxes, Royal Institution, London). Cornelius Varley's *Inventory* lists *Design Made for Royal Institution by C. Varley at the Request of Some of the Managers*. Though no date is given, it is clear from the projected design for the figures (Count Rumford, Davy, Cavendish and Faraday) that these cannot have been executed before Faraday's election as director of the laboratories in 1825.

171 Payne, 1993: 46–55.

172 Barrell, 1980: 116–17.

173 Barrell (1980: 144) sees this second mode as embodied in Constable's work. For a different reading of the role of labour in Constable, see Rosenthal, 1983.

174 I am grateful to Christiana Payne for her help in deciphering this inscription.

175 Graves, 1905–6, vol. 8, p. 74.

176 Information concerning this publication is difficult to acquire. Pidgley (1972: 785) states that there are only five etchings by Cornelius, implying that others are by his brother whose name is given as the co-publisher. But, since the subtitle to the work, of which the only copy I

could trace in a public gallery or library was in the British Museum, states that the etchings are by Cornelius, it follows that he was the only artist. There are also more than five etchings. The British Museum copy contains six etchings and four lithographs. A list of subscribers is included, which shows that Varley's buyers were mainly patrons, like Lady Rous and Sir John Swinburne (Mulready's patron), and artist friends. It is clear that the project never got beyond the publication of part one. Pidgley also mentions another edition of 1847 formerly in the Walker Collection which is 'not elsewhere recorded, and was perhaps never regularly issued' (p. 785). The existence of drawings and watercolours of boats and barges indicates that Varley later used his Graphic Telescope for such depictions (for example the coloured *Study of a Thames Barge*, dated 1 September 1823, in the Victoria and Albert Museum). Indeed, Varley (1845: 53) recommended the use of the Telescope for this purpose.

177 Christie's, 1 March 1977.
178 Sotheby's, 19 March 1981.
179 John Varley, *Sketchbook*, Victoria and Albert Museum.
180 For a detailed examination of the imagery of rivers and canals in British art at the beginning of the nineteenth century, see Hemingway, 1992: ch. 9.
181 William Godwin, *Diary*, 31 notebooks, 1788–1836, possession Lord Abinger, deposited in Bodleian Library, Oxford, Classmark Dep. e. 196–227; see, among others, the entries for 8 March 1802 (Dep. e. 206), 29 January 1803 (Dep. e. 206) and 15 March 1805 (Dep. e. 207).
182 Varley's wife is mentioned on 19 April 1805 (Dep. e. 207), and it is likely that John Varley's acquaintance with Godwin dates from as early as 1803, when Varley married her. She was the sister of John Gisborne, who was a friend of Shelley and Godwin, as noted by Story (1892: 229).
183 Allan Cunningham, *Lives of the Most Eminent British Painters*, vol. 2 (London, 1830) (Cunningham received a first-hand account of the friendship from Varley himself); Martin Butlin, *The Blake Varley Sketchbook of 1819 in the Collection of M.E.D. Clayton-Stamm* (London, 1969); Martin Butlin, 'Blake, the Varleys and the Patent Graphic Telescope', in Morton D. Paley and Michael Phillips, eds., *William Blake: Essays in Honour of Sir Geoffrey Keynes* (London, 1973): 294–304.
184 For a contemporary re-evaluation of Varley's position, see Fred Gettings, *The Hidden Art: A Study of Occult Symbolism in Art* (London, 1978): 109–25; and for a historical assessment, see Patrick Curry, *A Confusion of Prophets: Victorian and Edwardian Astrology* (London, 1992): ch. 1.
185 John Varley, *A Treatise on Zodiacal Physiognomy* (London, 1828).
186 J. Varley, 1828: iv.
187 Linnell and Cornelius Varley seem to have lost their close contact shortly after 1811 (entries referring to Cornelius in Linnell's *Journals* become fewer and fewer towards the close of 1811; vol. 1). A letter from Cornelius Varley of 2 July 1853 (John Linnell, *Letters*), answering Linnell's

request for information about photography, indicates that by that time they had become only distant acquaintances: he addresses Linnell as 'Dear Sir'. Eighteen years later Linnell seems to have written to Cornelius Varley again, asking for advice about his spectacles. In his reply of 2 October 1871, Varley addresses Linnell as 'Dear Friend' and ends: 'I don't think we have seen each other since you Banished Yourself from London. I am nearly through my ninetieth year, how much younger are you.–? P.S. – I think it was you who gave me a small coin found in the Red Hills many years ago. It represents the beginning of 12th Cap. of Rev. A woman clothed with the sun'. In a final letter of 5 October 1871, Varley expresses his support for Linnell in his public criticism of the Royal Academy. Other letters are preserved, written by Varley's son Frederick, thanking Linnell for his expression of sympathy after his father's death and a second one (dated 7 October 1873) in which Frederick asked for information about his father, presumably intended for the preparation of the anonymously published pamphlet (see n. 63 above).

188 Linnell, *Journals*, vol. 1; Linnell had already borrowed Paley's *Moral Philosophy* (he wrote 'mortal') from W. Colborne on 8 July. On 23 September and 3 October he borrowed the first and then the second volume of Paley's *Evidences* from Varley, and notes on 2 November that he wishes to belong to the Baptist Church and 'had some good communication with C. Varley on the thought'.
189 Linnell, 1864; also quoted in David Linnell, 1994: 28.
190 Jenkins, file 'William Henry Hunt' (letter to 'Friend Brown', 12 August 1863).

CONCLUSION

1 There is no evidence, however, that William Daniell's phenomenalism had any of these consequences.
2 To some extent, it was Dugald Stewart himself, as Yeo (1985: 265) has argued, who paved the path for this development by arguing that hypotheses are permissible if they are brought about by analogical reasoning, 'based on sound knowledge of one area before being applied to another'.
3 Ralph Hyde, *Panoramania!: The Art and Entertainment of the 'All-Embracing' View*, exhib. cat. Barbican Art Gallery (London, 1988).
4 For examples of such criticisms by Sir George Beaumont and Constable, see Scott B. Wilcox, in the introduction to Hyde, 1988: 25–9.
5 Wilcox, in Hyde, 1988: 28.
6 *The Eagle's Nest: Ten Lectures on the Relation of Natural Science to Art given before the University of Oxford in Lent Term 1872* (London, 1872): 142.
7 The watercolour is now in the City of Aberdeen Art Gallery and Museums Collections.
8 For a discussion of the different implications of geological

time in Victorian art, see Marcia Pointon, 'Geology and Landscape Painting in Nineteenth-Century England', in Jordanova and Porter, eds., 1979: 84–108.

9 'Lecture 4th, June 16th', *Memoirs of the Life of John Constable*, ed. C.R. Leslie (London, 1949): 343.

10 Gage, 1993: 176.

11 W.J.T. Mitchell, ed., 1994.

12 Mitchell, ed., 1994: 14. Not all of the contributors, however, adhere to this stricture as purely as Mitchell sets it out in his introduction.

13 Mitchell, ed., 1994: 2.

14 Benjamin, 1969; see also Karl Heinz Bohrer, *Plötzlichkeit: Zum Augenblick des Ästhetischen Scheins* (Frankfurt am Main, 1981).

BIBLIOGRAPHY

Adorno, Theodor W. *Ästhetische Theorie.* 1970. Frankfurt am Main, 1973.

Adorno, Theodor W., and Horkheimer, Max. *Die Dialektik der Aufklärung.* 1947. Frankfurt am Main, 1969.

Alison, Archibald. *Essays on the Nature and Principles of Taste.* Edinburgh, 1790. 2nd ed. 1811.

Andrews, Malcolm. *The Search for the Picturesque: Landscape Aesthetics and Tourism in Britain, 1760–1800.* Aldershot, 1989.

Anonymous. 'Review of Thornton's "A New Illustration"'. *Annual Review, and History of Literature, for 1803* 11 (1804): 873–82.

———. 'Review of Thornton's "A New Illustration"'. *Monthly Magazine, or British Register* 17 (1804): 346, 647.

———. *The Steam Boat Companion; and Stranger's Guide to the Western Islands and Highlands of Scotland.* 2nd ed. Glasgow, 1825.

———. *A Brief Notice of the Life and Labours of the Late Cornelius Varley.* London, [1874].

Badt, Kurt. *John Constable's Clouds.* London, 1950.

Bain, Ian. *William Daniell's A Voyage round Great Britain, 1814–1825: A Note on its Production and the Subsequent History of the Aquatint Plates Now Owned by Nattali & Maurice.* London, 1966.

Baldry, A.L. 'William Turner of Oxford, Water-Colour Painter, Born 1789, Died 1862'. *Walker's Quarterly* 11 (1923): 3–18.

Ballantyne, Andrew. 'Turbulence and Repression: Re-reading "The Landscape"'. In Stephen Daniels and Charles Watkins, eds. *The Picturesque Landscape: Visions of Georgian Herefordshire.* Exhib. cat. University Art Gallery Nottingham. Nottingham, 1994: 66–78.

Banks, Joseph. *Sketchbook of the Voyage to the Hebrides, Orkneys and Iceland in 1772.* 4 vols. British Library. BL Add. 15509–12.

———. *The Banks Letters: A Calendar of the Manuscript Correspondence.* Ed. Warren Dawson. London, 1958.

Barbier, Carl P. *William Gilpin: His Drawings, Teaching, and Theory of the Picturesque.* Oxford, 1963.

Barrell, John. *The Dark Side of Landscape: The Rural Poor in English Painting 1730–1840.* Cambridge, 1980.

———. *The Political Theory of Painting from Reynolds to Hazlitt: The Body of the Public.* New Haven and London, 1986.

———. *The Birth of Pandora and the Division of Knowledge.* London, 1992.

Bayard, Jane. *Works of Splendor and Imagination: The Exhibition Watercolor, 1770–1870.* Exhib. cat. Yale Center for British Art. New Haven, 1981.

Benjamin, Walter. 'Geschichtsphilosophische Thesen'. 1942. *Illuminationen: Ausgewählte Schriften.* Frankfurt am Main, 1969: 268–79.

Berger, John. *Ways of Seeing.* London, 1972.

Berman, Morris. *Social Change and Scientific Organization: The Royal Institution, 1799–1844.* London, 1978.

Bermingham, Ann. *Landscape and Ideology: The English Rustic Tradition 1740–1840.* London, 1987.

Bertelsen, Lance. *The Nonsense Club: Literature and Popular Culture, 1749–1769.* Oxford, 1986.

Blayney Brown, David. *Oil Sketches from Nature: Turner and his Contemporaries.* Exhib. cat. Tate Gallery. London, 1991.

Blunt, Wilfrid. *The Art of Botanical Illustrations.* London, 1950.

Bohrer, Karl Heinz. *Plötzlichkeit: Zum Augenblick des Ästhetischen Scheins.* Frankfurt am Main, 1981.

Brown, Theodore M. 'From Mechanism to Vitalism in Eighteenth-Century English Physiology'. *Journal of the History of Biology* 7 (1974): 179–216.

Browne, J. *Critical Examination of Dr. MacCulloch's Work on the Highlands and Western Isles of Scotland.* Edinburgh, 1825.

Browne, Janet. 'Botany for Gentlemen: Erasmus Darwin and "The Loves of the Plants"'. *ISIS* 80 (1989): 593–621.

Bryan, Michael. *Dictionary of Painters and Engravers.* 5 vols. London, 1903–4.

Bryson, Norman. *Vision and Painting: The Logic of the Gaze.* London, 1983.

Burbidge, Robert B. *A Dictionary of British Flower, Fruit and Still Life Painters.* 2 vols. Leigh-on-Sea, 1974.

Burke, Edmund. *A Philosophical Enquiry into the Origin of our Ideas of the Sublime and Beautiful.* [1757. 2nd ed. 1758.] *With an Introductory Discourse Concerning Taste.* Ed. J.T. Boulton. London, 1958.

——. *Reflections on the Revolution in France.* 1790, Ed. Conor Cruise O'Brien. London, 1968.

——. *The Correspondence of Edmund Burke.* Gen. ed. Thomas W. Copland. 10 vols. Cambridge, 1958–78.

——. *The Writings and Speeches of Edmund Burke.* Gen. ed. Paul Langford. 5 vols. to date. Oxford, 1981– .

Busch, Werner. 'Die autonome Ölskizze in der Landschaftsmalerei: Der wahr- und für wahr genommene Ausschnitt aus Zeit und Raum'. *Pantheon* 41 (1983): 126–33.

Busfield, Joan. *Managing Madness: Changing Ideas and Practice.* London, 1986.

Bush, Clive. 'Erasmus Darwin, Robert John Thornton, and Linnaeus' Sexual System'. *Eighteenth-Century Studies* 7 (1974): 295–320.

Butlin, Martin. *The Blake Varley Sketchbook of 1819 in the Collection of M.E.D. Clayton-Stamm.* London, 1969.

——. 'Blake, the Varleys and the Patent Graphic Telescope'. In Morton D. Paley and Michael Phillips, eds. *William Blake: Essays in Honour of Sir Geoffrey Keynes.* London, 1973: 294–304.

Butlin, Martin, and Joll, Evelyn. *The Paintings of J.M.W. Turner.* 1977. Rev. ed. 2 vols. New Haven and London, 1984.

Bynum, William F., Browne, E.J., and Porter, Roy, eds. *Macmillan Dictionary of the History of Science.* London, 1981.

Canovan, Margaret. 'The Un-Benthamite Utilitarianism of Joseph Priestley'. *Journal of the History of Ideas* 45 (1984): 435–50.

Cantor, Geoffry. *Michael Faraday, Sandemanian and Scientist: A Study of Science and Religion in the Nineteenth Century.* Basingstoke, 1991.

Cardew, F.M.G. 'Dr. Thornton and "The New Illustration" 1799–1807'. *Journal of the Royal Horticultural Society* 72 (1947): 281–5, 450–3.

Carlson, Eric, T., and Simpson. Meribeth, M. 'Models of the Nervous System in Eighteenth-Century Psychiatry'. *Bulletin of the History of Medicine* 43 (1969): 101–15.

Challinor, John. *The History of British Geology: A Bibliographical Study.* Newton Abbot, 1971.

Chitnis, Anand C. *The Scottish Enlightenment: A Social History.* London, 1976.

Christian, Jessica. 'Paul Sandby and the Military Survey of Scotland'. In Nicholas Alfrey and Stephen Daniels, eds. *Mapping the Landscape: Essays on Art and Cartography.* Exhib. cat. University Art Gallery, Nottingham. Nottingham, 1990: 18–22.

Christie, John R.R. 'Origins and Development of the Scottish Scientific Community, 1680–1760'. *History of Science* 12 (1974): 122–40.

——. 'The Rise and Fall of Scottish Science'. In Maurice P. Crosland, ed. *The Emergence of Science in Western Europe.* London, 1975: 111–26.

——. 'Ideology and Representation in Eighteenth-Century Natural History'. *Oxford Art Journal* 13 (1990): 3–10.

Christie's. *Catalogue of the Remaining Works of Dr. Thomas Monro.* Sales. cat. 26 June 1833.

——. *Catalogue of the Whole of the Remaining Works of Cornelius Varley.* Sales cat. 15 July 1875.

Clark, George. *A History of the Royal College of Physicians of London.* 3 vols. Oxford, 1964–72.

Clark, Kenneth. *Landscape into Art.* 1949. 6th ed. London, 1991.

Clarke, Edwin S., and O'Malley, C.D. *The Human Brain and Spinal Cord.* Berkeley, 1968.

Clarke, Michael, and Penny, Nicholas. *The Arrogant Connoisseur: Richard Payne Knight 1751–1824.* Exhib. cat. Whitworth Art Gallery. Manchester, 1982.

Colnaghi, P. & D. *Exhibition of Drawings and Watercolours by Cornelius Varley.* Sales cat. London, 1973.

Conisbee, Philip. 'Pre-Romantic Plein-Air Painting'. *Art History* 2 (1979): 413–28.

Constable, John. *John Constable's Correspondence.* Ed. R.B. Beckett. 6 vols. Ipswich, 1962–8.

Conybeare, Revd W.D., and Phillips, William. *Outlines of the Geology of England and Wales.* London, 1822.

Cooke, George, and Cooke, William. *Picturesque Views on the Southern Coast of England.* London, 1826.

Cooksey, Janet. *Alexander Nasmyth HRSA, 1758–1840: A Man of the Scottish Renaissance.* Haddington, 1991.

Copley, Stephen, and Garside, Peter, eds. *The Politics of the Picturesque.* Cambridge, 1994.

Cormack, Malcolm. *Oil on Water: Oil Sketches by British Watercolourists.* Exhib. cat. Yale Center for British Art. New Haven, 1986.

Cosgrove, Denis, and Daniels, Stephen, eds. *The Iconography of Landscape: Essays on the Symbolic Representation, Design and Use of Past Environments.* Cambridge, 1988.

Couzens Hoy, David, ed. *Foucault: A Critical Reader.* Oxford, 1986.

Craig, G.Y., ed. *James Hutton's Theory of the Earth: The Lost Drawings*. Edinburgh, 1978.

Crouan, Katharine. *John Linnell: A Centennial Exhibition*. Exhib. cat. Fitzwilliam Museum. Cambridge, 1982.

Cruikshank, George. *Scraps and Sketches*. 4 vols. London, 1828–32.

Cullen, William. *A Treatise of the Materia Medica*. 2 vols. Edinburgh, 1789.

Cumming, David A. 'John MacCulloch, Blackguard, Thief and High Priest, Reassessed'. In Alwyne Wheeler and James H. Price, eds. *From Linnaeus to Darwin: Commentaries on the History of Biology and Geology. Papers from the Fifth Easter Meeting of the Society for the History of Natural History 28–31 March*. London, 1985: 77–88.

Cunningham, Allan. *Lives of the Most Eminent British Painters*. 6 vols. London, 1829–33.

Curry, Patrick. *A Confusion of Prophets: Victorian and Edwardian Astrology*. London, 1992.

Curtis, William. *Botanical Magazine: Or, Flower-Garden Displayed*. 14 vols. London, 1787–1800.

——. *Lectures on Botany, as Delivered in the Botanic Garden at Lambeth. By the Late William Curtis, F.L.S.* Ed. Samuel Curtis. 3 vols. London, 1805 [with preface by R.J. Thornton].

Daniell, William. *Interesting Selections from Animated Nature with Illustrative Scenery*. 2 vols. London [1812?].

——. *A Voyage round Great Britain*. 8 vols. London, 1814–25. [text for vols. 1 and 2 by Richard Ayton].

——. *Illustrations of the Island of Staffa in a Series of Views: Accompanied by Topographical and Geological Description*. London, 1818.

Daniels, Stephen, and Watkins, Charles. 'Picturesque Landscaping and Estate Management: Uvedale Price and Nathaniel Kent at Foxley'. In Stephen Copley and Peter Garside, eds. *The Politics of the Picturesque*. Cambridge, 1994.

Darwin, Erasmus. *The Botanic Garden*. London, 1789–91. Part 1: 'The Loves of the Plants', 1789; Part 2: 'The Economy of Vegetation', 1791.

——. *Zoonomia: Or, the Laws of Organic Life*. 2 vols. London, 1794–6.

——. *Phytologia: Or, the Philosophy of Agriculture and Gardening*. London, 1800.

——. *The Temple of Nature*. London, 1803.

Davie, George E. *The Scottish Enlightenment*. The Historical Association's General Series 99. London, 1981.

Davies, Randall. 'John Varley'. *Old Water-Colour Society's Club* 11 (1924–5): 1–27.

Dayes, Edward. 'On Painting'. *Philosophical Magazine* 13 (1802): 122–9, 211–19, 348–54; 14 (1803): 31–41, 97–107, 218–28; 15 (1803): 12–15, 115–26.

——. *The Works of the Late Edward Dayes*. Ed. Mrs E. Dayes. London, 1805.

De Bolla, Peter. *The Discourse of the Sublime: Readings in History, Aesthetics and the Subject*. Oxford, 1989.

Denison, Cara D., Phimister, Evelyn J., and Wiles, Stephanie. *Gainsborough to Ruskin: British Landscape Drawings & Watercolors from the Morgan Library*. New York, 1994.

Deuchar, Stephen. *Sporting Art in Eighteenth-Century England*. New Haven and London, 1988.

Dobai, Johannes. *Die Kunstliteratur des Klassizismus und der Romantik in England 1700–1840*. 3 vols. Berne, 1974–7.

Doe, Donald B. *The Sublime as an Aesthetic Correlative: A Study of Late Eighteenth Century English Aesthetic Theory, Landscape Painting and Gothic Drama*. Diss. Ohio University, 1977. UMI, 1980, 48106.

Dunthorne, Gordon. *Flower and Fruit Prints of the Eighteenth and Early Nineteenth Centuries*. London, 1938.

Edwards, John. *A Collection of Flowers, Drawn after Nature, and Disposed in an Ornamental and Picturesque Manner*. London, 1801.

Edwards, Sydenham T. *Representation of 150 Rare and Curious Ornamental Plants*. London, 1809.

——. *Botanical Register, New Flora Britannica*. 14 vols. London, 1815–28.

Ehret, Georg D. *Trew's Plantae Selectae*. Norimbergae [Nuremberg], 1750–73.

Emsley, Clive. *British Society and the French Wars 1793–1815*. London, 1979.

Englefield, Henry C. *A Description of the Principal Picturesque Beauties, Antiquities, and Geological Phenomena of the Isle of Wight*. London, 1816.

Everett, Nigel H. *The Tory View of Landscape*. New Haven and London, 1994.

Eyles, V.A. 'Robert Jameson and the Royal Scottish Museum'. *Discovery: The Magazine of Scientific Progress* 15 (1954): 155–62.

Faigan, Julian. *Paul Sandby Drawings*. Exhib. cat. City of Hamilton Art Gallery. Sydney, 1981.

Farington, Joseph. *The Diary of Joseph Farington*. Eds. Kenneth Garlick, Angus Macintyre (and Kathryn Cave from vol. 7). 16 vols. to date. New Haven, 1978–.

Faujas de Saint-Fond, Barthélemi. *Voyage en Angleterre, en Écosse, et aux Iles Hébrides*. 2 vols. Paris, 1797. Eng. trans. as *Travel in England, Scotland, and the Hebrides*. 2 vols. London, 1799.

Finch, Francis O. *Memorials of the Late Francis Oliver Finch*. Ed. E. Finch. London, 1865.

Finley, Gerald. *Landscapes of Memory: Turner as Illustrator to Scott*. London, 1980.

Fittler, James. *Scotia Depicta*. London, 1804.

Forster, Thomas. *Researches about Atmospheric Phenomena*. London, 1813.

Foucault, Michel. *Historie de la folie*. Paris, 1961.

——. *Les mots et les choses: Une archéologie des sciences humaines* (Pairs, 1966); Eng. trans. as *The Order of Things: An Archaeology of the Human Sciences*. 1970. London, 1991.

Freeman, Michael. *Edmund Burke and the Critique of Political Radicalism*. Oxford, 1980.

French, Roger K. *Robert Whytt: The Soul, and Medicine*. London, 1969.

Fruchtman, Jack. 'Common Sense and the Association of Ideas: The Reid–Priestley Controversy'. In Melvin Dalgarno and Eric Matthews, eds. *The Philosophy of Thomas Reid*. Philosophical Studies Series 42. Dordrecht, 1989: 421–31.

Funnell, Peter D. 'Richard Payne Knight 1751–1824: Aspects of Antiquarianism, Aesthetic and Art Criticism in England in the Late Eighteenth and Early Nineteenth Centuries'. D.Phil. Thesis. Oxford University, 1985.

Furber, Robert. *Twelve Months of Flowers and the Flower Garden Display'd*. London, 1732.

Fyfe, Gordon, and Law, John, eds. *Picturing Power: Visual Depiction and Social Relations*. London, 1988.

Gage, A.T., and Stearn, W.T. *A Bicentenary History of the Linnean Society of London*. London, 1988.

Gage, John. *A Decade of English Naturalism: 1810–1820*. Exhib. cat. Norwich Castle Museum. Norwich, 1969.

——. 'The Distinctness of Turner'. *Journal of the Royal Society for the Encouragement of Arts* 123 (1975): 448–58.

——. *J.M.W. Turner: A Wonderful Range of Mind*. New Haven and London, 1987.

——. *George Field and his Circle: From Romanticism to the Pre-Raphaelite Brotherhood*. Exhib. cat. Fitzwilliam Museum, Cambridge. London, 1989.

——. *Colour and Culture: Practice and Meaning from Antiquity to Abstraction*. London, 1993.

Galassi, Peter. *Before Photography: Painting and the Invention of Photography*. Exhib. cat. Museum of Modern Art. New York, 1981.

——. *Corot in Italy*. New Haven and London, 1991.

Garfinkel, Norton. 'Science and Religion in England 1790–1800: The Critical Response to the Work of Erasmus Darwin'. *Journal of the History of Ideas* 16 (1955): 376–88.

Garnett, Thomas. *Observations on a Tour through the Highlands and Part of the Western Isles of Scotland, particularly Staffa and Icolmkill*. 2 vols. London, 1800.

Geikie, Archibald. *The Scottish School of Geology*. Edinburgh, 1871.

Geological Society of London. *Transactions of the Geological Society of London* 1 (1811): Preface.

——. *Annual Report of the Meeting of the Council and Museum Committee of the Geological Society*. 1815. George Bellas Greenough Papers and Correspondence. Manuscript Room, University College Library, London. Classmark 5/2.

Gerard, Alexander. *Essay on Taste*. London, 1759.

Gettings, Fred. *The Hidden Art: A Study of Occult Symbolism in Art*. London, 1978.

Gilpin, William. *Observations Relative Chiefly to Picturesque Beauty: Made in the Year 1776, on Several Parts of Great Britain, particularly the High-lands of Scotland*. 2 vols. London, 1789.

——. *Three Essays: On Picturesque Beauty; On Picturesque Travel; and On Sketching Landscape: to which is Added a Poem, On Landscape Painting*. 1792. 2nd ed. London, 1794.

——. *Observation on the Coast of Hampshire, Sussex, and Kent: Relative Chiefly to Picturesque Beauty; Made in the Summer of the Year 1774*. London, 1804.

Godwin, William. *Diary*. 31 notebooks. 1788–1836. Possession Lord Abinger. Deposited in Bodleian Library, Oxford. Classmark Dep. e. 196–227.

Gombrich, Ernst H. *The Story of Art*. 1950. London, 1992.

——. *Art and Illusion: A Study in the Psychology of Pictorial Representation*. 1960. Oxford, 1991.

——. 'Experiment and Experience in the Arts'. In R.B. McConnell, ed. *Art, Science and Human Progress*. London, 1983: 145–71.

Gordon, Catherine. 'The Illustration of Sir Walter Scott: Nineteenth-Century Enthusiasm and Adaptation'. *Journal of the Warburg and Courtauld Institutes* 34 (1971): 297–317.

Gould, Stephen J. *Time's Arrow, Time's Cycle: Myth and Metaphor in the Discovery of Geological Time*. London, 1988.

Gowing, Lawrence, and Conisbee, Philip. *Painting from Nature: The Tradition of Open-Air Oil Sketching from the 17th to the 19th Centuries*. Exhib. cat. Fitzwilliam Museum. Cambridge, 1980.

Grant, Maurice H. *A Dictionary of British Landscape Painters from the 16th to the 20th Century*. Leigh-on-Sea, 1952.

Graves, Algernon. *A Dictionary of Artists, who have exhibited Works in the Principal London Exhibitions, from 1760 to 1893*. London, 1901.

——. *The Royal Academy of Arts: A Complete Dictionary of*

Contributors and their Work from its Foundation in 1769 to 1904. 8 vols. London, 1905–6.

——. *The Society of Artists of Great Britain 1760–1791, The Free Society of Artists 1761–1783: A Complete Dictionary of Contributors and their Work from the Foundation of the Societies to 1791*. London, 1907.

Greenough, George Bellas. *Journals: Tour of Scotland, 1805*. George Bellas Greenough Papers and Correspondence. Manuscript Room, University College Library, London. Classmark 7/11 and 7/12.

Grigson, Geoffrey. 'Fingal's Cave'. *Architectural Review* 104 (1948): 51–4.

Grigson, Geoffrey, and Buchanan, Handasyde. *Thornton's Temple of Flora with the Plates Faithfully Reproduced from the Original Engravings*. 1951. 2nd ed. London, 1972.

Grose, Francis. *The Antiquities of Scotland*. 2 vols. London, 1789.

Gunnarsson, Torsten. *Friluftsmaleri före friluftsmaleriet*. Acta Universitatis Upsaliensis, Ars Suetica 12. Uppsala, 1989.

Halévy, Elie. *The Growth of Philosophic Radicalism*. London, 1928.

Hall, A. Rupert. 'The Royal Society of Arts: Two Centuries of Progress in Science and Technology'. *Journal of the Royal Society of Arts* 122 (1974): 641–58.

Hall, James. 'On the Vertical Position and Convolutions of Certain Strata, and their Relations with Granite' and 'On the Revolutions of the Earth's Surface'. *Transactions of the Royal Society of Edinburgh* 7 (1815): 79–108 and 139–211.

Hamilton, Jean. *The Sketching Society, 1799–1851*. Exhib. cat. Victoria and Albert Museum. London, 1971.

Hamilton, William. *Campi Phlegraei. Observations on the Volcanos of the Two Sicilies*. 2 vols. Naples, 1776. *Supplement*. Naples, 1779.

——. 'An Account of the Late Eruption of Mount Vesuvius'. *Philosophical Transactions of the Royal Society of London* 85 (1795): 73–116.

Hammond, John H. *The Camera Obscura: A Chronicle*. Bristol, 1981.

Hammond, John H., and Austin, Jill. *The Camera Lucida in Art and Science*. Bristol, 1987.

Hardie, Martin, and Clayton, Muriel. 'Thomas Daniell, R.A., William Daniell, R.A'. *Walker's Quarterly* 35–6 (1932): 1–106.

Hardie, Martin. 'William Turner of Oxford'. *Old Water-Colour Society's Club* 9 (1932): 1–23.

——. *Water-Colour Painting in Britain*. 3 vols. London, 1966–8.

Hartley, David. *Observations on Man, his Frame, his Duty, and his Expectations*. 2 vols. London, 1749.

Hawes, Louis. 'Constable's Sky Sketches'. *Journal of the Warburg and Courtauld Institutes* 32 (1969): 344–65.

Heleniak, Kathryn Moore. *William Mulready*. New Haven and London, 1980.

Hemingway, Andrew. 'The "Sociology" of Taste in the Scottish Enlightenment'. *Oxford Art Journal* 12 (1989): 3–35.

——. *Landscape Imagery & Urban Culture in Early Nineteenth-Century Britain*. Cambridge, 1992.

Henderson, Peter. *The Seasons or Flower-Garden*. London, 1806.

——. *Pomona*. London. 1808.

Herrmann, Luke. *Paul and Thomas Sandby*. London, 1986.

Hill, David. 'A Taste of the Arts: Turner and the Patronage of Edward Lascelles of Harewood House'. *Turner Studies* 4 (1984): 24–33.

Hipple, Walter J. *The Beautiful, the Sublime, and the Picturesque in Eighteenth-Century British Aesthetic Theory*. Carbondale, 1957.

Hirschman, Albert O. *The Passions and the Interests: Political Arguments for Capitalism before its Triumph*. Princeton, 1992.

Hoeldtke, Robert. 'The History of Associationism and British Medical Psychology'. *Medical History* 11 (1967): 4665.

Hole, Robert. *Pulpits, Politics and Public Order in England 1760–1832*. Cambridge, 1989.

Holloway, James and Errington, Lindsay. *The Discovery of Scotland: The Appreciation of Scottish Scenery through Two Centuries of Painting*. Exhib. cat. National Gallery of Scotland. Edinburgh, 1978.

Home, Henry (Lord Kames). *Elements of Criticism*. 3 vols. Edinburgh, 1762.

Howard, Luke. 'Considerations on Dr. Hutton's Theory of Rain'. *Philosophical Magazine* 14 (1803): 55–62.

——. 'On the Modification of Clouds, and on the Principles of their Production, Suspension, and Destruction'. *Philosophical Magazine* 16 (1803): 97–107; 17 (1803): 5–11.

Howard, Peter. 'Painter's Preferred Places'. *Journal of Historical Geography* 11 (1985): 138–54.

Hussey, Christopher. *The Picturesque: Studies in a Point of View*. London, 1927.

Hutchison, Sidney C. 'The Royal Academy Schools, 1768–1830'. *Walpole Society* 38 (1962): 123–91.

Hutton, James. 'Theory of the Earth: Or an Investigation of the Laws Observable in the Composition, Dissolution, and Restoration of Land upon the Globe'. *Transactions of the Royal Society of Edinburgh* 1 (1788): 209–304.

——. *Theory of the Earth with Proofs and Illustrations*. 3 vols.

Edinburgh, 1795–1899. [for further bibliographical details, see Chapter III, n. 67].

Hyde, Ralph. *Panoramania!: The Art and Entertainment of the 'All-Embracing' View.* Exhib. cat. Barbican Art Gallery. London, 1988.

Inkster, Ian, and Morrell, Jack, eds. *Metropolis and Province: Science in British Culture, 1780–1850.* London, 1983.

Irwin, Francina. *Turner in Scotland.* Exhib. cat. Aberdeen Art Gallery. London, 1982.

Jackson, Stanley W. 'Force and Kindred Notions in Eighteenth-Century Neurophysiology and Medical Psychology'. *Bulletin of the History of Medicine* 44 (1970): 397–410, 539–554.

Jacyna, L.S. *Philosophical Whigs: Medicine, Science and Citizenship in Edinburgh, 1789–1848.* London, 1994.

James, Frank A.J.L. 'Michael Faraday, the City Philosophical Society and the Society of Arts'. *RSA Journal* 140 (1992): 192–9.

Jameson, Robert. *A Mineralogy of the Scottish Isles.* 2 vols. Edinburgh, 1800.

Jefferiss, F.J.G. *Dr. Thomas Monro (1759–1833) and the Monro Academy.* Exhib. cat. Victoria and Albert Museum. London, 1976.

Jenkins, J.J. *Papers.* Royal Watercolour Society, Bankside Gallery, London.

Jordanova, Ludmilla J., and Porter, Roy, eds. *Images of the Earth: Essays in the History of the Environmental Sciences.* Chalfont St Giles, 1979.

Kallich, Martin. *The Association of Ideas and Critical Theory in Eighteenth Century England.* The Hague, 1970.

Kant, Immanuel. *Die Kritik der Urteilskraft.* 1790. Ed. Wilhelm Weischedel. Wiesbaden, 1957.

Kauffmann, C.M. *John Varley 1778–1842.* Exhib. cat. Victoria and Albert Museum. London, 1984.

Kemp, Martin. 'Alexander Nasmyth and the Style of Graphic Eloquence'. *The Connoisseur* 173 (1970): 93–100.

——. *The Science of Art: Optical Themes in Western Art from Brunelleschi to Seurat.* New Haven and London, 1990.

King, Lester S. *The Medical World of the Eighteenth Century.* Chicago, 1958.

King, Ronald. *The Temple of Flora by Robert Thornton.* London, 1981.

King-Hele, Desmond. *Erasmus Darwin.* London, 1963.

——. *The Essential Writings of Erasmus Darwin.* London, 1968.

——. *Doctor of Revolution: The Life and Genius of Erasmus Darwin.* London, 1977.

——. *The Letters of Erasmus Darwin.* Cambridge, 1981.

——. 'Erasmus Darwin. Master of Interdisciplinary Science'. *Interdisciplinary Science Reviews* 10 (1985): 170–91.

——. *Erasmus Darwin and the Romantic Poets.* London, 1986.

Kirwan, Richard. *Geological Essays.* London, 1799.

Kitson, Sydney D. *The Life of John Sell Cotman.* London, 1937.

Klingender, Francis. *Art and the Industrial Revolution.* London, 1947.

Knight, Richard P. *The Landscape: A Didactic Poem.* London, 1794. 2nd ed. London, 1795.

——. *The Progress of Civil Society: A Didactic Poem in Six Books.* London, 1796.

——. *An Analytical Inquiry into the Principles of Taste.* London, 1805.

——. *A Monody on the Death of the Rt. Hn. Charles James Fox.* London, 1807.

——. 'Review of "The Life of Sir Joshua Reynolds by James Northcote". *Edinburgh Review* 23 (1814): 263–92.

Knowles, Christiana. 'John Linnell: His Early Landscapes, to 1830'. M.A. Report. Courtauld Institute, London, 1990.

Kramnick, Isaac. *Republicanism and Bourgeois Radicalism: Political Ideology in Late Eighteenth-Century England and America.* New York, 1990.

Langford, Paul, ed. *Party, Parliament, and the American Crisis, 1766–74.* Gen. ed. Paul Langford. *The Writings and Speeches of Edmund Burke.* Vol. 2. Oxford, 1981.

——. *Public Life and the Propertied Englishman 1689–1798.* Oxford, 1994.

Laudan, L.L. 'Thomas Reid and the Newtonian Turn of British Methodological Thought'. In R.E. Butts and John W. Davis, eds. *The Methodological Heritage of Newton.* Oxford, 1970: 103–29.

Laudan, Rachel. *From Mineralogy to Geology: The Foundations of a Science, 1650–1830.* Chicago and London, 1987.

Lawrence, Christopher. 'The Nervous System and Society in the Scottish Enlightenment'. In Barry Barnes and Steven Shapin, eds. *Natural Order: Historical Studies of Scientific Culture.* London, 1979: 19–40.

Leslie, C.R., ed. *Memoirs of the Life of John Constable.* London, 1949.

Leslie, Margaret. 'Mysticism Misunderstood: David Hartley and the Idea of Progress'. *Journal of the History of Ideas* 33 (1972): 625–32.

Linnell, David. *Blake, Palmer, Linnell and Co.: The Life of John Linnell.* Lewes, 1994.

Linnell, John. *Autobiographical Notes.* Redhill, 1864. Linnell Trust.

——. *Letters.* Linnell Trust.

——. *Journals.* 15 vols. 1811–79. Fitzwilliam Museum, Cambridge.

Lister, Raymond. *The Letters of Samuel Palmer.* 2 vols. Oxford, 1974.

Long, Basil S. 'Cornelius Varley'. *The Old Water-Colour Society's Club* 14 (1936–7): 1–11.

Luc, Jean André de. *Letters on the Physical History of the Earth.* London, 1831.

Ludwig, Heidrun. 'Rediscovery of the Original Drawings of Georg Dionysius Ehret for the *Plantae selectae*'. *Archives of Natural History* 20 (1993): 381–90.

Lyell, Charles. *Principles of Geology: Being an Attempt to Explain the Former Changes of the Earth's Surface by Reference to Causes Now in Operation.* 3 vols. London, 1830–3.

Lyles, Anne. 'John Varley (1778–1842): A Catalogue of his Watercolours and Drawings in the British Museum'. M.A. Report. Courtauld Institute, London, 1980.

——. 'John Varley's Early Work'. *The Old Water-Colour Society's Club* 59 (1984): 1–22.

Lyotard, Jean-François. *Le différend* (Paris, 1983); Eng. trans. as *The Differend: Phrases in Dispute.* Manchester, 1988.

MacCulloch, John. 'On Staffa'. *Transactions of the Geological Society of London* 2 (1814): 501–9.

——. 'A Sketch of the Mineralogy of Sky'. *Transactions of the Geological Society of London* 3 (1816): 1–111; 4 (1817): 156–92.

——. *A Description of the Western Isles of Scotland.* 3 vols. Edinburgh, 1819.

——. *The Highlands and Western Isles of Scotland.* 4 vols. London, 1824.

——. *A System of Geology, with a Theory of the Earth.* London, 1831.

——. *Proofs and Illustrations of the Attributes of God, from the Facts and Laws of the Physical Universe: Being the Foundation of Natural and Revealed Religion.* 3 vols. London, 1837.

——. *John MacCulloch Drawings.* Geological Society of London. Ref. LDGSL 400.

MacKay, W.D., and Rinder, Frank. *The Royal Scottish Academy, 1826–1916.* Glasgow, 1917.

MacLeod, Roy M. 'Whigs and Savants: Reflections on the Reform Movement in the Royal Society, 1830–1848'. In Ian Inkster and Jack Morell, eds. *Metropolis and Province: Science in British Culture, 1780–1850.* London, 1983: 55–90.

Macmillan, Duncan. *Painting in Scotland: The Golden Age.* Oxford, 1986.

Malherbe, Michel. 'Thomas Reid on the Five Senses'. In Melvin Dalgarno and Eric Matthews, eds. *The Philosophy of Thomas Reid.* Philosophical Studies Series 42. Dordrecht, 1989: 103–17.

Martin, Martin. *A Description of the Western Islands of Scotland.* London, 1703.

Maslen, Keith. 'Printing for the Author: From Bowyer Printing Ledgers, 1710–1775'. *The Library.* Fifth Series. 27 (1972): 302–9.

McKenzie, Gordon. *Critical Responsiveness: A Study of the Psychological Current in Later Eighteenth-Century Criticism.* Berkeley, 1949.

McNeil, Maureen. *Under the Banner of Science: Erasmus Darwin and his Age.* Manchester, 1987.

Meek, Ronald L. *Social Science and the Ignoble Savage.* Cambridge, 1976.

Melvin, Peter H. 'Burke on Theatricality and Revolution'. *Journal of the History of Ideas* 36 (1975): 447–68.

Messmann, Frank J. *Richard Payne Knight: The Twilight of Virtuosity.* Studies in English Literature 89. The Hague, 1974.

Miller, David Philip. 'Method and the "Micropolitics" of Science: The Early Years of the Geological and Astronomical Societies of London'. In John A. Schuster and Richard Yeo, eds. *The Politics and Rhetoric of Scientific Method.* Dordrecht, 1986: 227–57.

Mitchell, Arthur. 'A List of Travels, Tours, Journeys, Voyages, Cruises, Excursions, Wanderings, Rambles, Visits, etc., Relating to Scotland'. *Proceedings of the Society of Antiquaries of Scotland* 11 (1900–1): 431–638.

Mitchell, L.G., ed. *The French Revolution 1790–1794.* Gen. ed. Paul Langford. *The Writings and Speeches of Edmund Burke.* Vol. 8. Oxford, 1989.

Mitchell, Timothy F. *Art and Science in German Landscape Painting 1770–1840.* New York, 1993.

Mitchell, W.J.T. *Iconology: Image, Text, Ideology.* Chicago, 1986.

Mitchell, W.J.T., ed. *Landscape and Power.* Chicago, 1994.

Monk, Samuel H. *The Sublime: A Study of Critical Theories in XVIII-Century England.* New York, 1935.

Morrell, J.B. 'The University of Edinburgh in the Late Eighteenth Century: Its Scientific Eminence and Academic Structure'. *ISIS* 62 (1971): 158–71.

——. 'Science and Scottish University Reform: Edinburgh in 1826'. *British Journal for the History of Science* 6 (1972): 39–56.

Mount, Harry T. 'The Reception of Dutch Genre Painting in England, 1695–1829'. Ph.D. Thesis. Cambridge University, 1991.

Munk, William. *The Roll of the Royal College of Physicians (1701 to 1800).* 2 vols. 1861. 2nd ed. 3 vols. London, 1878.

Napier, Robert W. *John Thomson of Duddingston, Landscape Painter: His Life and Work.* Edinburgh, 1919.

Nasmyth, James. *An Autobiography.* London, 1883.

Necker de Saussure, Louis A. *A Voyage to the Hebrides or Western Isles of Scotland.* London, 1822. [for further bibliographical details, see Chapter III, n. 54].

Newman, Charles. *The Evolution of Medical Education in the Nineteenth Century.* London, 1957.

Northcote, James. *Memoirs of Sir Joshua Reynolds, Knt.* London, 1813.

Olson, Richard. *Scottish Philosophy and British Physics 1750–1880: A Study in the Foundations of the Victorian Scientific Style.* Princeton, 1975.

Parris, Leslie, and Fleming-Williams, Ian. *Constable.* Exhib. cat. Tate Gallery. London, 1991.

Paulson, Ronald. *Emblem and Expression: Meaning in English Art of the Eighteenth Century.* London, 1978.

——. *Hogarth.* Vol. 3: *Art and Politics, 1750–1764.* 1971. 2nd ed. Cambridge, 1993.

Payne, Christiana. *Toil and Plenty: Images of the Agricultural Landscape in England 1780–1890.* Exhib. cat. Yale Center for British Art. New Haven, 1993.

Pennant, Thomas. *A Tour in Scotland.* Chester and London, 1771.

——. *A Tour in Scotland, and Voyage to the Hebrides.* 2 vols. London, 1774–6.

Phillipson, Nicholas T. 'Culture and Society in the Eighteenth-Century Province: The Case of Edinburgh and the Scottish Enlightenment'. In Laurence Stone, ed. *The University in Society.* Vol. 2. Princeton, 1975: 407–48.

Pidgley, Michael. 'Cornelius Varley, Cotman, and the Graphic Telescope'. *Burlington Magazine* 114 (1972): 781–6.

——. 'Introduction'. P. & D. Colnaghi. *Exhibition of Drawings and Watercolours by Cornelius Varley.* Sales cat. London, 1973.

Playfair, John. *Illustrations of the Huttonian Theory of the Earth.* Edinburgh, 1802.

Pointon, Marcia. 'Geology and Landscape Painting in Nineteenth-Century England'. In Ludmilla J. Jordanova and Roy Porter, eds. *Images of the Earth: Essays in the History of the Environmental Sciences.* Chalfont St Giles, 1979: 84–108.

——. 'Portrait-Painting as a Business Enterprise in London in the 1780s'. *Art History* 7 (1984): 187–205.

——. *Mulready.* Exhib. cat. Victoria and Albert Museum. London, 1986.

——. *Hanging the Head: Portraiture and Social Formation in Eighteenth-Century England.* New Haven and London, 1993.

Pollock, Martin, ed. *Common Denominators in Art and Science.* Aberdeen, 1983.

Porter, Roy. *The Making of Geology: Earth Science in Britain 1660–1815.* Cambridge, 1977.

——. *Disease, Medicine and Society in England 1550–1860.* Basingstoke, 1987.

——. *Mind Forg'd Manacles.* London, 1987.

——. *Doctor of Society: Thomas Beddoes and the Sicktrade in Late-Enlightenment England.* London, 1992.

Price, Uvedale. *An Essay on the Picturesque, as compared with the Sublime and the Beautiful.* London, 1794. 2nd ed. London, 1796.

——. *Thoughts on the Defence of Property.* Hereford, 1797.

——. *A Dialogue on the Distinct Characters of the Picturesque and the Beautiful: In Answer to the Objections of Mr. Knight.* Hereford, 1801.

Prideaux, Sarah T. *Aquatint Engravings: A Chapter in the History of Book Illustration.* London, 1909.

Pries, Christine, ed. *Das Erhabene: Zwischen Grenzerfahrung und Grössenwahn.* Weinheim, 1989.

Priestley, Joseph. *An Examination of Dr. Reid's Inquiry into the Human Mind on the Principles of Common Sense, Dr. Beattie's Essay on the Nature and Immutability of Truth and Dr. Oswald's Appeal to Common Sense on Behalf of Religion.* 1774. 2nd ed. London, 1775.

——. *Hartley's Theory of the Human Mind: On the Principle of the Association of Ideas.* London, 1775.

——. *Letters to the Right Honourable Edmund Burke.* Birmingham, 1791. French trans., Paris, 1791.

Primer, Irwin. 'Erasmus Darwin's Temple of Nature: Progress, Evolution, and the Eleusinian Mysteries'. *Journal of the History of Ideas* 25 (1964): 58–76.

Prince, Hugh. 'Art and Agrarian Change, 1710–1815'. In Daniel Cosgrove and Stephen Daniels, eds. *The Iconography of Landscape: Essays on the Symbolic Representation, Design and Use of Past Environments.* Cambridge, 1988: 98–118.

Pugh, Simon, ed. *Reading Landscape: Country-City-Capital.* Manchester, 1990.

Pye, John. *Patronage of British Art: A Historical Sketch.* London, 1845.

Radisich, Paula R. 'Eighteenth-Century Plein-Air Painting and the Sketches of P.H. de Valenciennes'. *Art Bulletin* 64 (1982): 98–103.

Rauschenberg, Roy A. 'The Journals of Joseph Banks' Voyage up Great Britain's West Coast to Iceland and to the Orkney Isles, July to October 1772'. *Proceedings of the American Philosophical Society* 117 (1973): 186–226.

Redgrave, Richard. *Richard Redgrave, C.B., R.A.: A Memoir, Compiled from his Diary.* Ed. Frances M. Redgrave. London, 1891.

Redgrave, Samuel. *A Dictionary of Artists of the English School.* London, 1874.

Reid, Thomas. *An Inquiry into the Human Mind: On the Principle of Common Sense.* Edinburgh, 1764.

——. *Essays on the Intellectual Powers of Man.* Edinburgh, 1785.

Reynolds, Joshua. *Discourses on Art*. Ed. Robert R. Wark. New Haven, 1981.

Robertson, Bruce. *The Art of Paul Sandby*. Exhib. cat. Yale Center for British Art. New Haven, 1985.

Robinson, Sidney K. *Inquiry into the Picturesque*. Chicago, 1991.

Roget, John L. *History of the Old Water-Colour Society*. 2 vols. London, 1891.

Root-Bernstein, Robert S. 'On Paradigms and Revolutions in Science and Art: The Challenge of Interpretation'. *Art Journal* 44 (1984): 109–18.

Rosenthal, Michael. *British Landscape Painting*. Oxford, 1982.

——. *Constable: The Painter and his Landscape*. New Haven and London, 1983.

Ross, R.N. '"To Charm the Curious Eye": Erasmus Darwin's Poetry at the Vestibule of Knowledge'. *Journal of the History of Ideas* 32 (1971): 379–94.

Ross, S. 'Scientist: The Story of the Word'. *Annals of Science* 18 (1962): 65–85.

Royal Institution of Great Britain. *Royal Institution Minutes of General Meetings*. Vols. 3–6. Royal Institution of Great Britain, London.

——. *Royal Institution Index to Lectures 1799–1929*. 7 boxes. Royal Institution of Great Britain, London.

——. *The Archives of the Royal Institution of Great Britain: In Facsimile Minutes of Managers' Meetings 1799–1900*. Eds. Frank Greenway et al. 12 vols. London, 1971–6.

Royle, Edward. *Modern Britain: A Social History 1750–1985*. London, 1987.

Rudwick, Martin J.S. 'Hutton and Werner Compared: George Greenough's Geological Tour of Scotland in 1805'. *British Journal for the History of Science* 1 (1962): 117–35.

——. 'The Foundation of the Geological Society of London: Its Scheme for Co-operative Research and its Struggle for Independence'. *British Journal for the History of Science* 1 (1963): 325–55.

——. 'The Emergence of a Visual Language for Geological Science 1760–1840'. *History of Science* 14 (1976): 149–95.

——. *The Great Devonian Controversy: The Shaping of Scientific Knowledge among Gentlemanly Specialists*. Chicago, 1985.

Ruskin, John. *The Eagle's Nest: Ten Lectures on the Relation of Natural Science to Art given before the University of Oxford in Lent Term 1872*. London, 1872.

——. *Modern Painters*. 1843–60. New ed. 5 vols. New York, 1880–1.

Rykwert, Joseph. *On Adam's House in Paradise: The Idea of the Primitive Hut in Architectural History*. New York, 1972.

Sandby, Paul. *The Virtuosi's Museum; Containing Select Views, in England, Scotland, and Ireland*. London, 1778.

Schaffer, Simon. 'Natural Philosophy'. In G.S. Rousseau and Roy Porter, eds. *The Ferment of Knowledge*. Cambridge, 1980: 55–91.

——. 'States of Mind: Enlightenment and Natural Philosophy'. In G.S. Rousseau, ed. *The Languages of Psyche, Mind and Body in Enlightenment Thought*. Berkeley, 1990: 233–90.

Schofield, Robert E. *The Lunar Society of Birmingham*. Oxford, 1963.

——. *Mechanism and Materialism: British Natural Philosophy in an Age of Reason*. Princeton, 1970.

——. 'Joseph Priestley: Eighteenth-Century British Neoplatonism, and S.T. Coleridge'. In Everett Mendelsohn, ed. *Transformation and Tradition in the Sciences: Essays in Honor of I. Bernard Cohen*. Cambridge, 1984: 237–54.

Schwarz, L.D. *London in the Age of Industrializations: Entrepreneurs, Labour Force and Living Conditions, 1700–1850*. Cambridge, 1992.

Scott, Walter. *The Provincial Antiquities and Picturesque Scenery of Scotland, with Descriptive Illustrations*. 2 vols. London, 1826.

——. *The Complete Poetical Works of Sir Walter Scott*. 11 vols. Edinburgh, 1833–4.

——. *Memoirs of the Life of Sir Walter Scott*. Ed. John G. Lockhart. 7 vols. Edinburgh, 1837–8.

Secord, James A. *Controversy in Victorian Geology: The Cambrian-Silurian Dispute*. Princeton, 1986.

Shapin, Steven. 'Homo Phrenologicus: Anthropological Perspectives on an Historical Problem'. In Barry Barnes and Steven Shapin, eds. *Natural Order: Historical Studies of Scientific Culture*. London, 1979: 41–71.

——. 'The Politics of Observation: Cerebral Anatomy and Social Interests in the Edinburgh Phrenology Disputes'. In Harry M. Collins, ed. *Sociology of Scientific Knowledge: A Source Book*. Bath, 1982: 103–50.

Sharpe, Richard. *An Annotated List of Works Relating to Iona and St Columba Including the Neighbouring Island of Staffa*. Forthcoming publication.

Smout, Christopher. 'Tours in the Scottish Highlands from the Eighteenth to the Twentieth Centuries'. *Northern Scotland* 5 (1982): 99–121.

Snell, K.D.M. *Annals of the Labouring Poor: Social Change and Agrarian England 1600–1900*. London, 1985.

Spillane, John. *The Doctrine of the Nerves: Chapters in the History of Neurology*. Oxford, 1981.

Stafford, Barbara M. 'Rude Sublime: The Taste for Nature's Colossi during the Late Eighteenth and Early Nineteenth Centuries'. *Gazette des Beaux-Arts* 1287 (1976): 113–26.

——. *Voyage into Substance: Art, Science, and the Illustrated Travel Account, 1760–1840.* Cambridge, Mass., 1984.

Stansfield, Dorothy A., and Stansfield, Ronald G. 'Dr Thomas Beddoes and James Watt: Preparatory Work 1794–96 for the Bristol Pneumatic Institute'. *Medical History* 30 (1986): 276–302.

Stevens, Francis. *Views of Cottages and Farm-Houses in England and Wales.* 1808. 2nd ed. London, 1815.

Stewart, Dugald. *Elements of the Human Mind.* 3 vols. London and Edinburgh, 1792–1827.

——. *The Collected Works of Dugald Stewart.* Ed. William Hamilton. 11 vols. Edinburgh, 1854–60.

Stolnitz, Jerome. 'Beauty: Some Stages in the History of an Idea'. *Journal of the History of Ideas* 22 (1961): 185–204.

——. 'On the Origins of Aesthetic Disinterestedness'. *Journal of Aesthetics and Art Criticism* 20 (1961): 121–32.

Story, Alfred. *The Life of John Linnell.* 2 vols. London, 1892.

——. *James Holmes and John Varley.* London, 1894.

Sutton, Thomas. *The Daniells: Artists and Travellers.* London, 1954.

Taylor, Basil. *Joshua Cristall (1768–1847).* Exhib. cat. Victoria and Albert Museum. London, 1975.

Templeman, William D. *The Life and Work of William Gilpin.* Illinois Studies in Language and Literature 24. Urbana, 1939.

Thieme, Ulrich, and Becker, Felix. *Allgemeines Lexikon der Bildenden Künstler von der Antike bis zur Gegenwart.* 37 vols. Leipzig, 1907–50.

Thornton, Robert J. *The Politician's Creed, Being the Great Outline of Political Science: From the Writings of Montesquieu, Hume, Gibbon, Paley, Townsend, &c.&c. by an Independent.* London, 1795.

——. *Medical Extracts: On the Nature of Health: With Practical Observations, and the Laws of the Nervous and Fibrous Systems.* New ed. 4 vols. London, 1796–7. 4th ed. 5 vols. London, 1799–1800.

——. *Advertisement to the New Illustration of the Sexual System of Linnaeus by Robert John Thornton, M.D. Late of Trinity College, Cambridge; Fellow of the Linnaean Society, &c.&c.* 1 January 1797.

——. 'Letters in Response to the Review, Published in the "Annual Review" of 1804'. *Philosophical Magazine* 18 (1804): 326–32; 19 (1804): 141–6, 218–60, 360–3.

——. *Dr. Thornton's Exhibition of Botanical Paintings. Now Open at No. 49 Bond Street: With the Poetic Compositives made on the Different Subjects, and Explanatory Notes.* London, 1804.

——. *A New Illustration of the Sexual System of Carolus von Linnaeus.* London, 1807. [for further bibliographical details, see Chapter II, n. 1].

——. *The Temple of Flora: Or, Garden of Nature. Part 3 of 'A New Illustration'.* London, 1807.

——. *The Philosophy of Medicine: Or, Medical Extracts on the Nature of Health and Disease.* 5th ed. 2 vols. London, 1813. [for earlier editions, see Chapter II, n. 18.].

——. *The Religious Use of Botany: Being an Introduction to the Science.* London, 1824.

Titterington, Christopher. 'William Turner of Oxford and British Romantic Naturalism'. *Old Water-Colour Society's Club* 59 (1984): 23–52.

Torrens, Hugh S. 'Patronage and Problems: Banks and the Earth Sciences'. In R.E.R. Banks et al., eds. *Sir Joseph Banks: A Global Perspective.* Kew, 1974.

UEA English Studies Group. 'Strategies for Representing Revolution'. In Francis Barker et al., eds. *1789: Reading Writing Revolution: Proceedings of the Essex Conference on the Sociology of Literature.* Essex, 1982: 81–100.

Varley, Cornelius. *Inventory.* Walker Collection.

——. *Cornelius Varley's Narrative Written by Himself.* Walker Collection.

——. 'On Atmospheric Phaenomena: Particularly the Formation of Clouds; their Permanence; their Precipitation in Rain, Snow, and Hail; and the consequent Rise of the Barometer'. *Philosophical Magazine* 27 (1807): 115–21.

——. 'Meteorological Observations on a Thunder Storm; with some Remarks on Medical Electricity'. *Philosophical Magazine* 34 (1809): 161–3, 201–2.

——. *Shipping, Barges, Fishing Boats, and other Vessels, Commonly Met with on the British Coasts, Rivers and Canals.* London, 1809.

——. *A Treatise on Optical Drawing Instruments: Also, A Method of Preserving Pictures in Oil and in Water Colours.* London, 1845.

Varley, John. *A Treatise on the Principles of Landscape Design.* London, 1821.

——. *A Treatise on Zodiacal Physiognomy.* London, 1828.

Vogler, Richard A. *Graphic Works of George Cruikshank.* New York, 1979.

Waddington, Conrad H. *Behind Appearance: A Study of the Relations between Painting and the Natural Sciences in this Century.* Edinburgh. 1969.

Wagner, Monika. *Die Industrielandschaft in der Englischen Malerei und Grafik, 1770–1830.* Frankfurt am Main, 1979.

Walford, Edward, and Thornbury, George W. *Old and New London: A Narrative of its History, its People, and its Places.* 6 vols. London, 1879–85.

Warren, Howard C. *A History of the Association Psychology.* London, 1921.

Waterhouse, Ellis K. *The Dictionary of British Eighteenth-Century Painters in Oils and Crayon.* Woodbridge, 1981.

Weindling, Paul J. 'Geological Controversy and its Historiography: The Prehistory of the Geological Society of London'. In Ludmilla J. Jordanova and Roy Porter, eds. *Images of the Earth: Essays in the History of the Environmental Sciences*. Chalfont St Giles, 1979: 249–71.

——. 'The British Mineralogical Society: A Case Study in Science and Social Improvement'. In Ian Inkster and Jack Morrell, eds. *Metropolis and Province: Science in British Culture, 1780–1850*. London, 1983: 120–50.

Weiskel, Thomas. *The Romantic Sublime: Studies in the Structure and Psychology of Transcendence*. Baltimore, 1976.

Whytt, Robert. *An Essay on the Vital and other Involuntary Motions of Animals*. Edinburgh, 1751.

——. *Observations on the Nature, Causes, and Cure of those Disorders which have been Commonly Called Nervous, Hypochondriac, or Hysteric*. 1765. 2nd corrected ed. Edinburgh, 1765.

Williams, Iolo A. *Early English Watercolours*. London, 1952.

Wilton, Andrew, and Lyles, Anne. *The Great Age of British Watercolours, 1750–1880*. Exhib. cat. Royal Academy of Arts. London and Munich, 1993.

Witt, John. *William Henry Hunt (1790–1864): Life and Work with a Catalogue*. London, 1982.

Wood, William. *Zoography: Or the Beauties of Nature Displayed*. 3 vols. London, 1807.

Wright, John P. *The Sceptical Realism of David Hume*. Manchester, 1983.

Yeo, Richard. 'An Idol of the Market-Place: Baconianism in Nineteenth-Century Britain'. *History of Science* 23 (1985): 251–97.

INDEX

Adorno, Theodor W., 4–5, 152
aesthetics, aesthetic theory, 7, 11–12, 57
　Alison on, 22–4, 25
　Burke on, 13–15
　Gerard on, 19, 157 n.32
　Gilpin on, 10–11, 26–7
　history of, 156 n.6 and n.8
　Home on, 19–20, 157 n.32
　Knight on, 29–32, 35
　Price on, 27–30, 35
　Stewart on, 24–6
aether, Newtonian, 12
　Cullen's modification of, 19
　Hartley's use of, 12–13, 18
　and Young's theory of light, 155 n.29,
　　161 n.160
Aikin, Arthur, 126
Alison, Archibald, 11, 12, 22–4, 25, 35, 67,
　　78, 83
　on contemporary society, 23–4
　Essays on the Nature and Principle of Taste,
　　22–4
　Hartley and, 23
　MacCulloch influenced by, 83
　Reid and, 23
　similarities with Kant, 23
　Smith's division of labour and, 23
　Stewart and, 24, 25
　on taste, 23–4
Alken, Samuel, 73
Allan, David,
　Thomas Graham, Baron Lynedoch, 60,
　　plate 36
Andrews, Malcolm, 170 n.37
animals,
　depicted in landscape settings, 68–70
Annual Register 64
aqueous theory, *see* neptunism
art,
　science and, 3, 5–6, 150–1
art history,
　landscape art and, 4–6
　science and, 5–6
association of ideas,
　Alison's theory of, 23–4

Burke's use of, 157 n.32
Chomsky against a modern version of,
　157 n.25
Erasmus Darwin and, 40
Hartley's theory of, 12–13
Knight and Hume's theory of, 30
Locke's principle of, 12
MacCulloch and, 82–3, 87, 94
Priestley and Hartley's theory of, 17
Reid's limited use of, 25
Stewart's theory of, 24–6
astrology,
　John Varley and, 145
Aurora Borealis, 127
Austin, Jill, 178 n.132

Bacon, Francis, 6, 171 n.84
Badt, Kurt, 127
Banks, Joseph,
　on Staffa, 68, 74–6, 80, 83, 85, 89
Baptist Church, 128, 147
Barker, Robert, 149
Barrell, John, 24, 155 n.21, 179 n.173
Bass Rock, *see* Scotland
Beaudrillard, Jean, 4
beautiful, the, (aesthetic category),
　in Alison's aesthetic theory, 23–4
　Burke on, 13–14
　landscape art and, 7, 9–10, 67, 70, 71
　Price on, 27–8
　in Stewart's aesthetic theory, 25–6
　Thornton's plants and, 37, 52–3, 57, 61,
　　65
beauty, 30
　see also beautiful
Beddoes, Thomas, 38, 164 n.39
Bell, Charles,
　WORKS:
　　Columnar Promontory of the Scure-Eigg, 81,
　　　82, **plate 51**; *View from Beinn,Na,
　　　Caillich in Skye*, 80, 90, **plate 50**
Benjamin, Walter, 4–5, 153
Bensley, Thomas, 65
Benthamism, 13, 159 n.82
Berger, John, 4

Berkeley, George, 20, 21
Bermingham, Ann, 155 n.21
Bethlem, 113
Blagden, Charles, 75
Blake, William, 144, 163 n.6
Botanical Magazine, 37, 46, 165 n.48, 166
　n.66
botanical treatises, 37, 49, 62
Brewster, David, 155 n.29, 161 n.160
Bridgewater, 3rd Duke of, *see* Egerton,
　Francis
British Mineralogical Society, 126
Brown, John, 163 n.11
Brown, Lancelot ('Capability'), 29, 32
Browne, Janet, 167 n.81
Brunonianism, 38, 163 n.11
Bryson, Norman, 4
Buckland, William, 88
Burke, Edmund, 11, 12, 13–17, 18, 27, 39,
　　61, 65
　and contemporary society, 15–17
　Hartley and, 13–14
　*A Philosophical Enquiry into the Origin of
　　our Ideas of the Sublime and Beautiful*,
　　13–16
　Price and, 17, 27
　Priestley and, 15–17, 18
　Reflections on the Revolution in France, 15–
　　16
　on taste, 15
Busfield, Joan, 175 n.60
Bush, Clive, 56, 163 n.5, 166 n.57 and
　n.65, 167 n.80

camera lucida, 131
camera obscura, 130–2
Canaletto (Giovanni Antonio Canal), 71,
　131
catastrophe (natural), 10, 77, 152
causation,
　divine, 77, 78, 88–9
　efficient,
　　Alison's abandonment of, 23
　　Burke's explanation of, 14
　　Gilpin does not identify, 27

Hartley adopts Newtonian aether as, 12

Knight takes up Scottish criticism of, 30

Newton's postulation of, 12

Price's explanation of, 27

Priestley's criticism of, 18

Reid's criticism of, 19, 20–2

Stewart's abandonment of, 24

Thornton's understanding of, 39

geology and, 76–9

meteorology and, 126–7

Chemical and Philosophical Society (Hatton House), 114

Cheselden, William, 25

chiaroscuro, 1, 29, 67, 73, 80, 85, 101, 106, 136, 138

Chitnis, Anand C., 20

City Philosophical Society, 126

Clark, Kenneth, 4

Claude, (Gellée, called Le Lorrain), 9–10, 42, 52, 70–1, 97, 106

Clerk of Eldin, John, 78

Cleveley, John,
    Fingal's Cave in Staffa, 75, **plate 46**

colour
    drawing instruments and, 133
    sketching in, 101–3, 106–11, 137
    vision, 22, 29–30, 157 n.20

common sense, *see* Scottish School of Common Sense

Conisbee, Philip, 106–7

Constable, John, 1–4, 5, 10, 35, 67, 105, 127, 150, 151
    on art and science, 150
    cloud studies and, 127
    WORKS:
    Boat Building, 105; *Flatford Mill*, 1–2, 105, 151, **plate 2**

Conybeare, W.D., 88

Cooksey, Janet, 173 n.158

Copley, Stephen, 161 n.177

Coruisk, Loch, *see* Scotland

Cosway, Maria, 41, 48
    see also Temple of Flora

Cotman, John Sell, 107, 111

cottage scenes, 135–8

Cox, David, 102

Cozens, John Robert, 29, 111
    Cetara, on the Gulf of Salerno, 29, **plate 7**

Cristall, Joshua, 119

Crome, John,
    Blacksmith's Shop Near Hingham, Norfolk, 136, **plate 100**

Crouan, Katherine, 130

Cruikshank, George, 140

Cuillin mountains, *see* Scotland

Cullen, William, 19

Cumming, David A., 169 n.8

Curtis, William, 37, 46, 165 n.48 and n.51, 166 n.66

Cuvier, Georges, 88

Dalton, John, 126–7

Daniell, Thomas, 67

Daniell, William, 8, 67–70, 74, 76–7, 80, 84, 85, 87, 89, 90–2, 93, 99, 101, 131, 151
    the *camera obscura* and, 131
    Interesting Selections from Animated Nature with Illustrative Scenery, 67–70, 74, 76–7
    sketching and, 101
    Thornton and, 69–70
    A Voyage Round Great Britain, 67–8, 80, 84, 85, 89, 90–2, 93, 99, 101, 131, 151
    WORKS:
    The Cave of Fingal, 67–8, 70, 74–5, **plate 41**; *The Coolin Taken from Loch Slapin*, 90–2, **plate 60**; *Entrance to Fingal's Cave, Staffa*, 67–8, 84, **plate 42**; *The Island of Staffa from the South West*, 85, **plate 56**; *Loch Coruisg Near Loch Scavig*, 90–2, 93, **plate 61**

Darwin, Charles, 40

Darwin, Erasmus, 39–40, 61, 62, 63, 65
    The Botanic Garden, 39–40, 62
    and contemporary society, 40
    Phytologia, 39, 61
    Zoonomia, 40, 61, 157 n.9

Davie, George E., 20

Dayes, Edward, 42, 48–9, 106

De Bolla, Peter, 156 n.8, 158 n.40

Descartes, René, 12

Desmarest, Nicolas, 76

De Wint, Peter, 102, 111, 155 n.29

Divine Providence,
    Burke and, 16
    Hartley's and, 13
    MacCulloch and, 88–9
    Thornton and, 62–4, 65

drawing instruments, 130–3

Dryander, James, 75

Dutch tradition, 57, 71, 144

Dyce, William,
    Pegwell Bay, Kent–A Recollection of October 5th 1858, 150, **plate 110**

earth, *see* history of the earth

earthquake, 77

ecology, 152

Edwards, Sydenham Teak, 37, 41, 42
    see also Temple of Flora

Egerton, Francis, 3rd Duke of Bridgewater, 144

Egremont, 3rd Earl of, *see* O'Brien, Sir George

Ehret, Georg Dionysius, 37, 166 n.66

Eigg, Isle of, *see* Scotland

electricity,

Newtonian aether and, 12

Thornton's understanding of, 39, 40, 61

Cornelius Varley's meteorological observations and, 127

empiricism, 6, 150
    versus phenomenalism, 5

enclosure, 6, 34, 137–8

Essex, Earl of, 115, 140–2

evolution, 40

Faraday, Michael, 126, 128, 179 n.170

Farey, J.,
    Camera Obscura, 130–1, **plate 95**

Farington, Joseph, 73–4, 95–6, 99, 107
    sketching and, 73, 95–6, 107
    tours in Scotland, 73–4, 95–6

Fast Castle, *see* Scotland

Faujas De Saint-Fond, Barthélemi, 75, 76
    Vue de la Grotte de Fingal, 75, **plate 47**

Fielding, Anthony Vandyke Copley, 88

Finch, Oliver Francis, 104

Fingal's Cave, *see* Scotland

Finley, Gerald, 173 n.151 and n.163

Fittler, James, 80

flowers,
    depicted in landscape settings, 8, 37–8, 42–64

Forster, Thomas, 127

Foucault, Michel, 6–7

Fox, Charles James, 16, 32, 34

French Revolution, 15, 16, 18, 20, 31, 32–4, 39, 40, 78, 143, 149

Fruchtman, Jack, 16

Furber, Robert, 62

Gage, John, 87, 172 n.110

Gainsborough, Thomas, 1–2, 4, 5, 11, 27, 60, 96
    WORKS:
    Coast Scene: Selling Fish, 96; *Wooded Landscape with Gypsy Encampment*, 27, **plate 5**; *Wooded Landscape with a Seated Figure*, 1–2, 11, **plate 1**

Galvani, Luigi, 40

Garfinkel, Norton, 164 n.40

Garnett, Thomas, 75

Garside, Peter, 161 n.177

Geological Society of London, 68, 75, 78–80, 82, 88, 102, 117, 126, 149
    Annual Report of 1815, 79
    phenomenalism of, 78–9, 88
    social context of, 79
    Transactions, 68, 78–9, 84–5, 90, 94

geology, 8, 67, 68, 70, 74–99, 149

Gerard, Alexander, 19, 157 n.32

Gilpin, William, 10–11, 26–7, 57, 73, 74, 95, 106, 107, 109
    Observation on the Coast of Hampshire, 95
    Observations of Scotland, 10, 73, 74

on the picturesque, 10–11, 26–7, 73
Price and, 27
Reynolds and, 155 n.5
on sketching, 106, 107, 109
Three Essays, 11, 27, 106, 109
WORK:
Dumbarton, 73, **plate 45**
Girtin, Thomas, 107, 111, 122, 175 n.42
Kirkstall Abbey, 107, 122, **plate 85**
Godwin, William, 144
Gombrich, Ernst, 4, 5, 154 n.15
Gould, Stephen J., 77
Graphic Telescope, 8, 130–5
Greenough, George Bellas, 79–80, 88
Griffiths, Moses, 68, 75, 89
Grose, Francis, 95
Tantallon Castle with the Bass & the Isle of May, 95, **plate 65**
Guettard, Jean Etienne, 76

Hall, James, 78, 97
Hamilton, William, 76
Hammond, John H., 178 n.132
Hardie, Martin, 114
Hartley, David, 11, 12–13, 17–18, 23
Alison and, 23
on contemporary society, 13
Observations on Man, 12–13
Priestley and, 17–18
Hatton House, *see* Chemical and Philosophical Society
Havell, William, 119
Hawes, Louis, 127
Heleniak, Kathryn Moore, 136
Hemingway, Andrew, 155 n.21, 156 n.6, 180 n.180
Henderson, Peter, 41, 47–8
see also Temple of Flora
Hipple, Walter, 23, 28, 156 n.6 and n.8, 158 n.40 and n.42, 160 n.135
history of the earth,
Erasmus Darwin's understanding of, 40
diluvian theory of, 88
Hutton's theory of, 77–8, 149
Lyell's theory of, 88
Hogarth, William, 38
Home, Henry, (Lord Kames), 19–20, 157 n.32
Howard, Luke, 126–7
Humboldt, Friedrich Heinrich Alexander von, 127
Hume, David, 12, 18, 20, 21, 30
Humphry, Ozias, 171 n.92
Hunt, William, 102, 111, 128, 135, 142, 144, 147
Study from Nature at Twickenham, 102, **plate 69**
Hussey, Christopher, 156 n.8
Hutton, James, 40, 70, 77–8, 79, 88, 97, 126, 149

hypotheses,
in the 1830s, 88, 99, 180 n.2
Hutton and, 78
theory of light and, 155 n.29, 161 n.160

igneous theory, *see* vulcanism
Impressionists, 151
instruments, *see* drawing instruments

Jacyna, L.S., 161 n.157
Jameson, Robert, 70, 76, 79, 80–1, 82, 90
WORKS:
Columnar Promontory of the Scure-Eigg, 81, 82, **plate 51**; *View from Beinn,Na,Caillich in Skye*, 80, 90, **plate 50**
Jenkins, J.J., 102, 104

Kames, Lord, *see* Home, Henry
Kant, Immanuel, 23, 156 n.6, 158 n.40
Kassel, 76
Kauffmann, C.M., 178 n.118, 179 n.161
Kemp, Martin, 97
King, Ronald, 41, 165 n.47, 166 n.64
King-Hele, Desmond, 164 n.40
Kirwan, Richard, 75, 77, 78
Klingender, Francis, 155 n.21
Knight, Richard Payne, 7, 12, 26, 29–35, 57
An Analytical Inquiry into the Principles of Taste, 29–32
on art, 32
on contemporary society, 30–1, 32–5
and J.R. Cozens, 29
Hume and, 30
The Landscape, 29, 30, 32–4, 35
A Monody on the Death of the Rt. Hn. Charles James Fox, 32
Price and, 29–30, 34–5
The Progress of Civil Society, 30–1, 34
Scottish Common Sense School and, 30
on taste, 30–2, 35
Knox, John, 93, 95
Loch Coruisk, Isle of Skye, 93, 95, **plate 63**
Kramnick, Isaac, 18

labourers, 34–5, 142
depiction of, 128, 130, 142–3
landscape art, 3, 9–10, 67, 99, 101–2, 150
art history and, 4–6
drawing instruments and, 130–3
flowers and, 8, 37–8, 42–64
geology and, 8, 68, 70, 74–99
see also beautiful; picturesque; sketching; sublime; topographical tradition; watercolours
landscape gardening, 29
Langford, Paul, 137–8
Lascelles, Edward, 140–2
Lawrence, Christopher, 19, 156 n.6, 159 n.85

Leslie, C.R., 87
Leslie, Margaret, 157 n.24
Lewis, George Robert, 102
Linnaeus, Carolus, 37, 39, 53, 62
Linnell, John, 102–4, 106, 128–30, 135, 136, 138, 142, 143, 144, 147, 163 n.6, 176 n.61
WORKS:
Bayswater, 129, **plate 92**; *Fields Where Gower Street Now Stands, Bedford Square*, 128, **plate 91**; *Kensington Gravel Pits*, 130, 142, 147, **plate 93**; *River Kennet, near Newbury*, 147, **plate 109**; *Russel Square*, 128, 143; *Study of Buildings*, 136, **plate 101**; *Study of a Tree*, 102, **plate 68**; *At Twickenham*, 102–3, 106, **plate 70**
Locke, John, 11, 12, 65
London,
artists' societies in, 102
Millbank, 102, 138–40, 178 n.118
T. Sandby's views of, 71
street scenes, 138–40
Twickenham, 102
London Gazette, 64
Long, Basil, 124, 176 n.63
Louterbourg, Philippe Jacques de, 10, 42, 96
WORKS:
An Avalanche in the Alps, 10, 42, **plate 4**; *Shipwreck*, 96
Lowry, Wilson, 126
Luc, Jean André de, 77
Lunar Society, 39, 40
Lyell, Charles, 88, 89
Lyles, Anne, 109, 174 n.6, 175 n.37
Lyotard, Jean-François, 4, 158 n.40

MacCulloch, John, 68, 80, 82–7, 88–9, 90, 94–5
association and, 82–3, 87, 94
A Description of the Western Isles of Scotland, 80, 82–7, 90, 94
The Highlands and Western Isles of Scotland, 83, 94, 172 n.109
phenomenalism and, 82–3, 85–6, 88
Proofs and Illustrations of the Attributes of God, 88–9
on Staffa, 68, 83–8
on Skye, 90, 94–5
A System of Geology, 88–9
WORKS:
Entrance of Fingal's Cave, Staffa, 84, **plate 54**; *View of the Scuir of Egg*, 82, **plate 52**; *View of Staffa from the South West*, 85, **plate 55**; *View at the Storr in Sky*, 90, **plate 59**;
Malherbe, Michel, 22
Martin, Martin, 74

medical education
    and Monro, 112–13
Meek, Ronald L., 160 n.107
Melvin, Peter, 15
meteorology, 126–7
Mill, John Stuart, 23
Millbank, *see* London
Miller, James,
    Fingal's Cave in Staffa, 75, **plate 46**
Miller, John F.,
    Fingal's Cave in Staffa, 75, **plate 46**
mind, 5, 7, 11
    Alison on, 23
    Hartley on, 17
    Knight on, 30–2
    Priestley on, 17–18
    Reid on, 21–2, 25
    Stewart on, 24–6
    Whytt on, 19
Mitchell, W.J.T., 4, 152, 154 n.10
Monk, Samuel H., 156 n.6
Monro Academy, 102, 111, 113
Monro, Thomas, 104, 110–13, 115, 128,
    135
Montagu, Elizabeth, 9
Monthly Magazine, 64–5
More, Jacob, 70
Morning Post, 124
Mount, Harry, 179 n.152
Mulready, William, 102, 128, 136, 142, 144,
    147
    Cottage and Figures, 136, **plate 102**

Napoleonic War, 62, 64
Nasmyth, Alexander, 8, 70, 96–7
    Tantallon Castle, 96–7, **plate 66**
Nasmyth, James, 97
Nattes, John Claude, 80, 89
    Fingal's Cave, 80, 89, **plate 49**
natural philosophy,
    ancient mythologies and, 63
    Erasmus Darwin's, 39–40
    Priestley's, 17
    radical politics and, 17, 26, 65
    Whytt on the limits of, 19
    see also geology; physiology; science;
        Thornton, Robert John
naturalism, 4, 5
    versus phenomenalism, 5
naturalist travellers, 74–86, 89–90
Necker de Saussure, Louis A., 75, 83
    WORKS:
    Fingal's Cave, 75, **plate 48**; *The Scuir of
        Egg from the East*, 83, **plate 53**
neptunism, 76–7, 78, 80–1, 85
nervous system, 11
    Brunonianism and, 163 n.11
    Burke on, 14–15
    Cullen on, 19
    Erasmus Darwin on, 40

Descartes' explanation of, 12
    Hartley on, 12–13
    history of theories of, 156 n.6
    Priestley on, 17–18
    Thornton on, 40
    Whytt on, 18–19
Newton, Isaac, 12
    Burke and, 14
    Hartley and, 12
    history of science and, 156 n.6
    Reid and, 21
Nonsense Club, 38

O'Brien, Sir George, 3rd Earl of Egremont,
    144
Olson, Richard, 26, 161 n.160
Opie, John, 41
    see also Temple of Flora

Paine, Tom, 15
Paley, William, 147
Palmer, Samuel, 111
panoramas, 149–50
Paulson, Ronald, 155 n.21
Payne, Christiana, 155 n.21, 174 n.17,
Pennant, Thomas,
    tours in Scotland, 68, 71, 74–5, 80, 81,
        89–90, 95, 98
perspective,
    Cornelius Varley and, 117, 126, 133
Pether, Abraham, 41–6, 61–2
    see also Temple of Flora
Petty, William, Marquis of Landsdowne
    (Lord Shelbourne), 15–16
phenomenalism, 5, 7, 26, 35, 79, 82, 83, 86,
    88, 95, 99, 101–2, 104, 105, 127, 130,
    140, 144, 147, 149–53
Philosophical Magazine, 49–52, 106, 126
Philosophical Transactions, *see* Royal Society
    of London
photography
    Cornelius Varley and, 8, 178 n.138
phrenology, 161 n.159
physiology, 7, 11
    in Burke's aesthetic theory, 14–15
    of Cullen's theory of the nervous system,
        19
    of Erasmus Darwin's theory of the
        nervous system, 40
    of Hartley's theory of association, 12–13
    in Knight's understanding of the
        picturesque, 29–30
    in Price's understanding of the
        picturesque, 27–8
    Priestley's criticism of received
        understanding of, 18
    Reid's understanding of, 21–2
    of Whytt's theory of the nervous system,
        18–19
picturesque, the, (aesthetic category),

in Alison's aesthetic theory, 23
    Clerk of Eldin's drawings and, 78
    Constable and, 105
    geologists and, 80–1, 84, 90
    Gilpin's definition of, 10–11, 26–7, 73,
    Knight on, 12, 29–30, 35
    landscape art and, 7, 10–11, 67, 72–4, 80,
        95, 101, 133
    Price on, 12, 27–9, 35
    Paul Sandby and, 72
    in Stewart's aesthetic theory, 25
    Thornton's plants and, 37, 42, 53–7, 61,
        65
    the Varley circle and, 102–3, 124, 125,
        128, 129, 135–6, 138, 144
Pidgley, Michael, 114, 179 n.176
Pitt, William (the Younger), 64
Playfair, John, 77, 97
plein-air sketching, *see* sketching
Pococke, Richard, 76
Pointon, Marcia, 136
Porter, Roy, 77
portraiture
    in landscape settings, 58–60
Pre-Raphaelites, 147, 150
Price, Uvedale, 7, 12, 17, 26, 27–30, 34–5,
        57, 65, 72
    adoption of Burke's aesthetic theory, 17,
        27
    on contemporary society, 34–5
    An Essay on the Picturesque, 17, 27–30
    Gainsborough and, 27
    Gilpin and, 27
    Knight and, 29–30, 34–5
    Thoughts on the Defence of Property, 34–5
Priestley, Joseph, 7, 11, 13, 15–18, 26, 39
    Burke and, 15–17, 18
    and contemporary society, 15–18,
    An Examination of Dr. Reid's Inquiry,
        16–18
    Hartley and, 13, 17–18
    Hartley's Theory of the Human Mind,
        16–18
    Reid and, 16
Prince, Hugh, 155 n.21
property, 15, 34–5
    depiction of, 71, 135–40
Providence, *see* Divine Providence

radicals, 15–16, 39, 65, 126, 144
Radisich, Paula R., 175 n.32
Raspe, R.E., 76
Redgrave, Richard, 138
Reid, Thomas, 7, 11, 12, 16, 19, 20–3,
        24–5
    Alison and, 23
    and contemporary society, 20–1
    Essays on the Intellectual Powers of Man, 22
    An Inquiry into the Human Mind, 20–2
    Newton's laws and, 21

opposes Berkeley, 20–1
opposes Hume, 20–1
Priestley's criticism of, 16
Stewart and, 23, 24–5
Whytt's influence on, 19
Reinagle, Philip, 41–2, 46–7, 52
    see also Temple of Flora
Repton, Humphry, 29
revolution, see French Revolution
Reynolds, Joshua, 10, 11, 32, 60, 106, 131,
    155 n.5
    the camera obscura and, 131
    Discourses on Art, 10, 11, 106
    Gilpin and, 155 n.5
    Knight's criticism of, 32
    WORK:
    Commodore Keppel, 60, **plate 35**
Robinson, Sidney K., 161 n.177
Robson, George Fennel, 93, 95
    Loch Coruisk and the Cuchullin Mountains,
        Isle of Skye, 93, 95, **plate 62**
Roget, John L., 174 n.9, 177 n.86 and n.93
Rooker, Michael Angelo, 27
    Interior of Ruins, Buildwas Abbey,
        Shropshire, 27, **plate 6**
Rosa, Salvatore, 9, 10, 70–1, 107
Rosenthal, Michael, 105, 155 n.21, 177 n.91
Royal Academy of Arts, London, 10, 30,
    32, 74, 107, 128, 150
Royal Institution, 114, 117, 142, 143
Royal Society of London, 39, 74, 76, 114
    Philosophical Transactions, 25, 76
Rudwick, Martin, 70
Runciman, Alexander, 70
Ruskin, John,
    on art and science, 150
    on geology and Turner, 93–4, 95
    and sketching, 105, 147
Russell, John, 41
    see also Temple of Flora
Rykwert, Joseph, 171 n.90

Sandby, Paul, 9, 71–3, 78, 107, 110
    Clerk of Eldin and, 78
    The Virtuosi's Museum, 71–3
    WORKS:
    Leith, 71–2, 107, **plate 44**; South Prospect
        of Leith, 71, **plate 43**; Village Street,
        Old Charlton, Kent, 110, **plate 76**
Sandby, Thomas, 71, 131
Sandemanian Sect, 128
scepticism, 4, 19, 20–1
Schaffer, Simon, 15, 156 n.6, 159 n.81
Schofield, Robert E., 18
science
    art and, 3, 5–6, 150–1
    Foucault and, 7
    phenomenalism and, 5, 88
    Reid's philosophy aspires to status of,
        21

Stewart's philosophy aspires to status of,
    25, 26
use of term, 154 n.1
Cornelius Varley and, 126–7, 130–3, 145
    see also geology; meteorology; natural
        philosophy; physiology
Scotland,
    Eigg, Isle of, 80–3
    Scottish Highlands, 10, 70, 73–4, 78–80
    Scottish Lowlands, 70–4, 78–80
        Bass Rock, 95–8
        Fast Castle, 99
        Tantallon Castle, 95–9
    Skye, Isle of, 79–81, 89–90
        Cuillin mountains, 90–5
        Loch Coruisk, 95
    Staffa, Isle of, 74–6, 79, 80, 83–9
        Fingal's Cave, 67–8, 70, 74–5, 80, 83–9
Scott, Walter, 87, 89–94, 98–9
Scottish School of Common Sense, 18, 20,
    26, 30
Secord, James A., 79
sexuality
    of plants, 39, 56, 61
Shapin, Steven, 156 n.6, 161 n.159
Shelbourne, Lord, see Petty, William,
    Marquis of Landsdowne
shipwreck, 96, 98
sketching (outdoor),
    Banks and, 170 n.44 and n.45
    of clouds, 127
    in colour, 101–3, 106–11, 137
    Constable and, 2, 105
    Cotman on, 107
    Daniell and, 101
    Dayes on, 106
    Farington and, 73, 95–6, 107
    Gilpin on, 106, 107, 109
    Girtin and, 107
    Knight on, 35
    Ruskin and, 105, 147
    Paul Sandby and, 71–2
    the Varley circle and, 101–26, 128–44,
        147
Sketching Society, 102, 124, 137
Skye, Isle of, see Scotland
Smith, Adam, 18, 20, 23, 30
Society of Arts (Society for the
    Encouragement of the Arts,
    Manufactures and Commerce), 126,
    143, 176 n.63
Society of Painters in Water-Colours, 102,
    107, 111, 124, 126, 137
Staffa, Isle of, see Scotland
Stafford, Barbara Maria, 6, 169 n.16
Stanhope, Charles, 3rd Earl, 114–15
steamboats, 87, 89
Stevens, Francis, 136–8
Stewart, Dugald, 11, 12, 20, 22–3, 24–6, 35,
    67, 78, 149

Alison and, 24, 25
on the beautiful and sublime, 25–6
Elements of the Human Mind, 22–3, 24–6
phenomenalism and, 26
Reid and, 23, 24–5
on taste, 26
Story, Alfred, 102, 114
stratigraphy, 78, 79, 82, 88
    palaeontological, 88
street scenes, see London
sublime, the (aesthetic category),
    in Alison's aesthetic theory, 23–4
    Burke on, 13–14
    Clerk of Eldin's drawings and, 78
    geologists and, 80–3
    Kant and, 158 n.40
    landscape art and, 7, 9–10, 67, 71, 99
    Lyotard and, 158 n.40
    Price on, 27–8
    in Stewart's aesthetic theory, 25–6
    Thornton's plants and, 37–8, 42, 53–6,
        57, 61, 65
    Cornelius Varley and, 102, 120–2, 124
    John Varley and, 120–2

Tantallon Castle, see Scotland, Scottish
    Lowlands
taste (formation of),
    Alison on, 23–4
    Burke on, 15
    Gerard on, 19
    Home on, 19–20
    Knight on, 30–2, 35
    Stewart on, 26
Telegraph, 114
Temple of Flora, 37–65
    WORKS:
    Maria Cosway: Flora Dispensing her
        Flowers on the Earth, 41, 48, **plate 9**
    Sydenham Teak Edwards: Hyacinths, 42,
        49, 56–7, 62, 167 n.86, **plate 10**
    Peter Henderson: The American Cowslip,
        58, 60, 63, **plate 34**; The Blue
        Egyptian Water-Lily, 52, **plate 29**;
        The China Limodoron, 52, **plate 27**;
        The Dragon Arum, 53–6, 61, 167 n.84,
        plate 30; A Group of Auriculas, 49,
        plate 21; A Group of Carnations, 49,
        plate 22; Indian Reed, 46, 52, **plate
        14**; The Maggot-bearing Stapelia, 57–8,
        plate 31; The Nodding Renealmia, 52,
        plate 26; The Pontic Rhododendron, 63,
        plate 40; The Quadrangular Passion-
        Flower, 47–8, 49, 52, 167 n.86, **plate
        19**; The Queen, 52, 62, **plate 25**; The
        Sacred Egyptian Bean, 52, 62, 167 n.86,
        plate 28; The White Lily, 47, 52, 60,
        167 n.86, **plate 15**; The Winged
        Passion-Flower, 47–8, 49, 52, 167 n.86,
        plate 18

Abraham Pether, *The Persian Cyclamen*, 46, 49, 57, 62, **plate 13**; *The Snowdrop*, 46, 52, 56–7, 60, 62, **plate 12**

Philip Reinagle and Abraham Pether, *The Night-Blowing Cereus*, 42, 53, 56, 61, 165 n.47, 166 n.66, 167 n.86, **plate 11**

Philip Reinagle, *The Aloe*, 49, 58, 61, 165 n.47, 166 n.63, 167 n.86, **plate 24**; *American Bog-Plants*, 62–3, 166 n.63, **plate 39**; *The Blue Passion Flower*, 47–8, 49, 52, 165 n.47, 167 n.86, **plate 17**; *Cupid Inspiring the Plants with Love*, 41, 164 n.42, 165 n.47, **plate 8**; *Large Flowering Sensitive Plant*, 60–1, 165 n.47, 167 n.86, **plate 38**; *The Narrow-leaved Kalmia*, 58, 166 n.63, 167 n.86, **plate 33**; *Oblique-leaved Begonia*, 52, 165 n.47, 167 n.86; *Pitcher Plant*, 58, 166 n.63, **plate 32**; *The Superb Lily*, 47, 52, 53, 60, 61, 164 n.42, 167 n.86, **plate 16**; *Tulips*, 49, 56–7, 61, 167 n.86, **plate 20**

John Russell and John Opie, *Aesculapius, Flora, Ceres and Cupid honouring the Bust of Linnaeus*, 41

Robert John Thornton, *Roses*, 48, 49, 53, 62, 167 n.86, **plate 23**

Thomson, John, 98–9

Thornton, Bonnell, 38

Thornton, Robert John, 8, 37–65, 67, 68–9
Advertisement to the New Illustration, 8, 37, 41, 52
on contemporary society, 38–9, 40, 64–5
Daniell and, 68–9
Dr. Thornton's Exhibition of Botanical Paintings, 41–62, 64
Erasmus Darwin and, 39–40, 61, 62, 63, 65
Lottery, 41, 64
A New Illustration of the Sexual System of Carolus von Linnaeus, 37–65
The Philosophy of Medicine, 39, 40, 61–2
The Politician's Creed, 38–9, 40, 60
The Religious Use of Botany, 42–6, 60, 62, 64
see also Temple of Flora

topographical tradition, 9, 71–4, 107, 108, 109, 110

Transactions, see Geological Society of London

Turner, Joseph Mallord William, 4, 5, 8, 10, 74, 87–8, 89, 93–5, 97–8, 111, 149
WORKS:

The Bass Rock, 97–8, **plate 67**; *Fingal's Cave*, 87, **plate 58**; *Loch Coruisk, Skye*, 89, 93–5, **plate 64**; *Staffa, Fingal's Cave*, 87–8, 89, **plate 57**

Turner of Oxford, William, 102, 178 n.114

Twickenham, *see* London

Vallin, Jacques-Antoine, 60
Dr. Forlenze, 60, **plate 37**

Van Dyck, Antony, 60

Varley, Cornelius, 8, 35, 99, 101–47, 151, 153
and contemporary society, 135–44
drawing instruments and, 130–5
meteorology and, 126–8
phenomenalism and, 104, 130, 140, 144
Shipping, Barges, Fishing Boats, and other Vessels, 126, 144
A Treatise on Optical Drawing Instruments, 133
WORKS:
Barmouth Vale from Cader Idris, 122, **plate 84**; *Beddgelert Bridge*, 122, **plate 86**; *Devil's Bridge*, 125, 126, **plate 90**; *Devil's Bridge* (sketch), 119, 124–6, **plate 89**; *Evening at Llanberis*, 120, **plate 82**; *The Graphic Telescope*, 130–3, **plate 94**; *Holland Street, Blackfriars Bridge*, 138–40, **plate 103**; *Lime Trees at Gillingham*, 115, **plate 78**; *Lord Rous's Park*, 115–17, **plate 77**; *Mountain Landscape, North Wales*, 120, **plate 80**; *Near Ross*, 153, **plate 111**; *Part of Cader Idris and Tal-y-Llyn*, 119–20, **plate 79**; *Patshul Staffordshire*, 133, **plate 97**; *River Wye*, 143, **plate 107**; *Ross Market Place, Herefordshire*, 107–8, 114, 124, 126, **plate 71**; *The Rows at Chester*, 109, **plate 73**; *Ruins of Kerry Castle*, 133–5, **plate 98**; *St. Albans, Hertfordshire*, 108, 124, **plate 72**; *Sawyers Clearing Timber from its Knots*, 142–3, **plate 106**; *Sketchbook: Lime Rocks Llangollen*, 120, **plate 81**; *Sketchbook: Wrekin Shropshire*, 124, **plate 87**; *Stacking Hay*, 144, **plate 108**; *The Traveller*, 124, **plate 88**; *View of a Farmyard*, 135–6, **plate 99**; *View from Ferry Bridge Yorkshire*, 133, **plate 96**

Varley, John, 8, 35, 99, 101–5, 109–11, 114, 120, 128, 135, 138–45
and contemporary society, 135–44
A Treatise on the Principles of Landscape

Design, 104–5
A Treatise on Zodiacal Physiognomy, 145
WORKS:
Looking down the High Street, Conway, 110, **plate 75**; *Mountain Landscape: View from Cader Idris*, 120, **plate 83**; *Pulling down Old Houses in Crooked Lane for approach to London*, 140, **plate 105**; *The Thames Near the Penitentiary, Millbank, London*, 140, **plate 104**; *View of Polesden, Surrey*, 110–11, **plate 74**

Varley, Samuel, 114–15

Vernet, Claude Joseph, 96

Vesuvius, 60, 76–7

Vision,
Burke on, 14
Hartley on, 13
Knight on, 29, 30, 32,
Price on, 29
Reid on, 22
Stewart on, 25

vitalism, 157 n.9, 159 n.88

vulcanism, 76–7, 78, 85, 97

Wagner, Monika, 155 n.21

Wales, 74, 102, 117–25, 126, 147

Walford, Edward, 138

war, *see* Napoleonic War

watercolours,
Monro's influence on development of, 110–13
technique and development of, 101–2, 137

Watercolour Society, *see* Society of Painters in Water-Colours

Watt, James, 38, 39

Webster, Thomas, 88, 117, 126, 142, 155 n.29

Weindling, Paul, 79

Weiskel, Thomas, 156 n.8

Werner, Abraham, 76–7, 79, 81, 82, 97

Whytt, Robert, 18–19, 21

Wilberforce, William, 142

Wilkes, John, 38

Williams, Iolo A., 114

Wilson, Richard, 10
View near Wynnstay, the Seat of Sir Watkin Williams-Wynn, Bt., 10, **plate 3**

Wollaston, William Hyde, 131

Wood, William, 168 n.2, 169 n.16

Yeo, Richard, 171 n.84, 180 n.2

Young, Thomas, 155 n.29, 161 n.160